ArtScroll® Tanach Series

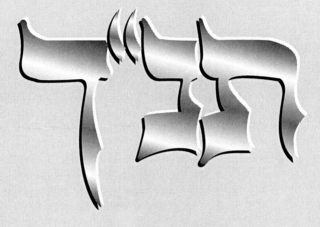

A traditional commentary on the Books of the Bible

Rabbi Nosson Scherman / Rabbi Meir Zlotowitz

General Editors

Foreword/ דברי פתיחה

HaGaon HaRav Mordechai Gifter

Telshe Rosh HaYeshivah

shir haShirim

SONG OF SONGS / AN ALLEGORICAL
TRANSLATION BASED UPON RASHI WITH A
COMMENTARY ANTHOLOGIZED FROM TALMUDIC,
MIDRASHIC AND RABBINIC SOURCES.

Published by

Mesorah Publications, ltd

Commentary compiled by
Rabbi Meir Zlotowitz

Allegorical translation, and Overview
by
Rabbi Nosson Scherman

FIRST EDITION
Seventeen Impressions ... January 1977 — June 2008
Eighteenth Impression ... March 2010
SECOND EDITION
Newly Typeset
First Impression ... October 2015

Published and Distributed by
MESORAH PUBLICATIONS, Ltd.
4401 Second Avenue
Brooklyn, New York 11232

Distributed in Europe by
LEHMANNS
Unit E, Viking Business Park
Rolling Mill Road
Jarrow, Tyne & Wear NE32 3DP
England

Distributed in Australia & New Zealand by
GOLDS WORLD OF JUDAICA
3-13 William Street
Balaclava, Melbourne 3183
Victoria Australia

Distributed in Israel by
SIFRIATI / A. GITLER — BOOKS
Moshav Magshimim
Israel

Distributed in South Africa by
KOLLEL BOOKSHOP
Northfield Centre, 17 Northfield Avenue
Glenhazel 2192, Johannesburg, South Africa

THE ARTSCROLL® TANACH SERIES
SHIR HASHIRIM / SONG OF SONGS
© *Copyright 1977-1996, 2015*
by MESORAH PUBLICATIONS, Ltd.
4401 Second Avenue / Brooklyn, N.Y. 11232 / (718) 921-9000 / www.artscroll.com

---

SHIR HASHIRIM / SONG OF SONGS
ISBN 10: 0-89906-000-5 / ISBN 13: 978-0-89906-000-2 (hard cover)
ISBN 10: 0-89906-001-3 / ISBN 13: 978-0-89906-001-9 (paperback)

FIVE-VOLUME MEGILLOS SET
ISBN 10: 0-89906-010-2 / ISBN 13: 978-0-88906-010-1 (hard cover)
ISBN 10: 0-89906-011-0 / ISBN 13: 978-0-89906-011-8 (paperback)

Typography by CompuScribe at ArtScroll Studios, Ltd.
4401 Second Avenue / Brooklyn, N.Y. 11232 / (718) 921-9000

Printed in the United States of America by Noble Book Press
Bound by Sefercraft, Quality Bookbinders, Ltd. Brooklyn, N.Y.

לזכר נשמות

Reb Yaakov Moshe Golding ז״ל

ר׳ יעקב משה ב״ר שמעון גדליה ז״ל

כ״ז שבט תשל״ד

Mrs. Chava Golding ע״ה

חוה בת ר׳ יעקב ע״ה

ט״ז אדר תשמ״ח

They added luster to one of the great family names
in American Orthodoxy.

The Torah was their only guide, and by its light
they sought out causes to foster and people to help.

At their table sat the leading sages of the era,
and the most helpless, indigent, and friendless —
and all were equally welcome.
She was at the beside of the ill,
and their families shared her home.

With warm hearts and open hands,
with modesty and elegance,
they left a legacy of loyalty to Torah
and to the perpetuation of its ideals.

תנצב״ה

Table of Contents

הסכמת הגאון האמיתי שר התורה ועמוד ההוראה
מורנו ורבנו מרן ר' משה פיינשטיין שליט"א

RABBI MOSES FEINSTEIN
455 F. D. R. DRIVE
New York, N. Y. 10002

ORegon 7-1222

משה פיינשטיין
ריש מתיבתא תפארת ירושלים
בנ"א יארק

בע"ה

הנה ידידי הרב הנכבד מאד מוהר"ר **מאיר יעקב בן ידידי הרב הגאון ר' אהרן זלאטאוויץ שליט"א** אשר היה מתלמידינו החשובים בהישיבה, וכל העת הוא מתנהג בכל העניינים כראוי לבני תורה ויראי ה', כבר חבר ארבעה ספרים חשובים: אחד על מגילת אסתר ואחד על מגילת רות ואחד על מגילת איכה ואחד על מגילת קהלת, בשפה האנגלית המדוברת ביותר במדינה זו, אשר קבץ דברים יקרים ופנינים נחמדים מספרי רבותינו נ"ע, אשר הם מעוררים לאהבת התורה וקיום המצות וחזוק האמונה בהש"ית, ונתקבלו אצל ההמון עם ההולכים בדרך התורה. ויש מזה תועלת לקרב לב הקוראים, אף מאלו שנתרחקו קצת, לאבינו שבשמים ולקיים מצותיו. ועתה חבר ספר כזה גם על מגילת שיר השירים שהוא קדש קדשים, וכבר ראה אותו בני הרה"ג ר' דוד שליט"א ושבחהו מאד, אשר על כן הוא מה שמדפיסו ומוציאו לאור עולם להגדיל אהבת השי"ת ותורתו הקדושה ואמונתנו בגאולה שהובטח לנו מהשי"ת וביותר בביאת הש"ם ע"י משיח צדקנו בקרוב.

וגם אני מברך את ידידי הרב הנכבד **מוהר"ר נתן שערמאן שליט"א** אשר הוסיף נופך לבאר תוכן כל מגילה ומגילה במקצת לפי דברי חז"ל בפתיחת הספר בדברים המושכין את הלב לתורה ויראת השי"ת שיצליח מאד בכל מעשיו בפרט בעבודת החינוך אשר עוסק בזה בכל כחו לקדש שם שמים. וע"ז באתי על החתום ביום ז' לסדר ותחי רוח יעקב כ' ו' טבת תשל"ז.

נאום משה פיינשטיין

מכתב ברכה מאאמו"ר
הרב הגאון ר' אהרן זלאטאוויץ שליט"א

מכתב ברכה
ממרן הגאון ר' מרדכי גיפטער שליט"א

בע"ה — ג', ה' חנוכה, תשל"ז

מע"כ ידידי היקר והנעלה

הרב ר' מאיר זלוטוביץ, נ"י, שלום וברכה נצח לו ולכא"ל !

אחדשה"ט באהבה ויקר,

באתי בזה להביע רחשי ברכה מקרב ולב על מפעלו הגדול בהוצאת כתבי הקדש בתרגום אנגלי חדש בצירוף לקט ביאורים באנגלית, יחד עם הקדמה השקפתית לכל ספר, מעשה ידי אומן, ידידנו הנעלה **הרב ר' נתן שרמן**, נ"י, שנושא גם בעול המערכת.

רואה אני בעבודה זו משום קדוש שם שמים, להציע בשפה השגורה פירוש וביאור כתה"ק ע"פ דברי רז"ל שהם הם מקור האמת וגם כמה תורה קשה להם לעמוד על הדברים במקורם, וכמה מהמתאמים לדבר ה' בדורנו רחוקים הם, לדאבוננו, ומתפתטים על דברי הבל והבאי של הכופרים למיניהם. ומזה הטעם רואה אני פרי ברכה גם בתרגום החדש שהוא קדש ומנופה מכל ההשפעות הזרות המצויות בתרגומים אחרים, לרבות אף כאלה המוחזקים לקדש.

יהא ה' עמו ועם ידידנו הרב ר' נתן נ"י ועם כל המסייעים על ידם, להגביר חילם במפעל קדוש זה, שיש בו משום קירוב לאותו היעוד של ,,ומלאה הארץ דעה את ה' כמים לים מכסים''

ידידו, דושה"ט באהבה,

מרדכי גיפטער

Preface

The preparation of this volume was approached בְּאֵימָה וּבְיִרְאָה בְּרֶתֶת וּבְזִיעָה, with feelings of awe, inadequacy, and trepidation. Rabbi Akiva had characterized Shir HaShirim as Holy of Holies, yet countless generations of readers had seen in it the opposite of holiness. Even the English versions often used by Orthodox readers fell short of offering the full range of perspective, insight, and interpretations of the Sages and the great commentators of succeeding generations. The result has been that the English-speaking reader was left defenseless in explaining Shir HaShirim to those who had been weaned on the cynical canards and misinterpretations of the ignorant and the unbelieving.

Therefore, although an acceptable translation and commentary to Shir HaShirim would be the most difficult of the ARTSCROLL TANACH SERIES, we felt that if the task could be done, it would be the most valuable of all the works thus far.

Several approaches were discussed and attempted. The impetus behind the formula finally adopted came from MARAN HAGAON HARAV YAAKOV KAMINETZKY שליט״א, Rosh HaYeshivah of Torah Vodaath, who graciously allowed us several hours of his time at his Monsey home. He urged that the only possible translation was one that reflected and incorporated the allegory, because a literal translation would be totally inadequate — even inaccurate — to convey the true meaning. He counseled that the translation must follow the unified approach of one major commentator, and that Rashi, the Father of Commentators, would be the logical one to use. He also cautioned that a literal translation not be neglected because it was Solomon's vehicle in conveying the allegory, and because the absence of a literal English translation — at least in the commentary — would unfairly deprive the English reader of an extra level of understanding.

In addition, Reb Yaakov lent us his worn and precious out-of-print copy of Divrei Yedidiah by Rav Yedidiah Lipmann Lipkin ע״ה, a nephew of Reb Yisrael Lipkin of Salant. The book, published in 1895, is a most profound commentary which Reb Yaakov urged us to draw from frequently.

We are deeply grateful to Reb Yaakov for his initial guidance. To speak with him is to feel a sense of awe and an appreciation of the greatness of a total Torah personality.

We HAVE *been privileged to draw guidance and inspiration from the Telshe Rosh HaYeshivah, HAGAON HARAV MORDECHAI GIFTER שליט"א. With graciousness beyond description, he has given of his time, sagacity, and guidance. Although "free time" is not in his vocabulary, he allowed us to meet with him in New York and at his home in Wickliffe. His conviction that the Tanach series is a vital contribution to Torah life and knowledge was a source of inexpressible inspiration. His sagely advice was crucial to the formation of the sefer and his generous willingness to read and comment upon the entire manuscript by mail and phone enhanced the work immeasurably. His comments are found sprinkled throughout the Overview and commentary, but his influence pervades the entire book.*

In addition, Harav Gifter consented to contribute a Hebrew Foreword that adds immeasurably to the reader's understanding of both Shir HaShirim and to Torah Hashkafah (perspective) in general. The Telshe Rosh HaYeshivah's incisive insight and originality of thought enhance greatly the quality of the book. Words do not adequately express our profound appreciation.

THE TRANSLATION

*A*s *the Foreword and Overview make abundantly clear, the only "literal" translation of Shir HaShirim is allegorical. Therefore our translation follows the allegory as interpreted by Rashi. Whenever the word "Translation" [with a capitalized "T"] appears in the commentary, it refers to the allegorical translation. For the English reader's convenience and so that he might better appreciate how the allegory is derived from the text, a literal translation of every phrase is included in brackets after each entry in the commentary. It should be noted, however, that even the literal translation hews to Chazal. As a single example, the word* שׁוֹשַׁנָּה *is universally translated in 2:1 as "lily," but we have rendered it as "rose" in consonance with Jewish tradition.*

SCOPE OF THE COMMENTARY

*T*he *commentary elaborates on Rashi's allegorical rendering in every instance, although he has not been translated verbatim. Additionally, the Talmud and Midrashim with the standard commentaries were consulted for those interpretations which were closest to* פְּשָׁט, *the more simple allegorical explanation which could meaningfully be incorporated into an English-language commentary.*

Next, the major commentators, Ibn Ezra, Ralbag, Ibn Aknin, Ramban, Arama, Alshich, Sforno, as well as Metzudas David, Tz'ror HaMor, and the later commentaries of Rav Dov Ber Treves, Rav Yechiel Heller, The Netziv, Rav Yedidiah Lipkin [see bibliography for full listing], were culled.

There are many commentaries on the book and nearly as many varied viewpoints on the general line of the allegory. To consistently cite all would have made our commentary so diffuse and unwieldy as to be almost useless. We have therefore been forced to somewhat limit the scope of the anthology to those commentaries closest to the main allegorical interpretation of the Sages as expounded by Rashi. Unfortunately, for this reason, we considered as outside the scope of this work the brilliant commentary of the Malbim as well as the esoterically profound commentaries of those kabbalistic giants, who view this work as essentially a craving dialogue between the rational soul and active intellect imprisoned within the human body — and the obstacles in the path of their union with HASHEM.

The readers will note that the various commentaries often appear to be mutually exclusive. They are not: they complement one another just as each of the many facets of a diamond plays a part in enhancing the brilliance of a precious stone. As the Talmud says:

> The school of Rabbi Ishmael taught: "[The word of God is] like a hammer that breaks a rock in pieces" (Jeremiah 23:29). Just as a hammer [striking a rock] divides into many sparks, so, too, every word emanating from the mouth of the Holy One, blessed is He, divides into seventy interpretations (Shabbos 88b).

SEVERAL WORDS OF CAUTION

We have prefaced our volumes with an urging to our readers that, far from a substitute for in-depth study of Talmud, Midrash, and commentaries in the original, this work should be taken as an introduction to their thought. Unfortunately, there is a sizable public who haven't either the time or the background to undertake such study. Nevertheless, we would urge everyone to see the ARTSCROLL TANACH SERIES as the merest taste of the richness awaiting readers who undertake a study of Torah with its original sources and commentaries. In addition, it must be understood that the commentary does not attempt to offer every word and certainly not every nuance of thought of those whom it quotes. Clearly, only highlights could be culled from the sources quoted. In many cases, study of the full commentaries in the original may lead the reader to different interpretations of the same commentary. This is natural and desirable, for the Torah greats of previous generations compared to us were, in the expression of the Sages, "like angels compared to men, or like men compared to donkeys."

ACKNOWLEDGMENTS

The sefer ב"ה complete, it is now our mutually pleasant duty to together thank the many people whose encouragement, advice, and criticism have made it worthy of the Torah public. Tens of friends responded with advice, read drafts, and generally inspired the undertaking of so sensitive a work. Many of these friends have been thanked in our earlier volumes, and our gratitude is to them again. Above all, we are indebted to:

HAGAON HARAV ARON ZLOTOWITZ'S, שליט"א, love of Torah and righteousness has been a beacon of inspiration. His is a Rav in the eternal tradition — Shas and poskim are on his fingertips, and he has given many hours to clarify obscurities and point out sources. May he and his rebbetzin, מנב"ת מרת פרומא תחי', be blessed with אריכות ימים ושנים, health and "nachas" from their children, grandchildren, and great-grandchildren.

HARAV DAVID FEINSTEIN, שליט"א, has again given unstintingly of himself to encourage and inspire, to criticize and perfect. He has read and commented upon nearly every selection, noting discrepancies, clarifying difficult passages, and guided us to new material. Also, his original insights were freely offered, and many of them are included in the Overview and commentary. Harav Feinstein generously opened the encyclopedic repository of his knowledge during the course of writing. He has our eternal gratitude.

HARAV DAVID COHEN, שליט"א, possesses a phenomenal breadth of knowledge and clarity of thought. Though his time is meticulously budgeted, he allowed us to call upon him almost at will. He advised, directed, read proofs, clarified, corrected, and gave freely from the spring of his original thought and scholarship. His stamp is indelibly on the book, and we are deeply grateful.

HARAV JOSEPH ELIAS, despite his heavy involvement with writing a commentary on the Passover Haggadah for the ArtScroll Series, graciously took time to read portions of the manuscript. His advice and encouragement, as always, were valuable and are greatly appreciated.

HARAV MOSHE EISEMANN of Baltimore generously sent tapes of his lectures on Shir HaShirim in the hope that they might be helpful. They were, and parts of the Overview reflect his material. The Jewish public is fortunate that this man of rare depth and exceptionally broad knowledge is working on a commentary to Yechezkel in the ARTSCROLL TANACH SERIES.

It is needless to re-emphasize that although all the above have generously left their mark on the book, since they have left final editorial discretion to us, they are absolved from any share of responsibility for any shortcoming in the final product. We bear that responsibility alone.

We are most appreciative to the members of the ARTSCROLL staff of typesetters, MRS. SHIRLEY KIFFEL, MRS. PEARL EIDLIS, and MISS ESTHER HARTMAN, who gave above and beyond the requirements of their duty in every aspect of the work, by volunteering their assistance outside of working hours. Special thanks are due to MRS. JUDY GROSSMAN and MISS RIVA ALPER, for their proofreading efforts.

The efforts of REB ZUNDEL BERMAN in disseminating this volume to the B'nai Yeshivos for whom it is primarily intended is again acknowledged.

Mention must also be made of the sincere efforts and assistance of MR. DAVID H. SCHWARTZ, RABBI BORUCH BORCHARDT, RABBI ELI MUNK, RABBI RONALD GREENWALD, RABBI NISSON WOLPIN, RABBI YOSEF WEINBAUM, RABBI YISRAEL H. EIDELMAN, MR. NAFTOLI HIRSCH, RABBI BURTON JAFFA, MR. JOSHUA GROSSMAN, and MR. CHARLES GRANDOVSKY. Their advice and encouragement are greatly appreciated.

A special note of thanks is due RABBI AVIE GOLD who graciously undertook to meticulously proofread and check the source references in this volume, trying to assure a nearly error-free publication. The several errors which remain — and which we will try to correct in future editions אי״ה — are due to technical reasons beyond his control. Avie did the bulk of the work during the "Shloshim" of his father, ר׳ יעקב בן ר׳ אברהם יצחק ז״ל. May this contribution to Torah knowledge bring an עליה לנשמתו.

There is one person who remained in the background but whose skill and dedication is all pervasive. REB SHEAH BRANDER is responsible for the highly praised graphics of the Series. But that is only part of his contribution. He has read and commented, discussed and criticized. He has put in unbelievable hours whenever the needs of the project called for it. In general, he has recognized the need for the Series and submerged all other interests for it. No thanks are adequate.

Our wives can be thanked only with a simple statement of fact. Paraphrasing Rabbi Akiva's statement about his wife: שלנו שלהן הוא, whatever we have accomplished is theirs. Jewish wives and mothers in the proudest tradition of the word, they have made their homes centers of kindness, extensions of the Beis Medrash, study hall, and academies where children are taught that Torah is life's greatest value. May they be granted their most fervent wish: that their children grow up firmly anchored in love of Torah and fear of HASHEM.

REFLECTIONS...

אָמַר ר' אֱלִיעֶזֶר מִכָּאן שֶׁעוֹשִׂין סְעוּדָה לִגְמָרָהּ שֶׁל תּוֹרָה
(שיה"ש רבה א:ט, עיין ענף יוסף)

When Solomon was given the blessing of wisdom, he brought countless sacrifices to express his gratitude to God. From this we learn that when someone completes a portion of the Torah, he should make a joyous feast
(*Midrash Anaf Yosef*).

A portion of the Torah has been completed. In less than a year we have ב"ה been granted the awesome privilege of completing five books of Tanach — the Five Megillos — and placing them before the Torah public. In the process, we have been done the inestimable honor of being granted the attention and cooperation of some of the greatest talmidei chachamim of our generation. We have been given the strength to go beyond what are considered the limits of endurance. Most of all, we are humbled, and grateful to Hashem Yisbarach for the סִיַעְתָּא דִשְׁמַיָא, heavenly assistance, without which the project would have remained but one more good intention that never reached fruition.

What began as a token gesture to memorialize a chaver tragically taken, Reb Mair Fogel ע"ה, has become — before his first Yahrzeit — a major venture that has merited the attention of tens of thousands of Jews from many backgrounds who are united by a thirst for Torah.

Our collaboration has become more than a joint effort of good friends enjoying אֶת וָהֵב בְּסוּפָה, the ultimate friendship of trying to understand the word of God; it has become a vehicle to enrich the public. Such a privilege becomes a duty. It will not be taken lightly as we pray that Hashem Yisbarach give us the wisdom, means, and health to continue in His service.

Rabbi Nosson Scherman / Meir Zlotowitz

Brooklyn, New York
Motzaei Shabbos, 18 Teves, 5737

דברי פתיחה / Foreword

◆§ Overview —
Shir HaShirim /
Symphony of Creation

דברי פתיחה

מאת מרן הגאון ר׳ מרדכי גיפטער שליט״א

ר״מ ישיבת טעלז

כל השירים קדש ושיר השירים קדש קדשים.

וביאור דבריהם:

א. תכלית הבריאה, הטבת הבורא ברוך הוא לזולתו, שיקבלו הברואים מאותו הטוב שאין מציאותו אלא בבורא ברוך הוא. ואי אפשר לברואים שיקבלו אותה הטובה אלא על ידי שיהיו דבקים בו.

ב. גדר האהבה — דבקות האוהב בנאהב, לא משום איזו תכלית ותועלת אלא מצד עצמו, שכל שהוא לאיזו תועלת יש בזה משום ריכוז בעצמו ולא בנאהב. ולכן למדונו רז״ל שלא לקיים מצוותיו יתברך על מנת לקבל פרס או לפרוש מהעבירה מפאת יראת העונש, אלא שתהא עשייתנו מאהבה.

ג. בהיות שגזרה חכמתו יתברך שיהא האדם מורכב מנשמה וגוף, אשר ביסודם הם הפכיים. נקבעה לו עבודתו להגביר כח הנשמה על הגוף ולזככו עד שיהא הגוף מתעלס באהבים עם הנשמה בעילוי נפלא. והמתחייב מזה שכל עניני הנשמה אי אפשר שיתקיימו באדם כראוי אם לא יעברו גם דרך הגוף, שירגיש בהם בחוש. לולא זאת אין כאן השלמות של זכוך החומר המתאחד בנשמה. ועיין פ׳ משפטים: "ואל אצילי בני ישראל לא שלח ידו ויחזו את האלהים ויאכלו וישתו" — ובגמרא ברכות י״ז, א׳ אמרו: "העוה״ב אין בו לא אכילה ולא שתי׳ וכו׳ אלא צדיקים יושבים ועטרותיהם בראשיהם ונהנים מזיו השכינה שנ׳ ויחזו את האלהים ויאכלו וישתו." ופירש״י: "שבעו מזיו השכינה כאילו אכלו

ושתו." ועיין ת"א על אתר — הרי שהנאת זיו השכינה מתוארת בלשון
אכילה ושתי', שאי אפשר לאדם בעל חומר להרגיש בעונג הנטול לגמרי
מהחושים החומריים. יצחק אבינו כשבקש לברך ברכתו בקש: "ועשה
לי מטעמים כאשר אהבתי והביאה לי ואכלה בעבור תברכך נפשי בטרם
אמות." ועיין פסחים ס"ח, ב': "א"ר אלעזר הכל מודים בעצרת שבעינן
נמי לכם מ"ט יום שניתנה בו תורה הוא — ופירש"י: "שישמח בו
במאכל ומשתה להראות שנוח ומקובל יום זה לישראל שנתנה תורה בו.
ועיין דברי רש"י בביצה ט"ז, א' בביאור ענין נשמה יתירה.

ד. אהבת ה' במלואה אומרת בטול גמור של האוהב אל הנאהב עד כדי
דבקות ואחוד, ולמען הגיע לידי כך צריך אדם להרגיש בגדר אהבה
כזאת דרך החוש. בבריאת האדם כתיב: "על כן יעזב איש את אביו ואת
אמו ודבק באשתו והיו לבשר אחד" — והוא הדבקות הגמורה של
האוהב בנאהב. ועיין שם ברמב"ן ובספורנו — ובהתקיים בו באדם זו
הדבקות, יוכשר להתעלות לאותה הדבקות השלמה של ביטול האוהב
בנאהב שבאהבת השם. ויתכן לפי זה להבין שמה שאמר ה': "לא טוב
היות האדם לבדו", הוא, כי אי אפשר שיגיע לתכלית השלמות של
דבקות בה' כל עוד שהוא לבדו, ולא ירגיש בחושיו ענין האהבה של
הדבקות הגמורה. ולכן למדונו רז"ל שכל אדם שאין לו אשה שרוי בלא
טובה דכתיב לא טוב היות האדם לבדו (יבמות ס"ב, ב') שהטובה שהיא
טובה בעצם היא הדבקות בה' יתברך אשר בזה זוכה לקבל טובתו של
השי"ת שהוא הטוב האמיתי, וכל שאין לו אשה אי אפשר להגיע לידי
כך.

וכל זה מבו' בדבריו של ר' יצחק דמן עכו ז"ל שהביא בראשית חכמה —
בסוף פ"ד משער האהבה — שמי שלא חשק לאשה הוא דומה לחמור
ופחות ממנו והטעם כי מהמורגש צריך שיבחין העבודה האלקית, ע"כ.

ה. וזהו ביאור דבריהם ז"ל שבשעת פגישת יעקב אבינו ע"ה עם יוסף
הצדיק היה קורא קריאת שמע, שבהגיעו לידי הרגשת אהבת אב לבנו
האהוב שהוא ממנו וחלקו — עיין נתיבות עולם בנתיב אהבת ה' — העביר
והעלה האהבה למקורה העליון — באהבת ה' — אשר זהו תכלית ענין
קריאת שמע.

ו. מתוך כך עומדים אנו על עומק המשל של אהבת ה' המשולה באהבת
איש ואשתו. תוקף התשוקה מתברר באשה בהיות שביסודה נבראת
למען יגיע האדם על ידה לדבקות בה' — ולכן האשה שאין לה דבקות
הבעל אלי' היא חסרת קיום — ולכן תגדל אצלה התשוקה — ולכן
במשל מוצאים אנו תשוקת ישראל לדבקות בה' נמשלת בתשוקת האשה
לבעל נעוריה, ועצם הדבקות של האהבה — קרבת ה' לעמו — נמשלת
באהבת הדבקות של בעל לאשתו.

ז. עניין הקדושה הוא השפעת השי״ת בהארת פניו למתקרב אליו ודבק בו — דרך ה׳, פרק ה׳ — ולכן כל השירים שעניינם הקירוב אל ה׳ יתברך בהכרת מלכותו וטובתו הם קדש, אבל שיר השירים שעניינו להורות על תכלית הדבקות במלואה ושלמותה, הנה היא הקדושה שאין למעלה הימנה, ושיר השירים קדש קדשים.

ח. ויש בזה עוד עומק, שכל הלשונות שבמשל הן עצמיים ובשרשם העליון עניינם נשגב למאד, אלא שהעניינים הרמים האלה משתלשלים ויורדים מעולם לעולם עד שמגיעים אלינו ומצטיירים לנו בצורה זו הנאותה לפי מציאות האדם בעולם הזה. (עיין נועם דברי השל״ה הקדוש בהקדמתו, ועיין מה שהאריך בזה מרן הגאון ר׳ יוסף ליב בלוך זצ״ל אב״ד ור״מ דטלז בשיעור דעת ״נשמת התורה״ ובשיעו״ד ״כי כל בשמים ובארץ״). ולפי מצבנו אנו הדברים הם דברי משל לנמשל נשגב ונעלה. אבל במציאות הדברים באמיתות שרשם העליון, אין כאן משל, אלא שהכל הוא לשון הנמשל עצמו.

ולכן עלינו לדעת שכל פרטי המשל אין בהם שום יתר, ח״ו, שאין המשל כמשלי בני אדם, שכל הנאמר ברוח הקודש מכוון הוא בדקדוק גמור אל הנמשל, ובפרט שלפי עומק הדברים בשרשם מדובר בנמשל עצמו.

ט. מכיון שהמדובר בשיר השירים הוא תכלית השלמות הגמורה שבדבקות האדם בה׳ יתברך, וקדושת אור פניו המתהוה בזו הדבקות, הרי זה מחייב שהשיר יכלול עניני האמצעים שעל ידם יגיע האדם לזו הדבקות, והם התורה והמצוות. ולכן כל המבואר בדבריהם ז״ל מעניינים אלה במדרשי שיר השירים הוא מוכרח מצד עצמו. וכן כל עניני גאולה וגלות, שכר ועונש, גילוי אורו והסתר פניו נמצאים הם בשיר השירים כפי שביארו לנו רז״ל.

י. כל האמור בזה אינו אלא ביאור קצר לדברי הרמב״ם בפרק יו״ד מה׳ תשובה, ה״ג: ״וכיצד היא האהבה הראוי׳ הוא שיאהב את ה׳ אהבה גדולה יתירה עזה מאד עד שתהא נפשו קשורה באהבת ה׳ ונמצא שוגה בה תמיד כאילו חולה חולי האהבה שאין דעתו פנוי׳ מאהבת אותה אשה והוא שוגה בה תמיד בין בשבתו בין בקומו בין בשעה שהוא אוכל ושותה. יתר מזה תהי׳ אהבת ה׳ בלב אוהביו שוגים בו תמיד כמו שצונו בכל לבבך ובכל נפשך, והוא ששלמה אמר דרך משל: ״כי חולת אהבה אני,״ וכל שיר השירים משל הוא לעניין זה״.

יעזרנו ה׳ ית׳ לאהבה וליראה אותו לטוב לנו כל הימים.

An Overview —

Shir HaShirim / Symphony of Creation

I. David — Source of Solomon's Temple

The Golden Era of Jewish history began when Solomon ascended to the throne of his illustrious father. The land was at peace, the world was awed at his wisdom and paid tribute to his greatness. But most of all, the splendor of the era would shine forth from the mountain in Jerusalem where Solomon was to build the *Beis HaMikdash*, the Holy Temple. Solomon built it, but it was not his. The Temple was King David's; its erection an outgrowth of his will and labor, its holiness a product of his august personality and righteousness.

The splendor of the era would shine forth from the mountain in Jerusalem where Solomon was to build the Beis HaMikdash, the Holy Temple. Solomon built it, but it was not his. The Temple was King David's.

In the year 2892 (868 BCE) King David moved his capital from Hebron to Jerusalem. He was finally the acknowledged king of all twelve tribes, his reign solidified. David looked about him and saw that something was lacking.

וַיֹּאמֶר הַמֶּלֶךְ אֶל נָתָן הַנָּבִיא רְאֵה נָא אָנֹכִי יוֹשֵׁב בְּבֵית אֲרָזִים וַאֲרוֹן הָאֱלֹהִים יֹשֵׁב בְּתוֹךְ הַיְרִיעָה. וַיֹּאמֶר נָתָן אֶל הַמֶּלֶךְ כֹּל אֲשֶׁר בִּלְבָבְךָ לֵךְ עֲשֵׂה כִּי ה׳ עִמָּךְ.

And the king said to Nathan the prophet, "See now, I am living in a house of cedar while the Ark of God dwells within 'the curtain!' " And Nathan said to the king, "Whatever is in your heart go and do, for HASHEM *is with you"* (II Samuel 7:2-3).

David was disturbed. In a kingdom that was more and more assuming the character of permanence, the Ark of HASHEM was still a wanderer. The Exodus from Egypt had taken place in 2448, more than four hundred forty-four years earlier. A year later, the Tabernacle in the desert had been dedicated. Never intended to be permanent, it had accompanied the Children of Israel through all their wanderings in the desert, being dismantled and reassembled with every journey. After Joshua led the people into Eretz Yisrael, the Tabernacle was erected in Gilgal.

In 2503, a new period began. A stone building covered with the tapestried roof of the Tabernacle was erected in Shiloh. It was to serve as the home of the Ark and the national altar until the destruction of Shiloh and the capture of the Ark by the Philistines (*I Samuel* Ch. 4) three hundred and sixty-nine years later. The national altar moved first to Nob and then to Gibeon.

David became king in 2884, but his reign was accepted only by his own tribe of Judah. After seven years of strife, he was finally accepted by all and, amid celebration and revelry, the Ark was moved to Jerusalem. But when David looked around him, his happiness was destroyed. From his own palace he could see the tent that housed the Ark. The Holy of Holies in a curtain dwelling! David knew that Mount Moriah in Jerusalem was steeped in history: past and future. Adam had erected an altar there on the very spot from whose earth he had been created; Cain and Abel sacrificed there; Noah did the same, and there Abraham had been ready to offer his son, Isaac, as an offering to HASHEM (*Rambam, Hilchos Beis Ha-Bechirah* 2:2). David knew the exact place because its location had been transmitted to him in a tradition beginning directly from Moses (*Yalkut Shimoni, I Chronicles* 1081).

But when David looked around him, his happiness was destroyed . . . The Holy of Holies in a curtain dwelling!

The Wish to Build So it was that David made known to Nathan his desire to build a Holy Temple for God. Nathan's affirmative reply was not based on his own surmise. He knew that the great David was indeed the ideal person whom God wanted as the builder of His Temple.

Nathan said, "Had not God intended that you
should build the Temple, it would not have even entered your mind to do so, for God commanded that
it be written about you, בִּקֵּשׁ ה' לוֹ אִישׁ כִּלְבָבוֹ, HASHEM
has sought for Himself a man after His own heart"
(I Samuel 13:14). [This was Samuel's declaration to
King Saul that God had sought a more worthy king,
i.e., David.] (Midrash Shocher Tov).

But that night, God appeared to Nathan again
with a new prophecy to David. The king's hope
was not to be realized; he would not build God's
Temple.

וַהֲקִימֹתִי אֶת זַרְעֲךָ אַחֲרֶיךָ ... הוּא יִבְנֶה בַיִת לִשְׁמִי
I shall raise up after you your offspring
... He shall build a House for My Name
(II Samuel 7:12, 13).

So the Temple would be built not by David, but
by his son. But what of God's earlier promise to
Nathan that the builder of the Temple would indeed
be David? How are we to resolve the contradiction between the two verses? Midrash Shocher Tov answers,
"Even though Solomon will build the Temple, it will
be called after your name [the Temple of David]."
David was surely worthy to build the Temple, but
Nathan the prophet came and said to him,

דָּם לָרֹב שָׁפַכְתָּ וּמִלְחָמוֹת גְּדֹלוֹת עָשִׂיתָ לֹא תִבְנֶה בַיִת
לִשְׁמִי כִּי דָמִים רַבִּים שָׁפַכְתָּ אַרְצָה לְפָנָי.
You have shed much blood and have made
great wars. You shall not build a Temple
for My Name's sake, for you have shed
much blood upon the ground before Me (I
Chronicles 22:8).

*David's
Dedication*

The Temple was dedicated with a song that be-
gins מִזְמוֹר שִׁיר חֲנֻכַּת הַבַּיִת לְדָוִד, A Psalm; a song of
the dedication of the Temple, by David (Psalms
30:1): David's dedication, David's song, David's
Temple. On its face, the psalm seems strange. It is
introduced as a hymn of dedication to the Temple,

yet the psalm does not speak about the Temple at all. *Rav S.R. Hirsch* in his *Commentary to Psalms* explains:

"It is a description of a lifetime of experiences, attesting to the healing and deliverance, trials and bliss which God sends to those who devote themselves to Him in love.

The nature and significance of the Temple, the Jewish House of God . . . is primarily intended to bring to mind the nearness of God on earth, the intimate relationship of God and man — the presence of the Lord in the midst of human endeavor as well as the heavenward striving of man toward Him. The Sanctuary of the Lord is nothing else but a concrete symbol of the truth that wherever all of man's spiritual and physical existence and striving is devoted to attain God's favor to the practical application of the law of God, then all of human life, both individual and communal, becomes a throne of Cherubim. [This is indicated by the command] to build a Sanctuary: וְעָשׂוּ לִי מִקְדָּשׁ וְשָׁכַנְתִּי בְּתוֹכָם, *They shall make a Sanctuary for Me — so that I may dwell among them* (*Exodus* 25:8) . . . We can readily understand the thought that led David to decide to build a permanent sanctuary for the Lord. David was imbued with the sense of the immediate nearness, guidance, and direction of God which he had experienced throughout all the years of his agitated life . . . "

The Temple was intended to be the earthly embodiment of the Revelation at Sinai. Just as the Godly Presence descended on Sinai, it was to rest upon the Tabernacle and the Temple; and just as God transmitted His message to man from Sinai, so would He transmit His word to man from atop the Holy Ark that contained the Tablets of the Law. *Ramban* (*Exodus* Ch. 25) draws several parallels between

Wherever all of man's spiritual and physical existence and striving is devoted to attain God's favor, then all of human life, becomes a throne of Cherubim.

the Giving of the Torah at Sinai and the role of the Tabernacle. It is plain from *Ramban* that the central role of the Temple is as the repository of the Tablets and the source of the word of God. The home of the Sanhedrin in close proximity to the Temple is dictated by the very mission of the Temple as the permanent embodiment of the Giving of the Torah. This central role of the Temple as continuation of the Sinaitic Revelation is the reason that the Altar and the sacrificial service are also there. Because the Temple is the home of Torah, the offerings that are the Divinely ordained device for drawing closer to Him must be in the same place (*Harav Gifter*).

The home of the Sanhedrin in close proximity to the Temple is dictated by the very mission of the Temple.

Why Not David

As the commentators have pointed out down the centuries, there is a spiritual content to the apparently "coincidental" history of the fathers of our nation. As Nathan told David (see above), the king could not have requested permission to build the Temple had not God selected him for the task. His request was not a coincidence; it indicated a deep, inner longing, one that reverberated in tune with the Heavenly will. Indeed, David's very being was like a harp in the hands of God. Not only his sweet songs, but his life was the instrument upon which the Heavenly score was played.

Indeed, David's very being was like a harp in the hands of God. Not only his sweet songs, but his life was the instrument upon which the Heavenly score was played.

Therefore, when David was chagrined that he was considered a shedder of blood and for that reason had become disqualified to build the Sanctuary, God reassured him by revealing the deeper meaning of Nathan's prophecy:

"Do not fear, David, by your life, all the blood you shed are considered before Me as if they were offerings. If you were to build it, it would last forever, never to be destroyed even though Israel would sin. It is revealed before Me that Israel will sin and, because the Temple will not be built by you, it will be possible to punish them by destroying the

Temple instead of destroying them" (Midrash Shocher Tov 62).

Thus we must see David's experiences in a new light. His wars were necessary preludes to the Temple, and his efforts to accumulate material and commitments for the future construction of the Temple were expressions of his own intimate and necessary relationship to the construction of the Sanctuary that would be called the House of David.

The True Struggle The Sages say that the Temple was called the House of David because he dedicated his life for it. David's physical wars and tribulations were the worldly guise of a spiritual struggle. When a human enemy sets itself up as an enemy of the Jewish nation, or of so supreme a figure as David who is the embodiment of the people, force of arms is a superficial aspect of the struggle. The true struggle is spiritual. That is why our Sages speak constantly of the Angel of Esau, the Angel of Egypt, the Angel of the Sea; *spiritual* forces of evil were attacking Israel's spiritual will for good.

If Israel's spirit were defeated, its armies would collapse. If its spirit remained strong, its mortal enemies would be vanquished. If Israel's spirit were defeated, its armies would collapse. If its spirit remained strong, its mortal enemies would be vanquished.

When Amalek attacked Israel soon after the Exodus, Joshua led Israel on the battlefield while Moses went up to a hilltop to pray.

וְהָיָה כַּאֲשֶׁר יָרִים מֹשֶׁה יָדוֹ וְגָבַר יִשְׂרָאֵל וְכַאֲשֶׁר יָנִיחַ יָדוֹ וְגָבַר עֲמָלֵק.

And it happened that when Moses raised his hand, Israel was stronger, and when he lowered his hand, Amalek was stronger (Exodus 17:11).

It was not Moses' hands which prevailed or lost the battle. He raised his hands in prayer to inspire Israel's eyes to rise to Heaven and its hearts to be dedicated to its Father in Heaven. When he lowered his hands, Israel turned its attention from God back to the human enemy. During those moments when they fought Amalek instead of fighting their own baseness, they were beaten back (*Rosh Hashanah* 29a, see *Tosafos Yom Tov*).

Jacob, too, was a great warrior on the battlefield with his sword and his bow. But there are other battlefields and other kinds of swords and bows than material ones. Shortly before his death, Jacob awarded Joseph the city of Shechem, אֲשֶׁר לָקַחְתִּי מִיַּד הָאֱמֹרִי בְּחַרְבִּי וּבְקַשְׁתִּי, *which I took from the hand of the Amorite with my sword and my bow* (*Genesis* 48:22). After Simeon and Levi killed the male inhabitants of Shechem, the neighboring Amorites assembled to avenge the decimated city. Jacob donned his sword and bow to fight them off (*Rashi*).

Targum renders the words *sword and bow* as בִּצְלוֹתִי וּבְבָעוּתִי, *with my prayers and supplications.* Some might see Jacob as the powerful warrior, the mighty man who could single-handedly remove large stones that a group of shepherds could not budge (ibid. 29:7-10). Eyewitnesses could report on his defense of Shechem with a flailing sword and powerful bow. But Jacob knew that his sword was lethal because behind it was a prayer; that his bow was invincible because behind it was a supplication. And he knew that just as a bow shoots more powerfully the tighter it is drawn, the greater the intensity of its devotion and concentration, the more a prayer can accomplish (*Kotzker*).

But Jacob knew that his sword was lethal because behind it was a prayer; that his bow was invincible because behind it was a supplication.

Preparing for Solomon — David's true war was the battle against the evil inclination, the יֵצֶר הָרָע. That battle had to be won before the Holy Temple could be built. Having subjugated the forces of evil, he had prepared the way for a more tranquil day, a more tranquil king:

הִנֵּה בֵן נוֹלָד לָךְ הוּא יִהְיֶה אִישׁ מְנוּחָה וַהֲנִיחוֹתִי לוֹ מִכָּל אוֹיְבָיו מִסָּבִיב כִּי שְׁלֹמֹה יִהְיֶה שְׁמוֹ וְשָׁלוֹם וָשֶׁקֶט אֶתֵּן עַל יִשְׂרָאֵל בְּיָמָיו.

Behold, a son will be born to you; he will be a man of rest, and I shall grant him rest from all his enemies all around, for his name will be Solomon, and I will bestow peace and tranquility upon Israel in his days (I Chronicles 22:9).

Solomon, the tranquil son who would be master of tranquility, heir to the legacy of holiness for which David had fought the inner enemy and the legacy of security for which he had fought the outer enemy, was born relatively late in David's life. He assumed the throne in 2924 when he was only 12 years old. First he assumed the reins of government and consolidated his dominion over the country. Then in the fourth year of his reign, four hundred eighty years after the Exodus (*I Kings* 6:1), he commenced the great work of his life, the construction of the Temple. Seven and a half years later, his work was completed (ibid. v. 38).

II. David and Solomon

(This section is taken from the *Overview* to the ArtScroll edition of *Koheles*. Further reading of that *Overview* is recommended for a fuller understanding of Solomon and, therefore, of *Shir HaShirim*.)

David and Solomon, father and son, were the greatest kings Israel ever had, but they were very different personalities with very different missions.

David and Solomon, father and son, were the greatest kings Israel ever had, but they were very different personalities with very different missions.

David was the king who, true to the example of his forefather, Judah, lived not for himself at all. He saw none of his greatness as belonging to himself; everything was at the service of his people. This attribute of unselfish majesty was a legacy of the forefather of the Davidic dynasty, Judah. He established the pattern of complete personal submersion to a mission. The name Judah — יְהוּדָה — has within it the Four-Letter Name of God. But it also has the letter ד, *dalet*, which means poverty. Judah could bear the greatness of his Creator, but, to himself, he was a pauper possessing nothing of his own. Because of this, he was king. (See

Overview to ArtScroll edition of *Ruth* for a more extensive treatment of King David.)

His prototype descendant, David, was the same way. He, the individual, did not matter at all. He was a servant of God and the nation. The name of David begins with a ד, *dalet*, symbolizing his humble origins. Then comes the letter ו, *vav*, a simple straight letter representing his uninterrupted spiritual ascent. But when it was all over and his greatness was acknowledged even by his bitterest enemies, his name concluded with another *dalet*. David remained a pauper: nothing that he had achieved was his own; all was a Heavenly gift to be held in safekeeping for the people because a king belongs to the people (*Chiddushei HaRim*).

David remained a pauper: all was a heavenly gift to be held in safekeeping for the people because a king belongs to the people

Only once in his lifetime do we find David asking for food and drink for himself. When, after David's heartbreaking fasts and prayers, the first offspring of his union with Bathsheba died, he arose from the floor where he had been begging for Heavenly mercy, and asked that his servants bring him a meal. It was his way of showing that he accepted God's decree: כְּשֵׁם שֶׁמְּבָרֵךְ עַל הַטוֹבָה כָּךְ מְבָרֵךְ עַל הָרָעָה, *just as one blesses for the good, one should also bless for the bad* (*Berachos* 48b); acknowledging that, whether in our unseeing eyes God's judgment seems to be benevolent or not, we accept it with the realization, if not the understanding, that whatever He does is truly good. With the exception of that celebration of acceptance, David's life was a chain of fasting and self-denial until he could say of himself that he had killed his evil inclination with fasting (*Pri Tzaddik*).

Solomon's mission was diametrically opposed. He, too, accepted God's will and subjugated his evil inclination. But his way of establishing God's kingdom within himself and Israel was to bring holiness into every aspect of luxurious living. Lavish feasts were everyday occurrences in Solomon's palace. Beauty and ostentation were the rule of the day. The harem held a total of a thousand wives and concubines. But feasts, beauty, and wives did not affect Solomon. It

Solomon's way of establishing God's kingdom within himself and Israel was to bring holiness into every aspect of luxurious living.

was through them that he proved that holiness can conquer every apparent manifestation of hedonism, and it was through his experience with them that he was able to proclaim, *"Futility of futilities, all is futile"* (Koheles 1:2).

David was a man of war; as he fought his evil inclination, so he fought his enemies. For, in truth, they were both the same. The Satan disguises himself in many ways: as Israel's desire and lust for sin, and as foreign enemies seeking to defeat the nation, or at least weaken its spirit. As David defeated his inner enemy, his outward enemy, too, fell defeated.

As David defeated his inner enemy, his outward enemy, too, fell defeated.

Solomon had no foreign enemies. Nor had he an inner enemy. He had defeated his evil inclination, and because he had, foreign enemies became his subjects. He surrounded his life with luxury — to show that it was meaningless; he seemed immersed in love — only to prove that all love belongs only to God. It is from the lavish feasts of Solomon that the Sages learn עוֹשִׂין סְעוּדָּה לִגְמָרָהּ שֶׁל תּוֹרָה, *one makes a feast upon completion of the Torah* (Midrash). Solomon's feasts were far from the gastronomical orgies portrayed by misreaders of Scripture; they were celebrations of Torah study, deed, and life.

Solomon seemed immersed in love — only to prove that all love belongs only to God.

Solomon's feasts were celebrations of Torah study, deed, and life.

Source of Greatness

Greatness is not a product born of complacency; it is forged from the tension of a struggle to emerge from darkness and create light. Solomon's lifework was to wallow in darkness that masqueraded as light; to indulge in comfort, pleasure, and luxury; to reign in peace and security — and still to recognize that the true light was spiritual, that great accomplishment was in the mind, heart, and soul; not in palaces, stables, and treasuries. He testifies in *Koheles* Ch. 2 that he denied himself virtually nothing. That and the astounding total of his wives paint the picture of what most people have taken to be the prototype of the Oriental potentate. But Solomon was as different from that popular stereotype as is light from darkness.

Of Solomon's three sacred books — *Shir HaShirim, Mishlei,* and *Koheles* — the one whose content *seems* least sacred is *Shir HaShirim.* Yet the *Midrash* says that all the books of Scripture are holy, but that *Shir HaShirim* is holy of holies. The Sages have their own definition of holy.

The Midrash says that all the books of Scripture are holy, but that Shir HaShirim is holy of holies

בְּכָל מָקוֹם שֶׁאַתָּה מוֹצֵא גֶּדֶר עֶרְוָה וְתַאֲוָה שָׁם אַתָּה מוֹצֵא קְדוּשָׁה.

Wherever you find a barrier against immorality and lust, there you find holiness (Midrash).

True holiness is not found in ceremonial robes, rolling eyes, and pious expressions, but in personal chastity and control. *Shir HaShirim,* an allegorical rendering of the love between God and Israel, shows Solomon as a passionate young man; the casual reader easily sees in it the Solomon who married a thousand wives and who indulged every mortal whim. How false a vision! *Shir HaShirim* is *holy of holies!* — because its author was a man who was able to descend to the murky depths of physical indulgence and remain complete, untouched, and unsullied. In Jewish belief, there is no such thing as a profane person producing a holy work. A book which is holy of holies can be produced only by a man who is holy of holies — and that holiness, by definition, means abstinence from lust and obsession with pleasure. For Solomon to achieve such holiness while living the sort of life that he did is the most eloquent testimony to the sort of human being he was: a holy of holies. His love was the antithesis of this world; it was a love that belonged purely to God and it was a paramount instance of the rule that light emerges from darkness. Only a heart that has tasted the extreme of earthly darkness and from there seeks Godliness in its revulsion to the pseudopleasures of animal lust can taste the utmost spiritual delight of the knowledge that, in the truest sense, the delusions of material necessity, reward, and joy are but a mirage, that they have no meaningful existence at all (*Resisei Layla*).

In Jewish belief, there is no such thing as a profane person producing a holy work. A book which is holy of holies can be produced only by a man who is holy of holies.

His love was the antithesis of this world; it was a love that belonged purely to God.

III. Essence of Song

פָּתַח רַבִּי יוֹסֵי וְאָמַר שִׁיר הַשִּׁירִים אֲשֶׁר לִשְׁלמֹה
שִׁירָתָא דָא אִתְּעַר לַהּ שְׁלמֹה מַלְכָּא כַּד אִתְבְּנֵי בֵּי
מַקְדְּשָׁא וְעַלְמִין כֻּלְּהוּ. אִשְׁתְּלִימוּ בִּשְׁלֵמוּתָא חֲדָא ...
וּבֵי מַקְדְּשָׁא אִתְבְּנֵי כְּגַוְונָא דִלְעֵילָא בְּשַׁעֲתָא דְּאִתְבְּנֵי
בֵּי מַקְדְּשָׁא דִּתַתָּא לָא הֲוָה חֶדְוָה קַמֵּיהּ קב״ה מִיוֹמָא
דְּאִתְבְּרֵי עַלְמָא כְּהַהוּא יוֹמָא.

Rabbi Yosi began: King Solomon was inspired to compose the Song of Songs when the Holy Temple was built and all the spheres, upper and lower, were completed with one wholeness ... and the Holy Temple was built as a replica of the Holy Temple above. When the Holy Temple was built below [on earth], there was no greater joy before the Holy One, blessed is He, from the day the world was created than on that day (Zohar).

W e can easily understand why the completion of the Temple should move Solomon to song.

Indeed, who would not sing when his eyes beheld the handiwork of human beings becoming the abode of the Divine Presence? But the *Zohar* attributes the song to more than the successful conclusion of many years of dreaming, planning, accumulating, and building. "All the spheres, upper and lower, were completed with one wholeness," the *Zohar* says. A mere building, no matter what the level of its magnificence, would not have inspired Song of Songs, the tribute which Rabbi Akiva calls Holy of Holies, the masterpiece of which he says, "the world was not worthy of the day when Song of Songs was composed." The building without the wholeness would have been nothing more than a brilliant example of Oriental splendor and opulence. Solomon was not the

only potentate who built a lavish, splendid temple, but he was the only one who built one worthy of the

Divine Presence, and he was the only one who composed a Song of Songs, an outpouring of Holy Spirit and passionate love of God that dwarfed every song in Scripture in its holiness and the joy it inspired in God.

Rabbi Akiva attributes the greatness of the day to its Song, rather than its Temple!

The Temple was completed on the day Song of Songs was composed, yet Rabbi Akiva attributes the greatness of the day to its Song, rather than its Temple! And the *Zohar* describes Song of Songs as the culmination of a "wholeness" greater than any that had ever come before, a wholeness sufficient to inspire the highest level of Divine joy.

Surely, the Torah's concept of "song" is as elevated from mere poetry as is the light of the sun from the glow of a candle. The *Targum* notes that only ten songs were composed to God;[1] of all the visions of the prophets, the psalms of David, and the unrecorded myriads of Heavenly praises composed by millions of inspired Jews, only ten are given the lofty title "Song," and Solomon's Song of Songs is elevated above them all.

What is "song"? What is "wholeness"? What is the unique greatness of Song of Songs?

Who Sings? Who sings the praise of the Creator? Man, even the greatest men, do it only infrequently. But the praises of God are sung constantly.

Who sings the praise of the Creator? ... The praises of God are sung constantly.

הַשָּׁמַיִם מְסַפְּרִים כְּבוֹד אֵל וּמַעֲשֵׂה יָדָיו מַגִּיד הָרָקִיעַ

The heavens declare the glory of God,

1. "Ten songs were sung in this world; this song [Song of Songs] is praised above all. The first song was sung by Adam when his sin was forgiven and the Sabbath came and protected him. He opened his mouth and said, *A psalm. A song to the Sabbath day* (Psalm 92). The second song was sung by Moses and the Children of Israel when the Master of the Universe split the sea ... *Then Moses and the Children of Israel chose to sing* (Exodus 15:1). The third song was sung by the Children of Israel when a well of water was given to them as it says, *Then Israel sang* (Numbers 21:17). The fourth song ... Moses ... said before he died ... *Give ear, O heavens* (Deut. 32:1). The fifth song was sung by Joshua ... when he stopped the sun ... *Then Joshua spoke* (Joshua 10:12). The sixth song was sung by Barak and Deborah when God delivered Sisera ... into their hands (Judges 5:1). The seventh song was sung by Hannah when a son was given to her ... (I Samuel 2:1). The eighth song was sung by David ... for all the miracles ... (II Samuel 22:1). The ninth song was sung by Solomon ... (Song of Songs). The tenth song will be sung by the Children of Exile when they are redeemed from their exile ..." (Isaiah 30:29).

and the firmament tells of His handiwork
(*Psalms* 19:2).

The psalmist says that all of creation tells of the glory of God. Our Sages go further in an esoteric but beautiful little book called פֶּרֶק שִׁירָה, *Chapter of Song.* In it the Sages tell us that every part of creation, from the mighty sun to the lowly ant, from the lilting songbird to the croaking frog, sings its unique song of praise to God composed of one or more verses from Scripture. The earth says that it and its fullness belong to God. The stars proclaim that God alone made the Heavenly hosts. A desert bird blesses the person who learns from it to trust that God will provide his food. The horse says that just as it looks to its master so must all look to God. The ant says that it shows the slothful person how much can be accomplished if he will but utilize the gifts God gave to him.

Every part of creation, from the mighty sun to the lowly ant, from the lilting songbird to the croaking frog, sings its unique song of praise to God.

These are only a few samples of the praises of *Perek Shirah.* What do they represent? Simply this: God's song of praise is sung when every part of creation performs its assigned task. In a symphony orchestra of a hundred musicians, when each player plays his assigned part, the result is an outburst of song that can seem almost heavenly in its beauty. But if there is no harmony, point and counterpoint, if each musician improvises as he pleases without regard to the fused outcome, the result will be not music, but noise: a deafening, horrendous noise. In creation as well, each player has a role: large and small, mighty and weak, each creature was made by God and placed in the universe for a Divine purpose. God asks nothing more than that each perform the task which was assigned to it.

God's song of praise is sung when every part of creation performs its assigned task.

God asks nothing more than that each perform the task which was assigned to it.

Man's Role

But their song cannot attain fulfillment unless man expresses the lessons they embody. The purpose of creation is man: his virtue ennobles it, his sin demeans it. When he hears the message of the sun and the ant and everything in between, creation becomes

But when man sees everything and perceives nothing, then the symphony of creation is playing for a tone-deaf critic. The creatures all perform their tasks, but their song is mute.

the symphony which God intended. But when man sees everything and perceives nothing, when his telescopes show him stars that are thousands of light-years away, and he can recite deadening statistics about the solar system and detail all the data indicating whether life does or does not exist on Mars — but he cannot say, *"The heavens declare the glory of God,"* then the symphony of creation is playing for a tone-deaf critic. He hears sound, but not music; cacophony, but not harmony. The creatures all perform their tasks, but their song is mute (*Yavetz; Sefas Emes*).

As *Rambam* says (*Yesodei HaTorah* 2:2):

> What is the path to His love and awe? When a person meditates upon His wondrous and great deeds and creatures and sees through them His incomparable, infinite wisdom, immediately he loves, praises, exalts, and feels a great urge to know His Great Name. As David said, *"My soul thirsts after the Lord, the living God."* And when he considers these very matters, he immediately trembles backward, fears, and recognizes that he is but a tiny, low, dark creature, standing with puny, insignificant wisdom before He Whose wisdom is perfect. As David said, *"When I see Your heavens, the work of Your fingers, what is man that You consider him?"*

Indeed, the purpose of creation is that man *recognize* purpose and mission in all about him. It is there, but it must be recognized and proclaimed *by him*.

When the Six Days of Creation were done, God said, וַיְכֻלּוּ הַשָּׁמַיִם וְהָאָרֶץ וְכָל צְבָאָם, *Thus the heavens and the earth were finished* (Gen. 2:1). The *Midrash* finds a deeper meaning in the word וַיְכֻלּוּ — שֶׁנַּעֲשׂוּ כֵּלִים, they [heaven and earth] became utensils. The physical aspects of creation, heaven and earth and everything they contained, became the tools by which man was to attain the heights which God intended for him, not for them. The centrality of creation is man's struggle between good and evil, his battle for perfection against the allure of physical existence: the combat between body and soul with each striving to subvert the other to its own ends. When man's soul triumphs over his body, his senses become heightened and he "hears" the song of heaven and earth and their creatures because he recognizes the hand of God in them and their allegiance to *His* will rather than to blind and mindless natural law.

When man's soul triumphs over his body, his senses become heightened and he "hears" the song of heaven and earth.

When man can do that, he becomes witness to creation. This mission of bearing witness is the particular responsibility of the Jew. אַתֶּם עֵדַי נְאֻם ה', *You are My witnesses — the word of* HASHEM *(Isaiah 43:10).* The greatest moments in Jewish history are the times when the nation perceived that the forces of nature are not blind automatons but that מְחַדֵּשׁ בְּכָל יוֹם תָּמִיד מַעֲשֵׂה בְרֵאשִׁית, *He [God] renews constantly, every day, the acts of creation (Sefas Emes).* Not only was the universe created by God, it is constantly recreated. It continues to exist by His grace and it never grows old, stale, and out of His control.

The Nation Doubts

The first time the entire Jewish nation perceived these truths in all their clarity was when, pursued by the attacking Egyptians and facing an impassable Red Sea, the Jews were without the means either to flee or to fight. The fainthearted among them thought they were doomed, that God had taken them from the "safety" of Goshen to face slaughter or even more merciless enslavement.

ה' יִלָּחֵם לָכֶם וְאַתֶּם תַּחֲרִשׁוּן. וַיֹּאמֶר ה' אֶל מֹשֶׁה מַה תִּצְעַק אֵלָי דַּבֵּר אֶל בְּנֵי יִשְׂרָאֵל וְיִסָּעוּ.

[Moses said,] "HASHEM *shall make war for you, and you shall remain silent." And* HASHEM *said to Moses, "Why do you cry out to me? Speak to the Children of Israel and let them journey forth" (Exodus 14:14-15).*

The *Midrash*, in commenting on these verses, quotes:

יִשָּׁקֵנִי מִנְּשִׁיקוֹת פִּיהוּ כִּי טוֹבִים דֹּדֶיךָ מִיָּיִן

Communicate Your innermost wisdom to me again in loving closeness, for Your love is dearer than all earthly delights (Shir HaShirim 1:2).

(This translation follows Rashi's allegorical interpretation as does the entire ArtScroll translation. Literally, however, the verse depicts Israel as asking God to bestow upon it "the kisses of His mouth.")

Rabbi Abraham of Slonim (in *Toras Avos*) explains the imagery of a "kiss" in this context of terror when Israel was beset on all sides and feared for its survival, when it cried out for God's mercy and it saw no natural means of escape. Scripture says,

נֶאֱמָנִים פִּצְעֵי אוֹהֵב וְנַעְתָּרוֹת נְשִׁיקוֹת שׂוֹנֵא

Faithful are the wounds inflicted by a friend; but superfluous are the kisses of a friend (Proverbs 27:6).

A kiss represents love and intimacy, it symbolizes a feeling that comes from the innermost depths of one person to another. It is a physical embodiment of an emotional, spiritual feeling.

Rebuke hurts. And because this is so, there is a natural tendency to appreciate a kiss and lash out against a rebuke.

Rebuke hurts. The average person resents the harsh words of criticism that can wound to the core, that can hurt more than physical wounds. And because this is so, there is a natural tendency to appreciate a kiss and lash out against a rebuke: because friends kiss and enemies rebuke, we tend to assume that whoever kisses is a friend and whoever rebukes is an enemy. "How could it be otherwise," people ask, "if he loved me, how could he hurt me so?"

Wise people know better, however.

Wise people know better, however. Unfortunately, every person has learned to his chagrin that not all kisses are sincere; some are meant only to camouflage hostility and lull the recipient into lowering his guard and relaxing his suspicion. And not every rebuke implies enmity. The true friend, the one who sincerely loves and cares for another, *must* chastise if the occasion demands it. And if the object of his harsh word feels hurt, if he is wounded enough to dislike the friend who loves him so much that he will even risk anger for the sake of friendship, that will not deter the true friend. He is more concerned with helping the object of his affection than in winning selfish popularity. This is Solomon's meaning when he says that the wounds of a friend are more faithful than the countless kisses of an enemy. How unfortunate that so many people are shallow enough to prefer the latter to the former.

The wounds of a friend are more faithful than the countless kisses of an enemy. How unfortunate that so many people are shallow enough to prefer the latter to the former.

Man's Role When the Children of Israel saw themselves entrapped in their Red Sea encampment, they saw only God's rebukes, but no kisses. Had all the miracles of Moses been but a device to lure them out of the security of slavery and make them the helpless prey of a vengeful Pharaoh? Was God Himself their enemy?

> וַיִּירְאוּ מְאֹד וַיִּצְעֲקוּ בְנֵי יִשְׂרָאֵל אֶל ה' ... הֲמִבְּלִי
> אֵין קְבָרִים בְּמִצְרַיִם לְקַחְתָּנוּ לָמוּת בַּמִּדְבָּר ... כִּי טוֹב
> לָנוּ עֲבֹד אֶת מִצְרַיִם מִמֻּתֵנוּ בַּמִּדְבָּר.

> *... And they were very frightened ... "Were there no graves in Egypt that you took us to die in the Wilderness? ... for it is better that we should serve Egypt than that we should die in the Wilderness (Exodus 14:10-12).*

What they did not realize at first was that they were being subjected to the *faithful wounds inflicted by a friend.* God was placing them in an impossible predicament so that they would be forced to see that salvation could come only from Him [see comm. to *Shir HaShirim* 2:14]. They cried out to Him in fervent prayer as they had not done under the lash of Egypt's slavemasters. That was what God wanted: He wanted their prayer, their realization that human devices were of no avail, their

That was what God wanted: He wanted their prayer.

recognition that *their* battle could be only against the inclination within themselves that sought to remove them from faith in God. To fight Pharaoh was futile and unnecessary. Pharaoh's power was simply a reflection of their own spiritual weakness. That was why, as the *Midrash* says, God appeared to them at the sea in the guise of a young warrior. He was making them understand that it was a time of spiritual warfare, of repentance, self-perfection, prayer. Once they had done that, God told them through Moses, מַה תִּצְעַק אֵלָי, *Why do you cry out to Me? (Exodus* 14:15) — I have already heard their outcry (*Midrash*). Because there were those among them who saw the truth and fought the personal spiritual battle, God appeared as a warrior ready to fight Egypt. He had shown them that all their fear and suffering had been for a purpose, that their night had been a prelude to the dawn, so that they might be ready to receive the light, so that they might better understand the difference between light and darkness, so that they might realize that God's rebukes are truly the most loving kisses.

Pharaoh's power was simply a reflection of their own spiritual weakness.

God's rebukes are truly the most loving kisses.

Sin Becomes Song

Beis HaLevi carries this theme further. When the sea had been split, the Jews saved and the Egyptians destroyed, Moses and the Children of Israel sang the Song at the Sea. He began those glorious words with the word אָז, *then.* The *Midrash* says:

אָמַר מֹשֶׁה: בְּאָז חָטָאתִי שֶׁאָמַרְתִּי „וּמֵאָז בָּאתִי אֶל פַּרְעֹה לְדַבֵּר בִּשְׁמֶךָ הֵרַע לָעָם הַזֶּה", בְּאָז אֲנִי אוֹמֵר שִׁירָה.

Moses said, I sinned with the word אָז, *then,* for I said: "*From then on* [וּמֵאָז] *when I came to speak to Pharaoh . . . he did evil to this people*" (*Exodus* 5:23). Therefore I use that same word, אָז, *then,* to begin my song.

When Moses came to Pharaoh to demand that Israel be permitted to bring offerings to God, the king became infuriated. In retaliation he increased the severity of the assigned labor. Brokenhearted, Moses complained to God that instead of helping the Jews, his mission had succeeded only in making their ordeal worse. He began his lament with the words, וּמֵאָז בָּאתִי אֶל פַּרְעֹה, *from then on when I came to speak to Pharaoh.*

If someone is helped out of distress, he will rejoice in the salvation, but he would still have preferred that the travail had never beset him at all. Not so when someone realizes that even his distress was truly for his benefit. Then he rejoices not only in the salvation but also in his newfound understanding of "travail" for he knows that each was a blessing.

The cruel slavery of Egypt was a national ordeal that very nearly destroyed the Jewish people. It plunged them to the forty-ninth level of impurity and so degraded them that the Angel of the Sea questioned the justice of drowning the Egyptians after saving the Jews: "These are idolaters and these are idolaters!" The liberation from Egypt was originally seen as a redemption from a plight that need never have come about.

Then Israel saw more deeply ... Because of their ordeals, God's glory on earth became known in a blaze of miracles. Then Israel saw more deeply. They saw that their enslavement in Egypt and their entrapments at the Sea both served a lofty purpose. They had been made the instrument of a revelation far beyond any that had ever occurred in human history. Because of their ordeals, God's glory on earth became known in a blaze of miracles. And the very severity of the degradation and extent of the danger showed how great was the mercy of God.

Thus, the thanksgiving and praise of Moses and Israel were not merely for the miracles but for the trial, not merely for the salvation but for the suffering. That was why Moses began the song with the word that recalled his sin; he was thanking God even for the predicament which had so plunged him into depression that he had dared question the purpose of his mission. Now he understood that the depth of his anguish was intended to heighten the glorification of God and Israel's perception of it.

This, then, is the deepest, truest meaning of the Torah's concept of "Song." There *is* a profound harmony in creation. Every part of God's handiwork plays its role in His design. Only one ingredient impedes its completion: man's lack of insight. When man fails to see the truth, the interaction, the harmony, then the song of creation remains unheard; because it is man's function to give it voice, it remains mute. At the Splitting of the Sea, Israel saw! It understood the purpose of its own suffering; it saw that every part of the universe, physical as well as spiritual, was a cog in the Heavenly mechanism. Because of what it actually experienced, it was able to have faith even in what was still beyond its ability to understand.

There is a profound harmony in creation ... Only one ingredient impedes its completion: man's lack of insight.

At the Splitting of the Sea, Israel saw!

After the salvation, the Torah tells us וַיַּאֲמִינוּ בַּה׳ וּבְמֹשֶׁה עַבְדּוֹ, *and they had faith in* HASHEM *and in Moses, His servant* (Exodus 14:31).

Because they believed, they were able to sing (*Tanchuma*). The attainment of belief when intellect combines with the subconscious goodness of the soul makes man hear the message of his innermost being that tells him, Sing! When man can so elevate himself that he hears and feels the call of his true self, he is separated from the vulgarity of his animal nature. A new world is revealed to him. In this material world, he sees the eternal world and he sings the song of eternity, the praise of the eternal God.

Because they believed, they were able to sing.

This song is constantly in man's soul. But there are only instants when he hears its notes, and then only when he brings belief in God to his everyday life on earth. If he can attain the height where faith is never-ending and he is always guided by its light, he will always hear the song in his heart. That is why such lofty songs are introduced by the Torah in future tense; why our Sages infer from this future tense such as that in the Song at the Sea — יָשִׁיר, *he "will" sing* — that the dead will rise again to new life, just as through faith they have sublimated their mortal lives. The future tense suggests timelessness,

If he can attain the height where faith is neverending and he is always guided by its light, he will always hear the song in his heart.

eternity, the conquest of animal existence and limitations (*Pirkei Emunah*).

Truth and Faith

Truth is what someone can see and touch. Faith is what he believes.

There is a difference between אֱמֶת, the perception of *truth*, and אֱמוּנָה, *faith*. Truth is what someone can see and touch. Faith is what he believes. In a sense, truth is firmer than faith because it is based on the tangible, on confirmed knowledge. But truth is also limited for precisely the same reason. At the Sea, Israel understood God's mercy then and there. They understood His purpose in having inflicted suffering upon them during the years of exile and slavery. That knowledge had become "truth" for them. But what of future trials? How would they and their descendants react to a different set of circumstances, one that cast them under a jackboot, clouded God's Presence, and masked His mercy? Would they have "*faith*" then when the "*truth*" could not be seen? The greatness of Israel at the Sea was such that the commonest maidservant saw prophecy beyond the visions of Ezekiel and even the children could perceive the reality of God so vividly that they could point with their fingers and say, זֶה אֵלִי וְאַנְוֵהוּ, "*This is my God!*" (*Exodus* 15:2).

They believed! So much was revealed to them that they had complete faith that every conceivable circumstance would be but another manifestation of God's will and mercy (*Chiddushei HaRim*).

They had complete faith that every conceivable circumstance would be but another manifestation of God's will and mercy.

This is the prerequisite of song: Man's perception is that everything plays its role and so he must give expression to the song of creation through his own deeds and the song that flows from the soul. All ten Scriptural songs listed by the *Midrash* were sung — *could* be sung — only during the highest levels of holiness. Even the miracle of Purim, one which by its very essence revealed that every "natural" sequence of events is but a glove enclosing the ever-present hand of God (see *Overview, Megillas Esther*, ArtScroll edition), could not produce a Divine song — it could not even be the cause of recitation of *Hallel*. Because it took place outside of the Holy Land, the wellspring of holiness, it could not result in the sort of outpouring of spirit that the Torah calls שִׁירָה, *song* (*Resisei Layla*).

Hallel, by its very nature, implies the perception of creation's message. In explaining why *Hallel* is not recited on Purim, the Talmud cites a version that מְגִילָּה קְרִיאָתָא זוֹ הִיא הַלֵּילָא, the very reading of the *Megillah* constitutes *Hallel*. True, the hiddenness of the Purim miracle precludes the singing of *Hallel*, a song declaring that God's hand is everywhere and that every part of creation sings a hymn of obedi-

The reading of the Megillah reveals that the hiddenness was but an illusion .... That recognition in itself is a form of Hallel.

ence. Nevertheless, the reading of the *Megillah* reveals that the hiddenness was but an illusion, that behind the appearance of coincidence is the reality of God's hand. That recognition in itself is a form of *Hallel* (*Harav Gifter*).

When King Solomon completed the Holy Temple, he did more than finish a building. He caused a Divine joy greater than any since creation. He built a Temple on earth that was a replica of the one on high. Like all Scriptural and Midrashic references to human replication of the heavenly, this connotes spiritual content. (This concept will be more fully dealt with later.) He said, בָּנֹה בָנִיתִי בֵּית זְבֻל לָךְ מָכוֹן לְשִׁבְתְּךָ עוֹלָמִים, *"I have surely built a house of habitation for You, the foundation for Your dwelling forever"* (*I Kings* 8:13). The same recognition that the angels have of the harmony of creation, the recognition that is expressed in their constant songs of praise to God, the recognition that is the essence of the "Holy Temple On High," was brought to earth in the Temple of Solomon. He led Israel in recognizing that all conditions of life on earth are God's product and in His service. This recognition *is* song; the words are but its outward expression.

This recognition is song; the words are but its outward expression.

Positive Peace This, indeed, is the very concept expressed in the name Solomon: שְׁלֹמֹה, *Shlomo*. The word *Shlomo* in Hebrew means שָׁלוֹם שֶׁלּוֹ, *peace is his*. Peace is only possible when each component of the world, a society, or even an individual human being, fulfills the role assigned to it. If a person feels frustrated because conditions of his life do not permit him to indulge a craving, or utilize a talent, or find sufficient time for Torah study, or to be enough at ease mentally so that he can fully assimilate and understand what he learns, then that person is not "at peace" with himself. Of course, a mature human being will learn to adjust; he will not become violent or lash out at everyone around him. He will learn to accept and cope with an unpleasant situation, but that is not peace; it is the absence of war.

Of course, a mature human being will learn to adjust ... But that is not peace; it is the absence of war.

In society, this idea is much more apparent. Crime may be controlled because of the efficiency of the police and the expeditious punishment of the courts. Or wars may not break out because of a balance of power or of terror; nations may not be willing to risk the enormous cost, carnage, and suffering of war. But greed, hatred, conniving, and suspicion remain. Remove the threat of retribution and, as the *Mishnah* in *Avos* puts it, one man would swallow his fellow alive. This, too, is merely the absence of war, not peace.

Peace, Solomon, and Temple

Peace, in Jewish thought, is a positive concept. It implies that every faculty within a person, every person within a society, every society within the world has the opportunity to fulfill itself, is satisfied with its role, carries out its role, and thereby contributes its distinctive tone to the symphony of creation.

The era of King Solomon was unique in history in its approach to that idea. The wars had been fought by David; he had conquered the enemy without and the enemy within, the physical and the spiritual. Solomon's time was one of tranquility, intense Torah scholarship providing peace for the mind and unusual wealth providing peace for material needs and desires. Nations far and wide came to honor the scholar king. They brought tribute to him. The world was at peace. With the completion of the Holy

Temple, offerings to God came from masters, lords, and rulers everywhere. It was truly a time of peace in its most positive sense.

All eyes turned toward the king and Temple: each representing the same ideal. Because just as the Temple was the resting place of the Divine Spirit, so was Solomon. Indeed, *Shalom* is a name of God because He is the ultimate source of all peace. And the *Shlomo* of Song of Songs is מֶלֶךְ שֶׁהַשָּׁלוֹם שֶׁלּוֹ, *the true King* — God — *to Whom peace belongs* (see comm. 1:1).

That is why God told David:

הִנֵּה בֵן נוֹלָד לָךְ הוּא יִהְיֶה אִישׁ מְנוּחָה וַהֲנִיחוֹתִי לוֹ מִכָּל אוֹיְבָיו מִסָּבִיב כִּי שְׁלֹמֹה יִהְיֶה שְׁמוֹ וְשָׁלוֹם וָשֶׁקֶט אֶתֵּן עַל יִשְׂרָאֵל בְּיָמָיו.

Behold, a son will be born to you; he will be a man of rest; and I shall grant him rest from all his enemies all around. His name will be Solomon, and I will bestow peace and tranquility upon Israel in his days (I Chronicles 22:9).

The Lord meant not merely the flesh-and-blood Solomon. He was promising David that a Temple would be built by an ideal person who would preside over an ideal world: a person who would make peace, embody peace, and, as the surrogate of the King to Whom peace belongs, sing the symphony of peace.

IV. Leadership in Song

Not only in the time of Solomon do we find that song as the recognition of the symphony of creation is an essential component of the highest level of spiritual life. Man's ultimate fulfillment has not yet come. That longed-for moment of human destiny will arrive with the coming of the Messiah. Then all the glorious prophecies of the End of Days will come to pass. There was a time when the Messiah very nearly arrived; he was only a murmur away, but . . .

בִּקֵּשׁ הקב״ה לַעֲשׂוֹת חִזְקִיָהוּ מָשִׁיחַ וְסַנְחֵרִיב גּוֹג
וּמָגוֹג, אָמְרָה מִדַּת הַדִּין לִפְנֵי הקב״ע וּמַה דָּוִד
מֶלֶךְ יִשְׂרָאֵל שֶׁאָמַר כַּמָה שִׁירוֹת וְתִשְׁבָּחוֹת לְפָנֶיךָ לֹא
עֲשִׂיתוֹ מָשִׁיחַ, חִזְקִיָהוּ שֶׁעָשִׂית לוֹ כָּל הַנִּסִּים הַלָּלוּ
וְלֹא אָמַר לְפָנֶיךָ שִׁירָה תַּעֲשֵׂהוּ מָשִׁיחַ?

The Holy One, blessed is He, wished to appoint Hezekiah as the Messiah and Sennacherib, Gog and Magog. The Attribute of Justice said before the Holy One, blessed is He, "Master of the Universe! If David, king of Israel, who recited so many songs and praises before You, You did not make the Messiah, then Hezekiah, for whom You performed all these miracles and yet he did not sing a song before You, will you make him the Messiah?" (Sanhedrin 94a).

All parts of creation fulfill their assigned functions, but they are incapable of bringing their song into reality without man. Only man, through his own service of God and his ability to recognize God's greatness and express it, can become the conductor of creation's song, the agent by which the potential of creation is brought to fruition. The Messianic era calls for such fruition. Hidden potential is not enough. It must be expressed by a great leader or by the entire Jewish nation. In the absence of national greatness, a leader can raise his people to such a level. But the outward expression must exist. The time of Messiah is by definition the era when the veils obscuring the Divine Presence are completely stripped away, when the insulation preventing people from hearing the message told by the heavens is removed, when all nations will form a single union performing the will of God.

The time of Messiah is by definition the era when the veils obscuring the Divine Presence are completely stripped away.

Hezekiah as an individual was great enough to be the Messiah, but he failed to sing the song of creation. Because he did not, he fell short, and the Messianic ideal could not be realized in his time (*Maharal, Chiddushei Aggados*).

Hezekiah as an individual was great enough to be the Messiah, but he failed to sing the song of creation.

As we have seen, David himself, despite his awesome greatness, could not be permitted to build the Temple. Nevertheless, it still could have been possible for the Temple to be built in his time. The people were at fault from the time when they entered the Land; they did not want a Temple enough to request permission to build it. It was not until David became chagrined at the contrast between his own dwelling and that of the Ark, that a Jew was filled with an insistent desire to build a worthy resting place for the Divine Presence. Where were the people? Why were they complacent with their curtained Ark? Had they too shared the craving of their king, a Temple would have been built. All David's wars and bloodshed would not have prevented it. But they didn't care, so the majestic task was left for Solomon (*Ramban, Korach*).

The people were at fault; they did not want a Temple enough to request permission to build it.

But what of the Midrashic statement that a Temple built by David could never have been destroyed, that a permanent Temple would have survived the destruction of the people?

It may very well be that what was lacking in David's time was a national recognition of the loftiness — the true nature — of David's songs. His psalms are full of recognition of the harmony of creation. The people, however, were not as great as their king; they failed to understand his songs as the literal expression of what was being sung continuously beneath their feet, before their eyes, and above their perceptions. That was why a Temple built by him would have been too great for the people; because *he* was too great for the people. They no more heard the full nuances and resonances of his song than they heard the tale of the heavens. David's songs contained everything, even the deepest and sublimest expressions of Torah itself. But his generation, great though it was, was unequal to his message.

David's songs contained everything, even the deepest and sublimest expressions of Torah itself. But his generation, great though it was, was unequal to his message.

That is why only David's song of triumph is among the ten songs of history (see *Targum* quoted in footnote, III above), but none of his psalms of praise. As the *Talmud* says in contrasting Hezekiah with David, David sang songs, but Hezekiah didn't. David sang, but his people didn't hear. Hezekiah could have raised the people up to his level, but he did not sing. By song, he could have made himself the Messiah; because he did not sing, his generation's ears remained closed.

Sometimes, leaders sing, but people don't hear. Sometimes the people can be made to hear, but the leaders don't sing. Sometimes, the people are great enough to sing themselves, but their song is diminished because their leaders are not part of the chorus.

When Leaders Are Lacking

אָז יָשִׁיר יִשְׂרָאֵל, וּמִפְּנֵי מַה לֹא נִזְכַּר מֹשֶׁה שָׁם? מִפְּנֵי שֶׁנֶּעֱנַשׁ עַל הַמַּיִם וְאֵין אָדָם מְקַלֵּס לַסְפַּקְלָטוֹר שֶׁלוֹ, וְלָמָּה אֵין שְׁמוֹ שֶׁל הקב״ה נִזְכַּר בָּהּ? מָשָׁל לְשִׁלְטוֹן שֶׁעָשָׂה סְעוּדָה לַמֶּלֶךְ, אָמַר הַמֶּלֶךְ פְּלוֹנִי אוֹהֲבִי שָׁם? אָמְרוּ לוֹ לַאו, אָמַר הַמֶּלֶךְ אִם אֵין אוֹהֲבִי שָׁם אֵינִי שָׁם.

"Then Israel sang" (Numbers 21:17). Why isn't Moses mentioned there? For he was punished because of water, and a person cannot praise his executioner. And why isn't the Name of the Holy One, blessed is He, mentioned in [the song]? It is like the example of a lord who made a banquet for the king. The king said, "Is my friend there?" They said to him, "No." The king said, "If my friend is not there, then I cannot be there" (Yalkut, Chukas).

When, close to the end of the forty years in the Wilderness, a well was miraculously created to supply water to the Jews, the people sang a song of praise to God. But Moses is not mentioned there despite the fact that he was their leader and that the well was created thanks to his and Aaron's merit. Because he sinned in connection with water and, as a result, was punished by being denied the opportunity to enter the Land, he could not praise the gift of water. And because the great Moses did not participate in the song, it was not lofty enough to include the Name of God.

How terrible it is when people are denied their leaders! How terrible it is when people are denied their leaders! At the Splitting of the Sea, Moses led the people in a song of praise. Through him, the people recognized God in His full glory. Even the humblest maidservants perceived and joined. But when forty years later the people — without Moses — saw God's glory and the obedience to it of all creation, their vision was blurred, their spiritual growth stunted. Without Moses, the song consisted of only a few verses, and it even lacked mention of God's Name.

Truly have the Sages taught,

קָשֶׁה סִילוּקָן שֶׁל צַדִּיקִים יוֹתֵר מִצ״ח קְלָלוֹת וְחוּרְבַּן בֵּית הַמִּקְדָּ׳ש.

The passing of the righteous is worse than the ninety-eight curses and the destruction of the Holy Temple (Midrash Eichah).

In the darkest period of Heavenly displeasure, even if the Temple is destroyed, the righteous exponents of Torah can still provide spiritual light and guidance for the people. Indeed, as we have seen above (see *Overview I, Ramban*) the Temple is the embodiment of the Revelation when the Torah was given. Its most essential nature is as a home for the Tablets of the Law rather than as the site of sacrifices. Torah without the Temple can still guide the *Torah without the Temple can still guide the people,* people, but when they are removed, all is plunged *but when they are removed, all* into darkness. Bereft of Torah leaders, the people *is plunged into darkness.* lack the guidance even to understand the meaning and message of the curses brought upon them. Even when the people raise themselves to the level of holy song, they are still unable to attain their potential heights if they are without their leaders (*Michtav Me'Eliyahu*).

V. Love in Its Highest Sense

(The following portions of the Overview are based in large part on the Foreword of Harav Mordechai Gifter שליט״א. The reader is urged to study the Foreword fully and carefully.)

One of the most challenging and difficult of all commandments is

וְאָהַבְתָּ אֵת ה׳ אֱלֹקֶיךָ
You are to love Hashem, your God.

It is a commandment that is constant and that has no limits, for love can always grow in intensity. Yet love cannot be legislated; it cannot be turned on upon someone's command. Therefore, righteous people throughout the ages have sought to find ways to develop a love of God, and then to increase it, intensify it, renew it. People whose consciousness of God never ceases utilize every opportunity to relate to God. Every moment of joy or fulfillment is His gift and therefore increases one's love for Him; every moment of sorrow or frustration is a manifestation of his displeasure and increases one's awe of Him, or, in the eyes of the most righteous people, even the seeming anger is nothing more than a level of mercy that is beyond their ability to recognize. And every earthly manifestation of joy, love, power, wisdom, or any other trait is utilized as a means of better comprehending God or turning one's feelings toward his love, awe, and service.

Righteous people throughout the ages have sought to find ways to develop a love of God.

Utilizing Love There are few moments in our history as poignant as the one when Jacob and Joseph met in Egypt after twenty-two years of separation during which Jacob thought that the finest of his sons was dead.

אָמוּתָה הַפַּעַם אַחֲרֵי רְאוֹתִי אֶת פָּנֶיךָ כִּי עוֹדְךָ חָי
Now I can die, after my having seen your face because you are still alive (Gen. 46:30),

said Jacob during their first meeting. The more deeply one understands the significance of Joseph in the life of Jacob, the patriarch's reasons for showing him obvious favor over his brothers despite the possible repercussions that very nearly came to a tragic fruition, and the role Joseph's descendants were to play in the future of the nation, the more one can appreciate the unimaginable joy Jacob felt when he saw Joseph for the first time after their long separation. Yet there is something truly remarkable in the narrative of that meeting.

וַיֶּאְסֹר יוֹסֵף מֶרְכַּבְתּוֹ וַיַּעַל לִקְרַאת יִשְׂרָאֵל אָבִיו גֹּשְׁנָה
וַיֵּרָא אֵלָיו וַיִּפֹּל עַל צַוָּארָיו וַיֵּבְךְּ עַל צַוָּארָיו עוֹד.

And Joseph harnessed his chariot and went up to meet Israel, his father, in Goshen. He appeared before him, fell on his neck, and he wept on his neck excessively (Genesis 46:29, see Rashi).

We have seen the intense emotion felt by Jacob; *Why didn't Jacob, too, fall on the neck of Joseph and weep for joy? The Sages explain that Jacob was reciting the Shema!* why then did only Joseph embrace and cry? Why didn't Jacob, too, fall on the neck of Joseph and weep for joy? The Sages explain that Jacob was reciting the *Shema*!

On the surface, it would appear to be an incomprehensible act. Had Jacob no other time to say the *Shema* that day? How could it be that he was occupied with its reading precisely at that moment of supreme ecstasy? No, Jacob's decision was no coincidence. Far from indicating a callousness toward the joyous occasion, it was caused by the very momentous nature of the meeting.

We can only begin to imagine what memories and thoughts went through Jacob's mind as he waited for the arrival of Joseph. Indeed, the Torah itself implies the exaltation of the moment by its reference to Jacob as Israel. The name Israel was given him to indicate that

שָׂרִיתָ עִם אֱלֹהִים וְעִם אֲנָשִׁים וַתּוּכָל

you have striven with the Divine and with men and have overcome (Genesis 32:29).

Jacob was called Israel only in his moments of spiritual exaltation. The verses leading up to his meeting with Joseph refer to him as Jacob, for he was frightened of the consequences of the descent to Egypt. But when he awaited Joseph he was Israel: joyous, confident, Godly. Then Joseph came and Jacob felt an upsurge of love such as he had quite possibly never before experienced. Any parent would have lavished that love on his rediscovered child, hugging, kissing, caressing, inquiring, scrutinizing. But not Jacob. Upon experiencing so powerful an emotion within himself, he turned it to the service of God. If indeed he were privileged to feel such superhuman love, then he would recite the *Shema* and pour all that love into the commandment to adore God (*Maharal*).

Complacency and greatness are incompatible. Even a Jacob in the moment when he is called Israel can experience a heightening of his awareness. And when he does, he transforms it into a means of adding a new dimension to his service of God.

The Love Is Yours!

The *Chofetz Chaim*, in eulogizing his departed son, told a heartbreaking yet inspiring tale about how even ordinary people were capable of keeping God uppermost in their minds in every possible experience. During the gruesome pogroms and bloodletting of the vicious Bogdan Chmielnicki and his barbarous Cossack hordes, a Jewish boy was murdered. He was the only child of his widowed mother. She knelt over his dead body, all alone in the world, and then looked up and spoke:

"Master of the Universe, until now half of my love went to You and half went to my son. Now that my son is dead, I give all my love to You."

The *Chofetz Chaim* concluded his tearful eulogy saying, "I try to serve God, but I am only a human being. No matter how much I love God, some of the love in my heart belongs to my children. Now my son is gone and, like that Jewish mother, I will take that love and give it all to God."

That story displays a degree of greatness and

single-minded devotion to God that is almost beyond comprehension. We might expect it from the saintly *Chofetz Chaim*, but surely not from an unlettered Polish widow. Truly did Rabbi Yerucham Levovitz say, "We are in the habit of saying that we cannot conceive of the spiritual loftiness of Abraham, Isaac, and Jacob. That statement is mistaken. We cannot even conceive of the spiritual greatness of our grandmothers."

We cannot even conceive of the spiritual greatness of our grandmothers.

The word "love" has become cheapened and degraded in today's common parlance. Today it is used as a synonym for gratification of the senses, but it means something else entirely. One of the masters of Mussar said, "When a person says he loves chicken, he doesn't love the chicken, he loves *himself*. If he loved the chicken, he wouldn't slaughter it and eat it." When the Torah uses the word "love," it is a lofty concept. The person who truly loves God negates his own existence entirely in the service of God. He serves God not because he fears punishment in this world or the next for flaunting the Divine will, not even because he anticipates reward in either world. The one who truly loves God serves Him because it is His will and for no other reason. Does a mother sacrifice her sleep, comfort, and convenience for her baby because she looks forward to old age when her grown child will serve her in return?

The person who truly loves God negates his own existence entirely in the service of God.

There is no human emotion more elevated than love, *true* love. The more genuine the love is, the more the lover abandons any thoughts of personal gain. Deep love is not based on reciprocity; it is entirely selfless. That mortal man can feel such sublime emotion is one of God's greatest gifts for it enables man to dedicate his entire being to God. An early Chassidic master said, "If I could have the opportunity to trade places with Abraham, I would not do it, for the glory of God would not be enhanced; there would still be only one Abraham!" The pride that *he* could be that Abraham did not enter into his equation. If God would have only one Abraham, what did it matter which person it was?

It has been said that the Hebrew word for love, אהבה, is related to the Aramaic word הב, *give*. To love is to give. Love in its truest form is selfless; to whatever extent it is self-serving it is not love at all.

The Battlefield This sublimation of human emotions and instincts for spiritual ends is more than praiseworthy and desirable; it is an absolute necessity for the fulfillment of man's mission on earth. The attainment of God's purpose by human beings demands the interplay of body and soul; that is why the soul was clothed in a body. Otherwise, a universe of angels would have been sufficient. Man is called upon to arbitrate the battle between his spirit and his flesh, to decide in favor of the spirit. The battle is constant; only the front changes. From the most immature, disinterested student to the greatest, holiest sage, the struggle exists. The schoolchild must triumph over the impulse that seeks to deny him even fifteen minutes of Torah study in the evening or on a Sabbath. The sage struggles against the inclination seeking to convince him that eighteen hours of intense, concentrated study and prayer is enough for one day. The

The battlefields are as far removed from each other as is the Bowery from Mount Sinai, but the struggle goes on.

battlefields are as far removed from each other as is the Bowery from Mount Sinai, but the struggle goes on (*Michtav Me'Eliyahu*).

At his holiest, man has converted his body into a repository of the spirit, exalted above the demands and weaknesses of the flesh. The Sages describe the death of Jacob as akin to taking off a jacket or drawing a hair from a cup of milk. So elevated had he become that even his bodily urges existed only as willing servants of the soul. At the other end of the spiritual spectrum, man can become so crass and venal that even his holy, Godly soul becomes contaminated. When that happens, his entire being becomes so earthly that the soul's attachment to spirituality becomes severed.

Sublimation of Pleasures But whatever the point of struggle, man must make use of his human desires for heavenly ends. The competitive desire for victory over one's opponents should be channeled into an insistence that the enemies of Torah cannot be allowed to triumph. The hunger for honor and recognition should become a need to create ever-greater glory for God and recognition of His greatness. Satisfaction in fruitful achievement should become joy in every gain for Torah. Human pleasures and passions should be recognized as a Divinely given means to show man that if bodily pleasures can be so gratifying, then the finest pursuit he can choose is the quest for spiritual joy.

העוה״ב אֵין בּוֹ לֹא אֲכִילָה וְלֹא שְׁתִיָּה . . . אֶלָּא צַדִּיקִים יוֹשְׁבִים וְעַטְרוֹתֵיהֶם בְּרָאשֵׁיהֶם וְנֶהֱנִים מִזִּיו הַשְּׁכִינָה שֶׁנֶּאֱמַר: „וַיֶּחֱזוּ אֶת הָאֱלֹהִים וַיֹּאכְלוּ וַיִּשְׁתּוּ". פֵּירֵשׁ״י שָׂבְעוּ מִזִּיו הַשְּׁכִינָה כְּאִילוּ אָכְלוּ וְשָׁתוּ.

In the World to Come, there is no eating or drinking ... only the righteous sitting with their crowns upon their heads enjoying the splendor of the Divine Presence, as the Torah says, "and they gazed at God yet they ate and they drank" (Exodus 24:11). Rashi explains, they were as sated from the splendor of the Divine Presence as if they had eaten and drunk (Berachos 17a).

Scripture compares the pleasure derived from the Divine Presence to the pleasure and gratification of eating and drinking. We do not have the comprehension to assimilate the true description of holiness. Flesh-and-blood people can no more envision the Divine Presence of the World to Come than a blind man can envision a sunset. But Scripture helps us along by telling us that the pleasures of that World are microcosmically similar to the contentment of a lavish banquet in congenial company with unsparing delicacies and the finest wines.

Flesh-and-blood people can no more envision the Divine Presence of the World to Come than a blind man can envision a sunset.

Thus we are given a lesson not so much in the actuality of spiritual joy — our very humanity forecloses its clear perception from us — but in how to view the world we live in.

Someone feels a tingle of pleasure in a sumptuous feast; imagine what the World to Come will hold!

One is grateful to an employer who appreciates and rewards dedication to a job; imagine what God's rewards will be!

One is grateful to an employer who appreciates and rewards dedication to a job; imagine what God's rewards will be! Someone helps a poverty-stricken cripple or a wealthy businessman threatened with financial ruin; imagine how much greater are the mercies of God! Traitors are severely punished; imagine what will happen when the Divine wrath is loosed against those who betray Him!

There is nothing more holy than a human being who can negate himself entirely without reservation to God. All human passions become but guideposts on the path to holiness. Jacob feels love; he pours it into an affirmation that Hashem is One and all-encompassing. An afflicted widow kneels over her murdered child watching all earthly purpose in her life drain out of his bleeding wounds, and she dedicates another portion of her heart to God.

Jacob feels love; he pours it into an affirmation that Hashem is One and all-emcompassing.

The Highest Love

Israel is God's beloved and He is its Beloved. The Sages ask:

הָנֵי תְּפִלִּין דְּמָרֵי עָלְמָא מַאי כְּתִיב בְּהוּ? א״ל „וּמִי כְעַמְּךָ יִשְׂרָאֵל גּוֹי אֶחָד בָּאָרֶץ.‟

These tefillin of the Master of the World, what is written in them? He answered: "And who is like Your people Israel, a unique nation on earth?" (I Chronicles 17:21) [Berachos 6a].

Tefillin, firmly bound on the arms and heads, the strength and intellect of all Jews, are the symbol of our eternal, unseverable bond with God. Our tefillin contain Scriptural chapters proclaiming that God is One, that He rewards and punishes, that He redeemed and hallowed us. What do His tefillin proclaim? That Israel is unique. That God and Israel are bound to each other in selfless devotion.

What do His tefillin proclaim? That Israel is unique. That God and Israel are bound to each other in selfless devotion.

This is the highest form of love. It is this love which is the subject of Song of Songs, the holiest of holies.

It is surely not coincidental that, of all the Sages, it was Rabbi Akiva who transmitted this perception to us. His story is well known. At the age of 40 he was an

It is surely not coincidental that, of all the Sages, it was Rabbi Akiva who transmitted this perception to us.

illiterate shepherd who so despised Torah scholars that
he would have violently attacked them had he been
given the opportunity. Rachel, daughter of one of
Israel's wealthiest men, saw a hidden spark in the lowly shepherd. Because she married him she was disin-
herited, ostracized by her family, and forced to live in
the most abject poverty. Her husband began to study
Torah and she sent him to learn in the academies of
Rabbi Eliezer and Rabbi Yehoshua, the great Sages of
the time. After twelve years he came home to visit her
and overheard her neighbors taunting her about the
"ignoramus" husband who had "deserted" her.

"He is studying Torah," she replied. "May he
spend another twelve years studying!"

Rabbi Akiva heard, turned around, and returned to
the academy without even pausing to greet his lonely
wife. Twelve years later he returned with twenty-four
thousand students sitting in the dust of his feet. He was
Rabbi Akiva, teacher of all Israel. Shabbily dressed, Rachel pressed through the welcoming throngs and threw
herself at his feet. Rabbi Akiva's students were aghast,
infuriated at the stranger's temerity. As they advanced
to remove her, Rabbi Akiva waved them away:

"Leave her, for all of my Torah and all of your Torah belong to her."

"Leave her, for all of my Torah and all of your
Torah belong to her."

Rabbi Akiva had seen in his own life what selfless devotion was.

Rabbi Akiva had seen in his own life what selfless
devotion was. Because of it an embittered shepherd
became his generation's greatest man. Who was more
qualified than Rabbi Akiva to perceive the holiness
of Song of Songs? (*Harav Avigdor Miller*).

VI. The "Simple" Meaning of Scripture

There is a passage in *Shabbos* 63a which, as interpreted by Harav Margulies in *HaMikra
V'HaMesorah*, illuminates the concept of Scriptural
meaning and interpretation. There is a dispute in the
Mishnah: The Rabbis hold that is forbidden to carry
swords and spears and the like in the street on the

Sabbath, while Rabbi Eliezer holds that it is permitted. The *Talmud* seeks to find a reason for the surprising view of Rabbi Eliezer. It explains:

מַאי טַעְמָא דְּרַבִּי אֱלִיעֶזֶר דִּכְתִיב ,,חֲגוֹר חַרְבְּךָ עַל יָרֵךְ גִּבּוֹר הוֹדְךָ וַהֲדָרֶךָ"?

Gird your sword upon [your] thigh, O mighty warrior, it is your majesty and your splendor (Psalms 45:4).

Since the verse describes a sword as the majesty and splendor of a warrior, it is plain that such implements are ornaments for the wearer and, therefore, may be worn on the Sabbath.

The scholar's mind — like sharpness of sword — is his real glory. Rabbi Kahana replied that the verse is allegorical; it refers to the words of Torah. The true sense of the verse is that the scholar's mind — like sharpness of sword — is his real glory. Mar answered Rabbi Kahana: אֵין מִקְרָא יוֹצֵא מִידֵי פְּשׁוּטוֹ, the verse cannot be divorced from its simple meaning. It is true that there is a deeper, homiletical significance to the verse — it is indeed a symbolic reference to the glory of a Torah scholar — but if the psalmist clothed his homily in the parable of a warrior and his arms, the simple meaning, too, has validity.

To this Rabbi Kahana replied:

כַּד הֲוֵינָא בַּר תַּמְנֵי סְרֵי שְׁנִין וַהֲוָה גְּמִירְנָא לֵיהּ לְכוּלֵּיהּ הַשַּׁ"ס וְלֹא הֲוָה יָדַעְנָא דְּאֵין מִקְרָא יוֹצֵא מִידֵי פְּשׁוּטוֹ.

When I was eighteen years old I had already completed the entire Talmud but I did not know that the verse cannot depart from its simple meaning.

His words are truly astounding, virtually incomprehensible. How can a rabbi of the *Talmud* not know what every schoolchild knows?

When Knowledge Is Ignorance

Harav Margulies explains that there are times when to understand a verse according to the simple translation of the words is not to understand it at all. As the Talmud says, כָּל הַמְתַרְגֵּם פָּסוּק כְּצוּרָתוֹ הֲרֵי זֶה בַּדַּאי, whoever translates a verse as it appears [without inquiring into its true meaning] is a fabricator (*Kiddushin* 49a).

One of Scripture's most familiar prophecies is Isaiah's idyllic description of the world following the coming of the Messiah:

וְגָר זְאֵב עִם כֶּבֶשׂ וְנָמֵר עִם גְּדִי יִרְבָּץ
The wolf will live with the lamb and the leopard will lie down with the kid (Isaiah 11:6).

On its face, the prophecy tells us that, in the End of Days, all natural antagonisms will vanish and even the most defenseless of animals will cavort peacefully with beasts of prey. This is indeed the view of most commentators. *Rambam* disagrees, however. In explaining the prophecy, he says that it is a mistake to think that the natural order of life on earth will change. Wolves will still prey on kids and leopards will still devour lambs. According to him, Isaiah's prophecy is to be understood as a poetic reference to nations. When God's truth becomes clearly and unmistakably revealed on earth, all nations will flock together to the mountain of Hashem to seek spiritual *The rivalries* fulfillment and wisdom. The rivalries and aggres-*and aggressions* sions of life today are the product of a refusal to see *of life today are* God's will. That obstinate blindness will give way to *the product of a refusal to see God's* a world of peace and knowledge of God. *will.*

In *Rambam's* interpretation, what is the simple meaning of the verse? Surely not that lambs and kids will lie with wolves and leopards. *Rambam* maintains that such a thing will never happen; hence it cannot be regarded as even the *simple* meaning of the verse.

True, the Torah very often speaks in similes and parables, but the verse does not always have two *true* meanings — the simple and the allegorical — both *When it is clear* of them equally valid. When it is clear that only the *that only the* deeper meaning is intended, then the poetic vehicle *deeper meaning is* intended, then the for that true meaning has no independent validity. *poetic vehicle for* This, then, was the difference of opinion between *that true meaning* has no independent Rabbi Kahana and Mar. Both knew full well that any *validity.* verse can be understood on many different levels,

ע׳ פָּנִים לַתּוֹרָה, the Torah has seventy facets. They differed in the interpretation of the verse then under discussion. Mar held that if the psalmist clothed his reference to a scholar and his wisdom in the simile of a warrior and his sword, then the parable, too, has a valid meaning. Just as Torah wisdom is the majesty and splendor of a scholar, so, too, a sword is the majesty and splendor — an ornament permitted on the Sabbath — of a warrior. Rabbi Kahana demurs. It cannot be that King David truly lauds a warrior and his implements of death in his sacred psalms. Psalm 45 is a soaring spiritual praise to God. It does *To interpret it* not speak of warriors and warfare at all. To inter-*literally is to* pret it literally is to misinterpret it entirely. Its *simple* *misinterpret it* meaning refers to words of Torah; its reference to a *entirely. Its simple* *meaning refers to* warrior is not meant to have any independent mean-*words of Torah* ing whatever.

Song of Songs

Song of Song of Songs is surely a song of love, but not of one *Songs* human's love for another. Our Sages and the commentators did not doubt for an instant that the only *simple* meaning is the allegorical one. The renderings and explanations of the so-called "simple" meaning, the references to feet, thighs, watchman, daughter, sheep, and so on are intended to do no more than to clarify the vehicle of the allegory. A careful description of a person will include full details about his clothing. Knowledge of the color, style, and appearance of the clothing will help identify the wearer; for the very perceptive listener it will tell much about the person's taste and economic circumstances and *But clothes are not* therefore about him. But clothes are not the person. *the person.* Only an imbecile would walk over to a suit of clothes on a hanger and address it by the name of its owner. *In the same way,* In the same way, Song of Songs is a Scriptural suit *Song of Songs is* of clothes for deep and Divine meaning. Only the *a Scriptural suit* *of clothes for* most ignorant could give the allegorical clothing an *deep and Divine* independent meaning of its own. *meaning.*

Indeed, the very necessity of an allegory to convey the lofty concepts of Song of Songs is proof of its elevated nature. We don't need fables and allegories to describe apples and oranges. We do need them to help bring lofty ideas down to a simple level of understanding.

The "Truth" of Parables

Is a king God? Surely not. But he is as close an approach as human experience can offer to the majesty of God.

Can we conceive of God? Of course not. Throughout the history of Torah literature, God is allegorically likened to a king. A monarch has absolute power, is the owner of all in the kingdom, and the life and death of his subjects depend on his whim. He can confer wealth and position, and remove them with a motion of his finger. Is a king God? Surely not. But he is as close an approach as human experience can offer to the majesty of God. Therefore, Torah literature is replete with parables in which a king represents God.

What does one tell a peasant with no knowledge of the king? In order to make him understand the majesty of the king, we would tell him that the king is even greater than the local warlord or the village elder. What does one tell a child who has never trembled at the warlord's displeasure or stood at rigid attention in the presence of the elder? That the elder or warlord is even greater than the greatest and most powerful person the child knows: his own father!

And what does one tell a child nowadays whose only knowledge of royalty is the queen of the British Empire or the other constitutional monarchs of Europe who have no power and have been shorn of much of their pomp? Can an American president be used as an allegorical example of God? He was never an absolute monarch, but in earlier times when he was an awe-inspiring, universally respected father figure, he could have conveyed a small sense of the majesty of God. But in recent years when presidents have become very life-size figures, and even most dictators must respond to public and world opinion, it may be that there are no earthly symbols left for the greatness of the Creator.

If human beings could understand the essence of God, such feeble attempts at likening it to something

The use of allegory in Song of Songs is itself the best indication that its true meaning is beyond the scope of human understanding.

in human experience would never have been necessary. The use of allegory in Song of Songs is itself the best indication that its true meaning is beyond the scope of human understanding.

A Drop of Ink

During the mid-nineteenth-century period of the most vicious czarist persecutions of Jews, it was common for the leading rabbis to visit St. Petersburg to plead the case of their people with the czar's ministers. During one of these visits a Russian official asked a visitor how he could account for the many Aggadic tales in the *Talmud* which were patently "inconceivable."

The rabbi answered, "You know very well that the czar and his advisers have often planned to promulgate decrees that would order the expulsion of the entire Jewish population. If God had not had mercy on us and thwarted your plans, the decree would have been written and placed before the czar for his signature. He would have dipped his pen into the inkwell and signed. His signature would have made final the greatest Jewish catastrophe in centuries. A poet might write that a drop of ink swept away three million people. All of us would have understood what he meant. But a hundred years later, someone might read it and consider it nonsense. In truth, the expression is apt and pithy; it is only a lack of knowledge that could lead a reader to dismiss it out of hand. So it is with many parables of our Sages. They were written in the form of a far-fetched story to conceal their meaning from those who were unqualified to understand. None of us are qualified, so we laugh at the stories instead of lamenting our puny stature." (See also *Maamar Al Ha' Aggados by Rabbi Moshe Chaim Luzatto.*)

In general history as well, many figures of speech have an obvious meaning to those familiar with them, but would be incomprehensible to the uninitiated. Everyone knows that a shot cannot be heard more than several hundred yards away. But every

A poet might write that a drop of ink swept away three million people. All of us would have understood what he meant. But a hundred years later, someone might read it and consider it nonsense.

American knows that "a shot heard round the world" began the American Revolution. We all long for the day when the problem of Jewish wandering and exile will finally be solved. If we didn't know its gruesome connotations, we might well feel that a "Final Solution" is something for which all Jews should pray.

True Definitions There is yet a deeper sense in which we must understand allegorical statements in the Torah. We are in the habit of thinking — as is held by many commentators — that when the Torah refers to the eyes or hands of God, for example, that it is using borrowed terms. God is incorporeal, He has no hands or eyes, but Scripture uses those expressions in the form of similes to make it easier for us to understand the context. Thus, when the *eyes of God* view the doings of man, we are being told that God somehow perceives what occurs as would a human being if he were peering with his eyes. But an eye is a human organ and a word that is relevant only to human beings.

The *Shelah HaKadosh* gives us a new and penetrating insight into the concept of borrowed words and simile, an insight that illuminates many areas of the Torah and especially of Song of Songs.

The word ayin, eye, refers to God's power and manner of sight.

Geshem, rain, refers not to the tangible drops of water that we call rain, but to God's power to stimulate the growth of vegetation.

The word *ayin*, eye, refers to God's power and manner of sight. The word *yad*, hand, refers to God's power to affect events on earth. This concept refers to other words as well. *Geshem*, rain, refers not to the tangible drops of water that we call rain, but to God's power to stimulate the growth of vegetation. Thus we have an entirely new understanding of countless verses in Scripture. God *does* have an *ayin* (eye); not an organ with a cornea, retina, and lens, but an *ayin* in the true sense of the word: the ability to perceive what occurs.

In creating human and animal life, God wished to endow His creatures with an ability akin to His Own ability to perceive occurrences. But no flesh-and-blood being can "see" as God sees. Therefore,

God took His lofty, spiritual quality of perception and brought it down to an earthly material state just as a teacher takes complex, lofty concepts and brings them down to the level of a 6-year-old. Thus we, too, have *eyes*, but our eyes are a far cry from the true *ayin* of God.

Ahavah, love, is the intimate spiritual closeness between God and righteous people. It is the emotion that Jacob felt when he turned his eyes from Joseph and read the *Shema*, that the *Chofetz Chaim* felt when he lost his son but won a new measure of love for God.

We take that ineffable term and use it for the closest possible relationship between two people because their selfless devotion to each other bears a resemblance to the holy concept of *Ahavah* that exists between God and Israel. Indeed, the portion of *Rambam's Mishnah Torah* that deals with the laws of *Shema*, Prayer, *Milah*, and the like — the observances that fasten and symbolize the closest relationship between God and His "firstborn son" — is called *Sefer Ahavah*, the Book of Love.

With this marvelous new understanding given us by the *Shelah*, we see Song of Songs in its clearest, truest light. The constant refrain of love, beloved, friend; of physical organs; of flitting to and fro in search of a lost lover, of animals, orchards, and mountains — these are indeed meant literally. They are literal in the same way that God's eyes, hand, and mouth are literal. When the commentators say that שְׁנֵי שָׁדַיִךְ, *your bosom*, refers to Moses and Aaron, they are not departing from the simple literal meaning of the phrase in the least. Song of Songs uses words in their ultimate connotations. Just as *geshem*, rain, means the power of stimulating growth, *shadayim*, the bosom, refers to the Heavenly power of nourishment. The most vital form of nourishment is spiritual, for what does it benefit a man if he is well-fed but spiritually starved? The body can thrive while the soul withers, but that person is truly dying of malnutrition in the most absolute sense. That is why the commentators define *your bosom* as

Moses and Aaron. They, Israel's sources of spiritual nourishment, are not implied allegorically or derived esoterically from the verse; the verse literally means them.

The True Light This sort of perception does not often come to human beings, but when it does, it must be fondled and treasured for it is the purpose of creation. The *Megillah* says that after the miracle of Purim, לַיְּהוּדִים הָיְתָה אוֹרָה, *to the Jews there was light*. The Sages comment אוֹרָה זוֹ תּוֹרָה, *light* is identical with Torah. We tend to regard this as a picturesque figure of speech;

"Know" that the sun is the source of light and that "Torah is light" only figuratively. But we are terribly wrong. we "know" that the sun is the source of light and that "Torah is light" only figuratively. But we are terribly wrong. The only true light is the spiritual brilliance, the splendor of the Divine Presence that is the very essence of Torah.

Can we cheapen the word "light" by saying that the blinding rays of the sun give more light than Torah? The true savant of spiritual light would no more say that than the nutritionist would say that a generous helping of strawberry shortcake is a better food than fish because it is more filling. Of course, the frail, mortal "eye" sees more light from the sun than from Torah, but the immortal "eye," the *true* eye, knows that there is only one form of genuine light:

Because the sun illuminates the material universe, just as the Torah illuminates the spiritual universe, we pay the sun the supreme compliment of using the same word for it that we use for Torah: אוֹרָה, light. Torah. The sun? Yes; because the sun illuminates the material universe, just as the Torah illuminates the spiritual universe, we pay the sun the supreme compliment of using the same word for it that we use for Torah: אוֹרָה, *light (Sefas Emes)*.

During the morning *Shacharis* prayer, the recitation of *Shema* is preceded by two blessings which go in ascending order. The first praises God for having created the Heavenly bodies, our sources of light. The second blesses God for having chosen Israel to receive the Torah. That blessing, too, praises God for giving light: the *literal* light. After praising Him for the important but relatively minor lights that decorate the firmament, we raise our vision to אורה זו תורה,

light *is* Torah, and praise Him for illuminating our lives with His wisdom and commandments (*Chasam Sofer*).

It is thus that we must read and understand Song of Songs. Let us pity those who see it as a sensual dialogue. Together with the Torah, let us don sackcloth and mourn that this Holiest of Holies is so reviled (see comm. 1:1). Nevertheless, the message of *Shir HaShirim* is so lofty, so exalted, so spiritual, so holy that God in His infinite wisdom knew that it could be presented to us only in its present form. Only in this manner could it engender the passionate love for God which is Israel's highest mission (see Foreword).

Has it been misinterpreted by fools and twisted by scoundrels? Most assuredly yes! But, God did not refrain from creating the sun because it would have worshipers.

Has it been misinterpreted by fools and twisted by scoundrels? Most assuredly yes! But: לֹא חָשׁ הקב״ה, לְהָאִיר הַחַמָּה מִפְּנֵי עוֹבְדֶיהָ, *God did not refrain from creating the sun because it would have worshipers.* And as the prophet says:

מִי חָכָם וְיָבֵן אֵלֶּה נָבוֹן וְיֵדָעֵם כִּי יְשָׁרִים דַּרְכֵי ה׳
וְצַדִּיקִים יֵלְכוּ בָם וּפשְׁעִים יִכָּשְׁלוּ בָם.

*Who is wise and will understand these things; [who is] understanding and will know them? For the ways of H*ASHEM *are straight; and the righteous walk in them, and sinners will stumble over them (Hoshea 14:10).*

Let us read and understand Shir HaShirim with the ecstasy of love between God and Israel.

But for ourselves, let us read and understand *Shir HaShirim* with the ecstasy of love between God and Israel which it expresses more than any other Song in the Torah. For it is in this intimacy with God that we can begin to turn all of creation into an orchestra resounding in a crescendo of God's symphony.

שִׁיר הַשִּׁירִים

Introductory Remarks
(Adapted from Rashi's introduction)

Solomon foresaw through רוּחַ הַקֹּדֶשׁ, the *Holy Spirit*, that Israel is destined to suffer a series of exiles and will lament, nostalgically recalling her former status as God's chosen beloved. She will say, *"I will go and return to my first husband* [i.e., to God] *for it was better for me then than it is now"* [*Hoshea* 2:9]. The Children of Israel will recall His beneficence and *"the treachery with which they betrayed Me"* [*Leviticus* 26:40]. And they will recall the goodness which He promised for the End of Days.

The prophets frequently likened the relationship between God and Israel to that of a loving husband angered by a straying wife who betrayed him. Solomon composed *Shir HaShirim* in the form of that same allegory. It is a passionate dialogue between the husband [God] who still loves his exiled wife [Israel], and a *"veritable widow of a living husband"* [*II Samuel* 20:3] who longs for her husband and seeks to endear herself to him once more, as she recalls her youthful love for him and admits her guilt.

God, too, *in all their troubles was troubled* [*Isaiah* 63:9], and He recalls the kindness of her youth, her beauty, and her skillful deeds for which He loved her [Israel] so. He proclaimed that He has *not tormented capriciously* [*Lamentations* 3:33], nor is she cast away permanently. For she is still His "wife" and He her "husband," and He will yet return to her.

[**Please note:** *The source for every excerpt in the commentary has been documented. Whenever M.Z. has inserted a comment or explanatory remark of his own, it is framed in square brackets.*]

I

1. שִׁיר הַשִּׁירִים — [lit., *The song of songs*.] I.e., the greatest of all songs uttered to the Holy One, blessed is He, by His people — the Congregation of Israel (*Rashi*).

— The best of songs, the most excellent of songs, the finest of songs (*Midrash*).

The *Targum* notes that ten songs were at various times uttered in this world. The best of all was this one. [See *Overview*.]

The idiomatic Hebrew expression שִׁיר הַשִּׁירִים, *Song of Songs*, meaning "most supreme song," is a common grammatical construction in Hebrew. It is similar to מֶלֶךְ מַלְכֵי הַמְּלָכִים, *King of kings' kings* — i.e., most regal in kingship; קֹדֶשׁ קָדָשִׁים, *holy of holies* — i.e., supremely holy. Conversely, when one wishes to describe a degenerate state, one uses a similar dual structure: הֲבֵל הֲבָלִים, *futility of futilities* — i.e., the utmost in futility; עֶבֶד עֲבָדִים, *slave of slaves* — i.e., the lowliest of servants (*Ibn Aknin*).

Rabbi Akiva said: "The entire universe is unworthy of the day on which the Song of Songs was given to Israel. All the כְּתוּבִים, *Writings* [Hagiographa], are holy, but the Song of Songs is the holy of holies" (*Mishnah, Yadayim* 3:5; *Rashi*).

Torah Temimah points out that in the *Yalkut* version of Rabbi Akiva's statement the words are: "... for all the *songs* [preserved in the Torah, or, of Solomon] are holy, but the Song of Songs is the holy of holies," i.e., although the other songs also contain sacred and esoteric allusions, they are open to simple and literal translation; whereas God forbid that the Song of Songs should be interpreted in any way but as its most sacred metaphor! [See *Foreword* and *Overview*.]

Additionally, in the other songs in Scripture, either God praises Israel or Israel praises Him. The other songs are thus referred to as "holy." Song of Songs, however, is referred to as "holy of holies" — i.e., supreme, dual holiness because it contains *reciprocal praises* between God and Israel (*Midrash*).[1]

As *Harav Mordechai Gifter* points out in the *Foreword*, every word of the parable is necessary and laden with allegorical implication. Nothing is extraneous or rhetorical. Whatever may strike the reader as inconsistent or superfluous is due to the limitations of his own intellect.

[The *Talmud* stresses the sanctity of the Song of Songs:] "Our Rabbis taught : He who recites a verse of the Song of Songs and treats it as if it

---

1. Of all the thousand and five "songs" (*I Kings* 5:12) attributed to Solomon, none compares to this, the most superior of all his songs. It contains hidden and sacred allusions to the entire historical span of the Jewish nation from the time of Abraham to the coming of the Messiah. One should not be astonished that the allegory presented the Congregation of Israel as a bride and God as her beloved. This was a common allegory of the Prophets. Isaiah used such metaphors as: *Now will I sing to my Beloved a song of my Beloved concerning His vineyard* (*Isaiah* 5:1); also: *As the bridegroom rejoices over the bride, so shall your God rejoice over you* (ibid. 62:5).

I
1-2

T*he song that excels all songs dedicated to God,*
Him to Whom peace belongs:

Israel: ²*Communicate Your innermost wisdom to me*
again in loving closeness, for Your love is

[Please refer to the Preface for methodology of the allegorical Translation.]

were a [secular] song ... brings evil upon the world. [When someone does so,] the Torah girds itself with sackcloth and stands before the Holy One, blessed is He, and laments before Him: 'Sovereign of the Universe! Your children have made me a harp upon which the frivolous play!' " (*Sanhedrin* 101a [*Maharsha*]).

According to one view in the *Midrash*, the phrase *Song of Songs* means "a double song" — "double and redoubled." [For example, the verse: *Behold, you are beautiful, my Beloved, behold you are beautiful* (1:15). This verse in itself is "double" (i.e., use is made of parallelism) and then the entire verse is "redoubled" in 4:7 (*Maharzu*). Others explain "double" as being composed of two strands: Israel's praise of God and God's praise of Israel, "redoubled" in its beauty and holiness (*Yefei Kol*).]

אֲשֶׁר לִשְׁלֹמֹה — *dedicated to God, Him to Whom peace belongs* [lit., *which is Solomon's*].

Noting that in Solomon's two other works, *Proverbs* (*Mishlei*) and *Ecclesiastes* (*Koheles*), his ancestry as בֶּן דָּוִד, *son of David*, is specifically mentioned, *Rashi* quotes the Sages as adducing that here [and in

most places throughout the Book] the word שְׁלֹמֹה standing by itself refers not to "Solomon" — although he is indisputably the author — but is interpreted as a dedication to מִי שֶׁהַשָּׁלוֹם שֶׁלּוֹ [or: מֶלֶךְ שֶׁהַשָּׁלוֹם לוֹ] — the King to Whom peace belongs [שְׁלֹמֹה = שָׁלוֹם לוֹ]; i.e., God, the Source of all peace, Who maintains peace among His creatures (*Shevuos* 35b; *Midrash*; *Yalkut* [see *Overview*]).

[See *comm.* to *Ecclesiastes* (*Koheles*) 1:1 (ArtScroll ed. pages 50-51) for Solomon/Hezekiah authorship of this Book.]

There is a difference of opinion in the *Midrash* as to the sequence in which Solomon composed his three Books: *Song of Songs*, *Proverbs*, and *Ecclesiastes*: Rav Yochanan argues from the way of the world. When a man is young, he composes songs [i.e., he couches his wisdom in the poetry of song, in reference to the *Song of Songs* (*Torah Temimah*)]. As he grows older, he couches his remarks in *Proverbs*. And, when he becomes an old man, he speaks of the futility of things [*Ecclesiastes* (*Koheles*), i.e., of mundane pursuits (*Torah Temimah*)].

2. יְשָׁקֵנִי מִנְּשִׁיקוֹת פִּיהוּ — [lit., *May He kiss me with* (or: *of*) *the kisses of His*

Ezekiel employed similar metaphors: [*Thus says* HASHEM, *God, to Jerusalem*] ... *you were naked and bare* (Ezekiel 16:3, 7).

Hoshea similarly said: *I will betroth you unto Me forever* (Hoshea 2:21). In *Psalms: a Maskil, a song of endearment* (45:1); *Hear, O daughter, and see, and incline your ear* (ibid. verse 11).

God forbid that one construe this as a love song or as anything but a metaphor! (*Ibn Ezra*).

mouth.] The exiled Israel says in her "widowhood": Let Him be intimate with me again, and communicate the innermost secrets of His Torah to me directly — פֶּה אֶל פֶּה, *mouth to mouth* — as He did at Sinai when He revealed Himself to us פָּנִים בְּפָנִים, *face to face* [Deuteronomy 5:4] (Rashi).[1]

Having been "separated" from God, Israel longs for Him and moans to herself, "O, let Him show me affection once again!" The speakers are not clearly identified, because it is the nature of allegory to be somewhat esoteric. However, the context makes clear the identity of the speakers (Metzudas David).

According to many commentators, the verse refers to the period of the Exodus from Egypt, and the metaphor reflects both the yearning of Israel for prophecy and direct communication from God. Both are manifestations of the allegorical term נְשִׁיקוֹת פִּיהוּ, *the kisses of His "mouth.";* Cf., e.g., Deuteronomy 18:18: נָבִיא אָקִים ... וְנָתַתִּי דְבָרַי בְּפִיו, *I will establish a prophet ... and I will place My words in his mouth;* and, similarly, Jeremiah 1:9. Thus, *kisses of God's mouth* refers to prophecy (Divrei Yedidiah).

Shir Chadash notes that the word מִנְּשִׁיקוֹת is prefixed by מ, *mem, of,* [lit., *of* the kisses] — a small measure of His kisses [i.e., intimacy] rather than *all* the kisses. The *Shechinah* is referred to as אֵשׁ אוֹכְלָה הִיא, *a consuming fire* [Deuteronomy 4:24]. Therefore, mortal man cannot bear the full extent of God's closeness. The most we can yearn for is מִנְּשִׁיקוֹת פִּיהוּ — a *small measure* of His closeness.

It has also been suggested that יִשָּׁקֵנִי may be related to the verb נשק, *sustenance,* as used in Genesis 41:40: וְעַל־פִּיךָ יִשַּׁק כָּל־עַמִּי, *by your mouth* [i.e., by your word] *shall all my people be sustained* [also Targum, Rashi]. Thus, our verse could be rendered as Israel's pleading before God: "*Sustain us* with an abundance of holiness, purity, and success, כִּי טוֹבִים דֹּדֶיךָ מִיָּיִן, *because Your love is greater than wine.* Because of adherence to *Your love* we have rejected all mundane pleasures [represented by 'wine'] and willingly endured constant exile and exposure to mortal danger עַל קְדוּשַׁת שְׁמֶךָ, for the Sanctification of Your Name" (Chavatzeles HaSharon).

כִּי טוֹבִים דֹּדֶיךָ מִיָּיִן — [lit., *for Your love* (or: *friendship*) *is better than*

1. The *Midrash* interprets this verse as referring to an incident that happened when Israel received the Torah at Mt. Sinai:

When Israel heard the first two commandments directly from God, the knowledge of Torah became rooted in their heart, and they did not forget anything. At the same time, the יֵצֶר הָרַע, *Evil Inclination,* was plucked from their heart [and no longer had control over them].

But overawed at hearing God's voice directly from the fire (Deuteronomy 5:21), Israel approached Moses and said: "Moses, become an intermediary between us," as it says *speak with us and we will hear, but let not God speak with us lest we die* (Exodus 20:16; Deuteronomy 5:22). [This is why in the first two commandments God refers to Himself in first person: *I am* HASHEM *your God,* and in the other eight, with Moses as the intermediary, God is referred to in third person (Vilna Gaon).]

At that moment their learning again became subject to forgetfulness ... and their Evil Inclination returned. So they returned to Moses and entreated him: "May God reveal Himself to us directly a second time — without an intermediary. *May He kiss us with the kisses of His mouth.* May He firmly root the knowledge of Torah in our hearts as it was! And, may He expel our Evil Inclination forever!"

"This cannot be now," Moses replied. "But it will be in time to come."

wine.] The love You manifested to Israel when You redeemed them from Egypt and when they stood before You at Mt. Sinai to receive the Torah was greater than all earthly pleasures, and we desire it again (*Metzudas David*).[1]

Rashi notes that in Hebrew, a festive, pleasure-filled banquet is idiomatically called יַיִן, *wine*, as in *Esther* 7:8; *Isaiah* 5:12, 24:9.

Ralbag adds that *wine* is the most common of bodily pleasures and stimulants. In order to represent physical gratification, therefore, Solomon found it sufficient to mention only *wine*, just as he did in *Koheles* 2:3: *I ventured to stimulate my body with wine* [see *comm.* to ArtScroll ed. ad loc.].[1]

The *Talmud* and many commentators allegorically explain יַיִן, *wine*, as a reference to the Torah (יֵינָה שֶׁל תּוֹרָה, *the wine of the Torah*), and דֹּדֶיךָ, *Your love*, is rendered *Your beloved ones*, i.e., the Sages.

What is the meaning of the verse: *for Your love is better than wine?* When Rav Dimi came [from Eretz Yisrael], he explained it thus: The Congregation of Israel declared to the Holy One, blessed is He: Master of the Universe! עֲרֵבִים עָלַי דִּבְרֵי דֹדֶיךָ יוֹתֵר מִיֵּינָה שֶׁל תּוֹרָה, *the words of Your beloved ones are more pleasant to me than the wine of the Torah* [i.e., the expositions of the Sages — דִּבְרֵי סוֹפְרִים — are more precious than the written words of the Torah (*Rashi*),

for the Oral, unwritten, Law supplements the Written Law and completes it] (*Avodah Zarah* 35a). [See, e.g., *Midrash*; *Mishnah Sanhedrin* 88b; *Eruvin* 21b.]

יַיִן, *wine*, stimulates joy. Therefore, because joy is a prerequisite to attainment of רוּחַ הַקֹּדֶשׁ, *the Holy Spirit, wine* sometimes metaphorically refers to spiritual attributes. In this verse, however, *wine* refers to Torah, while דֹּדֶיךָ, *Your love*, refers to אַהֲבַת ה' יִתְבָּרַךְ, *the love and awe of God.* Solomon declares that דֹּדֶיךָ, *the love and awe of God*, that results from Torah study is superior to the *wine of Torah* because the essence of Torah study is practice and fear of God (*Shir Chadash*).

The words of the Torah are compared to wine: Just as wine improves the longer it matures, so the words of Torah win a greater reputation for a man the longer they are ingrained in him ... Just as wine leaves its mark when drunk, so words of Torah leave their mark — people point a finger and say, "That is a scholar" ... Just as wine rejoices the heart, as it is written: *Wine gladdens the heart of man* [*Psalms* 104:15], so words of Torah rejoice the heart, as it says: *The precepts of Hashem are upright, gladdening the heart* [*Psalms* 19:9] ... (*Midrash*).

The *Midrash* offers an additional homiletical interpretation: *Your loved ones* — Israel — *are better than* יַיִן — the gentile nations.

---

1. *Malbim* points out that wine heightens man's ability, warms his natural feelings, and rejoices his spirit. But, alas, this enthusiasm is artificial because it is physically inspired. Like אֵשׁ זָרָה, *strange [foreign] fire* [cf. *Leviticus* 10:1], it originates from below and ascends from the body to the soul. Therefore, the joy it produces is profane. This is not true of the enthusiasm of the soul inspired by the Holy Spirit and prophecy — it is Godly happiness and the joy of holiness descending from Above — a Godly fire emanating from the soul to the body until physical barriers are smashed and subdued beneath the holiness of the soul. Therefore דֹּדֶיךָ, *Your spiritual friendship*, is preferable to יַיִן, *the physical stimulation of wine.*

ג לְרֵיחַ שְׁמָנֶיךָ טוֹבִים שֶׁמֶן תּוּרַק שְׁמֶךָ

ד עַל־כֵּן עֲלָמוֹת אֲהֵבוּךָ: מָשְׁכֵנִי אַחֲרֶיךָ

Seventy, the numerical value of יַיִן (י=10, י=10, נ=50), alludes to the seventy nations, to show that the people of Israel are more beloved before the Holy One, blessed is He, than all the nations.

[The commentators note the change in person in the verse. In the first half of the verse, נִסְתָּר, hidden, language (i.e., third person: "May He kiss ...") reflects the period of exile and estrangement between Israel and God into which Israel has fallen, by virtue of its moral decay. However, now that Israel seeks restoration of God's love, and, with it, the end of the estrangement, לְשׁוֹן נֹכַח, the familiar, direct form of communication (i.e., second person: "For Your love"), is used.]

Ibn Aknin stresses that shifts from second to third person are common in Scripture, and, in this case, the change could be a metaphorical indication of an ecstatic burst of passion.

Lekach Tov suggests that in the first stich the people of Israel (allegorized as a maiden among comrades) commiserate among themselves and long for the rebirth of God's love; therefore, they refer to Him in third person. Then, addressing the Shechinah directly, they exclaim the last stich in second person.

3. לְרֵיחַ שְׁמָנֶיךָ טוֹבִים — [lit., For fragrance your oils are good.] Rashi notes that oil is a metaphor for "fine reputation" [as in Koheles 7:1]. Therefore, the metaphor in this verse refers to the wondrous deeds

that God wrought for the Jews in Egypt, the "fragrance" of which was perceived to the ends of the earth.

Metzudas David interprets it as a prepositional phrase: "Because of the fragrance of your fine oils; ... therefore, Your Name is beloved among nations" [lit., maidens].

[The continuity of the verse may be explained as follows: We long after You not because we have empiric knowledge of You, but because we perceive Your presence through Your spiritual manifestations in Creation. The perception of His Presence is represented by scent — man's intellectual capacity to discern beyond what his other senses can define — a Presence that seduces the love of those who achieve its recognition.]

Do not wonder at how a mutual love can exist between God and Israel when Israel cannot see God. The verse alludes to this by inferring that just as one who passes a perfumery smells the scent although he cannot see the perfume, so do we perceive God's presence via the "scent" of His holy Torah and its multifaceted interpretations (Shir Chadash).

Ibn Aknin quotes the Midrash that the use of the plural שְׁמָנֶיךָ, Your oils, refers to God's dual and gracious manifestations: The Written Torah and the Oral Torah. The Torah was likened to oil to imply that just as oil in its original form [as olives] is bitter but afterward becomes sweet, so the study of Torah is at first laborious

dearer to me than all earthly delights. [3]Like the scent of goodly oils is the spreading fame of Your great deeds; Your very Name is "Flowing Oil," therefore have nations loved You.

[4]Upon perceiving a mere hint that You wished to draw me [near], we rushed with perfect faith after

but later becomes pleasant. Just as oil does not mix with other fluids, so Torah cannot mix with light-headed levity. As one becomes more frivolous, his Torah knowledge deserts him. Just as oil when mixed with other liquids always rises to the top, so Torah causes Israel to rise above all nations.

The *Midrash* [also *Ibn Ezra*] refers this verse to Abraham to whom God said, לֶךְ־לְךָ מֵאַרְצְךָ, *Go for yourself from your land* [*Genesis* 12:1]. He is likened to a flask of fragrant oil which emits its scent when moved from its place. So did Abraham go about and spread the knowledge of God among mankind.

Ibn Ezra continues that שֶׁמֶן תּוּרַק שְׁמֶךָ [*Your name is ointment poured forth*] refers to the fact that wherever Abraham sojourned, *there Abraham called on the name of Hashem* [*Genesis* 13:4].

שֶׁמֶן תּוּרַק שְׁמֶךָ — [lit., *Your Name is oil poured forth.*] I.e., Your reputation is

as widespread and far reaching as the fragrance of oil which is constantly poured forth, thus circulating its fragrance through the air. When fine oil is sealed in a flask, its fragrance does not diffuse, but when opened and poured forth into another flask, its fragrance spreads (*Rashi*).

Metzudas David renders: You are so permeated with fine oils with which you constantly anoint Yourself (i.e., Your wondrous deeds are so widely acclaimed) that you have rightly earned the title שֶׁמֶן תּוּרַק, *Flowing Oil.*[1]

Your Name is magnified by everyone who busies himself with the oils of Torah (*Midrash*).

The *Vilna Gaon* translates שֶׁמֶן תּוּרַק as *cosmetic ointment*, the word תּוּרַק being related to תַּמְרוּקֵי הַנָּשִׁים, *feminine cosmetics*, as in *Esther* 2:12.

עַל־כֵּן עֲלָמוֹת אֲהֵבוּךָ — [lit., *therefore do young maidens love you.*] The use of "maidens" in the allegory is consistent with the theme of the

1. [It must be understood that, aside from the שֵׁם הַמְפֹרָשׁ, *the Ineffable Name of HASHEM.* the concept of שֵׁם, *Name*, cannot be applied to God in its usual sense. It does not denote simply a title by which He is to be addressed. Rather, it reflects mortal man's limited comprehension of God's Attributes and Methods. When man perceives God's deeds as benevolent, he calls Him God of Mercy; when he perceives God as stern and demanding, he calls Him Lord of Justice. God is constant. His Names change to reflect mortal perceptions of Him.

Rav Sh. R. Hirsch points out, in his commentary to *Exodus* 6:3, that knowledge of God's Name is something that we will attain only "at the end of all the happenings in history." *Rav Hirsch* goes on to explain that, "Isaiah, speaking of the ultimate גְּאוּלָה, *Redemption*, says [*Isaiah* 52:6]: לָכֵן יֵדַע עַמִּי שְׁמִי, *Therefore My people shall know My Name.* It means: to understand God's methods of planning and ordering which are implied in this Name. This understanding can be completely achieved only out of the collective experience of all the ages."]

entire Song which is metaphorically couched in terms of man/woman. The reference is to the nations of the world: When יִתְרוֹ, *Jethro*, heard of God's deeds, he drew near and converted, as did Rachav who proclaimed [*Joshua* 2:10; 11]: "*For we have heard how* HASHEM *dried up the waters of the Sea of Suf before you when you came out of Egypt ... for* HASHEM *your God, He is God in heaven above ...*" (*Rashi*).

Alshich notes that the similes of wine and oil in these two verses refer to God's two methods of guiding the universe. All the world's destiny is determined בְּדֶרֶךְ הַטֶּבַע, *within the law of nature*. Although nature is a tool of God, He uses it when He does not wish to make His Hand obvious to all. Israel's destiny, however, is לְמַעֲלָה מִדֶּרֶךְ הַטֶּבַע, *higher than the law of nature ...*

Alshich continues with a parable: If people are drinking wine together and an unwanted guest joins them, they show him he is unwelcome by not offering him a taste of wine. But, if they are enjoying perfumes, they cannot prevent him from enjoying the fragrance.

Verse 2 thus refers to *wine* — God's special, gracious guidance of Israel, an attribute to which other nations are not privy; therefore, other nations are not mentioned there. Verse 3, however, refers to *oil*, God's goodness within natural law. Because that is enjoyed by all nations, the verse concludes with a reference to even their love of God: עַל־כֵּן עֲלָמוֹת אֲהֵבוּךְ, *therefore do other nations love You.*

The *Talmud* [*Avodah Zarah* 35b] homiletically refers the phrase to scholars: To what may a scholar be compared? To a flask of fragrant oils. When opened [i.e., when the scholar shares his knowledge with others], its fragrance is diffused; but, if covered up, its fragrance does not spread.

Moreover, things that are hidden become open to him as it is written: עַל־כֵּן עֲלָמוֹת אֲהֵבוּךְ, [*therefore young maidens love you*], which may be read עֲלָמוֹת, *the hidden love you* [i.e., אֲהֵבוּךְ], become revealed to you.

Moreover, even the Angel of Death loves him, for the words may be read to mean עַל מָוֶת אֲהֵבוּךְ, [he who is appointed] upon death loves you [for as pointed out in the *Talmud, Shabbos* 30a, in reference to David, as long as he was occupied in Torah study, the Angel of Death could not take his life (*Torah Temimah*)].

Still more, the scholar inherits both worlds — this world and the World to Come — for the words may be read to mean עֲלָמוֹת אֲהֵבוּךְ, *worlds love you.*

The *Midrash* offers further homiletical interpretations to עֲלָמוֹת: *Therefore do maidens* [i.e., Israel] *love You with youthful energy* [עֲלָמוֹת] *and vigor ...*

It can also be interpreted as עַל מָוֶת, *even unto death,* ... and refers to the martyrs through the ages, *Who love You* [God] *even unto death*, and of whom it is written [*Psalms* 44:23]: *For Your sake we are killed every day, we are considered as sheep for slaughter.*

4. מָשְׁכֵנִי אַחֲרֶיךָ נָרוּצָה — [lit., *Draw me, we will run after You!*] As reflected in the translation, *Rashi* does not render this phrase in its literal sense of *first draw me* and *then we will follow You*. He interprets that the Jews are recounting before God *the kindness of their youth, their love as a bride* [cf. *Jeremiah* 2:2]. Anticipating God's intention to draw them, they took the initiative and faithfully *followed Him into the desert* [ibid.] through a *land of waste and the shadow of death* [ibid. 2:6]. They prepared no provisions for the journey and trusted in Him and in His delegate [Moses].

The commentators note the use of the verb *run* — i.e., hurriedness, and apply it allegorically to Israel's immediate and anxious response at Mount Sinai: נַעֲשֶׂה וְנִשְׁמָע, *we will do and we will obey* [Exodus 24:7] (*Shevach Viy'kar*).[1]

Most commentators, however, see this phrase as Israel beseeching God to take the initial step and help them return to Him: "Draw me near You with only a slight gesture, and we will run after You with great alacrity" (*Metzudas David*); this similar desire is expressed in *Lamentations* 5:21: הֲשִׁיבֵנוּ ה' אֵלֶיךָ וְנָשׁוּבָה, [First] "*Bring us back to You, Hashem, and* [then] *we shall return*" [see comm. to *Eichah*, ArtScroll edition, p.140] (*Tz'ror HaMor*).

[All that Israel seeks — after its long exile — is a sign from God that He is receptive to ending the period of "estrangement" and we will jump at the opportunity. Compare David's prayer (*Psalms 86:17*): "*Display for me a sign for good.*"]

Midrash Lekach Tov compares Israel in exile to one imprisoned in a pit crying out for help: "Master of the Universe! Draw us out of our exile, and we will be free to pursue Your Torah and commandments."

Yalkut Shimoni comments: "Draw us [i.e., lead us] through our exile, so that in the future we can run after You."

"Guide me in Your truth and teach me, for, indeed, we will '*run the way of Your commandments*'" [*Psalms* 119:32] (*Sforno*).

Tiferes Shlomo homiletically comments:

The *Talmud* (*Kiddushin* 22) comments that מְשִׁיכָה, *drawing*, is a form of establishing ownership. There are two forms of drawing: *tugging* the animal so that it *follows* its new owner, or *striking* it so that it runs *ahead* of its new owner. We beseech God to "*draw us*" אַחֲרֶיךָ, *after You*, but not through blows and punishment. Our plea is that he *tug at us lightly* so that we may follow him.

The change from first-person singular ["draw me"] to first-person plural ["*we* will run"] is noted. *Tz'ror HaMor* comments that God's beneficence descends equally upon all, but people differ in their capacity to receive it. The verse begins in singular: מָשְׁכֵנִי, draw *me* [i.e., display the initiative toward me —

1. The *Midrash* homiletically connects the word מָשְׁכֵנִי to מַשְׁכּוֹן, *surety, collateral*, and relates that when Israel stood at Mount Sinai to receive the Torah, the Holy One, blessed is He, said to them: "Shall I give you the Torah? Bring good collateral that you will keep it and then I will 'give it to you.'"

"Sovereign of the Universe," they answered, "our Patriarchs will be our guarantors."
God rejected them.
"Then our prophets will be our guarantors," they suggested.
But God rejected them also and challenged them to bring better guarantors.
"Our children will be our sureties! [They will ensure the continuity of Torah]."
"They are, indeed, good guarantors," said God, accepting their pledge. "For their sake I will give you the Torah!"

[Thus, according to this *Midrash*, the verse would be homiletically rendered: מָשְׁכֵנִי, "By virtue of my מַשְׁכּוֹן, *surety*, אַחֲרֶיךָ נָרוּצָה, *we will run after You* and abide by Your Torah."]

נָרוּצָה הֱבִיאַנִי הַמֶּלֶךְ חֲדָרָיו נָגִילָה וְנִשְׂמְחָה בָּךְ נַזְכִּירָה דֹדֶיךָ מִיַּיִן מֵישָׁרִים אֲהֵבוּךָ:

ה שְׁחוֹרָה אֲנִי וְנָאוָה בְּנוֹת

the Community of Israel — as a collective entity], and אַחֲרֶיךָ נָרוּצָה, *we* [plural] *will run after You* [i.e., and "we," as a multitude of individuals, each according to his own capacity, will respond and run after You].

Alshich explains the change from "me" to "we" as referring to the spiritual and physical: Help "me" return in repentance; draw my soul to You in Your service, and "we" — all the organs of my body — will follow suit.

"We" refers to the עֲלָמוֹת, *the nations of the world*, alluded to in the previous verse: "Israel desires that God should draw it near ... then Israel and mankind will together follow the Divine ..." (*Rav W. Wolf*).

[I.e., the final perfection of creation will come about when Israel merits redemption and rises to such noble heights that all nations follow its example.]

הֱבִיאַנִי הַמֶּלֶךְ חֲדָרָיו — [lit., *the King has brought me into His chambers.*] Even in times of darkest exile, amid poverty and afflictions, they nostalgically reminisce at how God protected them by enveloping them in His cloud (*Rashi*).

Alshich and *Vilna Gaon* render this in the past perfect and apply the phrase to the redemption of the Temple: הֱבִיאַנִי הַמֶּלֶךְ חֲדָרָיו — "*When God will have brought me into His chambers in the Temple in a rebuilt Jerusalem and Zion,* נָגִילָה וְנִשְׂמְחָה בּוֹ, *all Israel will be glad and rejoice only in Him.*"

It is usual for a king to show those who run after him [i.e., his closest intimates] his chambers, the "chambers of the Torah" (*Shir Chadash*).

Tz'ror HaMor renders in the future tense, as a prayer: May it come to pass that, just as we have been privileged to recount Your love in gratitude for the redemption from Egypt, so may we be privileged to recount Your love in gratitude for the future, complete Redemption which will come to pass in the merit of those who love You sincerely.

נָגִילָה וְנִשְׂמְחָה בָּךְ — [lit., *We will be glad and rejoice in You.*] Israel — recalling God's beneficence — continues to delight in His Torah and rejoice in Him (*Rashi*), ... Because He is their God (*Sforno*).

As more chambers are revealed to us we will know You increasingly better so that we shall rejoice and delight in You — i.e., in our knowledge of You (*Shir Chadash*).

Malbim notes that נָגִילָה [*be glad*] denotes spontaneity while וְנִשְׂמְחָה [*rejoice*] denotes the long-lasting joy which outlasts a momentary outburst.

נַזְכִּירָה דֹדֶיךָ מִיַּיִן — [lit., *we declare* (or: *will commemorate*) *Your love* (*better*) *than wine.*] Even in exile as "a veritable widow of a living husband," she constantly recalls His former love as being superior to all mundane pleasures (*Rashi*).

Shir Chadash, following his thematic interpretation [see on verse 2]

I
5

You into the wilderness. The King brought me into His cloud-pillared chamber; whatever our travail, we shall always be glad and rejoice in Your Torah. We recall Your love more than earthly delights, unrestrainedly do they love You.

To the nations: ⁵*Though I am black with sin, I am comely with virtue, O nations destined to ascend to Jerusalem;*

of יַיִן as Torah and דּד as love of God and righteous deeds, renders: We will become aware of the required good deeds and attain love of God, through the study of Torah.

As the *Yalkut* comments: *"We recount Your love through wine, the wine of Torah"* [i.e., through the study of God's Torah, man can perceive His love for us].

[In a similar vein, the verse may be interpreted as a literal reference to wine: the wine of *Kiddush*, the Sanctification recited over a cup of wine on Sabbaths and festivals. Of these occasions, the *Talmud* (*Pesachim* 106a) comments: זָכְרֵהוּ עַל הַיַּיִן, *Remember it over wine.* Thus, the verse could be rendered: נַזְכִּירָה דֹדֶיךָ מִיַּיִן, *We recount Your love through wine,* the wine of *Kiddush* in which Your wondrous deeds and majesty are constantly recounted, זֵכֶר לִיצִיאַת מִצְרַיִם, *in commemoration of the Exodus from Egypt.* God's love for Israel — as manifested in this miraculous deed — was so open and unconcealed that the Sages note that "what a slavewoman witnessed at the (splitting of the) Sea, even Ezekiel did not witness in all his visions" (*Rashi to Exodus* 15:2).]

מֵישָׁרִים אֲהֵבוּךְ — [lit., *rightly do they love You*; or: *the righteous love You*.] The translation follows *Rashi*

who interprets מֵישָׁרִים [lit., *straightness*] as a modifying noun — *the sincerity of their love for You.* A strong love — straight, and void of deceit or roughness.

Ibn Aknin suggests: "For the righteousness of Your constant acts to them do they love You."

Many view the word as an adjective:

"How sincere were they that loved You! How constant were they that loved You! With great sincerity our ancestors did before You all that they did!" (*Midrash*).

"Our righteous ancestors loved You" (*Alshich*).

The *Netziv* allegorically paraphrases the verse: after running after God, entering His "chambers," rejoicing in His knowledge, then, מֵישָׁרִים אֲהֵבוּךְ, *with a straightforward intellect will they attain love of God.*

5. שְׁחוֹרָה אֲנִי וְנָאוָה — [lit., *I am black yet comely.*] I.e., "Do not think lightly of me because my 'Husband' has left me due to my swarthiness" — so declares Israel to the heathen nations. "I am blackened in consequence of my own deeds, but I am comely by virtue of the deeds of my forefathers. And, even among my own deeds, many are meritorious. Although I sinned regarding the Golden Calf [*Exodus* Ch. 32], in compensation I

[77]   *Shir HaShirim*

have the merit of having accepted the Torah" (*Rashi*).

The *Midrash* comments:

— *I am black* in my own sight, *but comely* before my Creator [i.e., when we recognize our faults we are comely in God's eyes].

— *I am black* all the days of the week [perhaps in the materialistic sense], *and comely* on the Sabbath.

— *I am black* all the days of the year, *and comely* on Yom Kippur.

— *I am black* in this world, *and comely* in the World to Come.

Ibn Aknin adds:

— *I am black* from the torturous tribulations of the exile, *but comely* at the prospect of Redemption and resumed service of God.

— *I am black* from the lime pits in Egypt, *but comely* with the blood of the paschal offering and blood of circumcision.

— *I am black* with the stigma of the generous offerings of the people to build the Golden Calf, *but comely* at their generosity in constructing the מִשְׁכָּן, the *Tabernacle*.

בְּנוֹת יְרוּשָׁלָם — [lit., *O daughters of Jerusalem*.] *Rashi* notes that the nations of the world are figuratively referred to as *daughters of Jerusalem* because, as the *Midrash* comments, Jerusalem will one day become the metropolis of all countries and draw people to her in streams to do her honor [and thus the nations of the world are poetically considered "daughters" of the great metropolis Jerusalem].

These are her neighbors who have witnessed her exiles and sufferings throughout the ages, and to whom Israel now addresses this dogmatic response (*Oteh Or*).

כְּאׇהֳלֵי קֵדָר כִּירִיעוֹת שְׁלֹמֹה — [lit., *like the tents of Kedar, like the curtains of Solomon*.] [The phrase is explained by most commentators as a parallelism to the opening phrase: *I am black* — like the tents of Kedar; *but comely* like the curtains of Solomon.]

Israel addresses the nations of the world: "Although I am as black as the tents of Kedar which constantly lay exposed to the elements, nevertheless, with a little effort, I can be washed as clean as the curtains of Solomon" (*Rashi*). I.e., "Do not think that God has rejected me utterly: He still loves me because of my merits. And, when I repent to Him, He will atone my sins" (*Metzudas David*). [As it is written (*Isaiah* 1:18): *If your sins are like scarlet, they will become white as snow*.]

[קֵדָר, *Kedar*, is a nomadic Bedouin tribe descending from Kedar, son of Ishmael (*Genesis* 25:13; *I Chronicles* 1:29). *Isaiah* (21:17) refers to the tribe as בְּנֵי קֵדָר, *the children of Kedar*, and David describes them as a barbarous people when he exclaims (*Psalms* 120:5): אוֹיָה לִי כִּי גַרְתִּי מֶשֶׁךְ שָׁכַנְתִּי עִם־אׇהֳלֵי קֵדָר, "*Woe is me that I sojourned in Meshech, that I dwelt in the tents of Kedar!*"]

The *Midrash*, consistent with its dictum (verse 1) that, in most places in this Book, שְׁלֹמֹה refers to מֶלֶךְ שֶׁהַשָּׁלוֹם שֶׁלּוֹ, *the King to Whom peace belongs*, comments that here, too, יְרִיעוֹת שְׁלֹמֹה refers to "the

though sullied as the tents of Kedar, I will be immaculate as the draperies of Him to Whom peace belongs. ⁶Do not view me with contempt despite my swarthiness, for it is but the sun which has glared

curtains of Him to Whom peace belongs" [i.e., the heavens, as it is written (*Psalms* 104:2): נוֹטֶה שָׁמַיִם כַיְרִיעָה, *Who stretches out the heaven like a curtain*].

According to the *Targum*, יְרִיעוֹת שְׁלֹמֹה refers to *the curtains of God* in the מִשְׁכָּן, *Tabernacle*, by virtue of which the Jews received atonement for the blackening sin of the Golden Calf.

6. אַל־תִּרְאֻנִי שֶׁאֲנִי שְׁחַרְחֹרֶת — [lit., *Don't look upon me that I am swarthy.*]

Rashi explains that *look*, in this verse, means *look contemptuously* (as in *I Samuel* 6:19), i.e., don't stare at me contemptuously because of my swarthiness; it is not a part of me, but caused by the sun and will fade when I go into the shade.

[Allegorically, then, according to this interpretation, the verse is to be rendered as a continuation of the previous verse in which the Community of Israel addresses heathen neighbors: "O nations of the world, do not rejoice in my sufferings. True, I am black with sin, but blackness is not my true complexion. It is artificial and I was coerced. If I return to God in true repentance, my sins will be atoned."]

The *Midrash* interprets this verse as Israel addressing her *prophets*: View us not with disdain because of our sins. No one loved us more than Moses; yet, because he referred to us as הַמֹּרִים, *the rebels* [*Numbers* 20:10], it was decreed that he should

not enter the Promised Land [*even as an individual*, because his sin of smiting the rock resulted in the *entire community* not being allowed to enter the Promised Land (*Yefei Kol*)]. Because Isaiah referred to us as עַם־טְמֵא שְׂפָתַיִם, *a people of impure lips* [*Isaiah* 6:5], he, too, was chastised by God ...

According to *Ibn Ezra*, שְׁחַרְחֹרֶת, *swarthy*, is a diminutive term of שָׁחוֹר, *black*; i.e., tan, tawny. Compare, i.e., the double forms: יְרַקְרַק, *greenish* [from יָרֹק, *green*], and אֲדַמְדָּם, *reddish* [from אָדֹם, *red*] (see also *Rashi* to *Leviticus* 13:19).

Alshich, Vilna Gaon, Tz'ror HaMor comment that שְׁחַרְחֹרֶת implies "intense blackness" in which case, according to them, the verse should be translated: *Do not stare at me as if I were intensely black; for only the sun has darkened me.*

The *Netziv* cites both views with support for each and concludes that its meaning — diminutive or accentuated — depends upon the context, in our case, favoring "intense blackness."

שֶׁשְּׁזָפַתְנִי הַשָּׁמֶשׁ — [lit., *because the sun has gazed upon me.*]

[The root, שׁזף, means, literally, *gaze, see*. It is so used in Scripture and translated by the commentators. It infers constant unshaded exposure to the rays of the sun; hence, in our context, it is translated by some as *tanned.*]

My darkness is not genetic, and

therefore it is removable; I am but superficially tanned by the sun; hence, I am subject to lightening by avoiding its direct rays (*Rashi*).[1]

The *Targum* renders:

"Despise me not, in that I am darker than you; it is because I have followed your actions and bowed down to the sun and moon."

בְּנֵי אִמִּי נִחֲרוּ־בִי — [lit., *my mother's sons quarreled* (or: *were incensed*) *with me.*]

Metaphorically בְּנֵי אִמִּי, *my mother's sons*, is explained by the commentators as referring to the nations of the world, "all of us being children of mother earth" (*Likutei Anshei Shem*).

Specifically, it refers to the Egyptians, i.e., the עֵרֶב רַב, *mixed multitude*, who accompanied the Jews at the Exodus, quarreled with them, and incited them to serve strange gods (*Rashi*).

According to the *Targum*, it refers to the false prophets:

"False prophets have been the cause of my sinful actions in order to draw upon me the fury and anger of God. They taught me to worship

your idols and follow your laws, while the Sovereign of the Universe, my own God, I did not serve. I did not follow His laws, nor did I keep His statutes nor His Torah."

Alshich interprets it as referring to the children of Esau.

According to several alternate interpretations, בְּנֵי אִמִּי, *children of my mother*, refers to בְּנֵי אוּמָתִי, *children of my nation*, rather than non-Jews:

— Dathan and Abiram who incited Pharaoh [against Moses] (*Midrash*).

— The false prophets who misled Israel [*Lamentations* 2:14] (*Lekach Tov*).

— The Jewish sinners who led Israel into sin (ibid.; *Tz'ror HaMor*).

— The Spies whose sin [of not believing that God had the power to conquer the nations of Canaan for the Jews] caused the Destructions of both Temples (*Ibn Aknin*).

שָׂמֻנִי נֹטֵרָה אֶת־הַכְּרָמִים — [lit., *they made me keeper of the vineyard.*]

I.e., figuratively, they enticed me into idol-worship; thus, I became "blackened" (*Rashi*).

---

1. Because the other nations taunt Israel, Israel replies to them: "If we who sinned only once are to be punished thus, how much more so, you." And Israel further says to the other nations: "We will tell you what we resemble. We are like a king's son who went out to the wasteland of the city, and the sun beat down on his head so that his face became swarthy. But when he went back to the town, with a little water and a little bathing, his skin became white again and his former good appearance was restored. So with us, the sun of idolatry may have tanned us, but its effects are not permanent. You, however, are swarthy from your mother's womb, for even there you served idols." When a woman is pregnant, she goes into her idolatrous temple and bows down to the idol along with her child (Midrash).

*upon me. The alien children of my mother incited
me and made me a keeper of the vineyards of idols,
but the vineyard of my own true God I did not keep.*

To
HASHEM:

*⁷ Tell me, O You Whom my soul loves: Where will
You graze Your flock? Where will You rest them under the fiercest sun of harshest exile? Why shall I be*

I.e., the Egyptians forced me to *guard their vineyards* — follow their evil ways — of which it is said [*Deuteronomy* 32:32], מִגֶּפֶן סְדֹם גַּפְנָם, *their vineyard is from the vineyard of Sodom* (*Akeidas Yitzchak*).

כַּרְמִי שֶׁלִּי לֹא נָטָרְתִּי — [lit., *my own vineyard I did not guard.*] The vineyard which was bequeathed to me as a heritage from my ancestors, I did not guard [i.e., I served strange gods, but the God of my fathers I did not serve] (*Rashi*).

Alshich and many others comment: "I was so pressured to guard others' vineyards that I was forced to neglect my own vineyard."

— "I neglected the Torah and good precepts handed down from my ancestors" (*Akeidas Yitzchak*).

The *Jerusalem Talmud* homiletically notes that the Community of Israel said to the Holy One, blessed is He: "Sovereign of the Universe! I must guard others' vineyards because I neglected to guard my own. I must now observe two days of festivals in exile and receive reward for only one of them because I neglected to proper- ly observe even one day while in Eretz Yisrael" (*Yerushalmi Eruvin* 3:9).

7. [Israel, allegorized here as sheep beloved by their shepherd, directly addresses God as a woman address- ing her husband and remonstrates with Him that the exile is too dif- ficult for her and unbecoming to Him.]

הַגִּידָה לִי שֶׁאָהֲבָה נַפְשִׁי — [lit., *tell me, Whom my soul loved.*] O, dear God, Whom my soul loves, even though our deeds are degenerate, neverthe- less tell us! (*Sforno*).

According to the *Midrash*, *Targum* [see below], and many commentators it is Moses who poses to God this question of Israel's fu- ture survival in exile: "*Tell me, concerning whom my soul loves* — this nation that my soul loves, this nation for which I have offered my life ... Now that You are removing me from the world, tell me: Who are the shepherds whom You are appointing over Your children?"

"... Who will guide and sustain them throughout their sojourns among the nations of the world?" (*Ibn Aknin*).

אֵיכָה תִרְעֶה אֵיכָה תַּרְבִּיץ בַּצָּהֳרָיִם — [lit., *where will You graze, where will You rest (Your flock) at noon?*]

Where [i.e., by what standard, with what Master Plan] will You pasture Your flock [i.e., the Jews] among the "wolves" in whose midst they dwell. Where will You rest them at noon during their long distressing exile? — "*noon*" being a time of distress for cattle (*Rashi*) because the "sun" is then most in- tense and there is no relief from the suffering (*Tz'ror HaMor*).

The *Vilna Gaon* perceives this verse as being posed in the form of a

פֶּרֶק א ח כְּעֹטְיָה עַל עֶדְרֵי חֲבֵרֶיךָ: אִם לֹא תֵדְעִי
ח לָךְ הַיָּפָה בַּנָּשִׁים צְאִי־לָךְ בְּעִקְבֵי הַצֹּאן

plaint by a forlorn exiled Israel, bereft of God's manifest nearness: "When You Yourself used to shepherd me, I lacked nothing. Now that You have 'left' me and I must tend for myself, I don't even recognize where I grazed. O God! Give me Your guidance throughout my exile! Where does one graze? Where does one rest? Why should I be forced to wander aimlessly about — unclothed?"

The *Midrash*, placing these words in the mouth of Moses, renders: "*Where will you graze them* — in the rainy season … when the foreign powers rise? *Where will you rest Your flock at noon* — when the foreign powers subjugate her?"[1]

The *Targum* paraphrases: "Inform me, I pray to You, how they will sustain themselves, and how they will live among the nations, whose decrees are as violent as the heat of the noonday sun in the summer solstice."

Many commentators — *Alkabetz, Ralbag, Eiger Chumash,* etc. — perceive in this verse Israel seeking comfort and comprehension of God's ways so they can return to Him. They render: "God, Whom my soul loves, teach me Your ways. *What is Your method of grazing,* etc., … i.e., of governing the universe. Let us discern Your love so we will be drawn to You in closeness and not stumble about in disgrace to Your Name." [See *Metzudas David* below.]

שֶׁלָּמָה אֶהְיֶה כְּעֹטְיָה — [lit., *for why should I be as one veiled.*]

… For it is not to Your honor that I go about as a mourner displaying grief (*Rashi*).

Metzudas David, translating כְּעֹטְיָה in the sense of "wandering about," renders: "Let me perceive Your ways so that I will be drawn to You and cleave to You; *why must I stumble about in constant quest, bewildered?*"

The *Midrash* offers the following interpretations:

— Let me not be like a mourner who covers [עֹטֶה] his upper lip and weeps [over Israel's distress] (cf. *Leviticus* 13:45).

— Let me not be like a shepherd who folds up [עָטָה] his garment and escapes (cf. *Jeremiah* 43:12).

— Let not Your children see that terrible distress is befalling them [וְיַטּוּ] and turn from You and cleave to the heathens.

עַל עֶדְרֵי חֲבֵרֶיךָ — [lit., *by the flocks of Your companions.*]

[*Companions* being understood by most commentators as the "kings and rulers" (*Rashi*), who "shepherd" the heathen nations.]

Divrei Yedidiah suggests that the reason that the heathen kings and rulers are referred to as His *companions* in government is because they rule by Divine sanction as noted in the *Talmud* (*Berachos* 58a): "Blessed

1. [It is perhaps possible to homiletically link תַּרְבִּיץ, *rest*, to the word רבץ as in הַרְבָּצַת תּוֹרָה, *dissemination of Torah.* Render thus: "By what method will You pasture Your flock in exile? Under such affliction, אֵיכָה תַּרְבִּיץ בַּצָּהֳרַיִם, how do You plan to disseminate Torah, i.e., how do You expect Torah to flourish, in the 'high noon' of affliction …?"

God gives His response in the following verse.]

like one veiled in mourning among the flocks of Your fellow shepherds?

Hashem: [8] *If you know not where to graze, O fairest of nations, follow the footsteps of the sheep, your forefathers, who traced a straight, unswerving path after My Torah. Then you can graze your tender kids*

is the Merciful One, Who established royalty on earth that reflects the royalty of Heaven and invested you with dominion ... For even a supervisor of irrigation is appointed from Heaven." Therefore the *flocks of Your companions* refers to the heathen nations.

It would be an insult to Heaven that Your children should be in distress and the flocks of Your "companions" in prosperity (*Midrash*).

According to *Ibn Ezra*, the verse allegorically portrays a repentant Israel asking God to enlighten them on how the Patriarchs conducted their lives so they might follow suit and not intermingle with followers of false gods who presume these gods to be His "companions."

In an alternate interpretation, the *Midrash* interprets חֲבֵרֶיךָ, *Your companions*, in the sense of "adherents," "devotees," referring to the Patriarchs, Abraham, Isaac, and Jacob; "When I go to Your companions [the Patriarchs)," exclaims Moses, "and they ask me about their flocks, what shall I tell them?"

[Compare use of *companions* in 8:13.]

8-11. [God is now the speaker responding to the inquiry of the previous verse. To fathom His ways, hold His love, and endure the travails of exile, Israel must follow the example of her forebears and cleave to His commandments.]

אִם־לֹא תֵדְעִי לָךְ הַיָּפָה בַּנָּשִׁים — [lit., *if you do not know, O fairest of women.*][1] "If you, whom your Shepherd no longer guides, ... if you, My beloved, fairest of all nations, do not know where to 'graze' in safety from those who distress you in order not to lose your children ..." (*Rashi*).

[הַיָּפָה בַּנָּשִׁים, *O fairest of women*, is allegorically explained by *Rashi* as meaning: *You, My beloved community, fairest of all the nations.*]

According to the *Midrash* [also *Targum*; see below], this verse is God's response to Moses' inquiries in the previous verse: "*If you do not know, O most eminent of prophets* ... even if you do not know at this moment, תֵדְעִי, you *will* know in due course." For, as the *Midrash* relates, before Moses died, God revealed the future history of Israel to him and showed him the leaders of forthcoming generations.

צְאִי־לָךְ בְּעִקְבֵי הַצֹּאן — [lit., *go out* (i.e., follow) *the tracks of the sheep.*] I.e., contemplate the actions of your

1. The *Midrash* notes that the prophets [or, depending upon the various interpretations of our verse, the Congregation of Israel or Moses,] are referred to as הַיָּפָה בַּנָּשִׁים, *fairest of women* — fairest among prophets, most eminent among prophets. Rav Yose ben Yirmiyah said: Why are the prophets compared to women? To illustrate that just as a woman is not

פֶּרֶק א

וּרְעִי אֶת־גְּדִיֹּתַיִךְ עַל מִשְׁכְּנוֹת הָרֹעִים: ט

לְסֻסָתִי בְּרִכְבֵי פַרְעֹה דִּמִּיתִיךְ

ancestors who accepted My Torah and observed My commandments, and follow their footsteps (*Rashi*). I.e., if you have difficulty in perceiving Me via your own intellect, then rely on the traditions [i.e., *footsteps*] of your ancestors and thus cleave to Me (*Metzudas David*).

Alshich renders: If you wish to seek the path by which I will return to you, then follow in the tracks of your holy ancestors.

Rav W. Wolf, seeing in the word עִקְבֵי, *heels*, the letters of יַעֲקֹב, *Jacob*, beautifully interprets this verse in the context of Israel's historic experience and its instructive purpose. He renders: אִם־לֹא תֵדְעִי לָךְ, *If you refuse to know your mission, then go into exile* ... "for this should give you the ability — toe and heel limping after עִקְבֵי הַצֹּאן (according to the immortal destiny expressed in the name יַעֲקֹב, *Jacob*) — to renounce all material force, and to see your power in the education of your youth for God's cause."

וּרְעִי אֶת־גְּדִיֹּתַיִךְ עַל מִשְׁכְּנוֹת הָרֹעִים — [lit., *and graze your kids by (upon) the shepherds' tents.*]

Then [if you follow in your ancestors' footsteps], you will merit the right to safely *graze Your children*

among the nations of the world (*Rashi*) ...

The Holy One, blessed is He, replied unto Moses, the prophet:

"If the Assembly of Israel, compared to a beautiful child, desires to wipe out the captivity, and make My soul compassionate toward her, let her walk in the ways of the righteous, and let her arrange her supplications by the mouth of the shepherds and leaders of the generation; let her instruct her children, compared to the kids of the goat, to assemble in synagogues and study-houses; then, by that merit, they will be sustained in exile, until I send their king, Messiah, who will lead them gently to their Dwelling Place, the Temple which David and Solomon, the shepherds of Israel, shall build for them" (*Targum*).

[גְּדִיֹּתַיִךְ, *kids*, are thus allegorically interpreted as children (cf. *Berachos* 63a); and *shepherds* are understood in the context of the previous verse as the leaders of the heathen nations.]

Not only צְאִי־לָךְ, should you yourselves follow in the path of your righteous forebears, but רְעִי אֶת־גְּדִיֹּתַיִךְ, *graze* even your children on these pastures, and then you will surely ascend עַל, *upon* — higher than — the heathen nations (*Alshich*).

ashamed to demand from her husband the requirements of her household [because household requirements affect him as well (*Torah Temimah*)], so the prophets were not ashamed to demand the requirements of Israel from their Father in Heaven [because the relationship between God and Israel is figuratively that of husband and wife, and the prophets perceive that Israel's needs, if one may so express himself, affect God [כִּי יִשְׂרָאֵל וְהַקָּבָּ"ה חַד הוּא, *for Israel and God are one* (*Torah Temimah*)].

Additionally, the prophets are compared to women because just as the responsibility for the well-being of the home and family rests upon the woman, so too the responsibility for the spiritual well-being of the nation rests upon the prophets (*Harav Gifter*).

even among the dwellings of foreign shepherds.
⁹*With My mighty steeds who battled Pharaoh's*

[The *Talmud* homiletically interprets מִשְׁכְּנוֹת, *dwellings*, as being related to מַשְׁכּוֹנוֹת, *sureties, pledges* (comp. 1:4, s.v. מָשְׁכֵנִי), and רֹעִים, *shepherds*, as referring to the צַדִּיקִים, *righteous men*, who are *shepherds of the generation*:] "When there are righteous men in the generation, the righteous men are sureties and are held accountable for the sins of the generation. But, when there are no righteous men in the generation, the תִּינוֹקוֹת שֶׁל בֵּית רַבָּן, *schoolchildren*, become sureties for the generation (*Shabbos* 33b) ..."

[Therefore render thus: "*If you do not understand how to keep God's commandments go out and learn them for the sake of your flocks*, i.e., your children, *and sustain your children for they are* מַשְׁכּוֹנוֹת הָרֹעִים, *the sureties*, עַל, *in lieu of*, *the righteous*."]

Shir Chadash relates it to the verse: מִשְׁכְּנוֹתֶיךָ יִשְׂרָאֵל, *Your tabernacles, O Israel* [*Numbers* 24:5], which the *Talmud* [*Sanhedrin* 105b] interprets as "your synagogues and study-houses"; and which, the *Midrash* notes, protect Israel "when the voice of Jacob [i.e., Torah-study] is heard therein." He therefore renders thus: "If you ask, 'אֵיכָה תִרְעֶה, *where to graze*,' then heed My advice and *graze your children in the spiritual pastures of the synagogues and study-houses*, and this will protect you."

Ibn Ezra comments that גְּדִיּתֶיךָ, *your kids*, refers not to *children*, but to the spiritually immature.

9. לְסֻסָתִי בְּרִכְבֵי פַרְעֹה — [lit., *to a steed in Pharaoh's chariot.*] *Rashi*

— as reflected in the allegorical translation — renders this verse as referring to God's wondrous deeds after the Exodus, in saving the Jews from Pharaoh's pursuing army and then drowning it in the Red Sea.

Metzudas David understands the simile as a generic reference to the Egyptian monarchy rather than to the particular Pharaoh who enslaved the Jews. It also refers to the fact that Egypt was the world's leading supplier of choice horses. He interprets this phrase as God's compliment to His beloved Israel, comparing them to the choicest of Pharaoh's personal horses: "To Me you are more beloved than all the nations of the world, even the choicest of them."

The finest of horses were bred in Egypt, and the choicest of them became part of the king's own stables. When harnessed to the king's chariot, they were bedecked with the finest of jewels. So God speaks of Israel as His choicest from among the nations, bedecked with ornaments as described in the following verses (*Vilna Gaon*).

Shaar Bas Rabim comments that the comparison of Israel to an Egyptian steed is apt. Usually it is the rider that directs his horse, but, as the *Midrash* in *Exodus* points out, although the fleeing Egyptians cried out in fright [*Exodus* 14:25]: אָנוּסָה מִפְּנֵי יִשְׂרָאֵל, "*let us flee from before Israel*," their horses led them into the water to drown. Similarly, God gives Israel the right to direct its own destiny and the destiny of the world through its righteous

conduct. As the Sages teach, ה' גּוֹזֵר
וְצַדִּיק מְבַטְּלָהּ, *God promulgates a decree, and a righteous man abrogates it.*

[The commentators note that סְסָתִי is the poetic feminine form of סוּס, *horse,* and means literally *mare.* The imagery conjured up in the literal interpretation of the parable is the comparison of her beauty to that of a superb Egyptian horse, the finest of which were especially chosen for Pharaoh's personal stable. It is noted several times in Scripture that Israel imported horses from Egypt. (See, e.g., *II Chronicles* 9:28.)]

דִּמִּיתִיךְ רַעְיָתִי — [lit., *I have compared you, My beloved.*] The allegorical translation, *I revealed that you are My beloved* [i.e., by performing miraculous deeds for you], follows *Rashi's* alternative rendering. In his primary comment, however, he relates the word to דֹּם, *silence,* and explains: "When you were imperiled at the Red Sea, I fought your battle and I bid you, '*Be silent, My beloved*' " [*Exodus* 14:14].

Alshich thematically connects verses 9-11 and explains them as God's response to Israel concerning their sin of עֵגֶל הַזָּהָב, *the Golden Calf.* He translates סְסָתִי as a possessive: *My horse,* and renders: See all the goodness I wrought for you! But you did

not respond in kind. *My horses —* horses that I created and gave him — Pharaoh harnessed and rebelliously turned against you and Me. I compare you, therefore, to these horses, My beloved nation, because you also took what is Mine and used it to sin against Me [next verses]. The booty from Egypt and the Red Sea was My gift to you [cf. לִי הַכֶּסֶף וְלִי הַזָּהָב נְאֻם ה' צְבָאוֹת, *Mine is the silver and Mine is the gold — the word of Hashem, Master of Legions* (*Haggai* 2:8)]. You gathered it and used it to fashion the Golden Calf!

This abuse of Heavenly gifts is the very essence of sin (*Tomer Devorah*).

10-11. [In these verses God continues recounting His beneficence to the Jews while, at the same time, implying their ingratitude.]

נָאווּ לְחָיַיִךְ בַּתֹּרִים צַוָּארֵךְ בַּחֲרוּזִים — [lit., *your cheeks are comely with circlets, your neck with strings of jewels.*]

Rashi, consistent with his thematic interpretation, explains that the ornaments in this verse are representative of the Egyptian booty which the Jews got at the Sea and in which they looked comely.

תּוֹרֵי זָהָב נַעֲשֶׂה־לָּךְ — [lit., *Wreaths of gold will we make for you.*][1] God recounts how He assured that Israel

1. [The plural form נַעֲשֶׂה, *we will make* — spoken by God — is noted by the commentators.
The same word נַעֲשֶׂה, *we will make,* is spoken by God in reference to creation of Man in *Genesis* 1:26. *Rashi* notes there that the plural form means to imply that God, in order to instruct man in proper behavior, consulted His "heavenly family" although, of course, the angels did not assist Him in His Creation of man. Although the plural form might lead heretics to

riders I revealed that you are My beloved. ¹⁰ *Your cheeks are lovely with rows of gems, your neck with necklaces, My gifts to you from the splitting sea,* ¹¹ *by inducing Pharaoh to engage in pursuit, to add circlets of gold to your spangles of silver.*

would be the recipient of this booty. He — along with His Celestial Court — influenced the Egyptians to wear their treasures while pursuing the Jews so that upon their defeat, Israel could claim the booty, represented by *wreaths of gold*. This was in addition to the less precious נְקֻדּוֹת הַכָּסֶף, *silver ornaments* [symbolic of the goods they carried out of Egypt], for as the Sages note: Greater was the בִּיַּת הַיָּם, *booty of the Sea* [represented in our verse by *gold* ornaments], than בִּיַּת מִצְרַיִם, *the booty of Egypt* [represented by *silver*] (*Rashi*).

עִם נְקֻדּוֹת הַכָּסֶף — [lit., *points of silver*.] *Rashi* explains this as silver ornaments which are striped and decorated with many colors. [According to his commentary the עִם, *with*, is to be understood as *additional* to the other gold ornaments.]

Ibn Ezra and *Vilna Gaon* explain this not as an additional piece of jewelry, but as a *silver overlay* upon the *wreaths of gold* mentioned in the beginning of the verse.

[The verses, explained by *Rashi* and many commentators with reference to God's gift to Israel of the boo-

ties of Egypt and the Sea, can best be understood with the following paraphrase of verses 10-11: *Perceiving how good you look bedecked in even simple silver ornaments, I arranged additional golden ornaments for you! Metzudas David*, who interprets the ornaments as an allusion to God's general gifts of abundant goodness in general, renders thus: "You are indeed worthy of being given much goodness; it befits you. And I will bestow blessing upon you commensurate with your worthiness and receptivity."]

The *Midrash*, however, perceives in these verses a reference to the Torah: לְחָיַיִךְ, *your cheeks*, refers to man's power of speech: "Just as the cheeks are made only for speech, so was Israel created only for the Torah" (*Yalkut Shimoni*)

The *Midrash* also interprets תֹּרִים homiletically as meaning תּוֹרוֹת, the two Torahs, Written and Oral.

The verse, then, according to these interpretations should be rendered: "Your power of speech is indeed comely when utilized to interpret and expound in matters of

conclude that there is ח"ו more than one creator, Scripture does not shrink from teaching us proper conduct and the trait of modesty, that the mighty should consult with and seek permission from the lowly.

Rav Hirsch, in his commentary to that verse explains, "the use of the *pluralis majestatis* [royal 'we') probably has its origin in the idea that the human ruler is not issuing orders in his own personal interest, but looks at himself as being at one with his people ... A similar concept can apply to the Creator. The *pluralis majestatis* occurs in the speeches of God in those cases where that, which on the surface appears to be restricting, disturbing, interference, is meant to be understood as being in reality something which causes happiness, brings rescue, and is necessary."]

Torah, thus, as it were, ornamenting the Torah itself" (*Shir Chadash*).

תּוֹרִים can also be homiletically interpreted, according to the *Midrash*, as related to the word תּוֹר, *turn*, as in *Esther* 2:12. Accordingly, our verse would be rendered thus: "The power of your speech is comely [i.e., most beneficial] when the Torah is expounded in its turn — i.e., on the proper occasions: the laws of Pesach on Pesach; the laws of Shavuos on Shavuos; and the laws of Succos on Succos."

צַוָּארֵךְ בַּחֲרוּזִים is homiletically interpreted in the *Midrash* as referring to students who eagerly חוֹזְרִים, *strain*, their necks to hear the words of the Torah from their teacher's mouth.

Shir Chadash notes that just as necklaces ornament their wearers, so does one who utilizes his neck [i.e., throat, voice] to study the Torah add charm and beauty to it [for as the *Talmud Eruvin* 54a comments: "Open your mouth and learn (aloud) Scripture, open your mouth and learn aloud the *Talmud*, that your studies may be retained and that you may live long"; as it is written (*Proverbs* 4:22): כִּי חַיִּים הֵם לְמֹצְאֵיהֶם, *for they* (i.e., the words of the Torah) *are life to those that find them*. Read not לְמֹצְאֵיהֶם, *to those that find them* (from root מצא, *to find*), but לְמוֹצִאֵיהֶם, *to those who utter them* (from root יצא, in *hifil*, to bring out, *utter*) with their mouth.

... For verbalizing makes succinct the thoughts of one's mind (*Harav Gifter*).

[It is perhaps possible, in keeping with the above interpretations of this verse, to suggest that חֲרוּזִים be interpreted as alluding to חֲרוּזִים, *rhymes of poetic prayer*. Render thus: *Comely are you when you utilize your speech for Torah study, and your throat for uttering prayer.*]

The *Vilna Gaon*, following the *Midrashim*, explains verse 11: תּוֹרֵי זָהָב refers to the Written and Oral Torah which God gave us and which (*Psalms* 19:11) *are more desirable than gold*. נְקֻדּוֹת כֶּסֶף refers to the ornaments of Torah, the esoterics, and the נְקֻדּוֹת, *the vowels*, by which many words of the Torah are exegetically expounded.

[Within the "simple" allegorical meaning of the verse, however, most commentators concur that the reference is to God's gifts at the Sea and Israel's lack of response as evidenced by their utilizing these treasures to fashion the עֵגֶל הַזָּהָב, *Golden Calf*.]

12-15. [As noted in the commentary to verse 2, the speakers of the various verses are not identified throughout the Book. In most cases, however, the gender of the verbs indicate who is being addressed. In the following verses, however, there is no definite way of establishing the identity of the speaker and this poses a difficulty even for those who interpret the מָשָׁל, the literal sense of the parable. The Sages, therefore, differ in their exegeses, demonstrating that there are, indeed, ע' פָּנִים לַתּוֹרָה, *seventy facets* (i.e., seventy modes) *to expounding the Torah* ....

In accordance with *Rashi*, the following verses are Israel's response

Israel: ¹²*While the King was yet at Sinai my malodorous deed gave forth its scent as my Golden Calf defiled*

to God. It may be summarized as follows: (v. 12) "True, beloved God. You did perform all those miracles for us at the Sea, and we sinned against You while You were still at Sinai; (v. 13) but You forgave us and consented to dwell among us; (v. 14) pardoning us for our many transgressions, (v. 15) and comforting us by telling us that because our iniquities are forgiven, we are beautiful again."]

12. עַד־שֶׁהַמֶּלֶךְ בִּמְסִבּוֹ נִרְדִּי נָתַן רֵיחוֹ — [lit., *while the King was* (still) *at His table, my nard gave forth its fragrance.*]

The allegorical translation follows *Rashi* who renders *my nard gave forth its fragrance* as a euphemism for *evil odor,* a distasteful term which Scripture avoided in speaking of Israel.

As the *Targum* paraphrases: "But while Moses was in the heavens to receive the Torah, the wicked ones of that generation — the mixed multitude among them — arose and made the Golden Calf. They corrupted their actions, and their evil name went forth against them throughout the world, whereas previously their scent went forth in the world as fragrance. Now, however, they were malodorous as nard."

The *Talmud* offers this comment: "Shameless is the bride who is unfaithful within her bridal canopy! [As was Israel who was unfaithful by making the Golden Calf at Mt. Sinai itself.] This is referred to in the verse, *While the King was still at His table, my nard gave forth* [i.e., *forsook* (Rashi)] *its fragrance.* Yet His love was still with us.

[I.e., although the incident depicted our degeneracy, God demonstrated His paternal love to us for, when recording the incident in Scripture,] He used the word *gave forth* instead of *became fetid* (*Shabbos* 88b).

This agrees also with the interpretation offered by Rabbi Meir in the *Midrash:* "While yet the Supreme King of kings, the Holy One, blessed is He, was at His 'table' in the heavens, Israel sent forth an offensive smell [i.e., became corrupt], and became involved with the Golden Calf."[1]

מְסִבּוֹ, *his table,* literally means *his reclining,* figurative of the reclining manner in which kings of ancient times would feast while reclining on a divan (*Metzudas Tzion*).

[נֵרְדְּ, *nard,* is an aromatic plant used as a perfume. The word appears in Scripture only here and below, 4:13-14, where it is listed with other spices. In the *Talmud* (*Kereisos* 6a)

---

1. The *Midrash* continues that Rav Yehudah disagreed with Rabbi Meir's interpretation and exclaimed: "Enough of this, Meir; the Song of Songs is not expounded in a bad sense but only in a good sense, for the Song of Songs was revealed only for the praise of Israel!" [Rav Yehudah then goes on to offer a favorable interpretation of the verse:] While the Supreme King of kings, the Holy One, blessed is He, was at His "table" in the heavens [i.e., even before He "descended" to Mount Sinai], Israel had already sent forth a fragrance before Mount Sinai and said [*Exodus* 24:7]:

כֹּל אֲשֶׁר־דִּבֶּר ה' נַעֲשֶׂה וְנִשְׁמָע, *"Everything that Hashem has said we will do and we will obey."*

פֶּרֶק א

יג צְרוֹר הַמֹּר | דּוֹדִי לִי בֵּין שָׁדַי יָלִין:

יד אֶשְׁכֹּל הַכֹּפֶר | דּוֹדִי לִי בְּכַרְמֵי עֵין

יג-יד

it is listed as an ingredient of the סַמָּנֵי הַקְּטֹרֶת, *compound of incense* used in the Temple.]

13. צְרוֹר הַמֹּר דּוֹדִי לִי — [lit., *a bundle of myrrh is my Beloved to me.*]

[According to *Rashi's* thematic interpretation, the myrrh of this verse compensates for the *nard* of the previous verse. *Nard*, as explained above, is a euphemism for the "offensive odor" of sin; the *bundle of myrrh* figuratively refers to her expiation.] I.e., my Beloved has become to me as one who possesses a bag of fragrant myrrh, and offering it to me says: "Here is a bag that will produce a finer fragrance than the one you lost." Similarly, God appeared after the incident of the Golden Calf, offering me an opportunity to acquire a "new fragrance": "Contribute toward the construction of the מִשְׁכָּן, *Tabernacle,*" He said, "and the act of repentance represented by the contribution of gold for the holy task of building the Tabernacle will expiate the sin of having given gold to make the Calf."

בֵּין שָׁדַי יָלִין — [lit., *lodged between my bosom.*] *Rashi* explains that these words indicate that the *Shechinah* dwelled between the two staves of the Ark: "Although I trespassed against Him, He forgave me and consented to 'dwell' there."

The simile of שָׁדַיִם, *bosom,* and staves of the Ark is elaborated upon in the *Talmud* where it is noted that although the staves were very long they were *perceivable from without,* but could not be *actually*

seen [cf. *I Kings* 8:8], because the twin poles pressed forth against the curtain, and only the twin bosomlike protrusions could be discerned from without (*Yoma* 54a; *Menachos* 98a).

[The *Talmud* homiletically interprets the words צְרוֹר הַמֹּר, *bundle of myrrh,* as מֵיצַר וּמֵימַר, *distressed and embittered*:] "The Congregation of Israel spoke before the Holy One, blessed is He: '*Though my Beloved has distressed and embittered me* [in consequence of the Golden Calf (*Rashi*)], yet בֵּין שָׁדַי יָלִין, *He* [nevertheless] *lodged between my bosom* [i.e., He forgave me and commanded us to immediately build Him a Tabernacle so He could 'dwell' between the staves of the Ark which protruded through the curtain" (*Rashi*)].

The word יָלִין, *lodge,* infers a temporary situation as one who "sleeps over" and then goes his way. Similarly God "lodged" within the Sanctuary, but when Israel sinned, the *Shechinah* "departed" to its "heavenly abode" and took up its lodging there (*Shevach Viy'kar*).

Metzudas David perceives this verse as Israel beseeching God: The fragrance of His bag of myrrh — containing many spices — is superior to my nard. The favors He lavished upon me are greater than my deeds, and I therefore beseech Him: בֵּין שָׁדַי יָלִין, *may He cause His Shechinah to dwell in my midst.* [My bosom being understood as "close to my heart."]

As *Ibn Ezra* translates: "Between the Cherubim, or in the midst of the

the covenant. [13]*But my Beloved responded with a bundle of myrrh, the fragrant atonement of erecting a Tabernacle where His Presence would dwell between the Holy Ark's staves.* [14]*Like a cluster of henna in Ein-gedi vineyards has my Beloved*

Congregation of Israel."

Shir Chadash interprets שָׁדַיִם, *bosom* — an allegorical reference to sources of nourishment — as an allusion to scholars who "nourish" others by instructing them in Torah. He renders: "If I provide spiritual nourishment for others, God will cause His Presence to 'dwell' upon me."

14. אֶשְׁכֹּל הַכֹּפֶר דּוֹדִי לִי בְּכַרְמֵי — [lit., *A cluster of henna is my Beloved to me, in the vineyards of Ein-gedi.*][1]

[Israel is still speaking.]

Rashi quotes the *Midrash* [*Yalkut Shimoni*] which states that the vineyards in Ein-gedi where henna is grown yield four or five crops a year. The allegory thus alludes to the expiations and pardons which God granted Israel for their many provocations against Him in the desert.

The allegorical interpretation of אֶשְׁכֹּל הַכֹּפֶר, *cluster of henna*, as referring to atonement and pardon is derived from the *Midrash* which expounds הַכֹּפֶר as being related to כַּפָּרָה, *atonement*.

The *Midrash* similarly suggests an allusion to Torah scholars: אִישׁ שֶׁהַכֹּל בּוֹ, *a man in whom is everything: the full spectrum of Torah-study,* for such people atone [מְכַפֵּר]

for the iniquities of Israel. [Render: *My beloved is to me like the Torah scholars of this world who atone for the iniquities of Israel.*]

According to the *Malbim*, this verse esoterically alludes to Divine spirituality which hovers outside human souls and which infuses all of creation, enabling Godly people to perceive even greater measures of spiritual richness. Although this source of Godliness is not within man, its "fragrance" can be perceived from afar.

He explains that Ein-gedi was in the wilderness (cf. *I Samuel* 24:2), thus it metaphorically alludes to a dwelling-place away from other inhabitants, yet because of its abundant growths of henna its scent is perceived from afar. So, too, the Divine which, so to speak, dwells from afar, yet He is like a cluster of henna whose scent permeates the world.

[The *Targum* on this verse asks where the Jews in the desert got wine to offer as oblation. Certainly the desert was no place fit for cultivation! He answers that they went to the vineyards of Ein-gedi from which they took clusters of grapes. They pressed wine out of them and offered it at the Altar.]

1. The *Talmud* explains אֶשְׁכֹּל as referring to God אִישׁ שֶׁהַכֹּל בּוֹ, *He to Whom all belongs*, and homiletically expounds the verse: "*He to Whom all belongs* [שֶׁהַכֹּל שֶׁלּוֹ = אֶשְׁכֹּל] *shall make atonement* [מְכַפֵּר = הַכֹּפֶר] *for me for the sin* [עָוֹן = עֵין] *of the kid* [גְּדִי = גֶּדִי = Kid = Golden Calf] *which I heaped up* [שֶׁבָּרַמְתִּי = בְּכַרְמֵי] *for myself*" (*Shabbos* 88b).

Metzudas David, interpreting the fragrance of the various spices mentioned in these verses as referring to God's favors to us, renders the verse thus: "The favors You bestowed upon us are so vast that they resemble a cluster of henna which grows in abundance and which gives off an aroma that can be perceived from afar. So are the wondrous and miraculous deeds You performed for us known to the ends of the earth" [cf. *Rashi's* comm. to verse 3].

15. הִנָּךְ יָפָה רַעְיָתִי —[lit., *you are beautiful, my love.*] According to *Rashi*, Israel is still the speaker. She recalls how God, perceiving her shame for her errant ways, strengthened her with the soothing words: "סָלַחְתִּי כִּדְבָרֶךְ, *I have forgiven because of your word* [Numbers 14:20]. *Now that you are forgiven,*" God continues, "הִנָּךְ יָפָה רַעְיָתִי, *you are [again] beautiful in deed and ancestry.*"

[The repeated usage of *you are beautiful* is expounded upon in the *Midrash* as emphasizing the various aspects in which spiritual beauty manifests itself. A selection:]

You are beautiful in the performance of mitzvos, *you are beautiful* in kind deeds.

You are beautiful in the performance of positive mitzvos, *you are beautiful* in abiding by the negative commandments.

You are beautiful with the mezuzah, *you are beautiful* with tefillin.

You are beautiful in repentance, *you are beautiful* with good deeds.

You are beautiful in this world, *you are beautiful* in the World to Come.

Shir Chadash says that the repetition of the phrase, *You are beautiful,* refers to the past and present. *You became beautiful* when you received the Torah at Mt. Sinai [for then your spiritual impurity and physical blemishes were removed (*Mechilta*)]. And *you are still beautiful.*

הִנָּךְ יָפָה עֵינַיִךְ יוֹנִים — [lit., *you are beautiful, your eyes are doves.*] I.e., you are beautiful — your eyes are *as* doves (*Ibn Ezra*).

[*Eyes* are mentioned because they are considered one of man's principal organs; as the *Talmud* says, "a blind man is considered like a dead man." Man's gaze, i.e., his outlook and perspective, is considered the barometer of his character, for, as the *Midrash* notes: "There are two hundred and forty-eight limbs in the human body, and they move only by the direction of the eyes."]

"If a bride's eyes are homely, it is indicative that one must survey the rest of her; but if her eyes are beautiful, one need look no further" (*Rashi; Midrash*).

The *Midrash* states that the *eyes* of the generation are its Torah leaders: the Sanhedrin. For just as the actions of the body are controlled by the eyes, so is Israel directed by its Torah leaders. [The verse would then be rendered allegorically: *You are beautiful, My beloved nation, you are beautiful. Your Torah leaders are like doves.*]

I multiplied His forgiveness to me.

15-16   ¹⁵He said, "I forgive you, My friend, for you are lovely in deed and lovely in resolve. The righteous among you are loyal as a dove."

¹⁶It is You Who are lovely, my Beloved, so pleasant

I.e., your righteous leaders have cleaved to Me as faithfully as doves who cling possessively to their mates and do not allow them to stray to others. Similarly the righteous sons of Levi stepped forward to do whatever God bid them [Exodus 32:26], because they alone did not stray in the incident of the Golden Calf (Rashi).

The Midrash notes several justifications for the metaphor of Israel and the dove: "As the dove is chaste, so is Israel; as a dove puts forth her neck for slaughter, so does Israel. As it says [Psalms 44:23]: For Your sake we are killed all the time. As a dove atones for iniquities [when offered as a sacrifice], so does Israel atone for the other nations. Since the seventy bulls that they sacrificed on Succos were offered only to protect the seventy nations, so the world should not be made desolate because of their sins. Just as from the time a dove recognizes her mate she never changes him for another, so Israel never exchanged the Holy One, blessed is He, for another, once they had learned to know Him."

It is the nature of doves to constantly glance back toward their nest, just as Israel always "glances" back to God, its Source, for rejuvenation ...

Rav Saadiah Gaon notes that this explains the comparison of Israel to a dove, and for the repetition of the phrase you are beautiful ...:

You are beautiful, My beloved; when you are My beloved and near to Me, you are surely beautiful, but even when you stray far away from Me, and cannot be properly called My beloved, even then You are beautiful because your eyes are as doves, i.e., you always look back and long after God.

16. [As evidenced by the masculine form in the words הִנְּךָ יָפֶה דוֹדִי (instead of the feminine הִנָּךְ יָפָה דוֹדָתִי), it is God, the male of the allegory, Who is now being referred to in this verse.]

הִנְּךָ יָפֶה דוֹדִי אַף נָעִים — [lit., You are handsome, my Beloved, indeed pleasant.]

Israel thus responds to God: The beauty is not ours but Yours: "You are the handsome one, my Beloved, אַף נָעִים, indeed pleasant, for having pardoned our iniquities and causing Your Presence to dwell among us" — cf. Leviticus 9:23, 24 (Rashi).

"We beseech You, dear God, not because of our merits, which are few, but for the sake of Your Name that It be sanctified and not profaned by the nations of the world. For it is Your Attribute to be beautiful, pleasant, and forgiving" (Tz'ror HaMor).

The Midrash homiletically interprets the word אַף [indeed] in its other meaning, anger, and renders: "Sovereign of the Universe, the

פרק א
יז

יז רַעֲנָנָה: קֹרוֹת בָּתֵּינוּ אֲרָזִים °רחיטנו
[°רָהִיטֵנוּ ק] בְּרוֹתִים:

anger [אַף] which You bring upon me is *pleasant*, because thereby You bring me back and turn me to better ways."

אַף־עַרְשֵׂנוּ רַעֲנָנָה — [lit., *even our couch is fresh* (or: *flourishing, full of vigor*).]

— As in *Psalms* 92:15: דְּשֵׁנִים וְרַעֲנַנִּים, *vigorous and fresh* (Metzudas Tzion).

Rashi explains that "couch" is a reference to the Tabernacle and the Temple. The existence of the Temple in Israel led to flourishing, vigorous growth of the Jewish population. Thus the verse says: *Because You were pleasant in forgiving us and allowing Your Presence to dwell among us despite our sins, our sons and daughters multiplied.*

Kitzur Alshich renders "couch" as a metaphor for intimate closeness. Thus the Temple is an allegorical reference to the intimacy between God and Israel: an association that is always רַעֲנָנָה, *vigorous and fresh.*

Couch refers to the Temple. It glorifies the nobility of a life dedicated to God in tangible images. Its teaching is the "couch" of humanity and it is always fresh and green (*Rav W. Wolf*).

[The word עַרְשֵׂנוּ, *our couch*, metaphorically refers to our prolificacy.] "Dear God, You are beautiful and pleasant only when Israel's prolificacy is רַעֲנָנָה, *vigorous and flourishing*, for only in this way is Your Name sanctified in the world ..."

As the *Targum* renders: "The Assembly of Israel replies to the Sovereign of the Universe, and says: How comely is Your Holy Presence at the time that You dwell in our midst, and receive our petitions with favor; at the time that You cause love to dwell in the home ('couch') and many children to be upon the earth, we increase and multiply, as the tree which stands by the spring of water, whose branches are fair, and whose fruit is plentiful!"[1]

---

1. The *Talmud* [*Taanis* 5b] tells us that Rav Nachman and Rav Yitzchak were taking leave of each other. The former asked the latter to bless him.

Rav Yitzchak replied: Let me tell you a parable. To what can your request be compared? To that of a man who was walking in a desert, suffering fatigue, hunger, and thirst, and then found a tree whose shade was pleasant and whose fruit was sweet with a brook flowing by it. He rested beneath its shade, ate from its fruit, and drank from its water. When he was about to leave, he said: "O tree, O tree! What blessing shall I bestow upon you? Shall I wish you that your shade be pleasant? Your shade *is* pleasant.

"Shall I wish you that your fruit be sweet? Your fruit *is* sweet.

"Shall I wish you that a brook flow by you? A brook *does* flow by you! Therefore I say, May it be the will of God that all shoots taken from you be like you."

"Similarly with you [concluded Rav Yitzchak to Rav Nachman], what can I wish you? Shall I wish you learning? You *have* learning. Wealth? You *have* wealth. Children? You *have* children! Therefore I say, May it be God's will that your descendants be like you!"

Shir Chadash finds this blessing alluded to in the phrase עַרְשֵׂנוּ רַעֲנָנָה, *may our couch be fresh.* "Couch" is an allusion to Jacob whose progeny were all perfect, unlike Abraham and Isaac who produced an Ishmael and an Esau. Jacob's descendants are blessed with *freshness*: may they ever be as "fresh" as a tree, with the ability to produce similar offspring.

*that You pardoned my sin, enabling our Temple
to make me ever fresh. [17] The beams of our houses
are cedar, our panels are cypress.*

17. קֹרוֹת בָּתֵּינוּ אֲרָזִים רַהִיטֵנוּ בְּרוֹתִים
— [lit., *the beams of our houses are
cedar, our panels are cypress.*]

[All the commentators agree that
this verse, following the reference to
the Sanctuary in the previous verse,
continues to extol the grandeur of
the dwelling place of God.][1]

This verse continues the thought of
the previous one. Verse 16 concluded
by saying that the sanctification of
God's Name demands the flourishing
growth of Israel. This verse continues
that God's beauty is "dependent"
upon His maintaining His beautiful
abode, the Temple. Therefore we ask
that He restore His Temple and protect it zealously (*Tz'ror HaMor*).

The *Targum* renders: "Solomon,
the prophet, speaks: How beautiful is
the Temple of HASHEM, built by my
hands, of cedarwood; but more beautiful still shall be the Temple which

shall in the time to come be built in
the days of King Messiah, the beams
of which shall be of the cedars of the
Garden of Eden, and the pillars of
firs, juniper, and cypress wood."

Sforno interprets קֹרוֹת, *beams*,
as a reference to the Torah sages of
each generation who are tall as cedar; and רַהִיטֵנוּ [lit., *our runners*] as
their students.

[The word רָהִיט is found nowhere
else in Scripture and the translation
is uncertain. *Rashi* comments that
he is uncertain whether it refers to
boards ("panels") or bolts; but the
Talmud, *Yoma* 38a (cited in the
footnote), relates it to the root meaning *runner*, and translates *door*
which "runs" to and fro, opening
and shutting; *Ibn Ezra* relates it to
רְהָטִים in *Genesis* 30:38 rendering
gutters; *Metzudas Tzion* renders:
runways, passageways.]

---

1. The *Talmud* interprets רְהִיטִים as "doors" and homiletically refers to the following miraculous incident:

"Nicanor had gone to fetch the doors [for the great eastern gate of the Temple Court] from
Alexandria of Egypt. Upon his return, a storm arose in the sea threatening to drown him.
Thereupon, they took one of his doors and cast it into the sea, and yet the sea would not stop
its rage. When, therefore, they prepared to cast the other into the sea, he rose and clung to it,
saying, 'Cast me in with it!' and the sea immediately stopped raging. He was deeply grieved,
however, about the other door. As he arrived at the harbor of Acco, it broke through [the surface of the sea] and came up from beneath the sides of the boat."

Referring to this incident, the Sages applied this verse: רַהִיטֵנוּ בְּרוֹתִים, *our doors are cypress*.
Do not read בְּרוֹתִים, *cypress*, but בְּרִית יָם, i.e., *covenant of the sea* [because it was as if it were
a covenant between the door and the sea (to preserve it) — *Rashi*].

"Therefore," continues the Talmud, "all the gates in the Sanctuary were later changed for
golden ones with the exception of the Nicanor Gates, because of the miracles wrought with
them" (*Yoma* 38a).

פֶּרֶק ב א אֲנִי חֲבַצֶּלֶת הַשָּׁרוֹן שׁוֹשַׁנַּת הָעֲמָקִים:
א-ב ב כְּשׁוֹשַׁנָּה בֵּין הַחוֹחִים כֵּן רַעְיָתִי בֵּין

II

1. אֲנִי חֲבַצֶּלֶת הַשָּׁרוֹן שׁוֹשַׁנַּת הָעֲמָקִים —
[lit., *I am a rose of the Sharon, a
rose of the valleys.*]

[There is a difference of opinion
among the commentators as to the
exact definitions of חֲבַצֶּלֶת, *chavatzeles*, and שׁוֹשַׁנָּה, *shoshanah*. *Rashi*
says they are synonymous (which
is in agreement with the *Midrash*:
"Is not *chavatzeles* the same as
shoshanah? While it is still small it
is called *chavatzeles* but when it is
fully grown it is called *shoshanah*").
Ibn Ezra, Ibn Janach, and *Radak*
understand *chavatzeles* as "rose";
Targum as "narcissus."]

Although the familiar translation of
שׁוֹשַׁנַּת הָעֲמָקִים is *lily of the valley*, we
have followed *Rashi* who holds that
chavatzeles and *shoshanah* are identical, as the above citations indicate.

[Although not explicitly stated
in *Rashi*, it would seem from his
interpretation of 1:16 being a modest exclamation יָפֶה דוֹדִי אַף נָעִים, *The
beauty is not ours but Yours,* that
in the dialogue between the speakers
this verse, too, is to be understood as
Israel's understated matter-of-fact
description of itself as a simple *rose
of the Sharon,* and *rose of the valleys,* the valley species of the flower
retaining its moistness because it is
not exposed to the scorching sun,
being of a more beautiful variety
than the mountain species.]

שָׁרוֹן, *Sharon,* is explained by the
commentators as a common noun
referring to a moist fertile area
(*Alshich; Metzudas David*), and
coastal plains (*Malbim*). *Rashi* on
Isaiah 33:9 identifies it as a pastoral
area. Many identify it with the plain
on the Mediterranean coast, extend-
ing from Jaffa to Caesarea.[1]

The *Midrash* and *Zohar* allegorize
Sharon as related to שִׁיר, *song,* and
comment: "Tomorrow when God will
deliver me from the shadow of ruling
powers I will blossom like a rose and
sing a new song before Him."]

Alshich, too, interprets the verse as
a modest statement: "We are only like
the rose of the moist plains and the
rose of the valley which need much
water and wither when the source of
water is removed, unlike the hardier
mountaintop roses which withstand
aridity better. We cried, נַעֲשֶׂה וְנִשְׁמָע,
'*we will do and obey!*' [*Exodus* 24:7]
at Sinai, but as soon as our source
of nourishment, Moses, went up to
heaven and was removed from us, our
resolve withered and we succumbed
to the allures of a Golden Calf."

Shir Chadash notes that it is un-
seemly for Israel to indulge in this sort
of self-praise. He interprets the verse
as a combination of fear and hope. As
noted above, the *Midrash* says that
chavatzeles and *shoshanah* are one
and the same: the former when it is

---

1. It is interesting to note that the *Talmud* mentions Sharon (*Yerushalmi, Yoma* 5:2) as being
included in the prayer of the High Priest on Yom Kippur. The bricks in that area were not
substantial enough to withstand the effects of the abundant rains and, as *Korban HaEidah* explains, the inhabitants had to renovate their homes twice every seven years for fear of sudden

II **I** *am but a rose of Sharon, even an ever-fresh rose*
1-2 *of the valleys.*

Hashem: ²*Like the rose maintaining its beauty among the*
thorns, so is My faithful beloved among the nations.

small and the latter when it is mature. Sharon is a sandy area [see footnote 1] and thus did not provide firm support for the roots of its vegetation, in contrast to the lush valley area. Thus, Israel states: "In my youth I am like a *young flower* in *Sharon,* always in danger of being uprooted just as immature youth is a time when fear of God is tenuous and endangered by outside influence. I pray that I may mature into a *rose of the valley,* firm, strong and secure."

"I am as vulnerable [without Eretz Yisrael]" or: in exile, complains the Congregation of Israel, "as a rose in the open plains, and as prone to be trampled upon as a rose in the valley" (*Ibn Ezra*).

[Other commentators — in contradistinction to the thematic interpretation suggested above of this verse as a humble declaration — perceive this verse as Israel's attempt to arouse God's love by this self-complimentary comparison:]

"I am like the hardy rose that thrives in fertile areas, and like the lily that maintains its moisture in the valleys and doesn't change; metaphorically, I always stand fresh and vigorous by virtue of my good deeds, and I walk a straight, unchanging course, clinging to the commandments" (*Metzudas David*).

2. כְּשׁוֹשַׁנָּה בֵּין הַחוֹחִים כֵּן רַעְיָתִי בֵּין הַבָּנוֹת — [lit., *As a rose among*

thorns, so is My beloved among the daughters.] Just as the rose retains its beauty and color although pricked by surrounding thorns, so does My beloved people maintain her faith despite the torments of her neighbors who try to sway her after their strange gods (*Rashi*).

[According to the interpretation of the previous verse this is God's response to Israel's modest declaration. "No, My beloved people," responds God, "you are not 'but a *simple* rose'! You possess the finest qualities manifested in roses: the ability to fend off the taunts and pricks of your neighboring 'thorns,' and not allow yourself to be swayed. You are indeed a beautiful, fragrant flower, but you had to overcome many obstacles to maintain your beauty."]

The following is God's response according to the various interpretations of the previous verse:

Alshich: True, your resolve withered and you succumbed to a Golden Calf, but you are as a rose that, although bruised by surrounding thorns, does not lose its beauty. Similarly, you were "bruised" by the influence of the Egyptian "daughters" in whose midst I set you, and by the עֵרֶב רַב, *mixed multitude,* who accompanied you in the desert. Were it not for their presence your beauty would be completely unblemished.

collapse. His prayer [also preserved in the Yom Kippur *Mussaf* service]: "May it be Your will, our God and God of our fathers, that the houses of the inhabitants of Sharon do not become their graves."

פרק ב

ג הַבָּנוֹת: כְּתַפּוּחַ בַּעֲצֵי הַיַּעַר כֵּן דּוֹדִי בֵּין

ג־ד הַבָּנִים בְּצִלּוֹ חִמַּדְתִּי וְיָשַׁבְתִּי וּפִרְיוֹ

ד מָתוֹק לְחִכִּי: הֱבִיאַנִי אֶל־בֵּית הַיַּיִן וְדִגְלוֹ

Ibn Ezra: True, you are vulnerable to trampling, but I will protect you from your fellows like a gardener protecting his prized rose from thorns.

Metzudas David: True, you are a hardy, beautiful rose. But just as a rose protects herself from intrusion by means of her prickly thorns in order to maintain its beauty, so should you comport yourself and fend off all foreign influence.

Rav Berachiah said: The Holy One, blessed is He, said to Moses: "Go and say to Israel: 'My children, when you were in Egypt you were like *a rose among thorns.* Now that you are entering the land of Canaan be also like a rose among thorns; take care not to follow in their ways' "; and so it says (*Leviticus* 18:3): *Do not perform the practice of the land of Egypt in which you dwelled; and do not perform the practice of the land of Canaan to which I bring you (Midrash).*

3. כְּתַפּוּחַ בַּעֲצֵי הַיַּעַר כֵּן דּוֹדִי בֵּין הַבָּנִים — [lit., *Like an apple (tree) among the trees of the forest, so is my Beloved among the sons.*]

Israel responds: Just as an apple tree among fruitless trees is beloved by virtue of its excellent fruit and fragrance, so is HASHEM superior to all the gods whom the heathen nations foolishly serve, and which are likened to insubstantial trees: simply *wood of the forest (Rashi; Yalkut Shimoni).*

[The translation of בָּנִים, *sons,* as an allegorical reference to alien gods

and heathen nations (cf. comm. to 1:7 s.v. חֲבֵרֶיךָ) agrees with most commentators. *Harav Gifter,* in his marginal notations to *Shir Chadash,* suggests that בָּנִים refers to the Jews who are בָּנִים ... לַה׳ אֱלֹקֵיכֶם, *children to HASHEM, your God* (*Deut.* 14:1). Therefore render: *As an apple tree adored by fruitless trees, so is God adored by His children, Israel.*]

בְּצִלּוֹ חִמַּדְתִּי וְיָשַׁבְתִּי וּפִרְיוֹ מָתוֹק לְחִכִּי — [lit., *in His (or its) shade I delighted and sat and His (or its) fruit is sweet to my palate.*] And therefore I delighted to sit in His shade (*Rashi*).

Rashi continues and quotes the *Midrash:* The apple tree [or, as translated by *Targum: esrog tree* (see *Tosafos, Shabbos* 88a)] is shunned by all people when the sun beats down because it provides no shadow. So did all the nations refuse to sit in the "shadow" of HASHEM on the day of the giving of the Torah. But I — the Congregation of Israel — longed for Him and sat; it was only I who longed, not the nations.

... It is *I* who perceived the eternal benefit of sitting in His shadow, unlike the others who saw only that there was no immediate glamor or benefit in accepting His Torah. For although the shade — i.e., reward — of Torah is not apparent, I acted from conviction and trust in His Redemption, unlike the heathen nations who were concerned only with ephemeral, existentialist recompense (*Yefei Kol*).

II Israel: ³*Like the fruitful, fragrant apple among the*
3-4 *barren trees of the forest, so is my Beloved among the*
gods. In His shade I delighted and [there] I sat, and
the fruit of His Torah was sweet to my palate. ⁴*He*
brought me to the chamber of Torah delights and

Even in turbulent exile when His "shade" is not so manifest compared to the tranquil shade of other nations, I delight in His shade (*Chavatzeles HaSharon*).

According to *Ibn Ezra's* thematic interpretation of the dialogue (see verses 1 and 2), Israel responds: "If You protect me, I will always repose in Your shade."

וּפְרִיוֹ מָתוֹק לְחִכִּי — [lit., *and His fruit is sweet to my palate.*] This refers to the twelve months which Israel spent before Mount Sinai regaling themselves with the words of the Torah, because *its fruit was sweet to my taste.* To *my* taste it was sweet, but to the taste of the other nations it was bitter like wormwood (*Midrash*).

Solomon also referred to Torah as fruit as it is written [*Proverbs 8:19*]: *My fruit is better than gold* (*Lekach Tov*).

4. הֱבִיאַנִי אֶל־בֵּית הַיַּיִן — [lit., *He has brought me to the house of wine.*] I.e., the אֹהֶל מוֹעֵד, *Tent of the Meeting*, in the Tabernacle where the details and explanations of the Torah were expounded (*Rashi*).

According to the *Midrash*, בֵּית הַיַּיִן, *the house of wine*, refers to Sinai [because the Torah was stored there in preparation for Revelation from the time of Creation just as wine is stored in a cellar (*Torah Temimah*)].

The *Vilna Gaon* comments that the numerical value of יַיִן is 70, alluding to ע' פָּנִים לַתּוֹרָה, *the seventy*

facets of Torah exegesis — an apt simile for the source of Torah revelation: Sinai, for it was the *house of* the seventy facets.

Ibn Ezra, however, allegorizes בֵּית הַיַּיִן as the Temple: מָקוֹם נִסּוּךְ הַיַּיִן, *the place where the libation of wine was offered.*

וְדִגְלוֹ עָלַי אַהֲבָה — [lit., *and His banner upon me is love.*] That He gathered the tribes about Him, i.e., His Tabernacle, in the desert, was an act of love (*Rashi*).

[In the most simple of allegorical interpretations this refers to the דְּגָלִים, *the standards*, under which the Tribes encamped (*Numbers* 2:2). It is this systematic encampment under the banner of God, so to speak, that is being recalled here. According to others, the "banner" refers to the Torah.]

Several homiletical interpretations of דִּגְלוֹ, *banner*, are offered in the *Midrash*:

— The numerical value of וְדִגְלוֹ is 49, equal to the forty-nine "gates" in which the Torah can be expounded;

[Or alluding to the Talmudic statement that there are fifty Gates of Understanding, of which Moses achieved the human ultimate of forty-nine (*Torah Temimah*).]

[Homiletically וְדִגְלוֹ = וְדִלְגוֹ:]

— If an ignorant, but sincere, man errs in reading the Torah, God says: "His mistake (*dilugo*) is beloved by Me."

— Even if a child skips the Name

of God many times, no harm is done. What is more, God declares: "His omission (dilugo) is beloved to Me."

— If a child mispronounces words, God says: "His babbling (liglugo) is beloved to Me."[1]

— "Even the 'deceits' of Jacob are blessed to Me."

[This refers to the episode in which Rebecca used goatskins (Genesis 27:16) to help Jacob deceive his father and obtain the Patriarchal blessings which Isaac had intended to bestow upon Esau. Even "his deceits (dilugo) are beloved by God." God completely forgave the deceit and caused His Name to symbolically rest upon the outcome by requiring goat hair in the construction of the Tabernacle. This was the eternal testimony that the act of Rebecca and Jacob was commanded by God (Exodus 26:7).]

Metzudas David interprets the verse as a wish, and poetically renders הֱבִיאַנִי in the future tense: O bring me into the banquet house — i.e., cause Your Shechinah to dwell among us in public assembly, and raise aloft Your banner demonstrating Your profound love for us to all the nations.

In the previous verse Israel expresses its desire to dwell under God's shade. The word חָמַדְתִּי, I delighted [lit., covet, desire], implies an emotional or physical desire. Because Israel had not yet become privy to the סוֹדוֹת הַתּוֹרָה, innermost secrets of the Torah, there was, as yet, no intellectual craving. However, this verse continues, when God led Israel into the house of wine (as explained in 1:2, the wine of Torah) and revealed the secrets of the Torah, then וְדִגְלוֹ, i.e., my awareness that He is דָּגוּל מֵרְבָבָה, pre-eminent above ten thousand [5:10], became the root of my love, because now I perceived firsthand the superiority of Torah over all other knowledge, and this enhanced my love for God (Netziv).

Harav David Feinstein notes in this context that the numerical value of יַיִן, wine [70], is equivalent to that of סוֹד, secret.

5. Poignantly wishing to demonstrate the profundity of her love, Israel depicts herself as a swooning, lovesick maiden in need of medicinal stimulants to help her revive herself (Ralbag), allegorically referring to exiled Israel's lovesickness for God, while it suffers affliction and awaits His return — lovingly serving Him while anxious for Redemption (Lekach Tov).

— סַמְּכוּנִי בָּאֲשִׁישׁוֹת רַפְּדוּנִי בַּתַּפּוּחִים [lit., Sustain me with dainties, spread out apples around me.]

---

1. Rav Levi Yitzchak of Berditchev once utilized this Midrashic interpretation when a misnagged taunted him that chassidim do not pray with the proper regard for correct pronunciation, and that they swallow their words.

Rav Levi Yitzchak responded that a toddler often makes sounds which are incoherent to anyone but his father who understands every gesture. Similarly we are considered children to God Who understands our every gesture, even if sometimes we do not express ourselves coherently. It is to this that the Sages alluded when they said that even when Jews skip (dilugo) or mispronounce a letter or word, they are beloved to Him, for they are His children.

clustered my encampments about Him in love.
⁵I say to Him, "Sustain me in exile with dainty
cakes, spread fragrant apples about me to com-
fort my dispersion, for, bereft of Your Presence,
I am sick with love." ⁶With memories of His

The exact meaning of אֲשִׁישׁוֹת is doubtful. *Rashi*, referring to *Hoshea* 3:1, renders "raisin cakes" or cakes made from fine pure flour.

Ibn Ezra translates אֲשִׁישׁוֹת as "glass flagons of wine"; others derive it from אֲשִׁישִׁים, *lentil cakes*, mentioned in the *Mishnah*, *Nedarim* 6:10.

The *Midrash* relates אֲשִׁישׁוֹת to אֵשׁ, *fire*: sustain me with two fires — The Written Torah and the Oral Torah [the Torah being called fire, as it says, "Is not My word like fire?" (*Jeremiah* 23:29)].

Tractate *Soferim* 16:4 allegorizes אֲשִׁישׁוֹת as the strong [הַמְאֻשָּׁשׁוֹת] well-founded *Halachos* and תַּפּוּחִים as *Aggados* which are "fragrant" like apples.

Rashi and most commentators render רַפְּדוּנִי, *spread out*, similar to יִרְפַּד, *he spreads himself*, in *Job* 41:22. *Ibn Ezra* relates it to the Arabic meaning "strengthen me."

[*Apples* were considered medicinal. The *Tosefta* (*Bava Metzia* 7:2) mentions that grapes and apples were brought to the sick.]

The *Midrash* makes a fascinating observation:

Formerly everyone had enough for his necessities and people were eager to study *Mishnah*, *Halachah*, or *Talmud*; but now that they haven't enough for their necessities, and moreover, are worn out by oppression, they want to hear only words of *Aggadah*, words of blessing and comfort. [Hence: "*Sustain me with dainties* — with the light and comforting spiritual food of *Aggadah, because I am love sick* — feeble in knowledge and worn out through suffering."]

כִּי־חוֹלַת אַהֲבָה אָנִי — [lit., *for I am sick with love.*] I.e., I am sick for want of His love,[1] I thirst for Him here in exile (*Rashi*);

My soul swoons for the return of the *Shechinah* (*Metzudas David*).

The *Midrash* comments:

The Community of Israel said before the Holy One, blessed is He: "Sovereign of the Universe: All the חֳלָאִים, *tribulations*, that You bring upon me are designed to make me more beloved to You [translating: *For my sickness is to bring about* אַהֲבָה, *love*].

---

1. The following is excerpted from *Rambam, Hilchos Teshuvah* 10:3:

What is the proper love for God? It is to love *Hashem* and be constantly enraptured by it like a lovesick individual, whose mind is at no time free from his passion for a particular woman, the thought of her filling his heart at all times, when sitting down or rising up, when eating or drinking.

Even more intense should love of *Hashem* be in the hearts of those who love Him, and this love should constantly absorb Him as commanded us in the phrase בְּכָל־לְבָבְךָ וּבְכָל־נַפְשְׁךָ, *with all your heart and with all your soul* [*Deuteronomy* 6:5]. Solomon expressed this allegorically in the verse כִּי־חוֹלַת אַהֲבָה אָנִי, *for I am sick with love.* The entire Song of Songs is indeed an allegorical description of this love. [See Foreword.]

Another explanation: "Sovereign of the Universe, all the sufferings which the nations inflict upon me are because I love You [and am, therefore, deserving of Your support and protection].

"Although I am sick [i.e., sinful], I am still His beloved."

Rav Saadiah Gaon renders the phrase חוֹלַת אַהֲבָה אָנִי, *For I am of weakening love.* Just as a sick person who feels his strength waning asks for stimulants, so in this verse the Community of Israel — perceiving and recalling the intensity of its love of God, and afraid that now, in its period of exile, her love is חוֹלָה, *sick, waning* — asks for His support and strength to stimulate her love for Him once again to its former vitality.

6. שְׂמֹאלוֹ תַּחַת לְרֹאשִׁי וִימִינוֹ תְּחַבְּקֵנִי — [lit., *His left hand is under my head and His right arm embraces me.*]

[As reflected in the Translation, *Rashi* views this verse as an ecstatic recollection of God's tenderness by Israel, sick for His love in exile. They recall the three-day journey to search out a resting place when they were accompanied by the Ark of HASHEM and enveloped in His Cloud [*Numbers* 10:33]. They also recall the manna He provided them as sustenance. Remembering this in the travail of bitter exile, they become enraptured and lovesick.]

[In connection with His behavior toward Israel, God's "right hand" refers to His attribute of mercy, while

His "left hand" refers to His attribute of justice. Thus, the verse may indicate that even when Israel is deserving of punishment, God supports its head with His left hand to prevent the destruction from being complete. When Israel earns His mercy, however, the embrace of His right hand is total.]

[Note also the contrast between God's compassionate, comforting use of His hand when Israel is deserving, and the *withdrawal of* His *right hand* (*Lamentations* 2:3,4) when they are unworthy. See comm. to ArtScroll *Eichah* ad loc.]

Alshich renders in the present tense: I am lovesick, because even when He afflicts me in exile, He nevertheless keeps His left hand beneath my head so I do not fall; and when I repent, His right hand embraces me in affection and forgiveness.

Metzudas David interprets the verse as a prayer: "O that He would once again manifest His love to me by 'embracing' me with His Presence." [See also 8:3.]

7. הִשְׁבַּעְתִּי אֶתְכֶם בְּנוֹת יְרוּשָׁלַם — [lit., *I have adjured you, O daughters of Jerusalem.*]

Rashi, Sforno, and *Metzudas David* explain this verse as Israel turning to her neighbors and so adjuring them. [For *daughters of Jerusalem* as a reference to the heathen nations, cf. 1:5.]

The *Talmud* (*Kesubos* 111a), *Midrash,* and *Alshich* interpret the verse as God speaking to Israel

loving support in the desert, of His left hand under
my head, of His right hand enveloping me. ⁷ *I adjure*
you, O nations destined to ascend to Jerusalem, for if
you violate your oath, you will become as defenseless
as gazelles or hinds of the field, if you dare provoke

[*daughters of Jerusalem* referring to the Jews as it does so often in *Lamentations*]; and *Tz'ror HaMor*, as God speaking to the heathen nations.

The *Midrash* appears to reconcile part of the apparent contradiction by commenting: There are two adjurations: one addressed to Israel, and one to the other nations. God adjured Israel not to rebel against the yoke of the governments, and He adjured the governments not to make their yoke too heavy on Israel lest they cause the end of exile to come before it was due. (Cf. *Kesubos* 111a cited below.)

Rashi concludes that although he is aware that the Sages derive various different interpretations from this verse [as to the identity of the speakers and the nature of their adjuration], he limits his commentary to the context of the verses as he perceived them, i.e., that Solomon envisioned concerning the Egyptian Exodus, the giving of the Torah, the entry into the Land, the Temple, and prophesied concerning the Babylonian Exile, the Second Temple, and its destruction.

The *Targum* renders this verse as Moses adjuring the Jews in the desert after the return of the Spies:

"Moses was informed by prophecy from HASHEM to send messengers to spy out the land. Returning from their mission, they brought an evil report concerning Eretz Yisrael and were detained for forty years in the desert. Then Moses said: I adjure you, O assembly of Israel, by the Lord of Hosts, and by the strength of the Land of Israel, that you presume not to go up to the land of Canaan until it be the will of Heaven, and until all the generation of the men fit for war be completely extinct from the camp; not as your brethren, the children of Ephraim, who, having left Egypt thirty years before the appointed time had arrived, fell into the hands of the Philistines dwelling in Gath and were killed [see *Ibn Ezra* in footnote below]. Rather, wait out the term of forty years, and then let your children go up and possess the land."

[Cf. comm. of *Divrei Yedidiah* to 3:5.]

בִּצְבָאוֹת אוֹ בְּאַיְלוֹת הַשָּׂדֶה — [lit., *by gazelles or by hinds of the field*.] I.e., [if you keep the adjuration, well and good; but if not,] you will become ownerless and your flesh will become prey like that of the animals of the field (*Rashi; cf. Kesubos* 111a).

The *Midrash* renders בִּצְבָאוֹת, *by the Hosts* — the heaven and earth: the Upper Hosts and the Lower Hosts, who were witnesses to this adjuration of the Jews to fulfill the Torah [cf. *Deuteronomy* 30:19]; אַיְלוֹת הַשָּׂדֶה, *and by hinds of the field* — the martyrs who poured out their blood for the sanctification of the Name, like the blood of the hind.

Ramban [as does the *Targum* cited above] takes צְבָאוֹת literally

ח תְּעוֹרְרוּ אֶת־הָאַהֲבָה עַד שֶׁתֶּחְפָּץ:
קוֹל דּוֹדִי הִנֵּה־זֶה בָּא מְדַלֵּג
ט עַל־הֶהָרִים מְקַפֵּץ עַל־הַגְּבָעוֹת: דּוֹמֶה
דוֹדִי לִצְבִי אוֹ לְעֹפֶר הָאַיָּלִים הִנֵּה־זֶה

as an oath in the Name of the *Lord of Hosts.* [Cf. ה' צְבָאוֹת שְׁמוֹ, *HASHEM of Hosts is His Name (Jeremiah 10:16,31:34 etc.).*]

אִם־תָּעִירוּ וְאִם־תְּעוֹרְרוּ אֶת־הָאַהֲבָה עַד שֶׁתֶּחְפָּץ — [lit., *If you will wake or rouse the love until it pleases.*]

[As reflected in the Translation, *Rashi* interprets תָּעִירוּ, *provoke hatred* (i.e., disturb), and עַד שֶׁתֶּחְפָּץ, *while it* is *still desirable,* i.e., while His love is still ingrained within me and He still desires me (similar construction to 1:12, עַד־שֶׁהַמֶּלֶךְ בִּמְסִבּוֹ, *While the King was still at His table*).

The other major interpretations of the verse are:

"If you, heathen nations, seize the opportunity of my sinful periods —

the times when I have incurred God's displeasure — to provoke me to further sin in the expectation that you will thereby cause God to discard me forever and to bestow His love upon you instead. When I repent and become worthy of God's love, however, nothing you do can estrange Him from me" (*Metzudas David*).

Or: "If you, Israel, will try, by prayer or other means, to arouse Him to manifest His love and end the exile prematurely — until the preordained time when it pleases Him to redeem Israel."[1]

8. *Rashi* explains that with this verse the author begins a recapitulation of God's remembrance of His people in Egypt, events which were

1. The *Midrash* (also the *Talmud, Kesubos* 111a with some variations) notes that this similar adjuration appears four times throughout *Shir HaShirim* (here, 3:5, 5:8, and 8:4): "God adjured Israel that it not rebel against governments; that it not seek to hasten [יְרְחֲקוּ] the end; that it not reveal its mysteries to the other nations; and that it not attempt to go up from גָּלוּת, *the diaspora,* by force."

The *Talmud,* ibid., lists the following: That Israel not go up [en masse as if surrounded] by a wall [individually, however, it is certainly permitted (*Maharsha*)]; that it not rebel against the nations of the world; and He adjured the idolaters that they not oppress Israel too much ...

And additionally: that [the prophets] shall not make known the end [of the exile; the beginning of the Messianic era]; that [the people] shall not יְרְחֲקוּ, *delay,* the end [by their misdeeds] (*Rashi*); or, according to *Maharsha,* shall not regard the end of the exile as being too far off and so lose hope.

Rashi suggests an alternate reading of יְרְחֲקוּ, "force by excessive prayer" (because if the Redemption comes at the predestined time, the transition has already been clothed in the natural cycle and will not be beset by preventive plagues by the Satan. But if the end is "forced," however, although God might accede to the prayer and bring the Redemption earlier, there will be many detractors and it will take place among much tribulation and oppression — *Arvei Nachal; Anaf Yosef*).

Ibn Ezra refers this verse to the Midrashic account of the "children of Ephraim" who [erroneously reckoning the 400 years of Egyptian bondage from the time when God announced the decree to Abraham (*Genesis* 15:13-17) instead of the time when Isaac was born,] took their wives and children and defiantly left Egypt before the End [and were slain]. (See *Midrash; Pirkei d'Rabbi Eliezer* 48; *Sefer HaYashar*.)

God to hate me or disturb His love for me while He still desires it.

⁸ The voice of my Beloved! Behold, it came suddenly to redeem me, as if leaping over mountains, skipping over hills. ⁹ In His swiftness to redeem me, my Beloved is like a gazelle or a young hart. I thought I would be forever alone, but behold! He was standing

alluded to only briefly and generally in the earlier verses.[1]

קוֹל דּוֹדִי הִנֵּה־זֶה בָּא — [*Hark!* (lit., *The sound*) *of my Beloved! Behold, he comes.*] An exclamation of unexpected joy [See comm. of *Rav Hirsch* to *Genesis* 4:10 where he suggests the translation for קוֹל, of *hark!* Cf. also 5:2: *A sound! My Beloved knocks!*]

מְדַלֵּג עַל־הֶהָרִים מְקַפֵּץ עַל־הַגְּבָעוֹת — [lit., *leaping upon the mountains, skipping upon the hills.*]

As reflected in the Translation, *Rashi* interprets this metaphorical image, if one may so express oneself, as if God hurriedly leaped and skipped to redeem the Jews before the predetermined End. This was in contrast to Israel's despair at the prospect of an additional 190 years of bondage to fulfill the prophecy of 400 years of bondage.

According to the account in the *Midrash*, the verse refers to Moses. When he came and said to Israel, "In

this month you will be delivered," they said to him, "Our teacher Moses, how can we be delivered? Did not God say to Abraham (*Genesis* 15:13): '*And they shall serve them,*' and *they shall afflict them* four hundred years, and so far only two hundred and ten have passed?" Moses answered: "Since God desires to deliver you, He disregards your calculations, but *leaps over the mountains*, the *mountains* and *hills* mentioned here referring to the calculations and periods. He *leaps over* these calculations and periods, and in this month you will be delivered."

Ibn Aknin quotes a *Midrash* that *mountains* refers to their זְדוֹנוֹת, *intentional transgressions*, which God *skipped over* [i.e., overlooked; forgave] and *hills*, to the less severe שְׁגִיאוֹת, *unintentional transgressions*.

9. דּוֹמֶה דוֹדִי לִצְבִי אוֹ לְעֹפֶר הָאַיָּלִים — [lit., *My Beloved is like a gazelle or a young hart*] — rushing to me in

1. [To properly understand the implication of these verses, it must be noted that at the בְּרִית בֵּין הַבְּתָרִים, *the Covenant between the Pieces* [*Genesis* 15:13], it was foretold to Abraham that his descendants would be enslaved in a strange land for four hundred years. According to the Sages, and as detailed by *Rashi* on *Genesis* 15:13, this calculation began from the birth of Isaac, with the result that the actual exile in Egypt was only 210 years, the numerical equivalent of רְדוּ, *go down* [to Egypt] (*Genesis* 42:2).

The figure of 210 is in accordance with the Rabbinic chronology that Yocheved, Moses' mother, was born as Jacob and his family entered Egypt, while she was 130 years old at Moses' birth. He came to deliver Israel from Egypt when he was 80 years old making a total of 210 years. No one knew until the fact of the Exodus that God would reduce the Egyptian years by beginning the reckoning of the 400 years from the birth of Isaac. It was as though He *leaped and skipped* — the similes employed in this verse.]

עוֹמֵד אַחַר כָּתְלֵנוּ מַשְׁגִּיחַ מִן־הַחֲלֹנוֹת
י-יא , מֵצִיץ מִן־הַחֲרַכִּים: עָנָה דוֹדִי וְאָמַר לִי
יא קוּמִי לָךְ רַעְיָתִי יָפָתִי וּלְכִי־לָךְ: כִּי־הִנֵּה

His fleetness and nimbleness (*Rashi*).

הִנֵּה־זֶה עוֹמֵד אַחַר כָּתְלֵנוּ מַשְׁגִּיחַ מִן־
הַחֲלֹנוֹת מֵצִיץ מִן־הַחֲרַכִּים — [lit., *behold,
He stands behind our wall looking
through the windows, peering
through the lattices.*][1] Israel was
like a woman resigned to being an
עֲגוּנָה, bereft of her husband while
still legally bound to him, for a still
undetermined period of time. Then,
suddenly, behold! He came to tell me
that He is peering through the "windows of the heavens" taking notice of
my plight, as is written [*Exodus* 3:7]: *I
have indeed seen the affliction of My
people who are in Egypt*, i.e., reassuring Israel that whatever its travail, He
never failed to keep the closest watch
over its fortunes (*Rashi*).

This verse indicates — in its broader
sense — that God, *hiding behind our
wall*, is in reality not far from us, but
near to our call. He remains "hidden"
so that we should not perceive His
Presence unless we actively seek Him
out, as it is written [*Deuteronomy*
4:29]: *If from there you seek HASHEM
your God, you shall find Him*. He
looks [i.e., *supervises*] *through the
windows*, however, to insure that the
afflictions do not consume us; and
simultaneously He *gazes from the
lattices of heaven* [*Psalms* 14:2]: *to see
if there is anyone who understands,
one who seeks God* (*Sforno*).

Even when we sinned so grievous-
ly that we erected a "wall" between
Him and ourselves, nevertheless, *He
stands behind our wall* compassion-
ately watching over us and peering
through the "windows" — the cracks
in the wall of sin — made by the virtue of our righteous (*Tz'ror HaMor*).

Alshich perceives the three
phrases, *standing behind the wall,
looking through the windows, and
peering through the lattices*, as the
progressive manifestations of God's
"involvement and concern" in redeeming us from Egypt. First, if it
may be so said, He kept "hidden,"
standing behind the wall, but listening attentively to our supplication;
later He actively *looked through the
heavenly windows*, until finally, He
intently *peered through the lattices*
implying even a greater manifestation of His interest.

[The *Midrash* also explains *our
wall* as referring to the כּוֹתֶל הַמַּעֲרָבִי,
the *Western Wall* of the Temple:]

Behold, He stands behind our wall
— behind the Western Wall of the
Temple. Why so? Because God has
sworn that it will never be destroyed.

[*Torah Temimah* notes that in the
parallel *Midrash* quoted in *Yalkut*,
the version reads: "Because the
Shechinah has never departed from
the Western Wall."]

1. [The metaphor *windows of heaven* occurs often. Biblically as אֲרֻבּוֹת הַשָּׁמַיִם (e.g., *Genesis*
7:11; *II Kings* 7:2; *Malachi* 3:10), and post-Biblically as חַלּוֹנֵי רָקִיעַ. (The concept also appears
to be synonymous with שְׁעָרִים, *Gates*.) *Yerushalmi, Rosh Hashanah* 2:4 notes that God
created 365 windows in heaven. *Midrash Gedulas Moshe* relates that when Moses ascended to

behind our wall, observing through the windows, peering through the lattices.
    ¹⁰When He redeemed me from Egypt, my Beloved called out and said to me, "Arise, My love, My fair one, and go forth. ¹¹For the winter of bondage

Alternatively, the *Midrash* renders: *He stands behind our wall* — the walls of synagogues and study-houses; *looking through the windows* — i.e., from between the shoulders of the priests [when they stand together to chant the priestly blessing]; *peering through the lattices* — from between the priests' outspread fingers. [Next verse:] *My Beloved called out and said to me:* What did He say? יְבָרֶכְךָ ה' וְיִשְׁמְרֶךָ, *May HASHEM bless you and safeguard you* [Numbers 6:24].

[On even a deeper, more general level, many commentators translate מַשְׁגִּיחַ as *regard, observe, supervise* — specifically referring to the fundamental doctrine of הַשְׁגָּחָה, *Divine Providence.* They perceive in this verse God's government of His Creation, and His accessibility to His creatures.

Thus, He stands ready to jump to our aid — swiftly — *like a gazelle* or *a young hart* although He maintains His aloofness *standing behind our wall.* He supervises the general welfare (הַשְׁגָּחָה כְּלָלִית) by *looking through the windows* of heaven, and also extends His supervision and Providence to individuals (הַשְׁגָּחָה פְּרָטִית) by symbolically *peering* (more closely) *through the*

lattices (Ibn Aknin; Ramban; Rav Saadiah Gaon; Netziv).]

10. עָנָה דוֹדִי וְאָמַר לִי — [lit., *My Beloved lifted His voice and said to me.*] He *lifted His voice* through Moses; *and said to me* through Aaron (*Rashi*).

[The Community of Israel is reminiscing how God, rushing to deliver her from Egyptian bondage, called upon her to bestir her to carry out His precepts to become worthy of deliverance. The time, He notes in the following verses, was indeed propitious for Redemption.

The word עָנָה is translated within this context according to *Rashi, Metzudas Tzion,* and *R' Hirsch* in its root meaning of "lifting up one's voice" as in *Deuteronomy* 27:14.]

The more common translation, *responded,* misses the point as the Beloved is making a statement uttering a call, not responding to a previous inquiry.

Nevertheless, in the allegorical context, the word עָנָה can perhaps be rendered *answered,* thus: *Responding* (to my prayers) my *Beloved said to me.*]

קוּמִי לָךְ רַעְיָתִי יָפָתִי וּלְכִי־לָךְ — [lit., *rise up for you My love, My fair one, and go for you.*] — i.e., bestir yourself, and *I will bring you up out*

the heavens he was shown — in the first heaven — many windows: the window of prayer and the window of supplication; of weeping and of joy; plenitude and starvation; wealth and poverty; war and peace; conception and birth; showers and soft rains; sin and repentance; life and death; sickness and health, etc.]

יב הַסְּתָו עָבָר הַגֶּשֶׁם חָלַף הָלַךְ לוֹ: הַנִּצָּנִים
יב-יג נִרְאוּ בָאָרֶץ עֵת הַזָּמִיר הִגִּיעַ וְקוֹל הַתּוֹר
יג נִשְׁמַע בְּאַרְצֵנוּ: הַתְּאֵנָה חָנְטָה פַגֶּיהָ

of the affliction of Egypt [Exodus 3:17] (Rashi).

"Arise!" He called to me through His prophets, "and improve your ways, away from exile" (Tz'ror HaMor).

The seemingly superfluous and redundant use of לָךְ, for you, is noted. Metzudas David suggests that it implies for your benefit: Arise, My love, for your benefit; and go for your own good.

[Compare Rashi's commentary to the similar construction in God's call to Abraham (Genesis 12:1): לֶךְ־לְךָ, "Go for your own benefit and your own advantage."]

The appellative רַעְיָתִי, My love, refers to the Community of Israel, as a whole; יָפָתִי, My fair one, refers specifically to the righteous (Divrei Yedidiah).

11-13. [The following verses paint a beautiful poetic picture describing the propitiousness of the season of Redemption. Metaphorically, the verses conjure up an image of the worst being over. Delivery is at hand.]

11. כִּי־הִנֵּה הַסְּתָו עָבָר — [lit., For, lo, the winter is past.] And travel is no longer difficult (Rashi).

Metaphorically, winter refers to the 400 years of bondage reckoned from the birth of Isaac which had now ended (Midrash; Rashi). [Cf. footnote to v. 8.]

The call — heralding the end of exile and bondage — was delivered through Moses to the Children

of Israel. It is the same call that was resounded again and again throughout Israel's history, and is the call that will precede our final Redemption as promised by the prophets. "Arise! The winter is over!" (Ibn Aknin).

הַגֶּשֶׁם חָלַף הָלַךְ לוֹ — [lit., the rain is over and gone.] As rain is the harshest part of winter, so the harshest part of the 210 years of Egyptian bondage was the 86 years from the birth of Miriam; they, too, are now over and gone (Midrash).

In a parenthetical phrase Rashi adds that she was called מִרְיָם [lit., bitterness] because from her birth the Egyptians increased the bitterness of the bondage upon the Jews [as it says (Exodus 1:14): וַיְמָרְרוּ אֶת חַיֵּיהֶם, they embittered their lives (Midrash)].

"The winter of history is past, the rains of the Galus [Exile] have fulfilled their purpose. They have penetrated deep into the soil, and have prepared it for the reception of spiritual seed" (Rav W. Wolf).

12. הַנִּצָּנִים נִרְאוּ בָאָרֶץ — [lit., The blossoms have appeared in the land.] Rashi, following Pesikta Rabbasi, interprets blossoms as a reference to Moses and Aaron who "blossomed" for all your needs.

The comparison of Moses and the prophets to blossoms is appropriate. Just as blossoms herald the imminent blooming flower, so do the prophets herald the oncoming Redemption (Ibn Aknin).

II

12-13 *has passed, the deluge of suffering is over and gone. ¹²The righteous blossoms are seen in the land, the time of your song has arrived, and the voice of your guide is heard in the land. ¹³The fig tree has formed its first small figs, ready for ascent to the Temple;*

[*Midrash Rabbah* interprets these verses to refer to the נְצוֹחוֹת, "conquering, victorious men," who spring up — like blossoms — in every era of Jewish history: Moses and Aaron; the נְשִׂיאִים, *princes* of the tribes (*Numbers* 34:18), in whose hands lay the duty of conquering the land and distributing the tribal inheritances among the families; Mordechai and his associates; Ezra and his associates; Elijah the Prophet, and Messiah.]

Have appeared in the land — to assist and deliver (*Sforno*).

עֵת הַזָּמִיר הִגִּיעַ — [lit., *the time of singing has come.*] I.e., the time when you are destined to sing a song praising God for splitting the sea (*Rashi*).

[The verse, according to this allegorical interpretation, is rendered: "Moses and Aaron have appeared in the land uttering promises of forthcoming redemption. The time is arriving when you will utter songs of praise at the sea. The voice of your guide Moses, or, alternatively, the news of Israel's turn for delivery is heard throughout the land."]

וְקוֹל הַתּוֹר נִשְׁמַע בְּאַרְצֵנוּ — [lit., *and the voice* (i.e., the cooing) *of the turtledove is heard in the land.*] I.e., the sound of the great Guide [תַּיָּר] (*Rashi*); Moses or Joshua, each of whom made proclamations and guided the people during the process of Exodus and conquest.

[Alternately, in consonance with the Midrashic interpretations attaching this verse to other epochs in Jewish history:] Cyrus, who issued the call to return from Babylonian captivity; and King Messiah.

Ibn Ezra renders: The sound that Israel's תּוֹר, *turn*, for Redemption has arrived, is finally heard throughout the land. [Cf. comm. to תּוֹר, 1:10.]

13. הַתְּאֵנָה חָנְטָה פַגֶּיהָ — [lit., *The fig tree has formed its first figs.*] I.e., the time is drawing near for you to enter the land so that you can bring בְּכוּרִים, *First Fruits*, to the Temple (*Rashi*).

The פַּגִּים, unripened *first figs*, are perceived by the Sages to refer to the wicked who are "unripened in their actions" (*Torah Temimah*). [As the *Pesikta* renders: *The fig tree drops her unripe figs, while the vines in blossom give forth their fragrance.*]

That is, the House of Israel drops her unripe figs, i.e., her wicked. This refers to the wicked ones among the Children of Israel who spurned redemption: Their lives were brought to an end by God during the three days of darkness [*Exodus* 10:22]. The rest of the verse [*while the vines in blossom*, etc.] refers to the others who repented and survived by the fragrance of their repentance which was accepted by God. "Thereupon Moses said to the Children of Israel: So many good fragrances are within you, and yet you are still here in Egypt! *Arise*

וְהַגְּפָנִים סְמָדַר נָתְנוּ רֵיחַ קוּמִי °לְכִי
יד [°לָךְ ק׳] רַעְיָתִי יָפָתִי וּלְכִי־לָךְ: יוֹנָתִי
בְּחַגְוֵי הַסֶּלַע בְּסֵתֶר הַמַּדְרֵגָה הַרְאִינִי
אֶת־מַרְאַיִךְ הַשְׁמִיעִנִי אֶת־קוֹלֵךְ כִּי־

My beloved, My fair one, and come away!" (Cf. Rashi; Pesikta d'Rav Kahana and Pesikta Rabbasi.)

וְהַגְּפָנִים סְמָדַר נָתְנוּ רֵיחַ — [lit., and the vines in blossom give forth fragrance.] The time for the נִסְכֵי הַיַּיִן, libation of the wine, the drink offerings, draws near (Rashi).

Rashi offers an alternate interpretation: The deeds of your righteous ones have formed and blossomed and emitted a pleasant fragrance.

Rashi also explains that סְמָדַר refers to the period when the blossom falls away and the individual grapes become visible.

According to Sforno the verse implies that the fruit of Canaan is ripe and the land is ready for Israel's habitation, for they would have entered the land upon receiving the Torah had they not sinned with the Golden Calf and the Spies.

Harav David Feinstein points out in this context that the symbolisms in these verses indicating — in the literal sense — the external signs which signal the propitiousness of Redemption are among those very same signs which will signal the future Redemption. He cites the Talmud, Sanhedrin 98a:

Rav Abba said: There can be no more manifest sign of redemption than that which is written [Ezekiel 36:8]: But you, O mountains of Israel, will give forth your branch, and bear your fruit for My people

of Israel for they are soon to come — and as Rashi, ad loc., comments: "When Eretz Yisrael becomes manifestly so very fertile, the Messiah's advent is clear, and there can be no greater sign than this."

קוּמִי לָךְ רַעְיָתִי יָפָתִי וּלְכִי־לָךְ — [lit., rise up for you, My love, My fair one, and go for you.]

The k'siv [Masoretic written form] of the word לָךְ, spelled לכי in this verse, has a superfluous yud, the numerical equivalent of ten. This suggests that the intent of the verse is: "Arise to receive the Ten Commandments, My love, My fair one" (Rashi).

Understanding לָךְ, for you, to imply for your sake, Rav W. Wolf translates: stand up, for your sake, My companion, My fair one, and go on further for your sake.

[With an identical expression to the opening phrase (verse 10) the call is poetically closed.]

14. יוֹנָתִי בְּחַגְוֵי הַסֶּלַע בְּסֵתֶר הַמַּדְרֵגָה — [lit., O My dove, in the crannies of the rock, in the covert of (i.e., hidden by) the step.]

Rashi explains that this verse refers to the time shortly after leaving Egypt, when Pharaoh was pursuing the Jews and found them encamped at the sea. The Jews were trapped with the sea before them and the Egyptian army behind them. What did they resemble? A dove which was fleeing from a hawk. It flew

*the vines are in blossom, their fragrance declaring
they are ready for libation. Arise, My beloved, My
fair one, and go forth!"*

*¹⁴ At the sea, He said to me, "O My dove, trapped
at the sea as if in the clefts of the rock, the conceal-
ment of the terrace. Show Me your prayerful gaze,
let Me hear your supplicating voice, for your voice*

into the cleft of a rock, and found a serpent lurking there. It could not enter because of the snake nor turn back because of the hawk.[1]

[On the simile of *dove*, see 1:15.]

מַדְרֵנָה is translated *step* by all the commentators. *Rashi* explains that it refers to the "steps" [terraces] dug into hills around fortifications.

God then said to them: הַרְאִינִי אֶת־מַרְאַיִךְ — [lit., *show Me your countenance*.] I.e., "Show Me the quality of your deeds," says God to the trapped Israel: "To whom

do you turn [i.e., direct your מַרְאֶה, *gaze*] when in trouble?" (*Rashi*).

הַשְׁמִיעֵנִי אֶת־קוֹלֵךְ — [lit., *let Me hear your voice*.][2] I.e., the voice of despair which I had already heard in Egypt (*Midrash*).

... *And they cried unto HASHEM* [Exodus 14:10] (*Rashi*).

Ollelos Ephraim perceives in this verse an insight that man's righteousness is evaluated not through his public conduct, but through his conduct in private. Thus the verse says: *In the crannies of the rock*,

1. The *Midrash* illustrates God's punishment of the Jews with a parable.

A king's only daughter refused to talk to him. He ordered, "Let all the people go out to the forum." When they went there, he gave a sign to his servants, and they fell on her suddenly like brigands. She cried, "Father, save me!" He said to her: "Had I not done this, you would not have cried out for my help."

So too, when the Egyptians oppressed the Jews, they began to cry and lift their eyes to the Holy One, blessed is He, as it says [Exodus 2:23]: *"During those many days it happened that the king of Egypt died, and the Children of Israel groaned and they cried out."* Immediately [ibid. v. 24], *And God heard their moaning*: the Holy One, blessed is He, heard their prayer and brought them forth with a strong hand and an outstretched arm.

Then, He hardened the heart of Pharaoh and he pursued them, as it is written [Exodus 14:8]: *And the Lord hardened the heart of Pharaoh, king of Egypt, and he pursued* etc. (It is also written [ibid. v. 10], וּפַרְעֹה הִקְרִיב, *And Pharaoh brought near*. What is meant by *brought near*? That he brought Israel near to repentance.)

The Children of Israel lifted up their eyes, and behold, the Egyptians were marching after them; and they were very afraid; and the Children of Israel cried out unto the Lord (14:10), in the same way as they had cried out in Egypt. When the Holy One, blessed is He, heard, He said: "Had I not done so to you, I would not have heard your voice." Referring to that moment He said, "My dove, in the crannies of the rock ... let Me hear your voice."

2. The *Koretzer* explained the verse as follows:

HASHEM declares to the righteous man: "Let Me be seen through your countenance," for God's image is reflected in the countenance of the righteous; "let Me be heard through your voice," for he who hears the words of a righteous man is inspired to improve himself and become closer to God.

Thus the verse is an appeal to Israel to learn from and follow its righteous men.

פרק ב

טו-טז קוֹלֵךְ עָרֵב וּמַרְאֵיךְ נָאוֶה:

טו אֶחֱזוּ־לָנוּ שׁוּעָלִים שֻׁעָלִים קְטַנִּים

טז מְחַבְּלִים כְּרָמִים וּכְרָמֵינוּ סְמָדַר: דּוֹדִי לִי

in the covert of the step, show me your countenance, let me hear your voice..., i.e., let me observe your conduct when in the privacy of your own home.

נָאוֶה וּמַרְאֵיךְ עָרֵב כִּי־קוֹלֵךְ — [lit., *for your voice is sweet and your countenance comely.*]

The *Midrash* explains the entire verse as referring to the Jews crossing the already split sea:

— *My dove in the crannies of the rock* refers to the Jews who were sheltered in the recesses of the sea;

— *Show Me your countenance,* as it says [*Exodus* 14:13]: *Stand and see the salvation of* HASHEM;

— *Let Me hear your voice* refers to the Song, as it says [ibid. 15:1]: *Then sang Moses;*

— *For your voice is sweet* refers to the singing;

— *And your countenance is comely* [מַרְאֶה, *your gaze,* i.e., the direction you point; נָאוֶה, *is comely* = אַנְוֵהוּ, *will glorify*], because the Jews, recognizing that their salvation was possible only through the help of God, pointed with their finger saying [ibid. v. 2]: זֶה אֵלִי וְאַנְוֵהוּ, *This is my God and I will glorify Him.*

Metzudas David thematically comments that HASHEM is addressing the Congregation of Israel as His *dove,* His loyal beloved. He tells her that now that He is assured of her unfailing love they should meet, if one may so express it, "intimately" in the wilderness in the recesses of Mount Sinai, where He will be attentive to the voice with which she expressed her allegiance by saying, נַעֲשֶׂה וְנִשְׁמָע, *we will do and we will obey!*

Alshich renders the verse as referring to the later exiles: God said, "Even when in *the crannies of the rock,* i.e., among your enemies who wish to annihilate you; *in the covert of the step,* in the bleakness of oppression, nevertheless *you are My dove,* loyal and devoted. *Show Me your countenance,* i.e., manifest the image of God upon you by displaying your righteousness and ingenuity; *let Me hear your voice* in supplicating prayer as you did in Egypt; *for your voice,* i.e., the fount of your prayers, *is pleasing to Me.* And then *your appearance will be as comely* compared to the other nations, as the day you departed from Egypt.

The *Midrash* queries: Why were the Matriarchs so long barren? Because God loved to hear their prayers. Hence it says, *for your voice is sweet and your countenance is comely.*

[The *Talmud* (*Kesubos* 75a) derives from this verse that "a harsh voice in a woman is a physical defect"; while in *Niddah* 31b the Sages comment: Why is a woman's voice sweet and a man's voice not sweet? Man derives his from the place from which he was created (i.e., the earth, which produces no resonant sound when it is pounded — *Rashi*); a woman derives hers from the place from which she was created (i.e., the

*is sweet and your countenance comely." ¹⁵Then
He told the sea, "Seize for us the Egyptian foxes,
even the small foxes who spoiled Israel's vineyards
while our vineyards had just begun to blossom."*

bone; when one beats with it, resonant sounds can be produced — *Rashi*.]

[The *Halachah* prohibiting listening to the singing of women (*Orach Chayim* 75:3; *Even HaEzer* 21:1) is also derived from this verse by the *Talmud, Berachos* 24a and formulated: קוֹל בְּאִשָּׁה עֶרְוָה, *A woman's voice is provocative.*]

15. [As reflected in the Translation, *Rashi* thematically interprets this verse as God's response to their cries when trapped at the sea:]

אֶחֱזוּ־לָנוּ שֻׁעָלִים קְטַנִּים מְחַבְּלִים כְּרָמִים וּכְרָמֵינוּ סְמָדַר — [lit., *the foxes have seized us, the little foxes that ruin the vineyard while (and) our vineyards were in blossom.*]

God responded by ordering the sea: *Seize* (i.e., drown) *these foxes* (i.e., the Egyptians); *the small along with the great,* for both participated in ruining our blossoming vineyards. *Rashi* goes on to cite the *Midrash* that the Jewish women, to avoid Pharaoh's harsh decree, would hide their infant sons in basements. The wicked Egyptians would take their own young children into the Jewish houses and pinch them to make them cry. In response to these cries, the Jewish children would commence crying and their hiding places would be discovered, resulting in their being cast into the river. [Thus, the young "foxes" (i.e., the Egyptians who were "cunning as foxes" — *Midrash*), as well as the adults, were implicated in murdering our children, our blos-

soming vineyards.] (cf. *Sotah* 12a).

[The literal translation follows most of the commentators who render אֶחֱזוּ in the past tense: *grasped, seized,* rather than in the more common imperative form: *grasp, seize.* For a similar form of vocalization used as the past tense, cf. *Judges* 5:28, אֶחֱרוּ, *were tardy.*]

[Also, לָנוּ, *us,* in the literal translation refers to the Jews themselves. In *Rashi's* interpretation, with God as the speaker, *Us* is the *pluralis majestatis* (see comm. to 1:11). Even within the context of *Rashi's* interpretation, however, the verse could be rendered in past tense, with Israel still as the speaker recollecting God's salvation of them at the sea: *He seized the foxes for us ... etc.* See also comm. of *Divrei Yedidiah* below.]

The *vineyards* signify Israel, as it is written: *For the vineyard of the Lord of Hosts is the house of Israel* (*Midrash*).

וּכְרָמֵינוּ סְמָדַר — [lit., *and our vineyards were in blossom.*] *Midrash Lekach Tov* renders: *nevertheless our vineyards blossomed,* i.e., despite all their afflictions, we thrived, as it is written [*Exodus* 1:12]: *But as much as they would afflict it, so it would increase and so it would spread out.*

Ibn Ezra and *Metzudas David* explain the metaphor of "foxes" as referring to the sly, "mixed multitude" who swayed Israel from the proper path into worshiping the Golden Calf while Israel, the tender blossoming vineyard, was still young and susceptible. This resulted in a separation between God and Israel for the duration of their journeys in the desert. Nevertheless [next verse], the relationship was not severed entirely. Israel remained His choicest, and He their God, but He rested His *Shechinah* upon the *roses*: Moses, Aaron, and the seventy Elders, who, in the "fragrance" of their actions, are compared to roses.

Divrei Yedidiah perceives this verse as being God's exhortation to the angels at the time of the future Redemption that they intercede and help save Israel from its oppressors, the *foxes*: the oppressive nations, great and small. In this context, לָנוּ, *us*, refers to God and the angels. Then [next verse], Israel will serve God, and God, their shepherd, will shower His abundance upon them, in tranquil pastures. All this is leading to the Day of Judgment when the shadows with which He protected the wicked will flee. And God will swiftly descend upon the rebuilt Temple. The הָרֵי בָתֶר, *split mountain*, is a reference to הַר הַזֵּיתִים, *Mount of Olives*, upon which God's *feet shall stand that day* [i.e., He will manifest His miracles], *and the Mount of Olives*

will be split. See *Zechariah* 14:4ff.

16. דּוֹדִי לִי וַאֲנִי לוֹ — [lit., *My Beloved is mine, and I am His.*][1] I.e., He makes demands upon me that He makes upon no other nation — for example, to offer the paschal sacrifice, sanctify the firstborn, construct a Tabernacle, and sacrifice burnt-offerings — *and I am His* — and I, in turn, rely on none other but Him (*Rashi*).

The *Midrash* offers many such examples of the reciprocity of love between God and Israel. Several are cited below [but, because of space limitations, the proof-verses quoted by the *Midrash* in support of the various concepts have been omitted]:

He is my God and I am His nation; He is a father to me and I am His son; He is my shepherd, and I am His flock; He sang of me and I sang of Him; when I required something I sought it only from Him and when He required anything He sought it only from me.

הָרֹעֶה בַּשׁוֹשַׁנִּים — [lit., *Who feeds among roses.*] I.e., God, Who grazes His sheep amid scenes of tranquil beauty (*Rashi*).

The *Midrash* infers from this verse that the rod of God falls only upon men whose hearts are pliant like roses [i.e., whose hearts are pliant to God's will and are ready to

---

1. The *Chiddushei HaRim* would meditate on this verse and say: "To the measure that I comport myself before HASHEM, to that degree can I be assured that He will act toward me."

Kedushas Levi interpreted the same concept in commenting upon the verse [*Psalms* 121:5]: ה' צִלְּךָ עַל־יַד יְמִינֶךָ, HASHEM *is your "shadow" at your right hand:* Just as one's shadow moves according to his movements, so God acts in accordance with the behavior of people.

16 *My Beloved is mine, He fills all my needs and I seek from Him and none other. He grazes me in roselike bounty.* **17** *Until my sin blows His friendship away and sears me like the midday sun and His protection departs. My sin caused Him to turn away.*

I say to him, "My Beloved, You became like a gazelle or like a young hart on the distant mountains."

accept their punishment as loving chastisement which inspire them to repentance].

The following illustration is offered: It is like a man who had two cows, one strong and the other weak. Which does he work hard? Is it not the strong one? So God does not try the wicked, because they could not withstand the trial ... whom then does he try? The righteous, as it says [*Psalms* 11:5]: *HASHEM examines the righteous.*

Ibn Aknin translates: He Who grazes the roses — i.e., Whose Providence is upon the righteous — the *roses* referred to above in verse 2.

17. עַד שֶׁיָּפוּחַ הַיּוֹם וְנָסוּ הַצְּלָלִים — [lit., *until the day blows* (or: *breathes*), *and the shadows flee.*]

Rashi, interpreting this verse in continuity with the previous one, renders: *My Beloved is mine, and I am His.* This condition prevailed until the day that my sin blackened me with the ferocity of the sun. I thus destroyed this intimacy by the sin of the Golden Calf and the Spies. *And the shadows flee* refers to the merits which formerly protected us: I cast off His yoke [and lost His protection].

[Some interpret the phrase literally: "until toward evening, when the power of the sun is spent and the shadows lengthen and fade." (See also on 4:6).]

סֹב דְּמֵה־לְךָ דוֹדִי לִצְבִי אוֹ לְעֹפֶר הָאַיָּלִים — [lit., *turn, my Beloved, and be like a gazelle or a young hart.*]

Rashi allegorically renders in past tense: "Through my sins I caused Him to [swiftly] depart from me." [See below.]

The *Midrash* renders: "O turn, my Beloved God from being executor of Justice to dispenser of Mercy, and hasten Your deliverance like a gazelle or young hart."

עַל־הָרֵי בָתֶר — [lit., *upon the mountains of separation.*] I.e., out of reach (*Rashi*).

[And thus, according to *Rashi's* interpretation the chapter closes with סִילוּק הַשְּׁכִינָה, *the departure,* in anger, *of the Shechinah,* which will be longingly sought after in the following verses.]

The *Midrash* relates בָתֶר, *separation,* to בְּתָרִים, *pieces,* and renders: "For the sake of the promise which God made to our father Abraham at the בְּרִית בֵּין הַבְּתָרִים, *Covenant between the Pieces,* saying [*Genesis* 15:18]: לְזַרְעֲךָ נָתַתִּי אֶת־הָאָרֶץ הַזֹּאת, *To your descendants have I given this land.*"

Alternatively, referring to another era, the *Midrash* relates it to בֵּתָר, *Beitar* [the city wherein the Bar-Cochba revolt (132-135 C.E.) ended with a disastrous defeat and

פֶּרֶק ג א עַל־מִשְׁכָּבִי בַּלֵּילוֹת בִּקַּשְׁתִּי אֵת שֶׁאָהֲבָה
א־ג ב נַפְשִׁי בִּקַּשְׁתִּיו וְלֹא מְצָאתִיו: אָק֫וּמָה
נָּא וַאֲסוֹבְבָה בָעִיר בַּשְּׁוָקִים וּבָרְחֹבוֹת
אֲבַקְשָׁה אֵת שֶׁאָהֲבָה נַפְשִׁי בִּקַּשְׁתִּיו וְלֹא
ג מְצָאתִיו: מְצָאוּנִי הַשֹּׁמְרִים הַסֹּבְבִים בָּעִיר

an incredible number of Jews slain by the Romans], and renders the verse: *Until God makes the day blaze with the fire of His wrath; and the shadows of distress and mourning flee, and He changes His treatment of us from the Attribute of Justice to the Attribute of Mercy and hastens our deliverance like a gazelle or a hart for what happened in Beitar.*

God said: "Even if I had no complaint against them [i.e., the Romans] except what they did in Beitar, My judgment would be executed upon them: What did they do in Beitar? Rav Yochanan said:

The emperor Hadrian slew in Beitar four hundred myriads of thousands of human beings.

[See also the comments related to this verse at the end of verse 15.]

Netziv interprets this verse as an epilogue to the foregoing verse which closes the previous Song. It is a prayer from Israel to God that "until the day of redemption comes about and the shadows of oppression fade, we beseech You, Beloved God, that You continue to cast Your Providence upon us and, like a gazelle or young hart, *skip* over the mountains of transgressions separating us."

III

1. עַל־מִשְׁכָּבִי בַּלֵּילוֹת בִּקַּשְׁתִּי אֵת שֶׁאָהֲבָה נַפְשִׁי — [lit., *Upon my bed at night I sought the one I love.*] In context with the previous verse, *Rashi* explains *night* as referring to the torment of Israel's thirty-eight-year sojourn in the desert in spiritual darkness when they were under the "Ban" [incurred because of the sin of the Spies who turned the people against the land. During this period, the *Midrash* (2:11) explains, God did not speak with Moses (see *Deuteronomy* 2:14-17). This verse metaphorically describes Israel's quest for God, *Whom my soul loves,* during these years of silence].

According to *Alshich*, the verse refers to the dark *nights* of the Egyptian and Babylonian exiles when Israel sought out their God to redeem them and resume His love for them.

[The imagery is poignant. It depicts the anguish of a tormented, insomniac Israel — bereft of its former open, uninhibited relationship with God — figuratively twisting and turning sleeplessly during its period of most pronounced separation, longing after Him, and a resumption of His love.]

The plural לֵילוֹת, *nights*, suggests incessant prayers, night after night — each going unanswered. Thus, the *Talmud* [*Berachos* 32b] comments:

As I lay on my bed in the night of my desert travail, I sought Him Whom my soul loves. I sought Him but I found Him not, for He maintained His aloofness. ²I resolved to arise then, and roam through the city, in the streets and squares; that through Moses I would seek Him Whom my soul loved. I sought Him, but I found Him not. ³They, Moses and Aaron, the watchmen patrolling the city,

"If one prays and is not answered he should pray again" (*Divrei Yedidiah*).

בִּקַּשְׁתִּיו וְלֹא מְצָאתִיו — [lit., *I sought Him but I found Him not.*] As He forewarned [*Exodus* 33:3]: *because I shall not ascend among you;* [*Deuteronomy* 1:42:] *for I am not among you* (*Rashi*).

He chose instead to remain hidden (*Alshich*).

2. אָקוּמָה נָּא וַאֲסוֹבְבָה בָעִיר בַּשְּׁוָקִים וּבָרְחֹבוֹת אֲבַקְשָׁה אֵת שֶׁאָהֲבָה נַפְשִׁי — [lit., *I will rise now and roam about the city, through the streets and through the squares, I will seek the one I love.*] The Jews did not remain apathetic. They did not slumber off in acquiescence, but instead were determined to arise and seek Him out by every possible avenue (*Alshich*).

This is alluded to in the verses [*Exodus* 32:11]: וַיְחַל מֹשֶׁה, *and Moses pleaded before God,* etc.; and [ibid. 32:30]: *I shall ascend to HASHEM* [*perhaps I shall make atonement for your sin*] (*Rashi*).

[The translation *streets* for שְׁוָקִים follows most commentators who also comment that it is synonymous with רְחֹבוֹת, here translated *squares*. *Divrei Yedidiah* suggests the more common translation: *Marketplaces and streets.*]

בִּקַּשְׁתִּיו וְלֹא מְצָאתִיו — [lit., *I sought*

Him, but I found Him not.] I.e., alas, my efforts were to no avail and I was nearly reduced to utter despair (*Alshich*).

I actively besought Him throughout the years in the wilderness, but He would not be appeased, nor did He consent to bring me immediately into the Land (*Metzudas David*).

According to *Rashi*, Moses' appeal resulted in God's decree [*Exodus* 32:34]: וּבְיוֹם פָּקְדִי וּפָקַדְתִּי עֲלֵהֶם חַטָּאתָם. וַיִּגֹּף ה' אֶת־הָעָם, *And on the day that I make My account, I shall bring their sin to account against them. Then HASHEM struck the people with a plague ...* [I.e., although God consented not to inflict *at a single stroke* the terrible punishments warranted by the sin of the Golden Calf, He said that whenever Jews are sinful, they would receive a *portion* of that punishment. (See footnote to verse 15.)]

3. מְצָאוּנִי הַשֹּׁמְרִים הַסֹּבְבִים בָּעִיר — [lit., *The watchmen who patrol* (or: *circle*) *the town found me.*]

[The commentators explain this as a reference to the leaders, Moses and Aaron, who "patrolled" among them to instill the populace with the love of God, guiding them, and inspiring them not to sin and to be patient, for Redemption was at hand.]

ד אֶת שֶׁאָהֲבָה נַפְשִׁי רְאִיתֶם: כִּמְעַט
ד-ה שֶׁעָבַרְתִּי מֵהֶם עַד שֶׁמָּצָאתִי אֶת
שֶׁאָהֲבָה נַפְשִׁי אֲחַזְתִּיו וְלֹא אַרְפֶּנּוּ עַד־
שֶׁהֲבֵיאתִיו אֶל־בֵּית אִמִּי וְאֶל־חֶדֶר
ה הוֹרָתִי: הִשְׁבַּעְתִּי אֶתְכֶם בְּנוֹת יְרוּשָׁלַם

The *Midrash* comments that this refers to the tribe of Levi [who, the Sages tell us, were not subjected to the Egyptian bondage, and who were the teachers and judges of Israel in Egypt].

Alshich comments that in addition to Moses and Aaron in the Egyptian Exile, *watchmen* refers to Ezra and Nechemiah who were "watchmen of HASHEM's vineyards" during the Babylonian Exile. He interprets these verses to allude to Israel's prayers for Redemption from both exiles. [Cf. comm. to *watchmen* in 5:7.]

אֵת שֶׁאָהֲבָה נַפְשִׁי רְאִיתֶם — [lit., *Have you seen Him Whom my soul loves?*]

[The Translation as a statement with an implied interrogation follows *Rashi*:] "Have you any word from Him?"

Have you *yourselves* perceived Him, and been directly assured of His Deliverance? (*Alshich*).

[Agitated and disquieted, she asks the question but does not wait for an answer] ... for there is no answer (*Sforno*).

Shir Chadash, who interprets watchmen as Torah scholars — "the guardians of the city" [cf. *Yerushalmi, Chagigah* 1:7] — notes that there is no interrogative participle in this phrase (although its absence is not idiomatically unusual in Hebrew). Accordingly, he renders it as a declaration: *Surely you have seen Him Whom my soul loves!*

4. כִּמְעַט שֶׁעָבַרְתִּי מֵהֶם עַד שֶׁמָּצָאתִי אֶת שֶׁאָהֲבָה נַפְשִׁי — [lit., *Scarcely had I passed them when I found Him Whom my soul loves.*][1] I.e., soon after *the watchmen*, Moses and Aaron, passed on — after forty years in the desert — God returned to Israel in the days of Joshua, helping it conquer the thirty-one kings (*Rashi*).

[According to those who interpret this as a reference to the Babylonian Exile, the meaning is: *Scarcely had the exile ended that I found God and clung to Him until the Temple was rebuilt.*]

אֲחַזְתִּיו וְלֹא אַרְפֶּנּוּ — [lit., *I grasped Him and I would not let Him go.*] I seized Him in great love and affection, and I would not allow Him to cease from accompanying me (*Alshich*).

1. Rabbi Bunam of Pesish'cha said:
   We can find God and achieve holiness only if we devote our leisure to holy studies and lead an exemplary life; not if we rest lazily in our homes or waste our time in pursuit of city enjoyments. So it says: *Upon my bed at night* [i.e., amid indolence] *I sought Him but I found Him not. I will rise now and roam about the city, through the streets and through the squares, I will seek the One I love. I sought Him but I found Him not ... Scarcely had I passed them when I found Him Whom my soul loves.* It is only *after* man puts away laziness and passes over the allures and pleasure-seeking in the city, that he finds God.

*found me. "You have seen Him Whom my soul loves;
what has He said?"* ⁴*Scarcely had I departed from
them, when, in the days of Joshua, I found Him Whom
my soul loves. I grasped Him, determined that my deeds
would never again cause me to lose hold of Him, until
I brought His Presence to the Tabernacle of my mother
and to the chamber of the one who conceived me.* ⁵*I
adjure you, O nations destined to ascend to Jerusalem,*

עַד־שֶׁהֲבֵיאתִיו אֶל־בֵּית אִמִּי וְאֶל־חֶדֶר הוֹרָתִי
— [lit., *until I brought Him to my
mother's house, and to the chamber
of her who conceived me.*] — until
I brought Him into מִשְׁכַּן שִׁילֹה, *the
Tabernacle at Shiloh* [i.e., I built a
dwelling for His Presence, in return]
for all that He wrought for me (*Rashi*).

Alshich, in consonance with his
comment to verse 3 referring the
verse to both exiles, explains *my
mother's house* as the First Temple
— dwelling place of my "mother"
(i.e., the *Shechinah*, which sustained
me like a mother); and *chamber of
her who conceived me* alluding to
the Second Temple (which was like
a mere chamber in comparison with
the grandeur of the First Temple). It
is referred to as חֶדֶר הוֹרָתִי, *the chamber of her who conceived me* [imply-
ing that the very existence of Israel
stemmed from it], for it was from the
Temple that תּוֹרָה וְהוֹרָאָה, *Torah and
instruction*, went forth to the world.

Midrash Lekach Tov, perceiving
the allusion to exile, paraphrases
verses 2-4 as follows: Verse 2: I will
therefore arouse myself to repentance, and will roam about the countries among whom we are dispersed
throughout the world. I sought out
the true Redemption but it eluded
me — for throughout the long and

bitter exiles, Israel often interpreted
signs to mean that delivery was at
hand, but its hopes were frustrated
each time. Verse 3: The watchmen,
i.e., the heathen nations in whose
midst I find myself in servitude,
found me and I asked them: "Have
you seen a God like ours? There is
no second unto Him! Woe is to us
that we neglect serving Him!" Verse
4: Once we pass through the exile,
however, I will have truly found
Him and I will grasp Him and there
will be no more exiles, as it is written [*Jeremiah* 31:11]: *and they shall
not languish in sorrow any more.*

5. This is the second of the four
places where similar adjurations appear in the Book. The comments on
this verse are limited to contextual
interpretations. [Refer to comm. on
2:7 for a fuller exposition of the
identical verse.]

הִשְׁבַּעְתִּי אֶתְכֶם בְּנוֹת יְרוּשָׁלַם — [lit.,
*I have adjured you, O daughters
of Jerusalem.*] I.e., you nations in
whose midst I dwell (*Rashi*).

[Now that she has *found Him
Whom her soul loves*, she repeats
the adjuration to the nations that
they not attempt to disturb her love
while it is so intense.]

Divrei Yedidiah thematically and
chronologically interprets this verse

פֶּרֶק ג | בִּצְבָאוֹת אוֹ בְּאַיְלוֹת הַשָּׂדֶה אִם־תָּעִירוּ
ו וְאִם־תְּעוֹרְרוּ אֶת־הָאַהֲבָה עַד שֶׁתֶּחְפָּץ:
ז מִי זֹאת עֹלָה מִן־הַמִּדְבָּר כְּתִימֲרוֹת
עָשָׁן מְקֻטֶּרֶת מוֹר וּלְבוֹנָה מִכֹּל אַבְקַת רוֹכֵל:

in the context of the Jews in the desert, where, after the sin of the Calf,[1] God decreed that the members of the generation twenty years of age and older would not enter the promised land. The younger generation which would enter the land after the forty years are called בְּנוֹת יְרוּשָׁלַיִם, *daughters of Jerusalem* [the Holy City being used as a figurative reference to the entire Land], because it was they who were destined to one day become its inhabitants. There was, accordingly, a double adjuration within the verse: (a) אִם־תָּעִירוּ, that they not sin and *provoke hatred* [see above on 2:7] by sinning again in the desert and causing further delay and wandering beyond the forty years; and (b) וְאִם־תְּעוֹרְרוּ אֶת הָאַהֲבָה עַד שֶׁתֶּחְפָּץ, *that they not arouse their love* for Jerusalem and Eretz Yisrael and attempt to enter the land *before the forty-year period ends, the time when God would deem it opportune*. It is noteworthy that the adjuration is directed to בְּנוֹת יְרוּשָׁלַם, i.e., the masses, and not רַעְיָתִי, *My beloved* — the specific designation of the righteous throughout the Book.

There is no fear that the righteous will act contrary to the will of God; adjuration is not necessary.

בִּצְבָאוֹת אוֹ בְּאַיְלוֹת הַשָּׂדֶה — [lit., *by gazelles* or *hinds of the field*.] As commented on 2:7, צְבָאוֹת refers to "the heavenly and earthly hosts," i.e., *angels*. He adjured that if they violate the oath they would be subject to punishment by the heavenly and earthly hosts and by אַיְלוֹת הַשָּׂדֶה, an allusion to beasts of the field (*Divrei Yedidiah*).

According to those who interpret this as an adjuration uttered by God that Israel do nothing to bring the Redemption before its appointed time [see comm. 2:7], its repetition here affirms that despite the praises of the previous verses indicating a growing closeness between God and Israel, the oath is still valid (*Shir Chadash*).

[It is also a reaffirmation that the travail is according to a Divinely arranged plan which must not be tampered with. When the predestined moment of Redemption is imminent, however, no obstacle will stand in its way.]

אִם־תָּעִירוּ וְאִם־תְּעוֹרְרוּ אֶת־הָאַהֲבָה עַד שֶׁתֶּחְפָּץ — [lit., *if you will wake or rouse the love until it pleases*.] I.e., if you will try to sway my Beloved's love for me by persuasion and incitement to abandon Him, while His love is still desirous of me (*Rashi*).

1. The narrative in *Numbers* 14 indicates that the decree was in punishment for Israel's sin in accepting the malicious report of the Spies, not, as *Divrei Yedidiah* says, for the Golden Calf. However, *Rashi* (*Numbers* 14:33) explains that the decree was originally conceived in response to the sin of the *Calf*, but God did not promulgate it until the incident of the Spies when Israel continued to sin (*Harav David Feinstein*).

III

6

for if you violate your oath, you will become as defenseless as gazelles or hinds of the field, if you dare provoke God to hate me or disturb His love for me while He still desires it.

Quoting the nations: ⁶ *You nations have asked, "Who is this ascending from the wilderness, its way secured and smoothed by palmlike pillars of smoke, burning fragrant myrrh and frankincense, of all the perfumer's powders?"*

Until such time that the Heavenly Kingdom shall please it of itself (*Midrash*).

6-11. The following verses follow Israel's adjuration to the nations of the world, as if to say, "Do not attempt to disturb God's love for us. It was *we* who followed Him into the desert; it was *we* whom He engulfed in His cloud; *we* accepted His Torah; *we* built the Tabernacle as He commanded; *we* crowned Him as our God. He will, therefore, surely resume His love for us, and I adjure you not to attempt to interfere with our love" (*Metzudas David* to verse 11).

6. מִי זֹאת עֹלָה מִן־הַמִּדְבָּר כְּתִימֲרוֹת עָשָׁן — [lit., *Who is this who rises up from the desert like columns of smoke?*]

According to *Rashi*, Israel is still the speaker. She is reminiscing how, when the Jews marched in the desert, they were led by the pillar of fire and the pillar of cloud [*Exodus* 13:21ff], which exterminated snakes and scorpions, and burned thorns and thistles to clear the way. The nations, witnessing this awesome sight, exclaimed: *Who is this* [i.e., how great is this spectacle] *that comes up from the desert?*

The *Midrash* elaborates: When Israel journeyed from one camp to another, the pillar of cloud descended and the pillar of fire sprang up. Smoke ascended from the Altar and two darts of fire were expelled from between the two staves of the Ark and burned up serpents, snakes, and scorpions from their path. When the other nations saw it, they feared Israel. Terror and trembling fell upon them as it says (*Exodus* 15:16): תִּפֹּל עֲלֵיהֶם אֵימָתָה וָפַחַד, *May fear and terror befall them.*

כְּתִימֲרוֹת עָשָׁן — [lit., *like columns of smoke.*] Tall and erect as a תָּמָר, *palm tree* (*Rashi*).

The contextual translation *columns* follows *Ibn Ezra*.

[The *Midrash* notes in this context that the smoke from the incense in the Temple used to ascend like a straight column.]

Metzudas David notes the use of the same term in *Joel* 3:3 [where the allusion is to God's manifestations].

מְקֻטֶּרֶת מוֹר וּלְבוֹנָה מִכֹּל אַבְקַת רוֹכֵל — [lit., *perfumed with myrrh and frankincense, of all powders of the merchants.*]

Biblically the burning of aromatic incense is referred to as קְטֹרֶת [here translated *perfumed*] (*Metzudas Tzion*).

The metaphor alludes to the עֲנַן הַקְּטֹרֶת, *cloud of the incense* [*Leviticus* 16:13], which rose up

זֵ הִנֵּה מִטָּתוֹ שֶׁלִשְׁלֹמֹה שִׁשִּׁים גִּבֹּרִים
ח סָבִיב לָהּ מִגִּבֹּרֵי יִשְׂרָאֵל: כֻּלָּם אֲחֻזֵי חֶרֶב
מְלֻמְּדֵי מִלְחָמָה אִישׁ חַרְבּוֹ עַל-יְרֵכוֹ
ט מִפַּחַד בַּלֵּילוֹת: אַפִּרְיוֹן
עָשָׂה לוֹ הַמֶּלֶךְ שְׁלֹמֹה מֵעֲצֵי הַלְּבָנוֹן:

from the Altar in the Inner Chamber; *powders* refers to the practice of crushing and grinding the spices fine as powder (*Rashi*).

לְבוֹנָה, *frankincense*, is so called because of its white color [לָבָן] (*Radak*).

Rashi renders רוֹכֵל, *a vendor of perfumes.*

7. הִנֵּה מִטָּתוֹ שֶׁלִשְׁלֹמֹה — [lit., *Behold, it is the litter* (lit., *couch*) of *Shlomo.*] I.e., referring to the אֹהֶל מוֹעֵד, *Tent of Meeting*, and Ark, which they transported in the desert. [The verse is thus allegorized as *behold, the resting place of God, King to Whom peace belongs, Shlomo* being a reference to God as noted in the comm. to 1:1] (*Rashi*).

שִׁשִּׁים גִּבֹּרִים סָבִיב לָהּ מִגִּבֹּרֵי יִשְׂרָאֵל — [lit., *sixty mighty (men) round about it, of the mighty (men) of Israel.*] I.e., a reference to the sixty myriads who were eligible to go to war. [*Rav Hirsch* expands this concept: instead of warriors, he translates "public servants"; see *Numbers 1:45*] (*Rashi*). And who were camped in the desert surrounding the Tabernacle (*Ibn Aknin*).

The *Midrash* perceives in this verse an additional allusion to the priestly blessing [*Numbers 6:24-26*]: *Behold*, מַטָּתוֹ, *the tribe of Shlomo* — God to Whom peace belongs: *Sixty mighty* refers to the sixty

letters of the priestly blessing; *of the mighty* — because they fortify Israel; *they all handle the sword* — because each of the blessings contains HASHEM's Name [and is thus fortified with strength, as the Sages proclaimed: Every prayer containing HASHEM's Name is like a sword that tears through all obstacles]. This is the implication of *girded with a sword*. [Cf. Jacob's statement (*Genesis 48:22*): בְּחַרְבִּי וּבְקַשְׁתִּי, *with my sword and my bow*, which the Sages interpreted: with my prayer using HASHEM's Name (*Torah Temimah*).] *Skilled in warfare* — because through their blessing they combat the visitations in the world (*Midrash*).

8. כֻּלָּם אֲחֻזֵי חֶרֶב מְלֻמְּדֵי מִלְחָמָה — [lit., *They all grasp the sword, skilled* (or *learned*) *in warfare.*] I.e., in the warfare of Torah. [Cf. *Chagigah 14a*: *Mighty men* refers to masters of traditions; *man of war* refers to one who knows how to dispute in the warfare of Torah (i.e., knows how to deal with the argumentation essential to the study of the Torah; a keen-minded debater).]

The verses also refer to priests who camped round about the Tabernacle and were skilled in the procedure of the Divine Service (*Rashi*).

אִישׁ חַרְבּוֹ עַל-יְרֵכוֹ מִפַּחַד בַּלֵּילוֹת — [lit., *each with his sword on his thigh,*

⁷Behold the resting place of Him to Whom peace belongs, with sixty myriads of Israel's mighty encircling it. ⁸All of them gripping the sword of tradition, skilled in the battle of Torah, each with his sword ready at his side, lest he succumb in the nights of exile. ⁹A Tabernacle for His presence has the King to Whom peace belongs made of the wood of Lebanon:

because of terror (or: fear) in the nights.]

Sword refers to "weapons" — i.e., the means to assure that the Torah is not forgotten and that it is transmitted intact from one generation to the next, for fear lest Torah be forgotten, and, if it is, that trouble will befall them (Rashi).

"They are all equipped for the battles of life with the weapon of the Torah. The precepts of the Torah which apply to all the problems of life give them the means to emerge victorious from the battle. Therefore, each wears it always at his side, to protect him in the difficult hours of the night" (Rav W. Wolf)

The opening phrase is literally they all grasp the sword, yet this phrase depicts the sword sheathed at their thigh! Megillas Sefer explains the apparent contradiction. Their hands did grasp the sword in anticipation and preparedness, but it stayed sheathed at their thigh, and was never drawn because peace pre-

vailed during Solomon's reign — a sword was not drawn in the land.

9. Having described the "couch" in general, the following verses proceed to describe it in detail (Vilna Gaon):

אַפִּרְיוֹן עָשָׂה לוֹ הַמֶּלֶךְ שְׁלֹמֹה מֵעֲצֵי הַלְּבָנוֹן — [lit., A sedan chair has King Shlomo made unto Him, of wood of Lebanon.]

This refers to the Tent of Meeting [described in verse 7] which was established in the Tabernacle of Shiloh. He made it as a sedan chair, a private chamber for His glory (Rashi).[1]

[He made is to be understood: He commanded to be made.]

[The word אַפִּרְיוֹן appears in Scripture only here and it is etymologically difficult. The translation sedan chair, a covered litter in which nobles and brides were transported, is based upon its usage in the Mishnah and Talmud (Sotah 12a). Allegorically it is interpreted to refer to the Tabernacle, the covered litter of Shlomo — God to Whom peace

1. The Midrash makes the following comparison:
A king had a young daughter whom he loved dearly. When she was young he would see her in the street and speak with her in public, but after she grew up he said that this was unbecoming and he ordered a pavilion constructed in which he could converse with her in privacy.
Similarly, when Israel was "young" in Egypt, God's communication and manifestations were public and obvious, and at the Exodus the Jews openly perceived Him [Exodus 12:23; 14:31; 15:2; 33:2]. But after Israel received the Torah at Sinai and became God's people, the Holy One, blessed is He, said: It is unbecoming that I should speak with them openly. Let them, therefore, make for Me a Tabernacle and whenever I require to speak with them, I will speak to them [through Moses] from its midst [Exodus 34:34; Numbers 7:8,9].

פֶּרֶק ג י עַמּוּדָיו עָשָׂה כֶסֶף רְפִידָתוֹ זָהָב מֶרְכָּבוֹ
י-יא אַרְגָּמָן תּוֹכוֹ רָצוּף אַהֲבָה מִבְּנוֹת
יא יְרוּשָׁלָם: צְאֶינָה וּרְאֶינָה בְּנוֹת צִיּוֹן
בַּמֶּלֶךְ שְׁלֹמֹה בָּעֲטָרָה שֶׁעִטְּרָה-לוֹ אִמּוֹ

belongs. *Metzudas David* notes that additionally the *Talmud* (*Kesubos* 10) explains the word as meaning *bed* from פּוֹרִיָה, *to be fruitful.*

[The *wood of Lebanon* refers to the finest Lebanese cypress and cedar that were used for the Tabernacle and also later for the Temple.]

10. עַמּוּדָיו עָשָׂה כֶסֶף — [lit., *He made its pillars of silver.*] I.e., the hooks of the Tabernacle's pillars. [See *Rashi* to *Exodus* 27:10 (*Midrash*).]

רְפִידָתוֹ זָהָב — [lit., *its hangings* (or: *spreads*; or: *beddings*; or: *inlay*; or: *coverings*) *were gold.*] I.e., His dwelling place upon the golden כַּפֹּרֶת, *the Covering* [of the Ark whence He spoke with Moses; cf. *Exodus* 27:17,22] (*Rashi*).

מֶרְכָּבוֹ אַרְגָּמָן — [lit., *its seat purple* (*wool*).] A reference to the פָּרֹכֶת, *the Curtain* [of purple (*Exodus* 26:31ff)] which was suspended from poles between the pillars (*Rashi*); and which was the partition between קֹדֶשׁ, *the Holy*, and קֹדֶשׁ הַקֳּדָשִׁים, *the Holy of Holies* [ibid. v. 33] (*Metzudas David*).

תּוֹכוֹ רָצוּף אַהֲבָה — [lit., *its inner side was decked with love.*] I.e., arranged with deckings that were all symbolic of the love between

God and Israel: the Ark, its Cover, Cherubim, and Tablets (*Rashi*).

Tz'ror HaMor elaborates. He relates רָצוּף, *decked*, with רִצְפָּה, *live burning coal*, as in *Isaiah* 6:6, and renders it: *Its inner side was decked with a hot coal of love* — burning love;. i.e., love which permeated the entire atmosphere of the Sanctuary (*Vilna Gaon*).

The *Midrash* interprets אַהֲבָה as a reference to the *Shechinah* [whose love and glory filled the inside of the Tabernacle].

מִבְּנוֹת יְרוּשָׁלָם — [lit. *by the daughters of Jerusalem.*] *Rashi* interprets the phrase in this case to refer to "the Jews" — "God fearing and complete [יְרוּשָׁלָיִם = יְרֵאִים וּשְׁלֵמִים] before the Holy One, blessed is He."

Throughout the rest of the Book (e.g., 1:5; 2:7; 3:5; 5:8; 8:4) *Rashi* interprets *daughters of Jerusalem* as a reference to the heathen nations [see comm. to 1:5]. Perhaps here the diminutive prefix — מ, *of* — indicates that the verse refers not to *all* nations, but to only "*a portion of*" the *daughters of Jerusalem. Rashi* contextually interprets that "*portion*" as referring to Israel (*Ohel David*).

11. צְאֶנָה וּרְאֶינָה בְּנוֹת צִיּוֹן בַּמֶּלֶךְ שְׁלֹמֹה — [lit., *Go forth and gaze,*

Yalkut Shimoni notes: One verse [*Exodus* 40:35] reads: *the glory of* HASHEM *filled the Tabernacle*, yet another verse [*I Kings* 8:27] reads: *behold*, (even) *the heavens and the heavens of heavens cannot contain you.* These seemingly contradictory verses can be explained by a comparison:

10 *Its pillars He made of silver; His resting place was gold; its suspended curtain was purple wool, its midst was decked with implements bespeaking love by the daughters of Jerusalem.* **11** *Go forth and gaze, O daughters distinguished by loyalty to God, upon the King to Whom peace belongs adorned with the crown His nation made for Him,*

O daughters of Zion, upon King Shlomo.]

As reflected in the Translation, *Rashi* (following the *Midrash*) interprets צִיּוֹן, *Zion,* as related to the verb צִיֵּן (mark, sign, distinguish), and renders the phrase: "children — i.e., Israel — who are מְצוּיָנִים, *distinguished,* as His, by virtue of circumcision, *tefillin,* and *tzitzis."*

Gaze upon King Shlomo — upon the King to Whom peace belongs; upon the King Who produced His creatures in their full שְׁלֵמוּת, *perfection* (*Midrash*).

בַּעֲטָרָה שֶׁעִטְּרָה־לּוֹ אִמּוֹ — [lit., *with the crown that his mother crowned him.*] I.e., with the אֹהֶל מוֹעֵד, *Tent of Meeting,* which was conspicuously *crowned* with blue, purple, scarlet, and fine linen [cf. *Exodus* 26:31] (*Midrash; Rashi*).

Shlomo — i.e., God *Himself* — cannot be perceived by man. Therefore the *daughters of Zion* are bid to gaze upon His *crown,* i.e., perceive Him through His earthly manifestation. The *crown* is the outward symbol of majesty, indicating the King's public grandeur. His essence, however, can never be known to those who see Him only in public. Thus it is a simile for God's earthly manifestation in His humanly perceived deeds (*Vilna Gaon*).

As reflected in the Translation, the Hebrew word אִמּוֹ [lit., *His mother*] is allegorically explained by the *Midrash, Zohar,* and *Rashi* as אוּמּוֹ, *His nation,* Israel [as in 1:6, בְּנֵי אִמִּי, *children of my mother* = *children of my* אֻמָּה, *nation*].

The simile of *mother* is appropriate because Israel is the nation with whom God conducts Himself — if one may so express it — in filial deference, as illustrated in the Talmudic concept: "God promulgates a decree and the righteous man abrogates it" (*Vilna Gaon*).

Mother is additionally explained as referring to the princes of the tribes who were metaphorically the "mothers in Israel" [i.e., sources of nourishment and comfort, and directly involved in the construction of the Tabernacle] (*Sforno*).

Markevos Ami and *Divrei Yedidiah* explain the term *his mother* differently: When a ruler refers to "his ministers," he does not mean that they have authority over him, but that the

"Rav Yehoshua ben Siknin said in the name of Rav Levi. The Tent of Meeting can be compared to a cave adjoining the sea. When the tide is high the water fills the cave, yet the sea loses nothing. Similarly, the Tent of Meeting was filled with the glory of the Divine Presence, and yet the world lacks nothing of the infinite Presence of the *Shechinah."*

בְּיוֹם חֲתֻנָּתוֹ וּבְיוֹם שִׂמְחַת לִבּוֹ:

א הִנָּךְ יָפָה רַעְיָתִי הִנָּךְ יָפָה עֵינַיִךְ יוֹנִים מִבַּעַד לְצַמָּתֵךְ שַׂעְרֵךְ כְּעֵדֶר הָעִזִּים ב שֶׁגָּלְשׁוּ מֵהַר גִּלְעָד: שִׁנַּיִךְ כְּעֵדֶר

---

ministers who hold dominion over others are beholden to him. Similarly, when Israel accepted the Torah, she became the spiritual אֵם כָּל הָאוּמוֹת, *mother of all mankind*. Despite her noble status, she remained the loyal servant of God. Thus, Israel — herself belonging to God — became *His mother* of all nations.

Rav W. Wolf beautifully translates: *The crown with which the nation He chose as the mother of mankind crowned Him on the day of His espousals, on the day of the gladness of His heart.*

בְּיוֹם חֲתֻנָּתוֹ וּבְיוֹם שִׂמְחַת לִבּוֹ — [lit., *on His wedding day and on the day of His heart's bliss*.]

On His wedding day — the day the Torah was given, when they crowned Him as King and accepted His yoke; *and on the day of His heart's bliss* — the dedication day of the Tabernacle in the desert (*Rashi*).

According to the *Talmud* (last *Mishnah* in *Taanis*) the former refers to the giving of the Torah, and the latter refers to the building of the Temple.

IV

הִנָּךְ יָפָה רַעְיָתִי הִנָּךְ יָפָה עֵינַיִךְ יוֹנִים **1.** — [lit., *You are beautiful, My love, you are beautiful, your eyes are doves*.]

Upon perceiving that the beloved delights in His love and has limitless faith in Him, He responds by extolling her with the following declaration: "Your deeds have been beautiful since you first became My beloved, and you have maintained your beauty throughout the time of our estrangement. Your Sages, who are the "eyes" of the community [*eyes* refer to your leaders, the members of the Sanhedrin (*Midrash*; cf. 1:15)], are pleasant and modest in their behavior

as doves that are modestly concealed behind a veil — away from the public gaze (*Metzudas David*).

[The verse is basically a repeat of 1:15; see commentary there for elaboration.]

Rashi explains the simile of *doves*: Your quality and actions are like the dove which is loyal to its mate. When it is to be slaughtered, it does not fidget, but [willingly] stretches forth its neck. So have you bent your shoulder to endure my yoke and my awe [see also comm. to 1:15].

מִבַּעַד לְצַמָּתֵךְ — [lit., *from behind your kerchief*.]

*on the day His Law was given and He became one
with Israel, and on the day His heart was gladdened
by His Tabernacle's consecration.*

Hashem:

IV

1-2

Behold, you are lovely, My beloved, behold you are
lovely, your very appearance radiates dove-
like constancy. The most common sons within your
encampments are as dearly beloved as the children
of Jacob in the goatlike procession descending the
slopes of Mount Gilead. ² Accountable in deed are

This literal translation follows *Rashi*
who explains in a long dissertation
that grammatically the word cannot
be derived from צָמַת, *veil*, but from
צָמָה, a *hair net, kerchief*.

[The phrase occurs again in verse
3. The *Midrash* homiletically explains it there as מְצוּמָתִים, the *self-
restrained* among you. See comm.
there.]

שַׂעְרֵךְ כְּעֵדֶר הָעִזִּים שֶׁגָּלְשׁוּ מֵהַר גִּלְעָד
— [lit., *your hair is like a flock of
goats streaming down from Mount
Gilead.*]

[Until this point, her *general*
beauty is praised. Now her *specific*
features are detailed and praised. It
must be remembered that in these
descriptions a double simile/ metaphor is taking place. Israel, allegorized throughout the Book as a beautiful woman, is now praised for the
specific beautiful characteristics that
have endeared her to her Beloved.
These features refer to events in
Jewish history. According to the
commentators, including *Rashi*,
the ensuing list of events does not
follow a strict chronological order.

Rather the verses reflect random
praises of exemplary periods in her
history.]

Rashi apparently disregards the
אֶתְנַחְתָּא pause *after* לְצַמָּתֵךְ מִבַּעַד,
which indicates that *your hair* begins
a new thought. Instead, he attaches
the preceding phrase to the succeeding one and renders: *From behind
your kerchief, your hair is like a
flock of goats ...*, i.e., "even from behind your kerchief your hair gleams
in its brightness like the white wool
of goats whose hair gleams from
afar, streaming down a mountain."
Metaphorically, the simile is: "Even
the emptiest [i.e., people whose merit
is the most hidden] among you are as
dear to Me [i.e., *shine forth*] as Jacob
and his sons who streamed down
Mount Gilead when Laban pursued
them there" [see *Genesis* 31:23ff.].

Additionally, according to *Rashi*,
the phrase alludes to those who
warred against the Midianites on the
east bank of the Jordan in the land
of Gilead [see *Judges* Chs. 11-12].

[The Halachic prohibition against
reciting the *Shema* in the presence of
a married woman with exposed hair

פרק ד

ג הַקְּצוּבוֹת שֶׁעָלוּ מִן־הָרַחְצָה שֶׁכֻּלָּם מַתְאִימוֹת וְשַׁכֻּלָה אֵין בָּהֶם: כְּחוּט הַשָּׁנִי שִׂפְתוֹתַיִךְ וּמִדְבָּרֵךְ נָאוֶה כְּפֶלַח הָרִמּוֹן רַקָּתֵךְ מִבַּעַד לְצַמָּתֵךְ:

(*Orach Chayim* 75:1) is derived from this verse by the *Talmud, Berachos* 24a and formulated: שֵׂעָר בְּאִשָּׁה עֶרְוָה, *a woman's hair is provocative.*]

2. שִׁנַּיִךְ כְּעֵדֶר הַקְּצוּבוֹת שֶׁעָלוּ מִן־הָרַחְצָה — [lit., *Your teeth are like a flock well counted, which have come up from the washing.*] Here, again, the allegory is couched in terms of physical beauty. The simile stresses the whiteness, regularity, and completeness of well-cared-for teeth, which are like carefully counted sheep whose wool is tended and washed by wise shepherds from the moment of birth (*Rashi*).

שֶׁכֻּלָּם מַתְאִימוֹת וְשַׁכֻּלָה אֵין בָּהֶם — [lit., *all of which are perfect and there is none blemished among them.*][1]

The verse allegorizes the mighty warriors of Israel who figuratively "tear apart and consume their enemies round about them with their teeth" but refrain from stealing and lewdness so they do not become tainted by sin [and thus are as if *they came up from the washing*]. Specifically, this refers to the 12,000 men who fought against Midian [*Numbers* 31:5], not even one of whom was "blemished" by being suspect of lewdness, as it is

written [ibid. v. 49]: *and not a man of us is missing* ["through indulgence in sin" (*Yevamos* 61a)]. So chaste were they that even for possibly licentious *thoughts* they would bring sacrifices of atonement. Although they had risked their lives in battle, they were even above the suspicion of taking spoils for themselves, as Scripture testifies of them [*Numbers* 31:11-12]: "And they took *all* the spoil ... and brought it to Moses and Eleazar," not even a single cow or donkey was missing (*Rashi*).

Divrei Yedidiah interprets this verse as referring to the priests in the First Temple [*teeth* alluding to their eating the sacrifices]. They were "numbered" in their service, for which they ritually washed, all of whom were perfect and there was no one blemished among them.

3. כְּחוּט הַשָּׁנִי שִׂפְתוֹתַיִךְ — [lit., *Your lips are like a thread of scarlet.*] As reflected in the Translation this refers to the sincerity and earnestness of the pledge which the Spies made to Rachav who sheltered them in Jericho. In gratitude, they pledged to guarantee her safety and that of her family when Israel occupied the city if she would display a scarlet

1. שֵׁן, in addition to *tooth*, can also be translated as *sharpness*. It is, therefore, used as a reference to "scholars" as in the Talmud (*Berachos* 36a; *Bava Kamma* 14a) where we find that Shmuel called his disciple, Rav Yehudah, שִׁינָּנָא, an affectionate designation, meaning "sharp-witted" in Torah learning.

[Compare, in this context, the Talmudic explanation of the verse (*Deuteronomy* 6:7): וְשִׁנַּנְתָּם לְבָנֶיךָ, *and you shall teach them diligently to your children*, as related to שֵׁן, keen, sharp:

your mighty leaders like a well-numbered flock come up from the washing, all of them unblemished with no miscarriage of action in them.

³Like the scarlet thread, guarantor of Rahab's safety, is the sincerity of your lips, and your word is unfeigned. As many as a pomegranate's seeds are the merits of your unworthiest within your modest veil.

thread as a signal to the conquering Jews [see *Joshua* Chapter 2] (*Rashi*).

The *Midrash* and many commentators see in this phrase a reference to the scarlet thread which was used on Yom Kippur. [The *Mishnah* (*Shabbos* 9:3; *Yoma* 4:2, 6:8) describes how the high priest tied part of the scarlet thread to the scapegoat and the other to a rock on the mountain from which the goat was thrown. When the thread turned white it was symbolic that the people's sins were forgiven as alluded to in *Isaiah* 1:18: *Though your sins be as scarlet, they shall be white as snow.*]

...Thus the simile is: "What emanates from your mouth is also as pure as that thread became" (*Shevach Viy'kar*).

וּמִדְבָּרֵךְ נָאוֶה — [lit., *and your speech* (or: *mouth*) *is comely.*] The *Midrash* renders מִדְבָּרֵךְ, *your desert*, and comments: This refers to the scapegoat [which was sent into the desert]. Israel proclaimed to God: "Sovereign of the Universe, [now that the Temple is destroyed] we have no scarlet strip nor scapegoat!" God replied: "*Your lips are like a thread of scarlet*"

— the utterance of your lips [i.e., the prayer which you now utter in place of the Temple service] is as beloved to Me as the strip of scarlet. *And your desert* [מִדְבָּר] *is comely* [i.e., just as I was pleased with the scapegoat (*Leviticus* 16:8-10,21-22) you sent into the wilderness, so am I pleased with your דִּבּוּר, *speech* (prayers), which now replaces it. This interpretation is derived from the fact that the Hebrew root דבר, *utter*, is found in the word מִדְבָּר, *your desert*.]

Metzudas David perceives a reference here to the pleasant chanting of the Levites during the Temple service.

כְּפֶלַח הָרִמּוֹן רַקָּתֵךְ מִבַּעַד לְצַמָּתֵךְ — [lit., *your temples are like a slice (a half — Rashi) of pomegranate, from behind your veil.*] *Rashi* interprets רַקָּתֵךְ as the upper part of the face, near the eyes, which in Talmudic language is referred to as רוּמָנֵי דְאַפֵּי [*Avodah Zarah* 30b]. The praise here, then, refers to the redness of the cheeks which, peeking through a kerchief, resemble the outside circumference of half a pomegranate. *Rashi's* allegorical interpretation is

"that the words of Torah shall be *clear cut* in your mouth" (*Kiddushin* 30a).]

Thus *Shevach Viy'kar* renders the verse: "Your scholars and righteous men are likened to well-numbered flocks whose studies *have come up from the washing*, i.e., are קַב וְנָקִי, 'small but clean' ('well sifted'). All of them are perfect, and even in exile there is none among them who is blemished through deviance from God's path."

פרק ד ד־ה

ד כְּמִגְדַּל דָּוִיד צַוָּארֵךְ בָּנוּי לְתַלְפִּיּוֹת אֶלֶף
ה הַמָּגֵן תָּלוּי עָלָיו כֹּל שִׁלְטֵי הַגִּבֹּרִים: שְׁנֵי
שָׁדַיִךְ כִּשְׁנֵי עֳפָרִים תְּאוֹמֵי צְבִיָּה הָרֹעִים

found in the Translation.

[The Sages relate רַקָּתֵךְ, *your temples*, to רֵקָנִים, *empty ones* (i.e., illiterate ones), and render allegorically, as God praising Israel:] *Even the illiterate ones among you are as full of precepts as a pomegranate is full with seeds.* For everyone who has the opportunity of committing a sin, and refrains from doing so, commits a good deed. How much more is this true of those, מִבַּעַד לְצַמָּתֵךְ, *behind your veil*, i.e, those among you who are צְנוּעִין וּמְצוּמָתִין, *modest and self-restrained!* [who renounce the allures of the world, restraining themselves for the exclusive study of Torah (*Torah Temimah*)] (*Midrash*).

4. כְּמִגְדַּל דָּוִיד צַוָּארֵךְ בָּנוּי לְתַלְפִּיּוֹת— [lit., *Your neck is like the Tower of David, built as a landmark.*] An erect posture in a woman is beautiful, and the simile to *Tower of David* refers to מְצוּדַת צִיּוֹן, *the Stronghold of Zion*, a beautiful, stately tower and fortification. So is your *neck* — i.e., the לִשְׁכַּת הַגָּזִית, *the Chamber of Hewn Stone* [the seat of the Sanhedrin], which was the spiritual stronghold of Israel (*Rashi*).

Built as a landmark. The word תַלְפִּיּוֹת is etymologically difficult and many interpretations are offered. The translation *landmark* follows *Ibn Janach*. *Rashi* renders: "built as an ornament, a model for all to gaze at and study its form and the beauty of its construction."

— "An edifice, taller than all others,

and visible from afar, used as a reference point by travelers to ascertain their direction" (*Metzudas David*).

— "Built for teaching" (*Targum*; *Metzudas David*) — from where Torah emanated to the world (*Tz'ror HaMor*).

The *Talmud* interprets this verse as referring to the Temple and renders תַּלְפִּיּוֹת as the תֵּל, *elevation* [i.e., Temple], toward which all פִּיּוֹת, *mouths*, turn [in fulfillment of Solomon's prayer at the consecration of the Temple, that God respond to those *that pray toward this place* (*I Kings* 8:29; *II Chronicles* 6:20)]. It is from these verses that the Sages ruled: A blind man ... should direct his heart toward his Father in heaven; one who is outside of Eretz Yisrael should turn toward Eretz Yisrael; one who is in Eretz Yisrael should turn toward Jerusalem; one who is in Jerusalem should turn toward the Sanctuary; one who is in the Sanctuary should turn toward the Holy of Holies ... In this way, all of Israel will be turning their hearts toward one place (*Berachos* 30a).

Tz'ror HaMor perceives in the word *neck* a reference to the righteous, upon whose necks rest the yoke of each generation. The simile of the *Tower of David* refers to the righteous who stand erect as a tower withstanding all hardship, in contrast to the wicked who buckle at the first blows of suffering and yield to idolatrous practices. The

⁴*As stately as the Tower of David is the site of your Sanhedrin built as a model to emulate, with a thousand shields of Torah armor hung upon it, all the disciple-filled quivers of the mighty. ⁵Moses and Aaron, your two sustainers, are like two fawns, twins of the gazelle, who graze their sheep*

significance of בָּנוּי לְתַלְפִּיּוֹת, *built as a landmark*, is that the sage serves as a model of behavior for all to emulate just as a landmark is a model of architecture.

אֶלֶף הַמָּגֵן תָּלוּי עָלָיו כֹּל שִׁלְטֵי הַגִּבֹּרִים — [lit., *a thousand shields are hung upon it* (i.e., the Tower); *all quivers of the mighty.*] In its literal sense, *Rashi* explains that this refers to the practice of warriors to hang their shields [triumphantly] upon the walls of towers. [See *Ezekiel 27:11.*]

Allegorically, this refers to the Chamber of the Hewn Stone, the seat of the Sanhedrin, from whence teaching went forth — Torah being Israel's "shield." Additionally, אֶלֶף הַמָּגֵן might be a reference to מָגֵן אֶלֶף, *the protector of a thousand* [i.e., the Torah, as in *Psalms 105:8; I Chronicles 16:15*]: *The Word He commanded for a thousand generations.*

Targum, consistent with its translation of אֶלֶף, *teaching*, renders: אֶלֶף הַמָּגֵן, the teaching (i.e., study of

Torah) which protected Israel in wars as if they were grasping all kinds of weapons.

כֹּל שִׁלְטֵי הַגִּבֹּרִים — [lit., *all quivers of the mighty.*] *Rashi* explains that students [children] are referred to in the context of *arrows* and *quivers*, as it is written [*Psalms 127:4-5* (significantly a psalm ascribed to Solomon!)]: *Like arrows in the hand of a mighty man, so are the children of youth ... Praiseworthy is the man who fills his quiver with them.*[1]

5. שְׁנֵי שָׁדַיִךְ כִּשְׁנֵי עֳפָרִים תְּאוֹמֵי צְבִיָּה — [lit., *Your bosom is like two fawns, twins of a gazelle.*]

Rashi explains *bosom* as referring to Moses and Aaron who "nursed" Israel. They are likened to the twins of a gazelle because they were equal one to the other. For this reason, sometimes Aaron is mentioned first (*Exodus 6:26*), and sometimes Moses (ibid. v. 27) to demonstrate that Moses was not greater than Aaron, nor was

---

1. *Rav Hirsch* elaborates: בְּנֵי נְעוּרִים, *children of youth*, refers to children of young parents ... Young parents will be successful in guiding their children resolutely to the one true goal for which God has entrusted these young souls to them. The arrow shot from a strong hand bears within itself the strength of the sharpshooter long after it has left its hand, and thus follows unswervingly and unhesitatingly the direction given it by the "mighty man."

So, too, children raised by parents of youthful vigor [*and trained from their earliest youth!*] will remain unerringly true to the direction and goal set them by the guiding hand of their father and mother, even long after they have matured and left the immediate sphere of their parents' guidance. For this reason precisely [is the man fortunate] who *has his quiver quite full of these arrows*, who has wealth in the form of many children who have been raised to set their hearts aright.

פֶּרֶק ד ו בַּשּׁוֹשַׁנִּים: עַד שֶׁיָּפוּחַ הַיּוֹם וְנָסוּ הַצְּלָלִים
ו-ח אֵלֶךְ לִי אֶל־הַר הַמּוֹר וְאֶל־גִּבְעַת הַלְּבוֹנָה:
ז-ח כֻּלָּךְ יָפָה רַעְיָתִי וּמוּם אֵין בָּךְ: אִתִּי

Aaron greater than Moses (*Midrash*).

Rashi alternatively interprets *bosom* as referring to the twin Tablets of the Law which are also *twins of the gazelle* inasmuch as the five commandments on one Tablet corresponded respectively to the five on the other Tablet:

— *I am HASHEM your God* corresponds to *You shall not murder*, for a murderer diminishes the Divine image [because he murdered someone who was created in the *image of God* (cf. *Genesis* 9:6)].

— *You shall have no other gods* corresponds to *You shall not commit adultery*, for one who engages in idolatry is comparable to *a wife that commits adultery, taking strangers instead of her husband* (*Ezekiel* 16:32) [because he has thereby broken his covenant with God (*Mechilta*)].

— *You shall not take the Name of HASHEM your God in vain* corresponds to *You shall not steal*, because one who steals will eventually swear falsely.

— *Remember the Sabbath day to sanctify it* corresponds to *You shall not bear false witness against your neighbor*, because he who profanes the Sabbath [symbol of God's having created the world and having "rested" on the seventh day] thereby testifies falsely against the Creator, denying that in the beginning He "rested" on the Sabbath.

— *Honor your father and mother* corresponds to *You shall not covet*,

for he who covets will ultimately beget a son who may curse his real father while giving filial honor to one who is not his father [see *Mechilta, Exodus* 20:13].

Translating the verse in chronological context of the Temple period, *bosom* refers to the king and high priest who jointly ruled the people with equal authority like two fawns, twins of a gazelle: the king caring for the physical needs of the nation, and the high priest for the spiritual needs (*Metzudas David*).

Additionally, *bosom* refers to the Written and Oral Torah which, like twins, complement and equal each other, and together lead us to graze in proper pastures (*Shevach Viy'kar*).

הָרֹעִים בַּשּׁוֹשַׁנִּים — [lit., *who feed among the roses*] — i.e., who graze their offspring in tranquil pastures (*Rashi*; cf. comm. to 2:16).

6-7. עַד שֶׁיָּפוּחַ הַיּוֹם וְנָסוּ הַצְּלָלִים — [lit., *until the day blows* (or: *breathes*) *and the shadows flee*.] [See comm. to 2:17.]

[The continuity of the verses is difficult and many interpretations are suggested by the commentators. *Rashi*, understanding verses 6-7 as a unit, perceives it as God's recounting to Israel how He had always been their shade in the "heat" of the days, protecting them, until they forfeited His protection by sinning. Later, when His anger was abated, He relocated His glory at Mount Moriah where once again they were

IV

6-7

in rose-like bounty.

⁶*Until My sunny benevolence was withdrawn from Shiloh and the protective shadows were dispersed by your sin. I will go to Mount Moriah and the hill of frankincense —* ⁷*where you will be completely fair, My beloved, and no blemish will be in you.*

---

entirely pleasing to Him, and their mutual love resumed:]

God says: "While the day was hot I protected you and you were acceptable to Me. But when, in the days of Hophni and Phinehas [the sons of Eli; cf. *I Samuel* 2:12 ff and Chapter 4], they sinned by profaning My holy things and despising My offerings, I departed from you and abandoned your Tabernacle ... allowing it to be destroyed by the Philistines" (*Rashi*).

אֵלֵךְ לִי אֶל-הַר הַמּוֹר וְאֶל-גִּבְעַת הַלְּבוֹנָה — [lit., *I will get Me to the mountain of myrrh, and to the hill of frankincense.*] ... and (after the heat of the day was over — i.e., My anger abated) I chose for Myself a new dwelling at Mount Moriah [Myrrh=Moriah], a house of eternity [the hill upon which frankincense was offered (*Targum*)] (*Rashi*).

Metzudas David, however, interpreting the verse as referring to evening [i.e., the total decline of the nation], renders: "Because of your lovely mannerisms and your inherent charm I will hurry — before 'evening' arrives — and cause My *Shechinah* to dwell in the Temple where incense, containing myrrh and frankincense, is offered."

This is in accord with the interpretation of *Divrei Yedidiah* who understands this verse as God's promise that by the time the day is

over and the "shade" of ancestral merits is abated, He will relocate His *Shechinah* and cause it to dwell in the Temple on Mount Moriah.

The *Zohar* interprets this verse as a statement regarding Israel's exiles in general. It is the Divine promise that Israel will be subjugated by the nations of the world — *until the long day of their dominion shall breathe its last,* and those that protect the nations [צְלָלִים], i.e., their rulers, shall dissipate. Anticipating that predetermined time of Redemption, God will establish Himself in Jerusalem on Mount Moriah awaiting Israel's resumption of His service. Then they will be forlorn no more.

7. כֻּלָּךְ יָפָה רַעְיָתִי וּמוּם אֵין בָּךְ — [lit., *You are entirely fair, My beloved, and there is no blemish in you.*] [In continuity of *Rashi's* interpretation of the previous verse: I will build a Temple at Mount Moriah] ... where I will again consider you beautiful and unblemished and will accept your sacrifices (*Rashi*).

"O Community of Israel, you are completely fair — there is not one among you who is blemished" (*Metzudas David*).

According to the *Midrash*, this verse refers to the time the Torah was given at Sinai: Rav Shimon bar Yochai said: At the moment when Israel stood at Sinai, there were

---

מִלְּבָנוֹן כַּלָּה אִתִּי מִלְּבָנוֹן תָּבוֹאִי
תָּשׁוּרִי | מֵרֹאשׁ אֲמָנָה מֵרֹאשׁ שְׂנִיר
וְחֶרְמוֹן מִמְּעֹנוֹת אֲרָיוֹת מֵהַרְרֵי נְמֵרִים:

among them neither persons with
unclean issue, nor lepers, nor lame,
nor blind, nor dumb nor deaf, nor
lunatics nor imbeciles, nor dullards,
nor doubters. With reference to that
moment it is written: *You are entirely fair, My beloved, and there
is no blemish in you.*

8. אִתִּי מִלְּבָנוֹן כַּלָּה אִתִּי מִלְּבָנוֹן תָּבוֹאִי
— [lit., *With Me from Lebanon,
O bride! With Me from Lebanon
shall you come.*] I.e., when you are
exiled from this "Lebanon" [sym-
bolizing the Temple (see below)], it
is *with Me* — says God — because
I shall go into exile with you; and
when you return from exile I will
return along with you *for in all
your afflictions, I, too, am afflicted*
[Isaiah 63:9]. The verse continues,
"With Me *from* Lebanon shall you
come" instead of "with Me *to* Lebanon shall you come" to stress God's
promise that in your every movement — both going and coming
— *from the moment you are exiled
from this place* until you return, I
will accompany you (*Rashi*).[1]

... And [*Exodus* 20:21]: *In every
place where I will cause My Name
to be pronounced, I will come to
you and I will bless you* (*Sforno*).

[On the connotation of *bride* see
also comment of *Divrei Yedidiah*

on verse 9 cited below.]

[*Lebanon* is understood by the
Sages to symbolize the Temple.
Note, for example, the verse in
Deuteronomy 3:25 where *Lebanon*
is translated by *Targum Onkelos*
as בֵּית מַקְדְּשָׁא, the *Temple*, based
upon the *Talmud: Yoma* 39b; *Gittin*
56b; and *Sifri*: "Why is the Temple
called Lebanon? שֶׁמַלְבִּין עֲוֹנוֹתֵיהֶם שֶׁל
יִשְׂרָאֵל — Because it whitens [לְבָנוֹן =
לָבָן] the sins of Israel."]

As *Midrash Zuta* comments:
Why is the Temple referred to as
Lebanon? Because whoever brings
his sacrifice there, and is sinful, does
not depart from there until his sins
become white as snow, in fulfillment of the verse [*Isaiah* 1:18]: *If
your sins be like scarlet, they shall
become white as snow.*

Ibn Aknin suggests that in the literal sense the appellation "*Lebanon*"
referring to the Temple might also
be due to the abundance of wood
from Lebanon that was used in its
construction.

[For the poetic form of this verse
and the next, where the opening
phrase is repeated, compare for example, *Psalms* 93:3: נָשְׂאוּ נְהָרוֹת ה'
נָשְׂאוּ נְהָרוֹת קוֹלָם, [like] *rivers they
raised, O HASHEM, [like] rivers they
raised their voice.*]

1. This verse refers to the oft-quoted concept of שְׁכִינְתָּא בְּגָלוּתָא, *the Shechinah [God's Pres-
ence] is in exile.* The *Talmud* comments:
Come and see how beloved are Israel in the sight of God, in that every place to which they
were exiled, the *Shechinah* went with them. They were exiled to Egypt and the *Shechinah*
was with them ... They were exiled to Babylon and the *Shechinah* was with them ... And
when they will be redeemed in the future, the *Shechinah* will be with them as it is written

8 *With Me will you be exiled from the Temple, O bride, with Me from the Temple until you return; then to contemplate the fruits of your faith from its earliest beginnings, from your first arrival at the summits of Senir and Hermon, the lands of mighty Sihon and Og, as impregnable as dens of lions, and as mountains of leopards.*

תָּשׁוּרִי מֵרֹאשׁ אֲמָנָה מֵרֹאשׁ שְׂנִיר וְחֶרְמוֹן מִמְּעֹנוֹת אֲרָיוֹת מֵהַרְרֵי נְמֵרִים — [lit., *look from the peak of Amanah, from the peak of Senir and Hermon, from the dens of lions, from the mountains of leopards*]

The translation reflects *Rashi's* primary interpretation of this verse. He understands תָּשׁוּרִי, *look*, in the sense of perceive, contemplate; רֹאשׁ, *head*, *peak*, as beginning; and אֲמָנָה as a form of אֱמוּנָה, *faith*, *trust*: Contemplate the rewards for the beginning of your trust in Me by having followed Me in the desert, traveling and camping at My command and your arrival at the peak of Senir and Hermon which were the *lions' dens* of Sichon and Og.

[This is in agreement with *Tanchuma Beshalach* 10: By which merit did the Jews deserve to [witness miracles and] sing the Song at the Sea? By merit of הָאֱמָנָה שֶׁהֶאֱמִינוּ תְּחִילָה, *the faith which they displayed first*, as it is written [*Exodus* 4:31]: *and the people believed.*

(The *Midrash* similarly translates רֹאשׁ אֲמָנָה as *the Prime Believer* — Abraham — by whose merit Israel deserved the miracles wrought for

them and in response to which they *sang* at the sea.)

Rashi bases his alternate explanation on the Midrashic interpretation of תָּשׁוּרִי as being related to שִׁיר, *song*, and Amanah in its literal sense as one of the mountains on the northern border of Eretz Yisrael ...

He therefore renders, according to this interpretation, *Sing from the peak of Amanah*, for when the exiles will be gathered they will reach these mountains — the border of Israel. Then, standing atop the mountains, they will view the Land and will ecstatically break out in song.

The *Mishnah* [*Sheviis* 6:1] refers to these mountains as טוּרֵי אֲמָנָה, *Taurus Manus*, the Mount of Amanon.

[*Targum Yonasan* identifies this with הֹר הָהָר, *the Mount Hor* (see his comm. to *Numbers* 34:7). The *Talmud*, *Gittin* 8a, notes that the inward slopes of these mountains are part of Eretz Yisrael, and the outward slopes are "foreign parts." (Note, however, that the Mount Hor mentioned in *Numbers*, ibid., as the northern border, is not to be confused with the mountain of a similar name in the wilderness of Zin in the

---

[*Deuteronomy* 30:3]: HASHEM *your God will return* [וְשָׁב] *with your captivity.* The verse does not read וְהֵשִׁיב, *and He shall bring back*, but וְשָׁב, *and He shall return.* This teaches that the Holy One, blessed is He, will return with them from the places of exile (*Megillah* 29a),

[See also comm. to *Eichah* 1:5 s.v. עוֹלָלֶיהָ, ArtScroll ed. page 59; and *Overview*, ibid., page xlii.]

לְבַבְתִּנִי אֲחֹתִי כַלָּה לְבַבְתִּנִי °בְּאַחַד ט
[°בְּאַחַת ק] מֵעֵינַיִךְ בְּאַחַד עֲנָק מִצַּוְּרֹנָיִךְ:

southeast on which Aaron died.)]

[*Mount Senir* is the name by which the Emorites call Mount Hermon (*Deuteronomy* 3:9), the snowcapped mountain range on northern Eretz Yisrael on what is today the border with Lebanon and Syria. *Rashi on Deuteronomy* ibid. notes that שְׂנִיר means "snow" in Ashkenaz (German = *schnee*) and in Canaanite. See also *I Chronicles* 5:23 where Senir and Hermon are listed separately, as in our verse.]

From the dens of lions, from the mountains of leopards [an obvious allegorical reference to the lair of Israel's heathen oppressors in exile].

(The *Midrash* [*Shemos Rabbah* 23:5] explains *lions' den* as referring to the exile in Babylon and Mede, and *leopards* to Edom. The *Midrash* to our verse refers *lions* to Sichon and Og [as noted in *Rashi* above] "who were proud and mighty like a lion; for there was but a day's journey between them and yet neither came to the aid of the other." *Leopards* refers to the Canaanites who were bold like leopards, for although their numbers were small they did not hesitate to sally forth against Israel.)

[In the literal sense, we learn from this verse that these mountain ranges were once the habitat of wild animals. Leopards are still found in the area, but lions, which inhabited the hills until the Middle Ages, are now extinct there.]

Shir Chadash notes that the reference is to the nations of our exiles whose language we do not understand. The comparison of the oppres-

sors to wild beasts is apt, he continues, and is alluded to in the curses in *Deuteronomy* 28:49: "HASHEM will bring a nation against you from the end of the earth ... *a nation whose language you shall not understand.*" Just as wild animals haven't the faculty of speech with which to understand your protestations of good will and lack of malice, similarly *that nation whose language you shall not understand.*

9. לְבַבְתִּנִי אֲחֹתִי כַלָּה — [lit., *You have captured My heart, My sister, O bride.*] I.e., you have drawn my heart to you (*Rashi*).

"To you is the '*heart*' of all the nations," says God. As the *Kuzari* notes: "Israel to the nations is like the heart to the body" (*Markevos Ami*).

[On the simile of *sister* cf. the use of אִמּוֹ, *His mother*, in 3:11.]

Divrei Yedidiah explains the connotation of *sister* as referring to זְכוּת אָבוֹת, *ancestral merit*, by virtue of which God showers His love upon us. Even a brother's daughter is sometimes called "sister" implying that this love is due to the filial relationship as Abraham said of Sarah, daughter of his brother Haran [*Genesis* 20:12]: *And moreover, she is indeed my sister, the daughter* [i.e., *granddaughter* (*Rashi*)] *of my father* ... Thus, in a deeply philosophical manner, God loves Israel — by virtue of their being the descendants of His beloved Patriarchs — and thus the term *sister* is expressive of this affinity. The very use of *sister* in these verses implies

⁹*You have captured My heart, My sister, O bride; you have captured My heart with but one of your virtues, with but one of the precepts that adorn you like beads of a necklace resplendent.*

this special relationship which Israel enjoys by virtue of their ancestral merit.

כַּלָּה, *bride*, refers to God's love which Israel enjoys by virtue of its own merits.

Therefore, in our verse, God refers to both *sister* and *bride* indicating the dual love. And similarly, throughout the Book.

In the previous verse which refers to Redemption of Israel after the Destruction, however, זְכוּת אָבוֹת, *ancestral merit*, does not apply, because it is noted in the *Talmud* (*Shabbos* 55a): "ancestral merit ceased" prior to the Destruction. Therefore, in that verse, God avoids the term *sister* and addresses her as *bride*.

Metzudas Tzion, however, regards *sister* as a term of great endearment and כַּלָּה as an adjective: "You, who are כְּלוּלָה, *embracing*, of all kinds of beauty and glory."

לִבַּבְתִּנִי בְּאַחַת מֵעֵינַיִךְ בְּאַחַד עֲנָק מִצַּוְּרֹנָיִךְ — [lit., *you have captured My heart with one of your eyes, with one bead of your necklace.*] I would have loved you exceedingly had you possessed only one of your endearing qualities. How much more so is My heart drawn to you seeing that you possess so many of them! Similarly, the *beads of your necklace* refers to the adornment of מִצְוֹת, *precepts*, by which Israel is distinguished [cf.

comm. to 3:11 s.v. צִיּוֹן] (*Rashi*).

Additionally, translating עֲנָק in its other meaning of *giant*, *Rashi* renders: [*You have captured My heart with*] one of your *giants* [i.e., *Patriarchs*], the individual referred to as *one* [*Ezekiel* 33:24]: Abraham. The Sages similarly apply the verse [*Joshua* 14:15]: *the greatest man among giants* to our father Abraham (*Soferim* 21:9).[1]

Consistent with the allegorical interpretation throughout the Book of עֵינַיִם, *eyes*, as referring to the righteous who are the "eyes" of each generation [cf. comm. 1:15, 4:1], *Rav Yechiel Heller* cites the Talmudic passage [*Yoma* 38b]: "The world exists even for the sake of one righteous person."

Additionally, precepts of the Torah are allegorized as beads, as in *Proverbs* 1:9: וַעֲנָקִים לְגַרְגְּרֹתֶיךָ, *and they* [i.e., instruction and Torah referred to in the previous verse] *shall be beads for your neck*.

He also notes that it is known that the performance of even one precept is sometimes sufficient to salvage one's soul from oblivion.

Rav Heller, therefore, renders our verse as God saying: *Even with one righteous person are you able to capture My heart; and even by performing a single precept do you gain this merit of drawing Me to you.*

1. The reference to necklace in association with Abraham is explained by most commentators as an allusion to the Talmudic statement: "Abraham had a precious stone hung around his neck. Any sick person who gazed upon it was immediately healed" (*Bava Basra* 16b).

מַה־יָּפוּ דֹדַיִךְ אֲחֹתִי כַלָּה מַה־טֹּבוּ דֹדַיִךְ · י

יא מִיַּיִן וְרֵיחַ שְׁמָנַיִךְ מִכָּל־בְּשָׂמִים: נֹפֶת תִּטֹּפְנָה

שִׂפְתוֹתַיִךְ כַּלָּה דְּבַשׁ וְחָלָב תַּחַת לְשׁוֹנֵךְ

יב וְרֵיחַ שַׂלְמֹתַיִךְ כְּרֵיחַ לְבָנוֹן: גַּן | נָעוּל

10. [God continues His praise of Israel. Their love, wherever they displayed it, is recognized.]

מַה־יָּפוּ דֹדַיִךְ אֲחֹתִי כַלָּה — [lit., *How fair was your love, My sister, O bride!*] I.e., how pleasing to Me is your love wherever you have displayed it: Gilgal, Shiloh, Nov, Gibeon [all of which were locations of either the Tabernacle or national altars], and the "House of Eternity" [the Temple in Jerusalem] (*Rashi*).

You endeared yourselves to Me when you had one giant [a reference to Abraham; see comm. to previous verse]. How much fairer are you now when you are an entire nation who loves Me! (*Markevos Ami*).

דֹּד, *love*, as expounded in 1:2 refers to God's beloved, the Sages: "Just as adornments beautify a bride, so do her Sages beautify Israel. Hence: *How fair are your Sages, O Israel*" (*Midrash Lekach Tov*).

מַה־טֹּבוּ דֹדַיִךְ מִיַּיִן וְרֵיחַ שְׁמָנַיִךְ מִכָּל־בְּשָׂמִים — [lit., *how much better your love than wine, and the fragrance of your oils than all perfumes!*]

Fragrance of your oils — i.e., your fine reputation (*Rashi*) [cf. comm. to 1:3].[1]

"Much better is your love than that

of יַיִן, the seventy nations [see comm. to 1:2], and the fine reputation of your righteous people is more pervading than all fragrances" (*Targum*).

Metzudas David interprets *love* as a reference to "faith." He, too, interprets *fragrance of oil* as a reference to "reputation," but explains it as referring to God's reputation. He renders thus: How goodly is your faith in Me ... and the fame of My Holy Name which you promulgate.

11. נֹפֶת תִּטֹּפְנָה שִׂפְתוֹתַיִךְ כַלָּה — [lit., *Sweetness* (or: "honey") *drops from your lips, O bride.*] — in discoursing upon Torah (*Rashi*).

— The Torah of which it is said [*Psalms* 19:11]: הַנֶּחֱמָדִים ... וּמְנֹפֶת צוּפִים, *more desired ... sweeter than the honeycomb*. This refers to the "revealed" portion of Torah which one is obligated to read publicly; hence the use of *lips* implying public speech (*Divrei Yedidiah*).

Divrei Yedidiah notes that because this verse describes the virtues of Torah which are not acquired by inheritance, the term אֲחוֹת, *sister*, denoting ancestral merit [see verse 9] does not apply here. Torah is acquired only by one's own personal diligence. Hence, כַּלָּה, *bride*, with its

---

1. *Rav Yechiel Heller* perceives in this verse God's praise of the Rabbinic ordinances which the Sages erected as "fences" around the Torah. As explained in the comm. to 1:2, דֹּדֶיךָ, *your love*, refers to "Your beloved ones," the injunctions of the Sages, which are more dear than יֵינָהּ שֶׁל תּוֹרָה, *the wine of Torah*. Similarly, prayer today replaces the incense in the Temple, as David beseeched God [*Psalms* 141:2]: *Let my prayer be set before You as the incense*. It is as if David said, "Master of the Universe! When the Temple exists, we offer incense to You, but

IV
10-12

¹⁰ *How fair was your love in so many settings, My sister, O bride; so superior is your love to wine and your spreading fame to all perfumes.*

¹¹ *The sweetness of Torah drips from your lips, like honey and milk it lies under your tongue; your very garments are scented with precepts like the scent of Lebanon.* ¹² *As chaste as a garden locked,*

connotation of personal merit is the appropriate appellation.

דְּבַשׁ וְחָלָב תַּחַת לְשׁוֹנֵךְ — [lit., *honey and milk are under your tongue*.] In continuity with *Divrei Ye-didiah's* interpretation of this verse, this phrase refers to סִתְרֵי תוֹרָה, *the esoteric portions of Torah*, which are also *sweet as honey*, but which must remain *under the tongue*, i.e., not be publicly expounded except to select individuals [see *Chagigah* 13a cited below]. As the *Talmud* [*Kiddushin* 25a] comments, the tongue is an organ that is sometimes exposed and sometimes concealed. Therefore, one must exercise discretion when he "exposes" what should be "hidden."

[The *Talmud* similarly views this verse as God's injunction to Israel not to reveal מַעֲשֵׂה מֶרְכָּבָה, *the Work of the Chariot*, i.e., the mysteries surrounding the visions of Ezekiel (1:4 ff) and Isaiah (Ch. 6):]

Honey and milk are under your tongue — i.e., the things that are sweeter than honey should remain *under* your tongue [in strict conceal-

ment; not to be taught] (*Chagigah* 13a; s.v. *Mishnah* ibid. 11b).

The *Midrash* homiletically comments: "If one discourses on the Torah and his words are not as tasteful as honey and milk, it were better that he had not spoken!"

[The *Kolbo* cites *honey and milk under your tongue* as a reason for the custom of eating dairy foods and honey on Shavuos, the holiday commemorating the giving of the Torah, which is symbolized by honey and milk.]

וְרֵיחַ שַׂלְמֹתַיִךְ כְּרֵיחַ לְבָנוֹן — [lit., *and the scent of your garments is like the scent of Lebanon.*]

And the scent of your garments alludes to the precepts associated with clothing: צִיצִית, *fringes*; תְּכֵלֶת, *purple thread*; בִּגְדֵי כְהוּנָּה, *priestly garments*; אִסּוּר שַׁעַטְנֵז, *the prohibition of wearing shaatnez* [a blend of linen and wool]; all of which God finds as pleasing *as the fine scent of Lebanon* (see below) (*Rashi*).

Scent of garments as explained by

when there is neither altar nor high priest, I beseech You, dear God, accept my prayers in their place" [cf. *Midrash Tehillim* 141].

Accordingly, he renders the verse as God's words of endearment to Israel throughout the generations:

"*How pleasing are your* דּוֹדִים, the extra *mitzvos* you proclaimed upon yourselves; those ordinances which you imposed as 'fences' to guard the Torah are more dear than יֵינָהּ שֶׁל תּוֹרָה, the 'wine' of Torah itself. And more pleasing is רֵיחַ שְׁמָנַיִךְ, the 'fragrance' of your prayers, which were ordained to be uttered in a soft, flowing voice, like oil. These prayers, so uttered, ascend to Me more than all perfumes — i.e., all the sacrificial incenses in place of which these prayers were instituted."

פֶּרֶק ד יג אֲחֹתִי כַלָּה גָּל | נָעוּל מַעְיָן חָתוּם: שְׁלָחַיִךְ

יג־יד פַּרְדֵּס רִמּוֹנִים עִם פְּרִי מְגָדִים כְּפָרִים עִם־

יד נְרָדִים: נֵרְדְּ | וְכַרְכֹּם קָנֶה וְקִנָּמוֹן עִם כָּל־עֲצֵי

לְבוֹנָה מֹר וַאֲהָלוֹת עִם כָּל־רָאשֵׁי בְשָׂמִים:

the *Vilna Gaon* refers to the מִדּוֹת, *manners*, character traits, which are the "garments" of man, because manners are not inborn, but must be acquired and "worn" like the garments with which man clothes himself. The *scent of garments* is the impression they make on others, i.e., the wearer's reputation and public acclaim, much of which is caused by his appearance. As such they are as pleasing to God as *the scent of Lebanon*, i.e., the scent of the sacrifices offered in the Temple [*Lebanon* referring to the Temple "which whitens the sins of Israel" — see comm. to verse 8].[1]

Like the scent of Lebanon — i.e., pleasing to both God and man (*Sforno*).

12. גַּן נָעוּל אֲחֹתִי כַלָּה — [lit., *A garden locked up is my sister, O bride.*] This verse refers to the modesty of the daughters of Israel who shun immorality (*Rashi*).

[The imagery is poignant. Her rare beauty and pervasive charm are controlled by innate modesty and purity. She is like a beautiful garden which is locked to all but its rightful owner.]

גַּל נָעוּל מַעְיָן חָתוּם — [lit., *a spring locked up, a fountain sealed.*] [Having compared her to a garden,

He embellishes the imagery and compares her to a spring and fountain of scarce, precious good water which were sealed by their owners to prevent intrusion by strangers. This is the *garden spring* described in verse 15.]

Rashi comments that גַּל can be translated *spring*, or alternately *gate* from the Aramaic, as in the *Talmudic* expression [*Berachos* 28a]: טְרוֹקוּ גָלֵי, *close the gate!*

The *Midrash* explains this verse as referring specifically to Jewish chastity in Egypt:

"Rav Abba bar Kahana said: Sarah went down to Egypt and guarded herself against immorality [*Genesis* 12:14ff] and all the women [generations later during the period of bondage] guarded themselves for her sake. Joseph went down to Egypt and guarded himself against immorality [*Genesis* 39:7ff] and all the men guarded themselves for his sake. Rav Pinchas said in the name of Rav Chiya: This avoidance of immorality was in itself sufficient merit to procure the deliverance of Israel from Egypt. How do we know? Because it says *a garden locked up is my sister, bride*; and it continues: שְׁלָחַיִךְ, *your*

1. This concept that God is pleased with someone of good character is additionally formulated in the *Talmud* (*Rosh Hashanah* 17a): Whoever forgives the affronts of others is forgiven his own sins; and in *Shabbos* 151b: Whoever displays compassion to his fellow man is shown compassion from Heaven; and in *Berachos* 5b: Whoever busies himself with acts of charity is forgiven all his sins. Thus, as in our verse, good manners achieve atonement for man like רֵיחַ לְבָנוֹן, the Temple sacrifices [see verse 8] (*Divrei Yedidiah*).

שיר השירים [140]

**IV
13-14**   *My sister, O bride; a spring locked up, a fountain sealed.* [13] *Your least gifted ones are a pomegranate orchard with luscious fruit; henna with nard;* [14] *nard and saffron, calamus and cinnamon, with all trees of frankincense, myrrh and aloes with all the chief spices;*

sending forth, i.e., your being sent forth from Egypt [is because you kept yourselves fenced in from immorality like] *an orchard of pomegranates.' "*

13. שְׁלָחַיִךְ פַּרְדֵּס רִמּוֹנִים עִם פְּרִי מְגָדִים — [lit., *Your arid areas* (or: *offshoots*) *are an orchard of pomegranates with precious fruits.*]

As reflected in the translation, *Rashi* explains שְׁלָחַיִךְ as an arid field in need of constant irrigation (comp. the Talmudic term בֵּית הַשְּׁלָחִין, *a field which needs irrigation* [Mishnah, *Moed Katan* 1:1]; antonym of בֵּית בַּעַל, *a field sufficiently watered by rain* and requiring no artificial irrigation [Mishnah *Bava Basra* 3:1]). He interprets the verse as praising the *dry ones* [alluding to those with little merit (*Tz'ror HaMor*)][1] and renders: *[Even] your arid ones are as full of goodness as an orchard of pomegranates [with precious fruits,* and the spices enumerated in the following verse]. This refers to the youngsters in Israel who strive to develop and increase [מַרְטִיבִין = *moisten*] good deeds like an orchard of pomegranates.

Interpreting this verse as the conclusion of v. 12, *Tz'ror HaMor* renders: Although the garden is now "locked up," in the future even its arid areas will be like an abundant pomegranate orchard.

[*Ibn Ezra, Metzudas Tzion,* and others translate שְׁלָחַיִךְ, *your offshoots* (lit., *your sendings forth*), i.e., your

branches which spring forth from you, as in *Isaiah 16:8:* שְׁלֻחוֹתֶיהָ נִטָּשׁוּ, *her offshoots were stretched out:*]

"Because of your many righteous deeds, and the modesty alluded to in the previous verses, I am confident that *your offshoots will be an orchard of pomegranates,* i.e., your offspring which will descend from you will be as full of wisdom as the pomegranate is full of seeds. And their fine character traits will be like the most precious fruit" (*Metzudas David*).

כְּפָרִים עִם־נְרָדִים — [lit., *henna with nard.*] — types of spices (*Rashi*); כְּפָרִים being the plural of כֹּפֶר as in 1:14; and נְרָדִים the plural of נֵרְדְּ (*Ibn Ezra; Ibn Janach*) — i.e., your descendants' reputation will waft as far as the fragrance of fine spices (*Metzudas David*).

14. נֵרְדְּ וְכַרְכֹּם קָנֶה וְקִנָּמוֹן עִם כָּל־עֲצֵי לְבוֹנָה מֹר וַאֲהָלוֹת עִם כָּל־רָאשֵׁי בְשָׂמִים — [lit., *Nard and saffron, calamus and cinnamon, with all trees of frankincense, myrrh, and aloes, with all the chief spices.*]

This verse continues to allegorize the "fragrance" of their highest virtues — equal to that of the finest spices (*Metzudas David*).

The *Midrash* identifies the various spices: *Nard* is nard oil; ... *cinnamon* used to grow profusely in Eretz Yisrael and the goats and deer grazed on it; *myrrh* is the oil of myrrh.

אֲהָלוֹת, *aloes,* is foliatum. Why

1. [Conversely, *moisture* refers to good deeds. See comm. to 6:11 s.v. לִרְאוֹת בְּאִבֵּי הַנָּחַל.]

פֶּרֶק ו טו מַעְיַן גַּנִּים בְּאֵר מַיִם חַיִּים וְנֹזְלִים מִן־לְבָנוֹן:
טו־טז טז עוּרִי צָפוֹן וּבוֹאִי תֵימָן הָפִיחִי גַנִּי יִזְּלוּ בְשָׂמָיו
יָבֹא דוֹדִי לְגַנּוֹ וְיֹאכַל פְּרִי מְגָדָיו:

is it called *ahalos?* Rav Adda explained it in the name of Rav Yehudah: Because it comes to us by way of אֲהָלִים [*ohalim*], *tents* [i.e., it is imported by Bedouin tent-dwellers (*Matnos Kehunah*)]. The Rabbis, however, say: Because it spreads in the Tent [i.e., when used as incense in the Holy Service, its smoke spread in the אֹהֶל מוֹעֵד, *Tent of Meeting* (*Radal*); or: its fragrance is pervasive enough to fill a tent (*Etz Yosef*)]. It was with this fragrance that the Jews perfumed themselves during their forty years in the desert.

15. מַעְיַן גַּנִּים בְּאֵר מַיִם חַיִּים — [lit., (you are) *A garden spring; a well of living waters.*] This verse continues the simile of arid fields begun in verse 13. God now praises Israel as the spring which enables the fields to be fruitful. Allegorically, this is God's praise of Jewish women who practice the ritual immersions and purifications (*Rashi*).

[The reference here to *spring* further describes the spring mentioned in verse 12, see comm. there.]

וְנֹזְלִים מִן־לְבָנוֹן — [lit., *and streams from Lebanon.*] From clean places, unclouded with mud (*Rashi*).

According to *Metzudas David*, this verse explains why *your offshoots will become an orchard of pome-*

granates [verse 13]: Because the spring which waters the garden is a well of running water, an uncontaminated well surrounded by a *locked-up garden* [verse 12] and furthermore these waters are sweet because they *stream down from the hills of Lebanon.* It is therefore only natural that such waters should succeed in producing a fine pomegranate orchard.

Allegorically: It is only just that Israel, whose ancestors are so righteous and modest, should produce offspring who so resemble them.

This verse also refers to the Torah, both its Written and Oral parts, which is a source of sustenance; *a garden spring, a well of living water which streams from Lebanon* — i.e., which emanates from God Who dwells in the Temple referred to as Lebanon (*Ibn Aknin*).

16. עוּרִי צָפוֹן וּבוֹאִי תֵימָן הָפִיחִי גַנִּי יִזְּלוּ בְשָׂמָיו — [lit., *Awake O north (wind) and come, O south! Blow (upon) my garden, let its spices flow out.*][1]

Having found delight in your fragrances — says God — and in the beauty of your dwellings, I hereby command the winds, north and south, to blow upon your garden to waft your fragrance afar. Allegorically this refers to the return of the dispersed exiles with

1. "In this world when the south wind blows, the north wind does not blow, and when the north wind blows, the south wind will not blow. But in the time to come, God will bring a strong wind on the world and drive the two winds together so that both will be in action" (*Midrash*).
North esoterically alludes to wealth, and *south* to wisdom [cf. *Bava Basra* 25b: "He who

15 *purified in a garden spring, a well of waters alive and flowing clean from Lebanon.*

16 *Awake from the north and come from the south! Like the winds let My exiles return to My garden, let their fragrant goodness flow in Jerusalem.*

Israel: *Let but my Beloved come to His garden and enjoy His precious people.*

the coming of the Messiah. The nations among whom they live will be so overwhelmed by the miracles preceding Redemption that they personally will deliver the Jews to Eretz Yisrael [see *Isaiah* 66:20] as their gift to God. When the Temple is built, the Jews will go there for the festivals and they will say to God, "Come to Your garden, O Beloved. If You are there, all is there" (*Rashi*).

God will thus awaken the slumbering exiles, as it is written [*Isaiah* 26:19]: *awake and sing, you who dwell in dust:* and [ibid. 43:6]: *I will say to the north, Give up; and to the south, Keep not back* (*Midrash Lekach Tov*).

This verse sums up God's manifold acclaim of Israel, praising her for maintaining His love throughout exile, and His promise to redeem her before *the day blows and the shadows flee.* He now blesses her that she maintain her vitality in the paths of Torah and precepts. He commands the north and south winds — symbolic of man's spiritual and physical requirements — to *blow* — i.e., be

bestowed in abundance — upon His *garden,* Israel, so that her *spices* can thrive and proliferate (*Markevos Ami*).

יָבֹא דוֹדִי לְגַנּוֹ וְיֹאכַל פְּרִי מְגָדָיו — [lit., *let my Beloved come to His garden and eat its precious fruit.*] If You are there, all is there (*Rashi*).

Israel, nurtured from God's beneficence, responds, *Come, my Beloved to His garden* [*His* being in the respectful third person] — i.e., Come, let Your *Shechinah* dwell upon Israel — even as they are dispersed in their exiles, *and let Him eat of His precious fruit,* i.e., and savor of the Torah and good deeds that I have been performing in exile, awaiting His redemption (*Markevos Ami*).

This is an appeal that God once again dwell in the Temple *and eat of its precious fruit,* i.e., the sacrifices (*Midrash Lekach Tov*); "and savor of the sacrifices which we shall offer up to Him" (*Targum*).

[To everyone else Israel is modestly *a garden locked up* (verse 12). It is only God, her *Beloved,* the lawful possessor of the garden Who is

desires to become wise should turn to the south," etc.]. This is the implied meaning of the above *Midrash.* In this world, he upon whom the wind [i.e., "spirit"] of wealth blows, the wind of wisdom does not blow. But in the time to come, both winds will blow together and תּוֹרָה וּגְדוּלָה, *Torah and greatness,* will reign united. The time will then be ripe for the Messiah to come (*Migdal David*).

בָּאתִי לְגַנִּי אֲחֹתִי כַלָּה אָרִיתִי מוֹרִי עִם־ א
בְּשָׂמִי אָכַלְתִּי יַעְרִי עִם־דִּבְשִׁי שָׁתִיתִי
יֵינִי עִם־חֲלָבִי אִכְלוּ רֵעִים שְׁתוּ וְשִׁכְרוּ

bidden to come and partake of its precious fruit.]

Israel says to the Holy One, blessed is He: Can the master of the house make a feast for his visitors and not join his guests? Shall a bridegroom prepare a feast and not sit down with them? If it pleases You: *Let my Beloved come to His garden and eat its precious fruit* — i.e., come dwell among us! (*Midrash, Numbers* 13:3).

V

Prefatory Remarks

[The division of the Bible into chapters is of non-Jewish origin, introduced in the Middle Ages by Christian Bible printers. Most Jewish Bibles followed these divisions for purposes of uniformity and identification. In Masoretic manuscripts the text is divided according to several traditional systems, some of which unfortunately have never found their way into printed editions. Most notable among the traditional systems are the פְּתוּחוֹת (open-line divisions) and סְתוּמוֹת (closed spaces), as found in ancient Hebrew manuscripts and Torah Scrolls.

According to the Masorah, therefore, this verse does not begin a new chapter and a new trend of thought. Hence, the commentators view this verse contextually as God's response to Israel's request that His Shechinah descend upon them "and eat of their precious fruit."

"I have already done as you requested!" He replies.]

1. בָּאתִי לְגַנִּי אֲחֹתִי כַלָּה — [lit., *I have come into My garden, My sister, O bride.*] When the Tabernacle was set up (*Rashi*).

As it is written [*Exodus* 40:33,34]: *And Moses completed the work. And the cloud covered the Tent of Meeting, and the glory of HASHEM filled the Tabernacle* (*Midrash, Numbers* 13:2).

Metzudas David interprets the verb בָּאתִי in the future-perfect tense and allegorically renders: God said, "Yes! I will come into My garden, i.e., cause My *Shechinah* to dwell in your midst; I will send down My fire to consume your many offerings [cf. *Leviticus* 9:24], and Aaron and his sons will then partake of the remainder."

אָרִיתִי מוֹרִי עִם־בְּשָׂמִי — [lit., *I have gathered My myrrh with My spice.*]

This refers to the incense which the princes of the tribes offered [at the Dedication (*Numbers* Ch. 7)] on the Outer Altar. *Rashi* [citing the *Midrash*] notes that this offering was doubly unusual; first, because incense was permitted only upon the inner Golden Altar, and because only at the dedication of the Tabernacle were individuals permitted to bring incense as a freewill offering — yet God accepted their sacrifice.

Harav Gifter points out that the decision of the princes to attempt such a proscribed offering was in the nature of הוֹרָאַת שָׁעָה [a temporary emergency measure permitted under highly unusual circumstances. The right to determine the existence of such conditions is given over only to acknowledged prophets or the Sanhedrin. (See

V HASHEM: *To your Tabernacle Dedication, My sister, O bride,*
1 *I came as if to My garden. I gathered My myrrh with My spice from your princely incense; I accepted your unbidden as well as your bidden offerings to Me; I drank your libations pure as milk. Eat, My beloved priests! Drink and become God-intoxicated, O friends!*

Rambam, Yesodei HaTorah 9:3)].

Only myrrh is mentioned explicitly, because it was one of the most important ingredients of the קְטֹרֶת, *mixture of incense*, used in the Temple (*Vilna Gaon*).

אָכַלְתִּי יַעְרִי עִם־דִּבְשִׁי — [lit., *I have eaten My honeycomb with My honey.*] The honeycomb is generally discarded after its honey is sucked out. But, out of intense love, I [i.e., God] "ate" both what is proper and what is not proper — i.e., I accepted the princes' קְטֹרֶת נְדָבָה, *freewill offerings of incense*, as well as שְׂעִירֵי חַטָּאת, *the goats for a sin-offering*, which the princes sacrificed and which I accepted that very day, although a sin-offering is otherwise not brought as a נְדָבָה, *freewill gift* (*Rashi*).

Divrei Yedidiah, however, comments that יַעְרִי, *My honeycomb*, alludes to the עוֹלָה, *burnt-offerings*, which were consumed on the Altar in their entirety — including the bones — hence the allusion of *honeycomb*, i.e., that which is usually discarded.

שָׁתִיתִי יֵינִי עִם־חֲלָבִי — [lit., *I have drunk My wine with My milk.*] This refers to the נְסָכִים, *wine-libations*, which were "sweeter" and more pure than milk (*Rashi*).

Divrei Yedidiah interprets חֲלָבִי [*My milk*] as referring to the חֵלֶב, *fat portions*, of the שְׁלָמִים, *peace-*

offerings. Since it melted into a liquid state when burned on the Altar, the verb *drink* is appropriate.

אִכְלוּ רֵעִים שְׁתוּ וְשִׁכְרוּ דּוֹדִים — [lit., *Eat, friends; drink and become intoxicated, O beloved.*]

Eat, friends — this refers to the priests who ate portions of most offerings. In the Tent of Meeting: Aaron and his sons, who were the only priests; in later years and in the Temple: all the priests. *Drink and become intoxicated, O beloved* is addressed to Israel who partook of the flesh of the peace-offerings which were offered at the dedication of the Altar (*Rashi*). [... As detailed in *I Kings* 8:62ff.]

Drink and become intoxicated refers in the literal sense only to the people, but not to the priests who were forbidden to drink wine or liquor prior to performing the Divine service (*Divrei Yedidiah*).

[The translation *become intoxicated* is literal. The implication as explained by the commentators is: *drink abundantly*. As reflected in the translation, the allegorical meaning is: *become God-intoxicated!* — i.e., a spiritual intoxication resulting from the love of God. See *Foreword* and *Overview*.]

The *Midrash* notes: "God was like a king who had made a feast and

פֶּרֶק ה ב דּוֹדִים: אֲנִי יְשֵׁנָה וְלִבִּי עֵר קוֹל | דּוֹדִי
ב   דוֹפֵק פִּתְחִי־לִי אֲחֹתִי רַעְיָתִי יוֹנָתִי תַמָּתִי
שֶׁרֹאשִׁי נִמְלָא־טָל קְוֻצּוֹתַי רְסִיסֵי לָיְלָה:

invited guests when it happened that an insect fell into the soup. Had the king refused to partake, all would have refused to partake, but when the king took some, all took [i.e., the freewill nature of the princes' incense and sin-offering, a disqualification under the law of the Temple service, is comparable to an insect falling into the soup. Therefore they required God's express command to partake thereof]" (*Midrash*).

[The *Midrash* also pictures God as the ideal host:] "God was like a king who made a feast and invited guests, and then went around among them saying: '[Eat friends] … I hope you like it, I hope you enjoy it.' "

2. [The following verses beautifully and tragically allegorize the period of the First Temple and its destruction; Israel's evil ways; God's many compassionate warnings to repent; their recalcitrance followed by His display of wrathful vengeance. They repented, but it was too late: His prophetically foretold Decree of imminent Destruction was not to be annulled.]

אֲנִי יְשֵׁנָה וְלִבִּי עֵר — [lit., *I (was) asleep but my heart (was) awake*.] Israel remorsefully recalls how, secure in the peaceful period of the First Temple, she neglected the service of God, as if she slumbered and slept; but, *my heart*, i.e., God, Who is *the Rock*

of my heart [Psalms 73:26], nevertheless was wakeful to guard me and grant me goodness (*Rashi* based upon *Pesikta d'Rav Kahana*).[1]

I.e., although I was neglectful of the commandments like one asleep, God remained ready to arouse me from my slumber (*Tz'ror HaMor*).

The *Targum* paraphrases: "After all this, the people of the House of Israel sinned, and He delivered them into the hands of Nebuchadnezzar, king of Babylon, and He led them into captivity; and in captivity they resembled a man in deep slumber who cannot be roused from his sleep. The voice of God enlightened them by means of the prophets. He would rouse them from the slumber of their hearts saying: Open your mouth, pray and praise Me, O My sister, My love, Assembly of Israel, resembling the dove in the perfection of your works, for [anthropomorphically] the hair of My head is full of your tears, as a man whose head is soaked with the dew of Heaven; and the locks of My hair are filled with the drops of your eyes, as a man whose locks of hair are filled with raindrops, that fall in the night."

קוֹל דּוֹדִי דוֹפֵק — [lit., *(Hark!) The sound of my Beloved knocking!*] I.e., [throughout all my slumbering] He caused His *Shechinah* to dwell upon the prophets issuing daily warnings

---

1. The *Midrash*, understanding *heart* also in its usual Biblical sense referring to the seat of intellect and emotion, interprets this verse as Israel addressing God: "Master of the Universe! Alas, *I am asleep* in lack of sacrifices, *but my heart is awake* for the recital of *Shema* and Prayer; *I am asleep* in lack of the Temple, but *my heart is awake* for synagogues and houses of study; *I am asleep* in ignorance of the time set for Redemption, nevertheless, *my heart is*

²I let my devotion slumber, but the God of my heart was awake! A sound! My Beloved knocks! He said, "Open your heart to Me, My sister, My love, My dove, My perfection; admit Me and My head is filled with dewlike memories of Abraham; spurn Me and I bear collections of punishing rains in exile-nights."

through them [a reference to *Jeremiah 7:25: From the day your forefathers left the land of Egypt until this day, I sent to you all My servants, the prophets, daily*] (*Rashi*).

[In the Hebrew, there is an accented pause after the word קוֹל, *the sound*, indicating that it is not modified by the word דּוֹדִי, *my Beloved*, but should be rendered as an exclamatory remark. A preferable literal translation might be: *A sound! My Beloved knocks!* For the translation *Hark!* in this context, see 2:8.]

פִּתְחִי־לִי אֲחֹתִי רַעְיָתִי יוֹנָתִי תַמָּתִי — [lit., *Open to Me* (i.e., *let Me in*), *My sister, My love, My dove, My perfect one.*] And do not cause Me to depart from you (*Rashi*).

It was with such terms of endearment [*sister, love,* etc.] that He constantly tried to arouse me to repentance (*Tz'ror HaMor*).

תַמָּתִי, *My perfect one* — i.e., nation which was commanded [*Deuteronomy 18:13*]: *You shall be perfect with HASHEM, your God* (*Akeidas Yitzchak*).

I.e., nation which endures exile and suffering with a perfect heart (*Alshich*).

The Holy One, blessed is He, said to Israel: "My sons, open for Me an opening of repentance no bigger than the eye of a needle, and I will make the opening wide enough for wagons and carriages to pass through" (*Midrash*).

[Cf. the Talmudic dictum (*Shabbos 104a*): "He who commences to purify himself is assisted from Heaven."]

שֶׁרֹאשִׁי נִמְלָא־טָל — [lit., *for My head is filled* (i.e., *drenched*) *with dew.*] I.e., I am drenched with pleasure at the Patriarch Abraham whose deeds were pleasing to Me as dew, and I now come to you ready to shower you with blessings and reward if you will but return to Me (*Rashi*).

קְווּצוֹתַי רְסִיסֵי לָיְלָה — [lit., *My locks* (are damp with) *the rains of the night.*] As reflected in the translation, *Rashi* explains that the phrase *rains of the night* has a harsher effect than dew and indicates hardship and punishment, thus indicating that this phrase is in contrast with the previous verse. Homiletically taking קְווּצוֹת as a homonym of קְבוּצוֹת, *collections*, he allegorically renders: *My collections contain punishments*, i.e., "I have a collection of punishments

awake, anticipating Redemption. *I am asleep* for lack of Redemption, but *the heart* of the Holy One, blessed is He, *is awake* to redeem me. As Rav Chiyah bar Abba noted, where do we find that the Holy One is actually identified as the 'heart' of Israel? In the verse [*Psalms 73:26*]: *God is the Rock, my heart.*"

פֶּרֶק ה ג פָּשַׁטְתִּי אֶת־כֻּתָּנְתִּי אֵיכָכָה אֶלְבָּשֶׁנָּה
ג-ה ד רָחַצְתִּי אֶת־רַגְלַי אֵיכָכָה אֲטַנְּפֵם: דּוֹדִי
שָׁלַח יָדוֹ מִן־הַחוֹר וּמֵעַי הָמוּ עָלָיו:
ה קַמְתִּי אֲנִי לִפְתֹּחַ לְדוֹדִי וְיָדַי נָטְפוּ־מוֹר
וְאֶצְבְּעֹתַי מוֹר עֹבֵר עַל כַּפּוֹת הַמַּנְעוּל:

with which to exact retribution from those who forsake and despise Me."

Alternately, *Rashi* suggests that *dew* and *rains of the night* might both be interpreted with a positive connotation as God saying: "I stand ready to shower you with reward for the *mitzvos* that are as easy to perform as *dew* as well as those *mitzvos* which are as difficult and inconvenient as *rains of the night*."

3. [Continuing the metaphor, Israel reacts to God's "knocking on the door" with the following rationale:]

פָּשַׁטְתִּי אֶת־כֻּתָּנְתִּי אֵיכָכָה אֶלְבָּשֶׁנָּה רָחַצְתִּי אֶת־רַגְלַי אֵיכָכָה אֲטַנְּפֵם — [lit., *I had (already) taken off my robe, how shall I don it? I had (already) washed my feet, how shall I soil them?*]

Allegorically: "I had already accustomed myself to the service of other gods and I had even accepted their ways as proper — how can I possibly return to HASHEM?" (The verse — in the literal sense — reflects the thoughts of a straying wife who did not wish to open the door for her husband) (*Rashi*).

... Hearing the above reply, the Sovereign of the Universe replied to them through the prophets: "And as for Me, I have already removed My Presence from your midst. How then can I return, seeing that you have done these evil things? And having cleansed My feet of your

uncleanness, how can I soil them in your midst through your wicked actions?" (*Targum*).

Metzudas David explains this as one, who, ready to retire, is reluctant to dress again. Allegorically he refers it to the Jews in Babylon who became acculturated in their new country and were not well disposed toward sustaining the hardships of travel back to Eretz Yisrael.

4. [But when, in response to her recalcitrance] ...

דּוֹדִי שָׁלַח יָדוֹ מִן־הַחוֹר — [lit., *My Beloved sent forth His hand from the portal* (or: *hole*) (of the door).] I.e., when I responded that I would not repent from my newly chosen idolatrous ways, *He sent forth His hand* and displayed His vengeance in the days of Ahaz [king of Judah], by bringing upon him the armies of Aram *who struck him and took a large number of captives from him. And Pekach son of Remaliah* [king of Israel] *killed a hundred twenty thousand people in Judah in one day* ... [see II Chronicles 28:5, 6] (*Rashi*).

The *Midrash* comments on the imagery of this verse: *He sent forth His hand from the portal of the door* — like a poor man asking for alms. [For despite its disloyalty and transgressions, God pleaded with Israel to repent.]

³ *And I responded, "I have doffed my robe of devotion; how can I don it? I have washed my feet that trod Your path; how can I soil them?"*

⁴ *In anger at my recalcitrance, my Beloved sent forth His hand from the portal in wrath, and my intestines churned with longing for Him.* ⁵ *I arose to open for my Beloved and my hands dripped myrrh of repentant devotion to Torah and God, and my fingers flowing with myrrh to remove the traces of my foolish rebuke from the handles of the lock.*

[After which Israel changed its ways]...

וּמֵעַי הָמוּ עָלָיו — [lit., *and my intestines stirred for Him.*] [*Intestines* being used interchangeably with *heart* as the Biblical term referring to the seat of emotion. Cf. *Jeremiah* 31:19; *Lamentations* 1:20, 2:11.]

5. ... [And becomes righteous in the service of God] ...

קַמְתִּי אֲנִי לִפְתֹּחַ לְדוֹדִי וְיָדַי נָטְפוּ־מוֹר — וְאֶצְבְּעֹתַי מוֹר עֹבֵר עַל כַּפּוֹת הַמַּנְעוּל [lit., *I rose to open for my Beloved and my hands dripped with myrrh; and my fingers flowing with myrrh upon the handles of the lock.*]

In eager and tender delight she rose to unbolt the door as one who perfumes herself to be endearing to her husband (*Rashi*).

Allegorically, *Rashi* explains that this refers to Israel's reaction to God's wrath as described in verse 4. Hezekiah, Ahaz's son, [reacted to His father's punishment by] repenting with all his heart and sought God. His entire generation was perfect and there never arose in Israel another generation like it. As the *Talmud* [*Sanhedrin* 94b] relates: [Hezekiah planted a sword by the door of the

house of study and proclaimed: "He who will not study the Torah will be pierced with the sword."] They searched from Dan to Beersheva and found no ignoramus; from Gabath to Antipris, and found no boy or girl, man or woman who was not thoroughly versed in the [intricate and difficult] laws of purity and impurity. This is the significance of *my hands dripped with myrrh*. [I.e., in my attempt to make myself as pleasing to Him as possible, I prepared myself by figuratively anointing and purifying myself with precious ointment — its effects overflowing — thus removing the foul odor of my past deeds (*Akeidas Yitzchak; Alshich; Metzudas David*).] ... Even of יֹאשִׁיָּהוּ, *Josiah*, is it recorded [*II Kings* 23:25]: *Before him there had never been a king like him who returned to* HASHEM *with all his heart* because he witnessed the punishment that befell [his grandfather] Menashe and [his father] Amon in fulfillment of: *He sent forth His hand from the portal of the door and my intestines stirred for him.*

The *Midrash* explains the seemingly redundant אֲנִי [I] to be an emphatic statement: "It was *I* who

פֶּרֶק ה ו פָּתַחְתִּי אֲנִי לְדוֹדִי וְדוֹדִי חָמַק עָבָר
ו־ז נַפְשִׁי יֵצְאָה בְדַבְּרוֹ בִּקַּשְׁתִּיהוּ וְלֹא
ז מְצָאתִיהוּ קְרָאתִיו וְלֹא עָנָנִי: מְצָאֻנִי
הַשֹּׁמְרִים הַסֹּבְבִים בָּעִיר הִכּוּנִי פְצָעוּנִי

rose — not the other nations."

The *Targum* explains the simile of *dripping myrrh* to allude to the sacrificial incenses. He paraphrases:

"And as the mighty stroke of God was heavy upon me, I was astounded at my actions. The priests brought the sacrifice and offered up sweet-smelling incense; but it was not accepted for the Lord of the Universe closed the doors of repentance in my face."

6. [But, alas, God's anger was not abated. His Decree was to be enforced.]

פָּתַחְתִּי אֲנִי לְדוֹדִי וְדוֹדִי חָמַק עָבָר — [lit., *I opened for my Beloved, but my Beloved had turned and gone.*] I.e., I responded to my Beloved but it was too late — He did not annul His decree, as it is said of Hezekiah [*Isaiah 39:6-7*]: *Behold, days are coming when everything in your house ... will be carried off to Babylonia ... and some of your children who will issue from you* — Daniel, Hananiah, Mishael, and Azariah. Similarly was Josiah forewarned by Chuldah, the prophetess [*II Kings 22:16*]: *I will bring evil upon this place and upon its inhabitants;* and in addition [ibid. 23:25]: *Before him there had never been a king like him, etc.* ... Nevertheless, HASHEM did not turn back from the fierceness of that great anger with which His anger burned against Judah, on account of all the provocation with which Menashe had provoked Him. And HASHEM said,

I will remove Judah also out of My sight as I have removed Israel, and I will cast off this city, Jerusalem, which I have chosen (Rashi).

נַפְשִׁי יֵצְאָה בְדַבְּרוֹ — [lit., *my soul departed* (i.e., I became faint) *as He spoke.*] I.e., as He uttered these harsh decrees ... because, in effect, He said: I will not now enter, since at first you refused to let Me enter (*Rashi*).

Others perceive *my soul departed* to imply intense prayer as in *my soul poured forth.* But alas, even prayer was of no avail (*Migdal David*).

בִּקַּשְׁתִּיהוּ וְלֹא מְצָאתִיהוּ — [lit., *I sought Him but did not find Him.*] And lest you say that Jeremiah prophesied during this period [(*Jeremiah 3:14, 22; 25:5; 35:15*]: *Repent, O faithless children;* and similarly (*Malachi 3:7*)]: *Return to Me and I will return to you* [i.e., prophecies which would indicate that their sincere repentance *should* have averted the Decree], be aware that the implication was not that repentance would avert the decree entirely but that it could soften the blows and help ease the rebuilding when the exiles eventually returned (*Rashi*).

קְרָאתִיו וְלֹא עָנָנִי — [lit., *I called Him but He did not answer me.*] I.e., I prayed but He did not respond. (Cf. *Jeremiah* Ch. 21,) when Zedekiah asked Jeremiah to inquire of God, and God answered with a stern prophecy of the disaster which was to befall the Jews. See also Chapter 37, and

שיר השירים [150]

⁶*I opened for my Beloved; but, alas, my Beloved had turned His back on my plea and was gone. My soul departed at His decree! I sought His closeness, but could not find it; I beseeched Him, but He would not answer.*
⁷*They found me, the enemy watchmen patrolling the city; they struck me, they bloodied me*

specifically 15:1: *Then said HASHEM to me: Even if Moses and Samuel were to stand before Me [and intercede] I would have no desire for this people* (*Divrei Yedidiah*).

7. מְצָאֻנִי הַשֹּׁמְרִים הַסֹּבְבִים בָּעִיר — [lit., *The watchmen who patrol* (or: *circle*) *the city found me.*] The *watchmen* metaphorically refers to Nebuchadnezzar and his forces who "patrolled" the city to wreak the vengeance of God [i.e., who acted as God's instrument in implementing His plan of retribution against the Jews. The Destruction of the First Temple was to begin] (*Rashi*).[1]

In 3:3, *Rashi* interprets the same word *watchman* as referring to Moses and Aaron whereas here, in 5:7, he renders it as referring to Nebuchadnezzar and his horde, an

apparent incongruity. In truth, however, there is no discrepancy. Any person who carries out the will of God is His *watchman*, whether he does it consciously as did Moses and Aaron, or like Nebuchadnezzar, without even knowing that he was God's instrument. Nebuchadnezzar's purpose, although he was not aware of it, was to force Israel to repent by making them realize that only in God lay their salvation. Therefore, Scripture calls him נְבוּכַדְרֶאצַר עַבְדִי, *My servant Nebuchadrezzar* [*Jeremiah* 25:9], and in that sense, he is here called God's *watchman* (*Harav David Feinstein*).

הִכּוּנִי פְצָעוּנִי — [lit., *they struck me, they wounded me*] [by wreaking Destruction upon Israel.]

[Note the contrast between the "watchmen" described in this verse

1. *Ibn Ezra* [following in part the *Targum* and *Midrash*] allegorically explains verses 2-8 as referring to a later period, beginning with the Babylonian exile, and culminating with the Second Temple.

[Verse 2:] During the Babylonian captivity, I was like a man in slumber, *but my heart was awake* in the deep-seated desire to reunite with the *Shechinah* as before. *The sound of my Beloved knocking* refers to the inspiration with which God stirred Cyrus, king of Persia, [to allow the rebuilding of the Temple in Jerusalem (see *Ezra* 1:1)] and to bid me to return to Eretz Yisrael. *For My head is drenched with dew*, which figuratively has God as saying: "I am drenched" [if one may so express it] "because I do not dwell in a House." Or, *dew* allegorizes the tears from Israel's prayers which ascended on high and *drenched* Him.

[Verse 3:] *I have already taken off my robe* ... refers to Israel's indolence in responding to the call to return to the Land and rebuild the Temple. [See *Overview* to ArtScroll ed. of *Esther* p. xvi: "The righteous Persian monarch gave the order that the Jews might go home again — and only forty-two thousand heeded his call! Forty-two thousand heard the call of prophecy but millions stayed behind."]

[Verse 4:] *My Beloved sent forth His hand* — i.e., His prophets, Haggai and Zechariah [who prophesied about the eventual restoration of the Temple and Jerusalem; see *Haggai* 1:8 and *Zechariah* 1:16] — *from the portal* of heaven.

who react violently by "striking and beating" to the reaction of the watchmen in a parallel verse in 3:3, who depart peacefully.

The contrast is poignant.

In 3:3, as explained in the commentary, Israel seeks her Beloved, God, not as a victim of His wrath, but in longing for Him after 38 years of Divine silence. Israel takes to the "streets" to demonstrate that she is determined to search vigorously for Him in every nook and cranny. The "watchmen" she meets — Moses and Aaron — are themselves searching for the word of HASHEM. Israel asks for their reassurance: *"Have you heard the word of HASHEM?"* They commiserate with her. But, unable to respond affirmatively, they depart, frustrated and silent.

In our verse, however, Israel *smarts* under God's wrath after hearing prophecies of impending destruction and His implacability. Distraught, she takes to the *street* to seek Him and

supplicate before Him; but her repentance is too little and too late. The *watchmen* she meets this time are made of different stuff: they are the villainous foe Nebuchadnezzar and his army who, seeing her distraught and separated from her Beloved, pounce upon her and submit her to the most brutal blows they can mete out. It is all part of God's plan: they are bent upon Israel's annihilation.]

נָשְׂאוּ אֶת־רְדִידִי מֵעָלַי שֹׁמְרֵי הַחֹמוֹת — [lit., *the guards of the walls stripped my mantle from me.*] Interpreting *guards of the walls* as the ministering angels who formerly guarded the walls of Jerusalem [cf. *Isaiah* 62:6], and *my mantle* as the Temple, *Rashi* explains this verse as alluding to the Midrashic account that even the angels assisted in the destruction of the Temple by kindling the fire, as explained in the verse [*Lamentations* 1:13]: *From on high, He sent a fire* [see footnote to *Eichah*, ArtScroll ed., p. 65].

[Verse 5:] *I rose to open for my Beloved* — i.e., I rebuilt the Temple, anticipating that the *Shechinah* would dwell therein as foretold by the prophets. But alas! *my Beloved had turned and gone* — the *Shechinah* did not enter therein as before. And this is the significance of *I became faint for His word* — i.e., as I recalled how He would speak with me previously. *I sought Him, but did not find Him* — [because of the absence of the *Shechinah* and because within forty years of the rebuilding of the Temple, prophecy ceased in Israel (*Or Yohel*)].

Ramban notes in this context the five things which the First Temple had but which the Second lacked: The Ark, the Ark Cover, the Cherubim; the Fire; the *Shechinah*; the Holy Spirit [of prophecy], and the *Urim VeTumim* (*Yoma* 21b).

[As the *Targum* renders: "I desired to ask instruction of the Eternal, but He had removed His Presence from me; my soul longed for the sound of His word, I sought the presence of His glory, but I found it not; I prayed to Him, but He covered the heavens with clouds and would not receive my prayer."]

[Verse 7:] *The watchmen*, i.e., the kings of Greece, *found me. They struck and wounded me* [by their evil decrees] and thus left me barren of *mitzvos* — but nevertheless I remained loyal to Him [v. 8]: and as you nations of the world can testify, *I am sick for His love.*

V

8

wreaking God's revenge on me. They stripped my mantle of holiness from me, the angelic watchmen of the wall.

⁸ I adjure you, O nations destined to ascend to Jerusalem, when you see my Beloved on the future Day of Judgment, will you not tell Him that I bore all travails for love of Him?

---

8. [Israel is in exile. But, faithfully enduring all suffering, they cling to their faith and address their captors:]

הִשְׁבַּעְתִּי אֶתְכֶם בְּנוֹת יְרוּשָׁלָם — [lit., *I adjure you, O daughters of Jerusalem.*] I.e., O nations who are destined to ascend to Jerusalem [see parallel verses in 2:7 and 3:5]. According to *Rashi*, the adjuration in this verse is addressed to Nebuchadnezzar and his armies: "who have seen Chananiah, Mishael, and Azariah submit themselves to the fiery furnace [*Daniel* 3:20], and Daniel cast into the lions' den [ibid. 6:17] in punishment for his praying; and to the generation of Mordechai in the time of Haman."

"So far the Song shows Israel in a dialogue with God and mankind. Now Israel summons mankind to prepare for the moment when it will conduct the dialogue for its part directly with God: You revealed your antithesis from God's love mostly in the way you treated me; therefore, in your first talk with God, you will have to give expression to the

understanding that you have regained for His love!" (*Rav Wolf*).

אִם־תִּמְצְאוּ אֶת־דּוֹדִי — [lit., *If you find my Beloved.*] I.e., in the future, on the Day of Judgment, when you will be called upon to bear witness for me, as is written [*Isaiah* 43:9]: *Let them bring their witnesses and they will be vindicated* (*Rashi*).[1]

Finding God alludes to occasions when you, O heathen nations, will be confronted with obvious manifestations of God's protection and supremacy, and even you will be moved to declare God's greatness, as was Nebuchadnezzar when Chananiah, Mishael, and Azariah survived the fiery furnace, and Cyrus when Daniel survived the lions' den (*Divrei Yedidiah*).

מַה תַּגִּידוּ לוֹ שֶׁחוֹלַת אַהֲבָה אָנִי — [lit., *What shall you tell him? That I am sick with love.*] [I.e., *what* in this context is rhetorical. The intended meaning could be rendered: *This is what you should tell Him.*] When you testify concerning me, tell Him

---

1. [*Rashi's* comment is based on the *Talmud, Avodah Zarah* 3a: The Holy One, blessed is He, will say [to the heathens]: Even some of you will testify that Israel observed the entire Torah. Let Nimrod come and testify that Abraham did not consent to worship idols; let Laban come and testify that Jacob could not be suspected of theft; let Potiphar's wife testify that Joseph was above suspicion of immorality; let Nebuchadnezzar come and testify that Chananiah, Mishael, and Azariah did not bow down to an image; let Darius come and testify that Daniel never neglected the prayers; let Bildad, Tzofar, and Eliphaz testify that Israel observed the whole Torah, as it is said: *Let them* [the nations] *bring their* [own] *witnesses, and they* [Israel] *will be vindicated* (*Isaiah* 43:9).]

פֶּרֶק ה ט מַה־דּוֹדֵךְ מִדּוֹד הַיָּפָה בַּנָּשִׁים מַה־דּוֹדֵךְ
ט-יא , מִדּוֹד שֶׁכָּכָה הִשְׁבַּעְתָּנוּ: דּוֹדִי צַח וְאָדוֹם
יא דָּגוּל מֵרְבָבָה: רֹאשׁוֹ כֶּתֶם פָּז קְוֻצּוֹתָיו

that only for loving Him was I afflicted [חָלִיתִי, *became ill*] with harsh suffering among them! Let Nebuchadnezzar come forth and testify! Let Eliphaz come forth, with Tzofar and all the heathen prophets, and testify that I fulfilled the Torah! (*Rashi*).

— Tell Him that I endured all the travails and sufferings of exile. Thus, my "sickness" is not due to suffering; it comes from being sick for His love (*Vilna Gaon; Metzudas David*).

… And, as a sick person yearns for healing, so do we yearn for deliverance (*Midrash*).

Divrei Yedidiah interprets differently: Israel says to the nations: When you recognize God's greatness testify that I realize that the cause of my suffering is not due to inability on His part to rescue me, or because He has decided to cast me off, never to return to me. I am fully aware that my travail is because חוֹלַת אַהֲבָה אָנִי, *I am sick by virtue of His love for me*: His chastisements are יִסּוּרִים שֶׁל אַהֲבָה, *chastisements of love*, designed to awaken me and bring me to repentance. As it is written [*Proverbs 3:11-12*]: *Do not despise* HASHEM's *discipline, and do not despise His reproof, for* HASHEM *admonishes the one He loves;* … and in the Torah [*Deuteronomy 8:5*]: *As a man will chastise his son, so* HASHEM, *your God, chastises you.*

[See also comm. to חוֹלַת אַהֲבָה in 2:5.]

9. מַה־דּוֹדֵךְ מִדּוֹד הַיָּפָה בַּנָּשִׁים — [lit., *what (makes) your Beloved (better)*

than *(another) beloved, O fairest among women?*] This was the response of the heathens to the Jews: In what way is your God so superior to other gods that you are ready to be burned and tortured for Him? You are handsome, you are mighty. Come intermingle with us (*Mechilta; Rashi*).

I.e., "Why are you so loyal to a God Who has forsaken you? Let us join and become one nation, and together let us serve our god" (*Metzudas David*).

"Why is your Beloved more than another beloved? Why is your God more than other deities? Why is your Protector more than other protectors?" (*Midrash*).

[The simile of *fairest among women* meaning *fairest among nations* appears also in 1:8 where it is uttered by God. Here, being mouthed by the nations it seems to be tinged with an overtone of derisive mockery.]

The nations taunt: Are you truly *the fairest among nations* by virtue of clinging to this God of yours? Surely not! Just look at yourselves; the reverse is true! Therefore, why do you insist upon the superiority of your God over all others, and so adjure us that we should not dare disturb your love and cause Him to love us? Never! It would be better for all if you forgot Him. Join us in serving our god and let us all prosper together (*Alshich*).

מַה־דּוֹדֵךְ מִדּוֹד שֶׁכָּכָה הִשְׁבַּעְתָּנוּ — [lit., *what (makes) your Beloved (better) than (another) beloved, that*

⁹*With what does your beloved God excel all others that you suffer for His Name, O fairest of nations? With what does your beloved God excel all others that you dare to adjure us?*

Israel: ¹⁰*My Beloved is pure and purifies sin, and is ruddy with vengeance to punish betrayers, surrounded with myriad angels.* ¹¹*His opening words were finest*

you so adjure us?] — to so testify about your love (*Rashi*); in that you cling so to Him until death (*Sforno*).

It is bad enough that you clung to Him so while you were the *fairest among nations.* But now that you are in the lowest of depths, why do you still consider Him so superior that you submit to every form of suffering for His Name's sake to such an extent that you obligate us to testify for you as if under oath? (*Tz'ror HaMor*).

10-16. [Israel responds to the nations: "I will describe my Beloved to you — but in the most anthropomorphic of analogies — as a maiden describes her bridegroom."] Then even you will agree that there is no other like Him (*Alshich*).

10. דּוֹדִי צַח וְאָדוֹם — [lit., *My Beloved is clear skinned and ruddy.*] *Rashi* translates צַח, *white* [or: *clear*], as in *Lamentations* 4:7: צַחוּ מֵחָלָב, *they were whiter than milk.*

I.e., He is anxious to "whiten" my deeds even when He sits in judgment as He is depicted [*Daniel* 7:9]: *His garment was white as snow, and the hair of His head was like pure wool* (*Rashi*);

... *And ruddy* [i.e., *red*] — in readiness to exact retribution from His enemies, as Isaiah declared [in surprise upon seeing a vision of God depicted as a solitary and majestic

figure in blood-red vesture approaching victoriously from the direction of Edom, after having wreaked vengeance on Israel's enemies]: *Why is there red on Your raiment, and [why are] Your garments like those of someone treading in a wine vat?* [*Isaiah* 63:2] (*Rashi*).

... *White* signifying purity and atonement and *red* signifying sin and punishment seemingly are contradictory attributes, both of which are embodied within Him simultaneously (*Netziv*).

דָּגוּל מֵרְבָבָה — [lit., *preeminent above ten thousand.*] I.e., preeminent among the many "soldiers" [*angels*] surrounding Him (*Rashi*).

— *Targum* renders: "while His [דֶּגֶל] banner waves over myriads of angels who minister before Him."

... As it is written of Him in *Daniel* 7:10: *a thousand thousands were serving Him and myriads were standing before Him* (*Ibn Ezra; Metzudas David*).

"Just as a [דֶּגֶל] banner is raised above the head of a marching army, so does He tower above all others in strength, eternity, might, and sovereignty" (*Ibn Aknin*).

11. רֹאשׁוֹ כֶּתֶם פָּז — [lit., *His head is (like) finest gold ...*] Interpreting רֹאשׁוֹ, *His head*, to mean *His beginning*, *Rashi* renders: The beginning

פֶּרֶק ה יב תַּלְתַּלִּים שְׁחֹרוֹת כָּעוֹרֵב: עֵינָיו כְּיוֹנִים
יב־יג עַל־אֲפִיקֵי מָיִם רֹחֲצוֹת בֶּחָלָב יֹשְׁבוֹת
יג עַל־מִלֵּאת: לְחָיָו כַּעֲרוּגַת הַבֹּשֶׂם
מִגְדְּלוֹת מֶרְקָחִים שִׂפְתוֹתָיו שׁוֹשַׁנִּים

of his words [i.e., the Ten Commandments, God's direct communication to the entire people] shone forth like the finest gold — as suggested by the verse [*Psalms* 119:130]: *The introduction of Your words illuminate.* By proclaiming the first commandment: *I am HASHEM your God,* He established His sovereignty over them, and then decreed His ordinances upon them.

Metzudas David interprets רֹאשׁוֹ, *His head,* in its literal sense: His *head* is like precious gold; it is more precious than any crown, so, allegorically, is God beyond mortal description; He is above praise.

קְוֻצּוֹתָיו תַּלְתַּלִּים — [lit., *His locks are wavy.*] *Rashi* comments: עַל כָּל קוֹץ וְקוֹץ תְּלֵי תִּלִּים שֶׁל הֲלָכוֹת, "Upon every one of its 'crowns' [i.e., the small lines adorning the tops of many letters in Scriptural Hebrew] there are mounds and mounds of *Halachos,* laws" (cf. *Eruvin* 21b).[1]

[With Torah still being allegorized as the subject, קְוֻצּוֹתָיו is thus regarded as alluding to קוֹץ, *crowns* (lit., *thorn*), and תַּלְתַּלִּים as a double form of תִּלִּים, *mounds.* Render: *The Torah's crowns are piled with mounds and mounds.*]

The *Vilna Gaon* points out that

the simile of *hair* to the "crowns" and minutiae of Torah is apt. Hair is considered by many to be superfluous because it is shorn and serves no useful purpose, but the *Zohar* stresses that much can be discerned from man's hair by those righteous people with the perception to delve into these hidden matters. Similarly, the seemingly superfluous "crowns" on the letters of the Torah unlock great storehouses of knowledge to the initiated (*Divrei Yedidiah*).

שְׁחֹרוֹת כָּעוֹרֵב — [lit., *black as the raven.*] An allusion that the Torah was written in black fire upon white fire (*Rashi*).

As the *Midrash* esoterically comments: The Scroll which God gave to Moses was of white fire and its writing was of black fire. It was itself fire and it was hewn out of fire; completely formed of fire and given in fire, as it says [*Deuteronomy* 33:2]: מִימִינוֹ אֵשׁ דָּת לָמוֹ, *from His right hand He presented the fiery Torah to them.*

12. עֵינָיו כְּיוֹנִים עַל־אֲפִיקֵי מָיִם — [lit., *His eyes are like doves beside brooks of water.*] *His eyes* alludes to God's governing of the Universe. As in *II Chronicles* 16:9: *For HASHEM's eyes roam throughout the land;* and *Psalms* 33:18: *the*

1. The reference is reminiscent of an incident related in the *Talmud, Menachos* 29b:
    When Moses ascended on high, he found the Holy One, blessed is He, making "crowns" for the letters in the Torah. [These are the *taggin:* the three small strokes written on top of the letters שעטנזגץ in the form of a crown.]
    "Why do you add these crowns?" Moses asked [i.e., is there anything lacking in the Torah making these additions necessary?].

שיר השירים [156]

V
12-13

gold, His crowns hold mounds of statutes written in raven-black flame.

¹²*Like the gaze of doves toward their cotes, His eyes are fixed on the waters of Torah, bathing all things in clarity, established upon Creation's fullness.* ¹³*Like a bed of spices are His words at Sinai, like towers of perfume. His comforting words from the Tabernacle are roses*

---

eye of HASHEM *is on those who fear Him* (*Divrei Yedidiah*).

Just as doves gaze toward their "windows" [i.e., "cotes" — see *Isaiah* 60:8], so are His eyes directed toward synagogues and study-houses from which emanates Torah which is compared to water (*Rashi*). [Cf. *Talmudic* dictum (based upon *Isaiah* 55:1): אֵין מַיִם אֶלָּא תּוֹרָה, *water refers to Torah* (*Bava Kamma* 17a).]

רֹחֲצוֹת בֶּחָלָב — [lit., *bathing in milk*.] I.e., when God's "eyes" hover in judgment, they establish the truth: acquitting the righteous and rewarding him for his righteousness; condemning the wicked and punishing him for his evil. [Thus, *milk* alludes to clarity (cf. on verse 10 above s.v. צַח); in this case, the clarity of God's perspective] (*Rashi*).

יֹשְׁבוֹת עַל־מִלֵּאת — [lit., *sitting upon the fullness*.] I.e., upon the fullness of the earth. *The eyes of* HASHEM — *they scan the whole world* (*Zechariah* 4:10) ... *seeing the evil and the good* [*Proverbs* 15:3] (*Rashi*).

Rashi offers an alternative commentary on this verse: *Eyes* refers to Torah scholars whom God provides with eyes to enlighten the world as

man's eyes enlighten him. Just as the dove wanders from cote to cote in quest of food, so do scholars go from the study-house of one sage to that of another seeking explanations of the Torah. *Besides the brooks of water* refers to the study-houses from which the "water" of Torah flows; *bathing in milk* — i.e., they glisten in the "milk" of Torah, whitening [i.e., clarifying] its innermost mysteries; *sitting upon the fullness* — i.e., properly assorting and explaining matters.

[In the literal sense, *Rashi* explains the phrase as a reference to jewels fitting properly in their setting: *fitly set*; neither too deep nor projecting.]

13. לְחָיָו כַּעֲרוּגַת הַבֹּשֶׂם מִגְדְּלוֹת מֶרְקָחִים — [lit., *His cheeks are like a bed of spices, banks (or: towers) of perfume.*] I.e., beds of spices containing banks of sweet herbs which are processed into perfumes (*Rashi*).

Allegorically, this refers to the Utterances at Mount Sinai during which God displayed a friendly, smiling demeanor (*Rashi*).

Cheeks are thus interpreted allegorically as the repository of His organs of speech (*Metzudas David*); the utterances of which are

---

"There will arise a man after many generations," answered God, "Akiva ben Yosef, by name, who will expound עַל כָּל קוֹץ וְקוֹץ, *upon every crown,* תִּלֵי תִּלִּים שֶׁל הֲלָכוֹת, *mounds and mounds of Halachos.*"

יד נְטְפוֹת מוֹר עֹבֵר: יָדָיו גְּלִילֵי זָהָב מְמֻלָּאִים
בַּתַּרְשִׁישׁ מֵעָיו עֶשֶׁת שֵׁן מְעֻלֶּפֶת סַפִּירִים:
טו שׁוֹקָיו עַמּוּדֵי שֵׁשׁ מְיֻסָּדִים עַל־אַדְנֵי־
טז פָז מַרְאֵהוּ כַּלְּבָנוֹן בָּחוּר כָּאֲרָזִים: חִכּוֹ
מַמְתַקִּים וְכֻלּוֹ מַחֲמַדִּים זֶה דוֹדִי וְזֶה רֵעִי
בְּנוֹת יְרוּשָׁלָם:

fragrant as spices. As the *Talmud* [*Shabbos* 88b] comments upon our verse: "With every single word that went forth from the mouth of the Holy One, blessed is He, the whole world was filled with spices [i.e., fragrance]," for His words spiritually purified and prepared the souls of the people, just as fragrant spices revive and rejuvenate the flesh (*Alshich*).

שִׂפְתוֹתָיו שׁוֹשַׁנִּים נֹטְפוֹת מוֹר עֹבֵר — [lit., *His lips are like roses; they drip flowing myrrh.*] I.e., His words in the Tent of Meeting, words of conciliation and atonement, teaching Israel the laws of the various offerings that please God and atone for sin (*Rashi*).

Metzudas David suggests that *His lips* might be interpreted as *His spokesman*, i.e., *His prophets*, who spread His word afar like the fragrance of spices.

The *Targum* paraphrases: "And as for the lips of His scholars engaged in the Torah, they distill taste on every side, while the word issuing from their mouths is as choice myrrh."

14. יָדָיו גְּלִילֵי זָהָב — [lit., *His arms are rods of gold.*] I.e., the Tablets which He gave with His right hand and which *were God's handiwork* [*Exodus* 32:16]. *Rods of Gold* are the עֲשֶׂרֶת הַדִּבְּרוֹת, *the Ten Commandments*, of which it is said [*Psalms* 19:11]: *They*

are more desirable than gold, than even much fine gold. גְּלִילֵי, *rods* [i.e., *rolls*], alludes to the *Midrash*: Rav Yehoshua ben Nechemiah said: The Tablets were of a miraculous nature: they were of hard stone, yet they rolled up [נִגְלָלִין] (*Midrash; Rashi*).

מְמֻלָּאִים בַּתַּרְשִׁישׁ — [lit., *studded with tarshish.*] The Ten Commandments are like rods of gold studded with precious stones because all 613 commandments are alluded to in the Decalogue (*Rashi*).

[*Tarshish* is a precious stone, described by the commentators as blue in color. The Bible names it (*Exodus* 28:20) as one of the stones set into the fourth row of the חֹשֶׁן מִשְׁפָּט, *breastplate of judgment*. Since there is no specific guidance on its identity, I have followed *Rav Hirsch* in *Exodus* ibid., and left the word untranslated. (But see *Rashi* to *Ezekiel* 1:16 where he seems to render "crystal.")]

According to others, the verse allegorizes the expanse of the heavens — product of *His hands* (cf. *Psalms* 8:4: *Your heavens, the work of Your fingers*) — which glow bright like gold, and are studded with jewel-like stars (*Alshich; Metzudas David*).

מֵעָיו עֶשֶׁת שֵׁן מְעֻלֶּפֶת סַפִּירִים — [lit., *his body* (or: *intestines*) *is as shiny as ivory overlaid with sapphires.*]

V
14-16

*dripping flowing myrrh. ¹⁴The Tablets, His handi-
work, are desirable above even rolls of gold; they
are studded with commandments precious as gems,
the Torah's innards are sparkling as ivory intricately
inlaid with precious stone. ¹⁵The Torah's columns are
marble set in contexts of finest gold, its contempla-
tion flowers like Lebanon, it is sturdy as cedars. ¹⁶The
words of His palate are sweet and He is all delight.
This is my Beloved and this is my Friend, O nations destined to ascend to Jerusalem.*

— This alludes to תּוֹרַת כֹּהֲנִים, the Book of וַיִּקְרָא, *Leviticus*, the third of the Five Books of the Torah: just as the intestines are in the midst of the body, *Leviticus* is in the center of the Torah. Although it [the Torah] appears smooth as ivory, in reality, it is full of detailed minutiae. Its phrases and words, despite a surface simplicity, are replete with nuances, meaning, and laws, like smooth ivory intricately overlaid with adornments. This is nowhere more evident than in the Book of *Leviticus* which contains more detailed precepts than any other Book (*Rashi*).

15. שׁוֹקָיו עַמּוּדֵי שֵׁשׁ מְיֻסָּדִים עַל־אַדְנֵי־פָז — [lit., *His legs are pillars of marble set upon sockets of fine gold.*] Legs refer to the columns of the Torah which are interpreted in connection with what follows and what precedes them. What do they resemble? A pillar which has a pedestal below and above. So the sections of the Torah are interpreted by relating them to what follows and what precedes them (*Midrash; Rashi*).

מַרְאֵהוּ כַּלְּבָנוֹן בָּחוּר כָּאֲרָזִים — [lit., *His appearance is like Lebanon, choicest among cedars.*] Whoever

contemplates upon His word finds flowers and shrubs like a blooming forest [*Lebanon* being a forest]. Such is Torah: Whoever meditates therein discovers limitless wisdom and understanding. He is the choicest, just as cedar is the choicest, for building, strength, and height (*Rashi*).

I.e., He so surpasses anything around Him that it is futile to attempt a description of Him by comparison with any other being (*Metzudas David*).

16. חִכּוֹ מַמְתַקִים וְכֻלּוֹ מַחֲמַדִּים — [lit., *His palate* (i.e., *mouth*) *is most sweet; and all of him is a delight.*]

It is written [*Amos 5:4*]: *For thus said HASHEM to the house of Israel: Seek Me and live. Could anything be sweeter than this?! And if a wicked man turns back from his wickedness and acts with justice and righteousness, he shall live* [*Ezekiel 33:19*] — i.e., if he is truly sorry for his misdeeds, his iniquities shall be counted as merits. Could anything be sweeter than this?! (*Rashi*).

זֶה דוֹדִי וְזֶה רֵעִי בְּנוֹת יְרוּשָׁלָם — [lit., *this is my Beloved, and this is my Friend, O daughters of Jerusalem.*] It is for all these virtues that "I am

פֶּרֶק ו א אָנָה הָלַךְ דּוֹדֵךְ הַיָּפָה בַּנָּשִׁים אָנָה פָּנָה

א-ג ב דוֹדֵךְ וּנְבַקְשֶׁנּוּ עִמָּךְ: דּוֹדִי יָרַד לְגַנּוֹ לַעֲרֻגוֹת

ג הַבֹּשֶׂם לִרְעוֹת בַּגַּנִּים וְלִלְקֹט שׁוֹשַׁנִּים: אֲנִי

sick for His love" (*Rashi*).

[This is the triumphant conclusion of her answer to the cynical question posed to her in verse 9. "This sums up the description of my Beloved, O nations of the world! This is why He is more beloved to me than any other, and why I willingly subject myself to every tribulation for the sanctification of His Name."]

VI

1. The nations continue to taunt Israel in future derision (*Rashi*):

אָנָה הָלַךְ דּוֹדֵךְ הַיָּפָה בַּנָּשִׁים — [lit., *Where has your Beloved gone, O fairest among women?*] Where has He gone? Why has He left you alone, widowed? (*Rashi*).

The inference here is: "If He is as you say He is, tell us where He has gone. We will help you in your quest and no longer attempt to sway you from Him" (*Metzudas David*).

This query refers to the period of 52 years after the Destruction of the First Temple during which Judah lay desolate; the roads and villages were deserted, not even cattle or birds inhabited the land [*Yoma* 54a; *Shabbos* 145b; see comm. to *Eichah* 1:1, ArtScroll ed. p.52] (*Divrei Yedidiah*).

There are two questions here.

(a) *Where has your Beloved gone?* and (b) *Where has He turned?* — i.e., with what does He occupy Himself? Since you yourselves don't know the answers, why do you rage so? (*Vilna Gaon*).

[The adjective *fairest among nations* in this context was used previously by the heathens in 5:9. See comm. there.]

[Several commentators, however, detect in these words a sincere appreciation and recognition of Israel's superior moral and ethical qualities. Although bereft of God, and subject to exile — beaten, downtrodden, and oppressed — Israel's sterling qualities shine forth. Even if the appreciation is tinged with envy and disdain, her qualities must be acknowledged.]

אָנָה פָּנָה דוֹדֵךְ וּנְבַקְשֶׁנּוּ עִמָּךְ — [lit., *Where has your Beloved turned, that we may seek Him with you?*]

This verse refers to the period when כּוֹרֶשׁ, *Cyrus*, was inspired by God to allow the rebuilding of the Temple in Jerusalem [see *Overview* to ArtScroll ed. of *Esther* pp. xv-xxii]. When the Jews commenced construction, the heathens harassed them and said: "Where has your Beloved turned? If He is returning to you, we will help you look for Him." In this manner it is recorded [*Ezra* 4:1-2]: *The enemies of Judah and Benjamin heard that the people of the exile were building a Sanctuary for HASHEM, God of Israel. They approached Zerubbabel ... and said: "Let us build with you, for like you, we will seek your God ..."* But

Where has your Beloved gone, O fairest among women? Where has your Beloved turned to rejoin you? Let us seek Him with you and build His Temple with you.

Israel: ² My Beloved has descended to His Temple garden, to His Incense Altar, yet still He grazes my brethren remaining in gardens of exile to gather the roseate fragrance of their words of Torah. ³ I alone

their intention was sinister, designed to disrupt the construction (*Rashi*).

2. דּוֹדִי יָרַד לְגַנּוֹ — [lit., *My Beloved has gone down to His garden.*] He commanded us to build His Temple, and He will surely be there with us (*Rashi*).

[Of course, the term יָרַד, *descended*, is not indicative of the actual direction of God's travel. He is omnipresent and, by definition, cannot "descend." Rather, the term indicates to our limited intellect what we comprehend to be a "descent" from His heavenly spheres to our earthly habitat.]

Israel is thus referred to as a *garden*, reminiscent of the verse [*Isaiah* 5:7]: *For the vineyard of* HASHEM, *Master of Legions, is the House of Israel, and the people of Judah are the shoot of His delight* (*Ibn Aknin*). [See also comm. to 4:12 s.v. גַּן נָעוּל.]

This, then, according to *Divrei Yedidiah*, is the answer of the Jews: When His *Shechinah* departed the Temple, it descended among His people, accompanying them into exile. [See footnote to 4:8.]

לַעֲרֻגוֹת הַבֹּשֶׂם — [lit., *to the beds of spices.*] I.e., the place where the sacrificial incense was burned (*Rashi*).

Metzudas David refers this to the synagogues and study-houses "where God surely 'descended' to

hear the sound of Torah and receive our prayers."

He looks down to and observes the ways of the righteous, the effect of whose deeds wafts in the air like the fragrance of spices (*Ibn Aknin*).

לִרְעוֹת בַּגַּנִּים — [lit., *to graze in the gardens.*] What is more, despite the fact that the Temple was built, He did not neglect those of His children who elected not to return to the Land. He "descended" to graze His sheep in "the gardens" of their dispersion — i.e., He caused His *Shechinah* to descend to the synagogues and study-houses of those "sheep" who remained in the lands of captivity (*Rashi*).

וְלִלְקֹט שׁוֹשַׁנִּים — [lit., *and to pick roses.*] [In consonance with previous references, *rose* is an allegorical allusion to righteousness:] God listens attentively to those who converse in Torah, gathering their merits, and recording them in a Book of Remembrance before Him, as it is written [*Malachi* 3:16]: *Then those who fear* HASHEM *spoke to one another, and* HASHEM *listened and heard, and a book of remembrance was written before Him* (*Rashi*).

The *Vilna Gaon* explains that they thus respond to the double question: (a) *My Beloved has gone down to His garden:* i.e., to His garden par excellence — the Garden of Eden; *to the beds of spices* — the company of the righteous — having removed Himself, so to speak, from this world; and (b) He occupies Himself by *feeding in the gardens,* i.e., by delighting in the presence of the righteous, *picking roses,* i.e., plucking their חִדּוּשֵׁי תוֹרָה, *Torah novellae.*

The *Midrash* interprets *picking roses* as an allusion to God "plucking away" the righteous of Israel at the appropriate time. The *Midrash* illustrates this by a reference to a gardener: Just as he knows the right time for plucking the fruit, so God knows precisely when the proper time comes to remove the righteous from this world, leading them into the Hereafter.

I.e., "He plucks His 'roses' [i.e., the remnants of His people] from among the thorns" (*Sforno*).

Divrei Yedidiah elaborates that the Jews in exile are referred to in 2:2 as a *rose among thorns.* Therefore, He accompanies them in exile anticipating the moments of Redemption when He will *pluck them up* from the midst of the heathen nations.

3. In reply to the offer of the nations that they would help Israel seek God and build a Temple for him, Israel answers (*Rashi*):

אֲנִי לְדוֹדִי — [lit., *I am my Beloved's.*] I.e., *I,* alone, am my Beloved's. You are not His, neither will you assist us in the construction, as it is written [*Ezra* 4:3]: *It is not for you together with us to build a Temple for our God,* and [*Nehemiah* 2:20]:

You have no portion, nor right, nor remembrance in Jerusalem (*Rashi*).

וְדוֹדִי לִי — [lit., *and my Beloved is mine*] [I.e., this exclusive love is mutual.]

This is the ultimate justification. The Community of Israel addresses the nations: "What right have you to ask about Him when you have no share in Him? *I am my Beloved's and my Beloved is mine!* Once I have attached myself to Him, can I separate myself from Him? Once He has attached Himself to me, can He separate from me?" (*Midrash*).

And although *my Beloved has gone to His garden* — i.e., has "confined" Himself to His heavenly spheres, and holds Himself aloof from me — nevertheless, I am confident that *I am [still] my Beloved's and my Beloved is mine.*

For just as I have never forsaken Him for another god, so has He never entirely forsaken me. He is attentive to my studies and prayers and He will yet recompense me for my good deeds (*Metzudas David*).

Rabbi Joseph Elias points out [in his *Passover Haggadah,* ArtScroll ed., comm. to *Kiddush*] that the special mutual relationship between God and Israel is epitomized in our verse. It manifests itself in several ways. For example, we find that God commanded Moses to *take vengeance for the Children of Israel against the Midianites* while Moses told the Jews *to inflict HASHEM's vengeance against Midian* [*Numbers* 31:2-3]. Similarly, he quotes Rabbi Levi Yitzchak of Berditchev who explains

VI

4

am my Beloved's and my Beloved is mine, He Who grazes His sheep in roselike pastures.

HASHEM: ⁴ *You are beautiful, My love, when your deeds are pleasing, as comely now as you once were in Jerusalem*

that the Torah refers to Passover as *the Festival of Matzos*, a name that gives praise to the Jews who left Egypt with nothing but a few matzos, while the Jews refer to it as *Pesach* [the day when God *passed over* our houses], a name that gives praise to God Who saved us.

הָרוֹעֶה בַּשׁוֹשַׁנִּים — [lit., *who feeds (others) among roses*.] I.e., God, Who grazes His sheep amid scenes of tranquil beauty (*Rashi*).

Esoterically: I receive from my Beloved, and He is to me the One Who grazes among the roses, indicative of the Upper Wisdom — everything feeding on that which is above it and being thereby sustained in a series of intertwined mutual relativities — each one dependent upon the spiritual sustenance it derives from the sphere above it (*Ramban*).

4. In the following verses — culminating in verse 11 — God praises Israel even further for all of the above (*Rashi*):

יָפָה אַתְּ רַעְיָתִי כְּתִרְצָה — [lit., *You are beautiful, My love, as Tirzah*.] *Rashi*, quoting the *Sifri*, allegorically interprets *Tirzah* not as a reference to a place, but as a form of the word רְצוּיָה, *pleasing*, *desirable*, and comments: You are beautiful, My love, when you are desirable [i.e., when

you perform deeds that please Me].

I.e., "You are beautiful when you appease [תִּרְצֶה] My anger" — as *Rashi* comments on the verse [*Leviticus* 26:34], אָז תִּרְצֶה הָאָרֶץ: "Then the land *will appease* the wrath of God" (*Tz'ror HaMor*).

The *Midrash* renders in consonance with this: "You are beautiful, My beloved, כְּשֶׁאַתְּ רוֹצָה, *when you desire*. When you desire [to serve God], you have no need 'to learn from anyone else.' "[1]

[*Tirzah*, as explained by the commentators, refers to the ancient Canaanite city of that name (*Joshua* 12:24) which was captured by Joshua. It was subsequently made a royal city by Jeroboam (*I Kings* 16:23), and served as the capital of Israel, i.e., the Northern Kingdom (ibid. 16:8, 15), until the time of Omri, who replaced it with Samaria (*I Kings* 16:23). The city, renowned for its beauty, is also mentioned as the center of the revolution of Menachem (*II Kings* 15:14-16) (*Ibn Ezra; Metzudas David*).]

נָאוָה כִּירוּשָׁלָם — [lit., *comely as Jerusalem*.] I.e., you are as comely now as was Jerusalem in its prime (*Rashi*).

[Jerusalem — the city which was referred to as *perfect in beauty* (*Psalms* 50:2; *Lamentations* 2:15).]

As the *Targum* paraphrases:

---

1. *Harav Gifter* points out that this is alluded to in the *Talmud* [*Berachos* 17a]: "Sovereign of the Universe: It is known full well to You that our will is to fulfill Your will. And what prevents us? The yeast in the dough" [i.e., the evil impulse, which causes a ferment in the heart].

We thus beseech Him to view us from the perspective of our inherent will to do His will. And HASHEM sees us in the light of that beauty.

ה אֲיֻמָּה כַּנִּדְגָּלוֹת: הָסֵבִּי עֵינַיִךְ מִנֶּגְדִּי שֶׁהֵם
הִרְהִיבֻנִי שַׂעְרֵךְ כְּעֵדֶר הָעִזִּים שֶׁגָּלְשׁוּ מִן־
הַגִּלְעָד: שִׁנַּיִךְ כְּעֵדֶר הָרְחֵלִים שֶׁעָלוּ מִן־
הָרַחְצָה שֶׁכֻּלָּם מַתְאִימוֹת וְשַׁכֻּלָה אֵין בָּהֶם:

ה-ו

"Beautiful is the [Second Temple] which you have built for Me, as was the First Temple which King Solomon built for Me in Jerusalem."

אֲיֻמָּה כַּנִּדְגָּלוֹת — [lit., *awe inspiring as an army with banners*.] [The literal translation follows *Ibn Ezra*. See also verse 10.]

Rashi, as reflected in the Translation, interprets this verse thematically as a reference to awe of the Jews which God cast upon the angels while the Second Temple was being built: *I will cast your awe upon the legions of angels to deter them from interfering with your task* [cf. *Ezra*, Chapter 5].

Targum interprets that Israel's dread is upon all the people now, just as it was when their regiments marched in the desert.

Sforno perceives in this phrase an additional allusion to the awe which Alexander felt for Shimon the Righteous.[1]

5. "You are beautiful," says God, "but in the Second Temple I will maintain a hidden aloofness. My *Shechinah* will not descend — neither will you have all the holy utensils you had in the First Temple" (*Divrei Yedidiah*).

הָסֵבִּי עֵינַיִךְ מִנֶּגְדִּי שֶׁהֵם הִרְהִיבֻנִי — [lit., *Turn your eyes away from me,*

for they overwhelm me.] In the literal sense, *Rashi* explains הִרְהִיבֻנִי from the root רהב, *pride, conceit* (cf. *Psalms* 90:10 וְרָהְבָּם, *and their pride*), and comments: It is as if a bridegroom addresses the fiancee whom he adores, "Turn away your eyes from me, for when I look upon you, my heart becomes conceited and haughty beyond control."

Allegorically, God addresses the Jews concerning the appurtenances of the Second Temple. [Truly you are as beautiful to Me now as you always were. But beware:] In this Temple, it will be impossible to return the Ark, Cherubim, and Curtain — those things שֶׁהִרְהִיבֻונִי, *which excessively endeared you to Me*, in the First Temple and inspired Me to manifest a special love to you — until you were faithless to Me. [That excess of love caused you to take Me for granted and led you to betray Me. It was more love than you could bear.]

Another interpretation: "Turn your pleading eyes from Me," says God. "Endure the exile, and don't anticipate the End — because there is an appointed time for every event. Your eyes overwhelm Me and fill Me with compassion — but the edict has already been proclaimed; until the pre-established time, You must

---

1. The *Talmud* [*Yoma* 69a] relates that when he met Shimon the Righteous garbed in his priestly garments, Alexander descended from his carriage and bowed down before him. His attendants asked him: "A great king like yourself should bow down before this Jew?"

"It is his image [which appears before me in battle and helps me win]" (*Maharsha*).

VI

5-6

of old, hosts of angels stand in awe of you. ⁵Turn your pleading eyes from Me lest I be tempted to bestow upon you holiness more than you can bear. But with all your flaws, your most common sons are as dearly beloved as the children of Jacob in the goatlike procession descending the slopes of Mount Gilead. ⁶Your mighty leaders are perfect, as a flock of ewes come up from the washing, all of them unblemished with no miscarriage of action in them.

faithfully bear the yoke. Rather, turn away your eyes, and if you repent, I will respond accordingly by redeeming you sooner" (*Midrash Lekach Tov; Vilna Gaon*).

Ibn Ezra, however, interprets *turn your eyes away from Me* as referring to the fact that prophecy [the *eyes* of Israel as allegorized in previous references to *eyes* in this Book] ceased in the Second Temple, as Daniel prophesied [*Daniel* 9:24]: *and to seal vision and prophet* [which is explained by *Ibn Ezra* and *Rav Saadiah Gaon* ad loc., that from the time of the Second Temple there were no prophets in Israel except for those who relied on a בַּת קוֹל, *heavenly voice* (*Or Yohel*)].

["But (following *Rashi*) aside from not permitting these appurtenances in the new Temple," God says, "because they invoke special love in Me which cannot surface now that you have sinned. Nevertheless, be aware that in every other way you have maintained all the former virtues that endeared you to Me. These qualities are":]

שַׂעְרֵךְ כְּעֵדֶר הָעִזִּים שֶׁגָּלְשׁוּ מִן־הַגִּלְעָד [lit., *your hair is like a flock of goats streaming down from Gilead*.] Even the young, tender, and

insignificant among you are praiseworthy (*Rashi*).

[*Rashi's* interpretation of *hair* as an allusion to unimportant people would thus seem to be compatible with the commentary of the *Vilna Gaon* quoted by *Divrei Yedidiah* on 5:11 s.v. קְוֻצּוֹתָיו תַּלְתַּלִּים. Thus, hair — usually regarded as "superfluous" — is allegorized as an allusion to the seemingly superfluous (i.e., insignificant) young and tender ones — the flock of "goats" — who, despite popular derogation, are indeed considered praiseworthy by God.]

[See parallel verses in 4:1ff for additional commentary.]

Others [e.g., *Ibn Ezra, Metzudas David*, etc.] see *hair* as an allusion to the nazarites, who had long flowing hair. In exile they could not offer a sacrifice at the completion of their period of nazarite vows; nevertheless, they were beloved of God.

6. שִׁנַּיִךְ כְּעֵדֶר הָרְחֵלִים שֶׁעָלוּ מִן־הָרַחְצָה — [lit., שֶׁכֻּלָּם מַתְאִימוֹת וְשַׁכֻּלָה אֵין בָּהֶם *Your teeth are like a flock of ewes* [fem. sheep] *who have risen from the washing which are perfect and there is none missing among them.*]

Your teeth, i.e., the leaders and mighty ones among you, are entirely

פרק ו ז כְּפֶלַח הָרִמּוֹן רַקָּתֵךְ מִבַּעַד לְצַמָּתֵךְ:
ח שִׁשִּׁים הֵמָּה מְלָכוֹת וּשְׁמֹנִים פִּילַגְשִׁים
ט וַעֲלָמוֹת אֵין מִסְפָּר: אַחַת הִיא יוֹנָתִי תַמָּתִי
אַחַת הִיא לְאִמָּהּ בָּרָה הִיא לְיוֹלַדְתָּהּ

good *like a flock of ewes.* [The simile of Israel to the ewe is appropriate because] the ewe can be utilized entirely for holy purposes: Its wool is used for תְּכֵלֶת, the purple-thread of *tzitzis* (ritual fringes on four-cornered garments); its flesh for sacrifice; its horns for the *shofar*; its leg [bone] for the flutes; its sinews for harpstrings; its skin for the timbrel [i.e., the musical instruments in the Temple]. The heathen nations, conversely, are compared to dogs, for they are entirely unusable for holy purposes (*Rashi*).

Teeth refers to the priest who eats the sacrifices; *ewes* to the righteous; *washings* — pure in repentance (*Divrei Yedidiah*).

7. כְּפֶלַח הָרִמּוֹן רַקָּתֵךְ מִבַּעַד לְצַמָּתֵךְ — [lit., *Your temples are like a slice (a half — Rashi) of pomegranate, from behind your veil.*]

"Even the illiterate ones among you are as full of precepts as is a pomegranate full of seeds" (*Midrash*).

… But, lacking the knowledge of certain commandments due to ignorance, they are compared to only a *part* of a pomegranate (*Divrei Yedidiah*).

[See also 4:3 for parallel commentary.]

Divrei Yedidiah makes the further observation that in Chapter 4, many more virtues are listed which are absent here. That is because Chapter 4 refers to the period of the First Temple when Israel attained its greatest

heights. This chapter, however, allegorizes the period of the Second Temple in which Israel lacked many of the qualities enumerated earlier.

8-9. [True, there are many peoples in the world — but for God, there is only one, His "dove" — the perfect one, Israel.]

8. שִׁשִּׁים הֵמָּה מְלָכוֹת — [lit., *There are sixty queens.*] I.e., the family heads who descended from Abraham: the sixteen of Keturah; Isaac and his two children; Ishmael and his twelve family heads; the twelve sons of Jacob; and the sixteen family heads of Esau; a total of sixty (*Rashi*).

וּשְׁמֹנִים פִּילַגְשִׁים — [lit., *and eighty concubines.*] Refers to Noah and his descendants until Abraham. The family heads descending from those leaving the Ark to rebuild and repopulate the earth add up to eighty. And just as queens are superior to concubines, so are Abraham and his descendants more esteemed than all others … (*Rashi*).

וַעֲלָמוֹת אֵין מִסְפָּר — [lit., *and maidens without number.*] each of the above having branched out into many families (*Rashi*).

[Allegorically, therefore, render *nations without number.* The use of *maidens* for *nations* is consistent with its use in 1:3, עַל כֵּן עֲלָמוֹת אֲהֵבוּךְ, "therefore have *maidens* — i.e., nations — loved you." See comm. there.]

9. אַחַת הִיא יוֹנָתִי תַמָּתִי — [lit., *One*

⁷ *As many as a pomegranate's seeds are the merits of your unworthiest within your modest veil.* ⁸ *The queenly offspring of Abraham are sixty, compared to whom the eighty Noachides and all their countless nations are like mere concubines.*

⁹ *Unique is she, My constant dove, My perfect one. Unique is she, this nation striving for the truth; pure is she to Jacob who begot her.*

(alone) *is My dove, My perfect one.*] Of all the nations mentioned above, she [i.e., Israel] is My chosen one, like a perfect dove, wholehearted with her mate (*Rashi*).

... As it is written [*II Samuel 7:23*]: *And who is like Your people, like Israel, a unique nation on earth?* (*Ibn Ezra*).

תַּמָּתִי, *My perfect one:* The Jews, children of Jacob, אִישׁ תָּם, *the "perfect" man* [*Genesis 25:27*] (*Midrash Lekach Tov*) — the nation which wholeheartedly [בִּתְמִימוּת] endures punishment without complaint (*Tz'ror HaMor*).

"One is this nation which has followed Me into the desert without questioning from where their sustenance will come, trusting in Me implicitly." This is the meaning of *My perfect one* — the one who has accompanied Me בִּתְמִימוּת, *in absolute perfection* (*Alshich*).

[For *My dove, My perfect one,* see also comm. to 5:2 where *Metzudas Tzion* alternatively renders: *My undefiled one.*]

אַחַת הִיא לְאִמָּהּ — [lit., *she is* (the only) *one to her mother.*] The word אִמָּהּ [*her mother*] in this verse is understood [as it is in 1:6 and 3:11] allegorically to mean אוּמָה, *nation.* It is this interpretation that is reflected

in the translation. *Rashi* accordingly explains the phrase in the context of the entire verse: "*My dove, My perfect one, is unique above all the others"* — *she is unified as a nation* — for despite the many arguments [in matters of Law] that take place in the study-houses, all Jews share one lofty motive: to comprehend Torah in its fundamentals and its truth (*Rashi*).

Are we to imagine that the disciples pursue different lines? Not so, since it says, *One is My dove, My perfect one.* They all base themselves on *halachah,* on one *gezeirah shavah* [when a law is derived from two similar Scriptural expressions that clarify each other], on one *kal vachomer* [a fortiori] (*Midrash*).

[In a more literal sense, the phrase is translated: *She is the special one to her Matriarch* (see *Alshich,* on next phrase).]

She is thus compared to an only daughter for whom a mother experiences great longing and love (*Shir Chadash*).

Tz'ror HaMor renders לְאִמָּהּ, *to her mother,* as a reference to the *Shechinah,* i.e., she is the only nation that deserves having the *Shechinah* dwell within it.

בָּרָה הִיא לְיוֹלַדְתָּהּ — [lit., *she is pure to the one that begot her.*] I.e., to the

פֶּרֶק ו י רָאוּהָ בָנוֹת וַיְאַשְּׁרוּהָ מְלָכוֹת וּפִילַגְשִׁים
וַיְהַלְלוּהָ: מִי־זֹאת הַנִּשְׁקָפָה כְּמוֹ־שָׁחַר
יָפָה כַלְּבָנָה בָּרָה כַּחַמָּה אֲיֻמָּה כַּנִּדְגָּלוֹת:

Patriarchs, suggestive of the verse [*Isaiah 51:1,2*]: *Look to the rock from which you were hewn, and to the hollow of the pit from which you were dug. Look to Abraham your father and to Sarah who bore you, for when he was yet one alone did I summon him* (*Alshich*).

By her every action, it is obvious that she descends from the blessed seed of Abraham, Isaac, and Jacob (*Netziv*).

The verse refers to the perfect integrity of his progeny [lit., *bed*] that Jacob foresaw and for which he praised God, as the commentators explain on the verse [*Genesis 47:31*]: *And Israel prostrated himself toward the head of the bed* [i.e., he thanked God that all of his children were righteous] (*Rashi*).

רָאוּהָ בָנוֹת וַיְאַשְּׁרוּהָ מְלָכוֹת וּפִילַגְשִׁים וַיְהַלְלוּהָ — [lit., *maidens saw her* — i.e., saw Israel in her glory (*Rashi*) — *and acclaimed her; queens and concubines, and they praised her.*]

The verse also alludes to the praise which even the heathen kings felt compelled to utter when confronted with the obvious manifestations of God's omnipotence for the benefit of His people, as foretold by Malachi [*3:12*]: *And all the nations shall praise you;* also by Isaiah [*49:23*]: *And kings shall be your nurturers and their princesses your wet nurses. With faces to the ground they will prostrate themselves to you; they will lick the dust of your feet ...*

... It refers especially to Nebuchadnezzar's declaration upon the departure of Chananiah, Mishael, and Azariah unharmed from the fiery furnace [*Daniel 3:28ff*]: *Blessed is the God of Shadrach, Meshach, and Abednego!* [the Babylonian names of Chananiah, Mishael, and Azariah, ibid. 1:7] ... *for there is no other god able to rescue in this manner* (*Shir Chadash*).

Alshich refers this verse to the Jews who accepted the Torah and exclaimed: *We will do and we will hear! The maidens* — i.e., the celestial beings — *saw her and praised her. Queens and concubines* — i.e., the heathen kings and ministers — *and they praised her.* As the Sages tell us: When the nations heard the thundering and saw the lightning accompanying the Giving of the Torah, they ran to Balaam and asked him, *What are these thunderous sounds?* "God is giving His Torah to the Jews," he replied. Immediately, they all arose and blessed her.

10. [As explained by *Rashi*, the following is the "acclaim and praise" of the heathen nations — the *maidens, queens,* and *concubines* referred to in the previous verse — and God now quoted it to Israel:]

מִי־זֹאת הַנִּשְׁקָפָה כְּמוֹ־שָׁחַר — [lit., *Who is that gazing down like dawn?*] I.e., Who is peering down upon us, the nations, from the heights of the Temple — highest of places

Nations saw her and they extolled her; queens and concubines, and they praised her: [10] *"Who is this that gazes down from atop the Temple Mount, brightening like the dawn, beautiful as the moon, brilliant as the sun, awesome as the bannered hosts of kings?"*

on earth — like the dawn, which begins in darkness but increasingly brightens and intensifies?[1] So was Israel when God spoke to Haggai commanding him to tell Zerubbabel, governor of Judah, that the time had come to build the Second Temple [*Haggai* 1:1-3]. During its early years, Israel was subject to Persia and Greece, but after the Hasmoneans triumphed, they themselves reigned (*Rashi*).

The implication of מִי זֹאת, *who is this?* in this verse is similar to the same phrase in 3:6 (*Ibn Ezra*).

According to *Ramban*, this verse also contains an allusion to God, Himself, recalling the verse [*Psalms* 14:2]: HASHEM *gazed down from heaven upon mankind;* also [*Deuteronomy* 26:15]: *Gaze down from Your holy abode, from heaven.*

יָפָה כַלְּבָנָה בָּרָה כַּחַמָּה — [lit., *beautiful as the moon, pure as the sun.*]

Israel, in the days of the building of

the Second Temple, was granted self-government at the pleasure of King Cyrus. Therefore, it is compared to the moon which does not possess the power of illumination, but can only reflect the light of the sun ...

"At this time of mankind's transition from God-remoteness to God-nearness, Israel appears on the stage of history in the light of the dawn of the nations. The fairness of the moon that stood in the night-sky of mankind during the long spell of the *Galus* [exile] joins with the brightness of the sun from which the eternal perfected day of history now shines. Attired in this double adornment of 'the moon and the sun,' God presents Israel to mankind. He brings to culmination in it the number of excellencies whose observances can provide them with the understanding of their own problems and tasks and their ability to solve them" (*Rav Wolf*).

1. The reference to *dawn* is also perceived in the *Midrash* as symbolic of the increasing intensity of Israel's future deliverance:

It is related that Rav Chiya and Rav Shimon ben Chalafta were once walking in the valley of Arbel in the early morning, and they saw the dawn coming up.

Rav Chiya said: "Similarly will the deliverance of Israel break forth, as it is written [*Micah* 7:8]: *though I sit in darkness, HASHEM is a light to me.* At first it comes on little by little, then it begins to sparkle, then it gathers strength, and then it spreads over the sky."

This is further indicated by the following verses. At first, *In those days, while Mordechai was sitting at the king's gate* [*Esther* 2:21]; then [ibid. 8:15]: *Mordechai left the king's presence clad in royal apparel;* and finally [ibid. v. 16]: *The Jews had light and gladness.*

Divrei Yedidiah adds that this is further alluded to by the Talmudic interpretation [*Yoma* 29a] that אַיֶּלֶת הַשַּׁחַר, *strengthening of the dawn* [*Psalms* 22:1, *Hirsch* transl.], alludes to Esther.

פֶּרֶק ו יא אֶל־גִּנַּת אֱגוֹז יָרַדְתִּי לִרְאוֹת בְּאִבֵּי הַנָּחַל
יא־יב יב לִרְאוֹת הֲפָרְחָה הַגֶּפֶן הֵנֵצוּ הָרִמֹּנִים: לֹא
יָדַעְתִּי נַפְשִׁי שָׂמַתְנִי מַרְכְּבוֹת עַמִּי נָדִיב:

אֵימָה כַּנִּדְגָּלוֹת — [lit., *awe inspiring as an army with banners*.] I.e., awesome with its mighty men, as the bannered hosts of kings (*Rashi*). [See comm. to verse 4.]

The verse means: Who is this nation that arose from slavery in Egypt, growing in greatness like the dawn's increasing light: being first a pale reflection like the moon, and then becoming as pure as the strength of the sun itself, until it became as *awe inspiring as an army with banners*? — I.e., its fear was upon all the nations, as it is written [*Deuteronomy* 28:10]: *Then all the peoples of the earth will see that the Name of* HASHEM *is proclaimed over you, and they will be afraid of you*. For when the Jews marched in the desert, banners held high, surrounded by the Pillar of Cloud and Fire, smoke rising [see above 3:7], the nations witnessed this awesome sight and were filled with fear. And this is the meaning of אֵימָה כַּנִּדְגָּלוֹת, *awesome as an army with banners*, for in heathen eyes, the camps of the Jews were like camps of the *Shechinah* (*Alshich*).

... As the *Targum* renders the verse: "The nations exclaimed: How brilliant are the deeds of this people like the morning dawn! Her youths are beautiful as the moon, and her merits bright as the sun, while the dread of her was upon all the inhabitants of the land at the time when she went forth in the desert in four regiments."

11. [The Holy One, blessed is He, continues His praise of Israel:]

אֶל־גִּנַּת אֱגוֹז יָרַדְתִּי — [lit., *I went down to the garden of nuts*.] I.e., I have come to the Second Temple unto you (*Rashi*).

"The Lord of the Universe spoke: [At the beginning of] the Second Temple, built through the hands of Cyrus, I caused My Presence to dwell in order to see the goodly actions of My people, to see if perchance the wise men had increased and multiplied, those who are compared to the vine, and if their scions were filled with good deeds like pomegranates" (*Targum*).

Rashi explains that Israel is compared to a nut. Upon looking at a nut, one sees only a shell, but its nutritious content is not visible. When it is opened, however, it is full with nutritious food. Similarly, Israel is modest and unpretentious; her scholars are not conspicuous, nor do they praise themselves publicly. But, when they are examined, they are found to be full of wisdom. Also, when a nut falls in dirt, its contents are not defiled. So, too, although Israel, exiled among the nations, endures great tribulation, its actions are not defiled.

לִרְאוֹת בְּאִבֵּי הַנָּחַל — [lit., *to look at the green plants of the vale*.] I.e., at the fresh, moisture-filled plants that grow at the riverbed, as in *Job* 8:12: עֹדֶנּוּ בְאִבּוֹ, *while it is still fresh* [moist] (*Metzudas Tzion*).

VI
11-12

11*I descended upon the deceptively simple holiness of the Second Temple to see your moisture-laden deeds in the riverbeds; to see whether your Torah scholars had budded on the vine, whether your merit-laden righteous had flowered like the pomegranates filled with seeds.*

Israel: 12*Alas, I knew not how to guard myself from sin! My own devices harnessed me, like chariots subject to a foreign nation's mercies.*

Allegorically: To examine the [vitalizing] sap [or: "moisture"] of good deeds that I could find in you (*Rashi*).[1]

I.e., My eye and heart are upon Israel [*Psalms* 14:2]: *to see if there exists a reflective person who seeks out God* (*Ramban*).

לִרְאוֹת הֲפָרְחָה הַגֶּפֶן — [lit., *to see whether the vine has "budded."*] I.e., to see whether sages and scholars will bud before Me (*Rashi*).

[The comparison of Israel and Torah to the vine is found in the *Talmud, Chullin* 92a. Perhaps, since wine allegorically refers to Torah-study (see comm. to 1:2), the vine refers here to the scholars who learn and expound it.]

הֵנֵצוּ הָרִמּוֹנִים — [lit., *if the pomegranates were in flower.*] I.e., if those who ["flowered"] and performed *mitzvos* were full of merit [as a pomegranate is full of seeds] (*Rashi*).

12. [Israel, hearing God's praise of her glorious past, reflects on her current plight and responds sadly:]

לֹא יָדַעְתִּי נַפְשִׁי שָׂמַתְנִי מַרְכְּבוֹת עַמִּי נָדִיב — [lit., *I did not know; my soul set me (as) chariots of a noble nation.*]

[In the literal sense, this verse, both in continuity and translation, is difficult, nearly incomprehensible. But the allegory is clear:] I did not know how to avoid sin in order to remain in my glory and greatness. Instead, I stumbled into the sin of causeless hatred and controversy which reached a peak in the time of the Hasmonean kings Hyrkenos and Aristoblus [two brothers who battled each other for the throne], until one of them invited Rome to enter the land. He accepted the throne from Rome, and became its vassal. From that point on, my own soul caused me to become as a chariot ridden upon [i.e., persecuted] by the nobility of foreign nations (*Rashi*).

---

1. [My father שליט״א points out that the concept of "moisture" meaning good deeds — i.e., the "vitalizing sap of good deeds" — is echoed in *Sanhedrin* 92b, in the context of Ezekiel's vision of the valley of the "dry bones" which allegorized "the entire House of Israel": אֵלּוּ בְּנֵי אָדָם שֶׁאֵין בָּהֶן לַחְלוּחִית שֶׁל מִצְוָה, *They were the men who lacked the "moisture" of mitzvos.*]
[Conversely, *your arid ones* alludes to those with little merit. See comm. to 4:13 s.v. שְׁלָחַיִךְ.]

נַפְשִׁי שָׂמַתְנִי, *my soul set me,* means according to *Rashi:* "I have brought these evils upon myself."

[I.e., without giving any thought to the matter, I obeyed the impulse of my nature, and found myself like a chariot ridden upon by foreigners.]

— I have no idea what I expected to accomplish by foolishly remaining in exile (*Sforno*).

— I did not have the perception to "open the door" to my Beloved [5:2,3] — and leave Babylon en masse in response to the Divine call to return to Eretz Yisrael[1] — and my soul thus brought upon itself the derision it suffers in exile (*Metzudas David*).

Divrei Yedidiah explains that historically this refers to the relative prosperity and freedom from persecution that the Jews enjoyed under the reigns of Cyrus and Darius. Secure, and thinking that this security would continue forever, they shrank from the call to return to Eretz Yisrael and rebuild the Temple. But in the thirty-fourth year of the Second Temple, Alexander the Great conquered the world and overran Persia, ushering in a period of great suffering for the Jews. Israel thus lamented: *I did not know,* i.e., I could not foresee the suffering which would result from my decision to remain in exile. I wallowed in the false security of captivity, thinking the security would continue forever; *my soul set me,* i.e., I brought this evil upon myself, causing me to be crushed by the chariots of those tyrants whom I always viewed as being *my own princely people.*

— I was not cognizant of the damage I was bringing upon myself until I became as one trampled by the nations. This refers to the Second Temple which was destroyed because of causeless hatred which led to Israel's exile (*Ibn Ezra*).

עַמִּי is translated *nation:* the suffix י, *yud,* according to most commentators being the poetic form as רַבָּתִי, שׁוֹכְנִי, הַמַשְׁפִּילִי (*Rashi; Ibn Ezra; Metzudas Tzion*).

[The *Midrash,* however, interprets this verse differently. Interpreting עַמִּי נָדִיב in the possessive: "the chariots of *my* noble people, Israel," it explains the verse as Israel's declaration of astonishment at her sudden elevation from derision to grandeur:]

Rav Chiyah said: We may compare Israel to a king's daughter who was gathering sheaves with her companions. One day the king passed by and recognized her and had her taken and placed before him in the carriage.

Her astonished friends exclaimed: "Yesterday you were gathering sheaves, and today you are sitting in the royal carriage near the king!"

"Just as you are astonished at me," she replied, "I, too, am astonished!" Applying the verse, *I did not know, my soul set me on the chariots of my princely people,* I am astounded at my elevation.

It applies to the Jews in Egypt: When they became free men, the nations asked them: "Yesterday you were repulsive and worked with brick and mortar, and today you

---

1. [See *Overview* to ArtScroll ed. of *Esther* p. xvi: "The righteous Persian monarch gave the order that the Jews might go home again, and only forty-two thousand heeded his call! Forty-two thousand heard the call but millions stayed behind."]

are free and lord it over the whole world: "I, too, am astonished." [I.e., "I don't know by what merit I was liberated and achieved this elevation. It is only to God's mercy that this can be attributed." (And similarly in the subsequent excerpts — *Torah Temimah*:)]

It applies to David: Yesterday he was fleeing from the Land, and today he reigns over all of Israel [*II Samuel* 8:15].

It applies to the righteous Joseph: Yesterday [*Psalms* 105:18] *they afflicted his leg with fetters; his soul came into irons,* and today [*Genesis* 42:6] *Joseph was the viceroy over the land.*

It also applies to Mordechai: Yesterday [*Esther* 4:1] *He donned sackcloth and ashes;* today [ibid. 8:15] *Mordechai left the king's presence clad in royal apparel.*

It also applies to Israel (at the future Redemption) who will be surprised at her elevation: She says to the other nations [*Micah* 7:8]: *Do not rejoice over me, my enemy; for though I fell, I shall rise; though I sit in darkness,* HASHEM *is a light to me.* And she will apply to herself this verse.

Additionally, the *Midrash* homiletically reads the phrase נָדִיב עַמִּי, *with me the Benefactor.* I.e., Israel declares: *with me* walks נְדִיב חַי עוֹלָמִים, the Benefactor par excellence — Sustainer of the Universe.

Metzudas Tzion makes the etymological comment that a nobleman is referred to as נָדִיב because it is a nobleman's nature לִנְדֹּב, to give charity and bestow gifts.

שׁוּבִי שׁוּבִי֙ הַשּׁוּלַמִּ֔ית שׁוּבִי שׁוּבִי וְנֶחֱזֶה־
בָּ֑ךְ מַה־תֶּחֱזוּ֙ בַּשּׁ֣וּלַמִּ֔ית כִּמְחֹלַ֖ת הַֽמַּחֲנָֽיִם:

VII

1. [According to *Rashi*, Israel is still the speaker, recalling how the heathens tried to entice her to join with them:]

שׁוּבִי שׁוּבִי הַשּׁוּלַמִּית — [lit., *Turn, turn, O complete one.*] "They say to me, turn away, turn away, you who are perfect [שְׁלֵמָה] in your faith in Him" (*Rashi*).

[הַשּׁוּלַמִּית (usually translated *The Shulamite*) is allegorically regarded by the commentators as an adjective related to the root שלם, *complete, whole.*]

The *Midrash* renders Shulamite: "The nation which God will one day settle in an abode of peace [*O Shalom*]; the nation that completes [*mashlemes*] the stability of the world."

Ibn Ezra suggests that it refers to *Jerusalemites* — residents of *Shalem*, the ancient name of Jerusalem. [Cf. *Genesis* 14:18.]

[The term שׁוּבִי, *turn*, is repeated for emphasis. This form is not unusual in Scripture. Cf. for example, *Judges* 5:12: עוּרִי, עוּרִי דְּבוֹרָה, עוּרִי עוּרִי, *awake, awake Devorah, awake, awake.*]

שׁוּבִי וְנֶחֱזֶה־בָּךְ — [lit., *turn, turn, that we may gaze at you.*] *Rashi*, following the *Midrash*, interprets וְנֶחֱזֶה not as "gaze" in its usual sense, but as "discern," "discover," "provide," as in the verse [*Exodus* 18:21]: וְאַתָּה תֶחֱזֶה מִכָּל־הָעָם, *and you shall discern from among the entire people* — as if to say: "Turn away, turn away to us *and we shall select from among you* commissioners and rulers."

Additionally, the word *gaze*

implies "and you will become the 'mirror' of the world [which all will gaze at and emulate — from מַחֲזֶה, *a vision*] (*Midrash*); and we will *discern* [i.e., contemplate] what greatness to bestow upon you" (*Rashi*).

Others translate שׁוּבִי in the sense of *return, repent* [the four times the word "return" is used here correspond to the four foreign powers that subjected Israel, indicating that Israel came under their sway unscathed and *returned* from it unscathed (*Midrash*)].

[Others understand God as the Speaker:]

"Return unto Me, O Assembly of Israel, return unto Jerusalem, return unto the House of Torah-instruction, return to receive prophecy from the prophets who preach in the Name of Hashem" (*Targum*).

Following this trend, *Sforno* interprets the chapter as a dialogue between the prophets and Israel. This verse evokes the memory of the Divine calls voiced through the prophets [*Malachi* 3:7]: שׁוּבוּ אֵלַי וְאָשׁוּבָה אֲלֵיכֶם, *return to Me, and I will return to you*, and [*Zechariah* 2:10,11]: *... flee from the land of the north — the word of Hashem — for I have scattered you like the four directions of the heavens ... Escape, O you who dwell with the daughter of Babylon.* Thus in our verse this call is echoed with the admonition that Israel repent and thereby reestablish its residence in the Land. The prophets say to Israel, "With the return to the Land, the *Shechinah* will

VII

1 Nations: The nations have said to me, "Turn away, turn away from God, O nation whose faith in Him is perfect, turn away, turn away, and we shall choose nobility from you."

Israel: But I replied to them, "What can you bestow upon a nation of perfect faith commensurate even with the desert camps encircling?"

dwell in your midst and then וְנֶחֱזֶה בָּךְ, we will again envision prophecies [from חָזוֹן, prophecy, vision] in your behalf because [בָּךְ = in your merit and by virtue of you (Harav Gifter)] if you repent fully, we will then be recipients of the word of God."

[Israel responds incredulously to the heathen offers to honor her:]

מַה־תֶּחֱזוּ בַּשּׁוּלַמִּית כִּמְחֹלַת הַמַּחֲנָיִם — [lit., What will you gaze at the complete one like a dance of the camps?] What can you discern in the complete one, i.e., what greatness can you confer upon me that would be commensurate with my own greatness? Your highest honors are not equal even to the greatness of the banners of the encircling encampments in the desert (Rashi).

[The literal meaning of כִּמְחֹלַת הַמַּחֲנָיִם is obscure, and the literal translation, which follows Metzudas Tzion, reflects this ambiguity. Allegorically, however, the phrase is quite clear as reflected in Rashi, above, and in the following comments.]

The Midrash interprets Israel's answer: What can you offer me? Have you ever heard of Abraham, Isaac, and Jacob worshiping idols that their descendants after them should so worship? Our fathers did not worship idols and we will not worship idols! And what can you do for us? Can you arrange such a

dance for us as was provided for our father Jacob when he went out of the house of Laban? For the Rabbis say a hundred and twenty myriads of angels danced and leapt before Jacob our father when he left the house of Laban [Genesis 32:3]: and Jacob said when he saw them: This is a Godly camp. And he called the name of that place Machanaim [two camps].

Israel continues: Your offer is meaningless. Remember that we once occupied the most lofty position at Mt. Sinai where there were מַחֲנָיִם, two camps: God with his שּׁוּלַמִּית "camp" of ministering angels [and the camp of Israel] (Midrash).

[According to the Targum's interpretation of the verse, the stich is a continuation of God's exhortation. Apparently relating תֶּחֱזוּ to חִזָּיוֹן, vision, prophecy; שּׁוּלַמִּית to יְרוּשָׁלַיִם, residents of Jerusalem; and מְחֹלַת to the root חלל, defilement, he renders:] "What good is it to you, O you false prophets, to mislead the people of Jerusalem by means of your messages of prophecy which you utter in rebellion against God, and to defile the camp of Judah and Israel?"

In continuation of Sforno's interpretation above, this is Israel's recalcitrant response to the true prophets who called for her return to God and the Land: What visions could you possibly see? Do you expect to reveal a new Torah, similar to the Revelation in the Sinai Desert that occurred when the encampments of Israel encircled the two other camps, i.e., the Camp of the Divine Presence and the camp of the Levites?

Alshich concurs with *Sforno's* interpretation but differs in that he ascribes the last stich, כְּמֶחֹלַת הַמַּחֲנָיִם, to be the prophet's response to Israel's recalcitrant query, *What visions could you possibly see?* They reply: If you will better your ways you will now deserve to depart from your present captivity as gloriously as your ancestors departed from Egypt with the "dancing" encampments. As the *Talmud* [*Berachos* 4a] comments: Israel would have been worthy of miracles in the days of Ezra, similar to the miracles of the days of Joshua, but their sins prevented it.

2. [Following *Rashi*: The nations answer:]

מַה־יָּפוּ פְעָמַיִךְ בַּנְּעָלִים בַּת־נָדִיב — [lit., *How lovely are your steps in sandals, O daughter of nobility!*] We ask you to join us because of your beautiful deeds which we had observed in you when you were still in your full beauty, i.e., your own land. *How lovely were your steps*, Jewish nation, *daughter of nobility*, on your pilgrimages to the Temple to celebrate the Three Festivals: Passover, Shavuos, and Succos (*Succah* 49b; *Rashi*).

[From the parallel comment in *Yalkut Shimoni* it is evident that the above interpretation is based upon translating פְעָמַיִךְ (*your steps*)

to mean *your times*, alluding to the שָׁלֹשׁ פְּעָמִים, *the three times* (*Deut.* 16:16) that the male Israelites made pilgrimages to the Temple. Accordingly, the verse should be allegorically paraphrased: "How lovely were your times (i.e., festivals) when you donned sandals to make your pilgrimage, O princely daughter."]

O daughter of nobility means daughter of our father Abraham [a general reference to the Jews] who is called נָדִיב, *noble*, as in the verse [*Psalms* 47:10]: *The nobles of the peoples gathered, the people of the God of Abraham.* The *Talmud* asks, *The God of Abraham* — and not the God of Isaac and Jacob? But the meaning is, *The God of Abraham* who was the first proselyte (*Succah* 49b).

Sforno: The prophets answered: To the contrary! *How lovely are your steps in sandals, O princely daughter* — i.e., return to the Land! The very possibility of being able to join in the festival pilgrimages should be incentive enough!

חַמּוּקֵי יְרֵכַיִךְ כְּמוֹ חֲלָאִים מַעֲשֵׂה יְדֵי אָמָּן — [lit., *the roundness of your flanks are like jewels, the work of a master's hand.*] [The literal translation of חֲלָאִים, *jewels*, follows most commentators (*Ibn Janach; Targum, Metzudas Tzion; Tz'ror HaMor*) as well as *Rashi* who notes that a heap of gold ornaments is referred to as חֲלִי כֶתֶם (lit., *jewels of gold*).]

Allegorically, however, חֲלָאִים refers to *entrenchments, excavations*, as in the Talmudic phrase חֲלִיַת

VII Nations: ²*But your footsteps were so lovely when shod*
2-3 *in pilgrim's sandals, O daughter of nobles. The*
rounded shafts for your libations' abysslike
trenches, handiwork of the Master Craftsman.
³*At earth's very center your Sanhedrin site is*
a crescent basin of ceaseless, flowing teaching;

הַבּוֹר, *excavation of a ditch* [*Eruvin*
78a; *Shabbos* 99a]. It is in this sense
that the Sages applied this verse to
the שִׁיתִין, the *pits* under the Altar,
which existed since the Six Days of
Creation [and were חֲמוּקִים, *hidden*],
and into which the wine flowed after the libation. They were rounded
like a thigh and descended to the
תְּהוֹם, *abyss. The work of a master's
hands* means that they were the
handiwork of the Holy One, blessed
is He (*Succah* 49a; *Rashi*).

The *Targum*, however, renders
this phrase as Solomon, inspired by
the spirit of prophecy, addressing
God about Israel and alluding to
*the children, products of their loins
who are beautiful as sparkling
jewels set in the Breastplate which
Bezalel the master craftsman fash-
ioned for Aaron.*

3. שָׁרְרֵךְ אַגַּן הַסַּהַר — [lit., *your umbilicus is like a round basin.*] *Umbilicus* allegorically refers to the
Chamber of Hewn Stone [the seat of
the Sanhedrin in the Temple] which

was situated בְּטַבּוּר הָאָרֶץ, at the umbilicus [the navel; i.e., the center] of
the world; אַגַּן — because justice,
represented by the Sanhedrin, protects [מֵגִין] the whole world; הַסַּהַר
— because it was moon-shaped [סַהַר,
moon; i.e., the members of the Sanhedrin were seated in a semicircle, like
the crescent moon, so they should be
able to look upon one another and
communicate properly and be able to
come to the true decision] (*Sanhedrin*
37a; *Rashi*).[1]

[In the literal sense סַהַר refers to
a large bowl used to serve drinks.
In the next stich, the praise is that
drinks do not cease flowing from it.]

Rashi explains סַהַר as an ivory
basin of fresh water from which
people wash.

אַל־יֶחְסַר הַמָּזֶג — [lit., *wherein no
mixed wine is lacking.*] I.e., wherein
teaching never ceases. Thus, the basin of water (see above), representing the Sanhedrin, is a never-ending
source of wisdom (*Rashi*).

[מֶזֶג literally refers to the fact that

1. *Divrei Yedidiah* places this entire chapter in the chronological context of the Talmudic period after the Destruction of the *Second* Temple, when [in verse 1] the Sages called upon Israel
who were *whole in faith* to repent, although they had sinned; like friends, calling for peace
between a husband and wife who argue but don't reject each other.
[Verse 2] Their "steps" are praised — i.e., those Sages who travel about from town to town,
village to village, to teach Torah [see *Eruvin* 54b], בַּת נָדִיב, daughter of the charitable nation,
nation of "volunteers": some volunteer their minds and bodies to travel and study, and their
brethren volunteer their wealth to support them in their quest; *children of the loins*, i.e., teachers who mold them in the way of Torah.
[Verse 3] This verse refers to the Sanhedrin, which, as noted in the *Talmud* [*Rosh Hashanah*
31b], continued to function even after the Destruction.

פֶּרֶק ז בִּטְנֵךְ עֲרֵמַת חִטִּים סוּגָה בַּשּׁוֹשַׁנִּים:
ד-ה ד שְׁנֵי שָׁדַיִךְ כִּשְׁנֵי עֳפָרִים תָּאֳמֵי צְבִיָּה:
ה צַוָּארֵךְ כְּמִגְדַּל הַשֵּׁן עֵינַיִךְ בְּרֵכוֹת

the strong wine from the soil of Israel could not be drunk undiluted, and therefore was mixed with water before serving. So strong was the wine that the *Midrash* recommends that the proper proportion in mixing wine is one-third wine to two-thirds water (*Tanchuma, Bamidbar* 4). So widespread was this practice that the *Talmud* even refers to serving wine as מְזִיגַת הַכּוֹס, lit., *mixing the cup* (*Shabbos* 66; *Pesachim* 114a).]

[The *Talmud, Sanhedrin* 37a, allegorically applied this two-to-one mixing requirement implied by our verse to the Sanhedrin. The Great Sanhedrin in Jerusalem consisted of seventy-one members. The full membership was required for their primary types of decisions, but the presence of a minimum of twenty-three judges — roughly one-third of the membership was required during all sessions ... . This quorum, twenty-three, was also the membership requirement of the minor Sanhedrins in all provinces and cities. ... Since the Great Sanhedrin was required to maintain a minimum number of twenty-three sitting judges during all sessions, a member was permitted to leave for personal reasons only if the minimum quorum of twenty-three remained there in his absence. Thus, allegorically, אַל-יֶחְסַר הַמָּזֶג, *the mixture* (a one-to-two ratio of judges) *was never lacking* (*Sanhedrin* 37a; see *Maharsha*).]

בִּטְנֵךְ עֲרֵמַת חִטִּים סוּגָה בַּשּׁוֹשַׁנִּים — [lit., *your stomach is like a heap of wheat hedged about with roses.*]

Your stomach is like a heap of wheat — which all require [i.e., wheat — the staple of life; cf. the Talmudic dictum "all require the owner of wheat" (*Berachos* 64a)] (*Rashi*).

... As the *Talmud* [*Sanhedrin* 37a] comments: Just as all benefit from a heap of wheat, so do all benefit from the deliberations of the Sanhedrin.

[בִּטְנֵךְ, *your stomach*, must therefore be understood, according to this interpretation, as allegorically synonymous with שָׁרְרֵךְ, *your umbilicus*, in the first part of this verse: both refer to the Sanhedrin.]

[*Midrash Tehillim* also interprets *stomach* (in the sense of *your essence*) as referring to Israel in general:]

"Is not a heap of pepper plants or a heap of cedar cones more beautiful than a heap of wheat? [I.e., why is a heap of wheat used for the simile in our verse rather than the more beautiful pepper plants of cedar cones?] Because the world can live without pepper plants and without cedar cones, but the world cannot live without wheat; likewise, the world cannot live without Israel."

סוּגָה בַּשּׁוֹשַׁנִּים — *Hedged about with roses* — even through a hedge of roses they would make no breach (ibid.).

— I.e., the lightest barrier is sufficient to keep them from sin. For it is the way of the world that a man marries a woman, and yearns greatly for his bride. After the wedding feast he approaches her, but if she says to him: "I have seen what looks like a red rose," he will draw away

שיר השירים [178]

your national center an indispensable heap of nourishing knowledge hedged about with roses. ⁴Your twin sustainers, the Tablets of the Law, are like two fawns, twins of the gazelle. ⁵Your Altar and Temple, erect and stately as an ivory tower; your wise men aflow with springs

from her. What causes the man not to come near her? What wall is there between them? What fence? What serpent bit him? What is it that restrains him? The words of the Torah that are as delicate as roses! ...

Similarly, a hungry traveler sees a cluster of dates on a tree and puts forth his hand to partake of it, but if others point out to him, "It is private property," he instantly draws his hand away, so as not to steal. What causes the hungry man not to eat ... [It is the moral deterrent] ... "of the hedge of roses." ...

Similarly, if a dish of meat is brought to a hungry man and he is told: "A piece of forbidden fat has fallen into the dish," he will instantly draw his hand away from the dish and will not eat of it. What causes this hungry man not to eat of the dish? ... "The hedge of roses!" (*Midrash Tehillim* 2:15; *Rashi*).

A hedge of roses is hardly an imposing barrier. Despite its thorns it can be trampled easily by anyone disposed to do so. Its true effectiveness is in its beauty; only a callous person would trample roses. Therefore, however, it can only deter those who appreciate its beauty; for those with no esthetic perception of its beauty it is no barrier at all. Similarly, the sanctions of the Torah and of Rabbinic ordinance are effective only for those who understand the greatness and majesty

of Torah. The word of Torah is the gentle reminder to refrain from trespass against the human soul, handiwork of Almighty God (*Harav Gifter* as heard from *Gedolei Telz*).

In an entirely different interpretation, *Metzudas David* understands these verses as God's moral exhortation to His children, Israel. He renders *stomach* as an allusion to *the fruit of the stomach* — the children: "May your children be as profligate as the seeds in a heap of wheat and may they be protected by exceedingly pleasant hedges lest they trespass and stumble on forbidden matters."

4. שְׁנֵי שָׁדַיִךְ כִּשְׁנֵי עֳפָרִים תָּאֳמֵי צְבִיָּה — [lit., *Your bosom is like two fawns, twins of a gazelle.*] I.e., the twin Tablets of the Covenant, or, alternately, the king and high priest [see extensive comm. to 4:5 where the same praise is uttered by God] (*Rashi*).

Thematically, *Metzudas David* interprets this verse as an exhortation regarding the *bosom* — i.e., sources of Israel's nourishment, the king and high priest who are admonished to conduct themselves as *two fawns, twins of a gazelle* by complementing each other and striving for mutuality: the king in affairs of state, and the high priest in the service of God.

5. צַוָּארֵךְ כְּמִגְדַּל הַשֵּׁן — [lit., *Your neck is like a tower of ivory.*] The Sanctuary and Altar which stand erect and tall — and the Chamber of Hewn Stone as well [see comm. to 4:4]

בְּחֶשְׁבּוֹן עַל־שַׁעַר בַּת־רַבִּים אַפֵּךְ כְּמִגְדַּל   **פרק ז**
הַלְּבָנוֹן צוֹפֶה פְּנֵי דַמָּשֶׂק: רֹאשֵׁךְ עָלַיִךְ   ו
כַּכַּרְמֶל וְדַלַּת רֹאשֵׁךְ כָּאַרְגָּמָן מֶלֶךְ

— provided spiritual strength and protection like an ivory tower (*Rashi*).

— *Your neck* is as sturdy to bear the yoke of *mitzvos* as a tower of ivory (*Alshich*).

עֵינַיִךְ בְּרֵכוֹת בְּחֶשְׁבּוֹן עַל־שַׁעַר בַּת־רַבִּים — [lit., *your eyes are (like the) pools in Cheshbon by the gate of Bas Rabim.*] *Rashi* paraphrases: Your eyes — like the pools in Cheshbon that draw water — are your wise men as they sit at the gates of Jerusalem, the city בַּת רַבַּת עָם, *greatly populated* [cf. *Lamentations* 1:1], involved in calculation [חֶשְׁבּוֹן] of the season and constellations. Their wisdom and intellect, manifested to all the nations (cf. *Deuteronomy* 4:6), draw your interest and allegiance like pools of water [cf. *Shabbos* 75a].

[*Cheshbon* is thus allegorically interpreted as "calculation." In the literal sense, however, Cheshbon is the ancient capital of Sichon, king of the Amorites. It was originally a Moabite city (*Numbers* 21:26). Shortly before his death Moses assigned it to Reuben (*Numbers* 32:3,37), but the hold of the Jews upon it was very insecure. It was famous for its beauty, fertility, and reservoirs.]

According to *Metzudas David*: May your scholars — the *eyes* of the community — exercise vision in instructing their community in following the proper path. May they be like pools of clear water nourishing the garden.

אַפֵּךְ כְּמִגְדַּל הַלְּבָנוֹן צוֹפֶה פְּנֵי דַמָּשֶׂק — [lit., *your nose is like the tower of Lebanon facing toward Damascus.*] *Rashi* comments: I cannot translate אַפֵּךְ as "nose" — either literally or allegorically. For what praise could there possibly be in a nose as large as a tower? Therefore, I say that the word means *face, countenance*. The reason the singular form of אַפֵּךְ instead of אַפַּיִךְ is used [although "face" in Hebrew is generally in the plural] is to specify the most distinctive portion of the face — the forehead, as alluded to in the verse [*Isaiah* 3:9]: הַכָּרַת פְּנֵיהֶם עָנְתָה בָּם, *the recognition of their faces testifies against them.* [The *Talmud* (*Yevamos* 120a) cites the verse in defining the distinguishing features in regard to positive identification of a dead man. Those features are the forehead and nose. Thus, אַפֵּךְ could be understood in our verse as: *your distinctive features are as outstanding as the tower of Lebanon.*]

Rashi adds that the rendering of *forehead*, rather than nose, is further supported by the fact that the praises in these verses are given in ascending physical order [beginning with *your steps* in verse 2, and going from organ to organ, culminating in *your hair* in verse 6. Since the eyes were already praised in the previous verse, and hair in the next, then it must be the forehead that is referred to here. A reference to "nose," however, would be out of sequence here. Compare the praise [*Ezekiel* 3:8]: *I have made your*

of complex wisdom at the gate of the many-peopled city; your face, like the tower of Lebanon, looks to your future boundary as far as Damascus.

⁶The Godly name on your head is as mighty as Carmel; your crowning braid is royal purple, your King

forehead strong against their foreheads, where the *forehead* is used as a symbol of strength.[1]

Like the tower of Lebanon facing [or: *gazing*] *toward Damascus.* Rashi cites a *Midrash* that this refers to *"the House of the Forest of Lebanon"* [I Kings 7:2] which King Solomon built. One who stood upon it could gaze forth and count the houses in Damascus. Additionally, *Rashi* comments that *gazing toward Damascus* is explained in the *Sifri* to allude to the prophetic vision that in the future the "gates of Jerusalem will stretch forth until Damascus."

This interpretation is elaborated upon in the *Midrash* which derives it from *Zechariah* 9:1: *The prophecy of the word of* HASHEM *in the land of Hadrach, and in Damascus shall His resting place be.* This is interpreted to mean *as far as* Damascus will His resting place be; however, His primary resting place remains the Temple.

6. רֹאשֵׁךְ עָלַיִךְ כַּכַּרְמֶל — [lit., *Your head upon you is like (Mount) Carmel.*] This refers to the *tefillin* of the head, of which the verse says [*Deuteronomy* 28:10]: *Then all the peoples of the earth will see that*

the Name of HASHEM *is proclaimed over you, and they shall be afraid of you.* The *tefillin* are Israel's strength; they are as awe inspiring as the cliff of the mountains — and Carmel is the loftiest of mountains.

The *Midrash*, according to which God is the speaker, homiletically renders רֹאשֵׁךְ, *Your head*, as related to רָשׁ, *the poor one*, and comments: your poor people [in *mitzvos*] *are as dear* to Me *as Elijah who ascended Mt. Carmel* [cf. *I Kings* 18:42].

Alshich renders: Those of your captors who are your *heads* in exile overshadow you like Mt. Carmel.

וְדַלַּת רֹאשֵׁךְ כָּאַרְגָּמָן — [lit., *and the hair* (or: *locks*) *of your head are like purple.*] I.e., and the braided locks of your nazarites demonstrating their compliance with the commandments are as comely as garments of braided purple wool [the color of royalty] (*Rashi*).

The *Midrash* [see above] continues: And the דַּלִּים, *needy*, and poor ones in Israel are as dear to Me as ... Daniel of whom it is written [*Daniel* 5:29]: *They clothed Daniel in purple.*

Following *Alshich*: The lowlier of your *heads* [see *Alshich*, above] —

1. *Harav David Cohen* suggests that "nose" might be an allusion to the *great men of the generation* who are great in stature *like the tower of Lebanon.* He derives this from the *Talmud, Taanis* 29a where during the wars preceding the destruction of the Second Temple, Rabban Gamliel's life was sought by the government. To alert Rabban Gamliel that his life was in imminent danger, a nobleman called out into his study-house: "The master of the nose is sought, the master of the nose is sought!" whereupon Rabban Gamliel, understanding the reference to himself, got up and fled.

פֶּרֶק ז ז אָסוּר בָּרְהָטִים: מַה־יָּפִית וּמַה־נָּעַמְתְּ אַהֲבָה
ז־ח ח בַּתַּעֲנוּגִים: זֹאת קוֹמָתֵךְ דָּמְתָה לְתָמָר

i.e., the commissioners and prefects, whose faces were אַרְגָּמָן, *purple, in display of their viciousness.*

מֶלֶךְ אָסוּר בָּרְהָטִים — [lit., *a king bound in tresses.*] This alludes to the fact that the Name of God [i.e., the King] is associated with the hair [of a nazarite] as it is written [concerning a nazarite (in *Numbers* 6:7)]: נֵזֶר אֱלֹהָיו עַל רֹאשׁו, *the crown of his God is upon his head* (*Rashi*); and this is the cause of the heathens' esteem for the Sages of Israel (*Netziv*).

[Alternatively rendering רְהָטִים in its meaning of *haste*, *Rashi* comments:] *The King* — i.e., God — is *bound* in love to the *mitzvos* and *to the haste* with which you run before Him.

And, according to the *Midrash: A king* refers to Moses, of whom it says [*Deuteronomy* 33:5]: *And he was a king in Jeshurun. Bound* — because it was decreed that he should not enter the Promised Land. On account of what? On account of the רְהָטִים, *streams,* of the waters of Meribah (*Numbers* 20:13). [Accordingly, the verse would be allegorically rendered: "A king [Moses], suppressed because of the streams [of Meribah]."

[*Metzudas David*, relating the

word רְהָטִים to רָהִיטֵנוּ as used in allusion to the Temple (in 1:17), comments:] If you continue to conduct yourself in this lofty manner, you will be so desirable that God Himself — if it may be so expressed — will be bound to you in the Temple, never to depart from there.

Alshich: But through it all, God was bound in love to Israel because of the *running* [as per *Rashi's* second interpretation above] of Abraham; and because of Jacob who "peeled the rods" in the רְהָטִים, *watering troughs* [*Genesis* 30:38; *Targum* below].

A king bound in tresses esoterically refers also to Messiah who figuratively is "bound up" and prevented from revealing himself (*Ibn Ezra*).

The *Targum* sums up many of the Midrashic interpretations cited above as he paraphrases this verse: "The king appointed to be the *head* [=רֹאשׁ] over you is as righteous as Elijah the prophet who showed his zeal for the God of Heaven when he slew the false prophets on Mount Carmel and restored the Jews to the fear of God. And the *poor* [= דַּלַּת] among the people who walk with *bowed head* [= רֹאשֵׁךְ] because they are in want, these

Rashi there explains "master of the nose" as meaning: בַּעַל קוֹמָה וְצוּרָה, *man of stature,* and גָּדוֹל הַדּוֹר, *leader of the generation.* [Maharsha explains that Rabban Gamliel, who was the prince of that generation, is compared to a "nose" — loftiest of the vital organs; the organ of life — the organ into which *God breathed the breath of life.*]

Harav Gifter points out that the "nose" in this context alludes to the Torah Sages' capability of being able to "sniff out" the good and bad in situations where others cannot differentiate between them. This is borne out by the Talmudic interpretation [*Sanhedrin* 93b] of the verse in *Isaiah* 11:3: ... וַהֲרִיחוֹ בְּיִרְאַת ה', *and he shall smell him* [i.e., "sniff out" and perceive beyond that which seems obvious] *with fear of God, and shall not judge* [merely] *after the sight of his eyes, nor decide* [merely] *after the hearing of his ears.* (See also *Ibn Ezra* ad loc.)

is bound in naziritic tresses. [7] How beautiful and pleasant are you, befitting the pleasures of spiritual love. [8] Such is your stature, likened to a towering palm tree,

shall in time to come be clothed in *purple* [= כְּאַרְגָּמָן], as were Daniel in Babylon and Mordechai in Shushan, through the merit of Abraham who in days of old ascribed *Sovereignty* [= מֶלֶךְ] to the Lord of the Universe, through the piety of Isaac whom his father *bound* [= אָסוּר] for the purpose of sacrifice, and through the saintliness of Jacob who 'peeled the rods in the *watering troughs*' [= בָּרְהָטִים]."

מַה־יָּפִית וּמַה־נָּעַמְתְּ אַהֲבָה בַּתַּעֲנוּגִים **.7** — [lit., *How beautiful you are, and how pleasant, love in delights.*] The last stich in the verse is obscure. *Rashi* comments: Having praised her in detail, the nations now praise her entirely: "How completely beautiful you are, and how pleasant it is to cleave to you with a love in which properly to take pleasure" [i.e., a spiritual love based upon lofty ideals].[1]

[Compare God's similar praise of Israel in 1:15 and their response in 1:16.]

"How beautiful you are in the performance of *mitzvos*, and how pleasant in the exercise of charity!" (*Midrash*).

Even a *halachah* is thus applied to this verse:

The Chanukah menorah should be placed by the door near the public domain [so it should be seen from the street] in such a manner that the *mezuzah* should be on the right and

the menorah on the left to fulfill what is stated: *how beautiful you are and how pleasant — how beautiful* with the *mezuzah, and how pleasant* with the menorah [i.e., that you are surrounded with commandments symbolizing beauty and pleasure] (*Soferim* 20:5; see *Orach Chayim* 671:5,7).

"How beautiful you are, O Assembly of Israel, when you hear the yoke of My Kingdom, when I chasten you with afflictions for your misdeeds and you receive them lovingly, for they appear in your sight as delights" (*Targum*).

Alshich perceives this verse as Israel's response: How wonderful and how pleasant was God's love for me when I experienced it בַּתַּעֲנוּגִים, *in the delight*, of my own Land — not amid the affliction of exile!

The *Beis Yitzchak* once homiletically commented: O! How indeed beautiful and pleasant it is to show love for God and to serve Him amid luxury, rather than, God forbid, poverty ...

And as *Rav Naftali Ropshitzer* said: "What is so great about serving God when one is impoverished and seeks His aid? The true test of the love of God is when one is בְּתַעֲנוּגִים, immersed *in delights!*"

זֹאת קוֹמָתֵךְ דָמְתָה לְתָמָר **.8** — [lit., *This, your stature, is like a palm tree.*]

---

1. Love of God gives joy and delight to the soul ... and Solomon praises this kind of love above all others: *How beautiful you are, and how pleasant, love in delights.* The meaning is, How superior is the beauty and the pleasure of the love of God to those of any other love, for this love is one of delights ... Other kinds of love give a person great pain before he obtains the object of his love. When he obtains a little thereof, he finds pleasure, but the pain increases

וְשָׁדַיִךְ לְאַשְׁכֹּלוֹת: אָמַרְתִּי אֶעֱלֶה ט
בְתָמָר אֹחֲזָה בְּסַנְסִנָּיו וְיִהְיוּ־נָא שָׁדַיִךְ
כְּאֶשְׁכְּלוֹת הַגֶּפֶן וְרֵיחַ אַפֵּךְ כַּתַּפּוּחִים:

[This is a continuation of the praise of Israel's neighbors:] We witnessed your lovely stature in the days of Nebuchadnezzar. All the other nations succumbed and bowed down to the statue [cf. *Daniel* Chapter 3] but you remained upright as this palm tree (*Rashi*).

The *Targum* perceives in the imagery of this verse an allusion to the priests as they bless the congregation: "When your priests spread forth their hands in prayer and pronounce the blessings upon their brothers, the House of Israel, their outspread hands resemble the branches of a palm tree, while your congregation stands facing the priests, their countenances lowered toward earth like a cluster of grapes."

וְשָׁדַיִךְ לְאַשְׁכֹּלוֹת — [lit., *and your bosom is like clusters.*] Your bosom, i.e., Daniel, Chananiah, Mishael, and Azariah were your sources of spiritual nourishment, just as clusters of grapes are sources of wine. Similarly, they inspired everyone with the knowledge that there is no fear of

God like yours (*Rashi*).

And following *Alshich*: God responds: "Yes; My love was most delightful in your own land. But that was when your stature was like a palm tree, displaying a unified heart to Me as the palm tree which has only one *heart* [*Succah* 45b], and when your *bosom*, i.e., your Torah-leaders who nourish you, instilled Torah into the hearts of the people. That is why you merited the love which you have since forfeited."

In continuity with his interpretation of these verses as God's ethical admonition to His people, *Metzudas David* interprets: "Be sure that *the moral stature* of your entire nation *be upright and straight as a palm tree*. Then be assured that *your bosom*, i.e., the king and high priest who nurture the people, will flow forth with abundant goodness *like clusters of grapes* flowing forth with abundant wine."

9. Thus far it was the heathen nations who have sung their praise

until he obtains it entirely, since it is possible to obtain. And when he obtains it entirely. his love ceases and his desire subsides. [I.e., because mortal love can be attained, man is not content until he reaches his goal. After he attains it, he tires of it.]

But the love of God is different … Man takes delight in that which he obtains, without any addition of pain because he knows that God cannot be entirely obtained. Therefore, he delights in the little that he attains, and as he attains more, his love and delight increase. Moreover, this love cannot cease because the object is infinite, and man is constantly eager to obtain more … For, the greater the worth of the object desired, the greater the delight in its attainment.

True love is the love which man has for the beloved for the sake of the beloved alone, having no other purpose than to do the will of the beloved …. such love which is for the sake of the beloved solely will last as long as the beloved endures. And since God endures forever, love for Him never ceases (*Sefer Halkkarim* [III:36]; see *Foreword* and *Overview*).

VII
9

from your teachers flow sustenance like wine-filled clusters.

HASHEM: ⁹ I boast on High that your deeds cause Me to ascend on your palm tree, I grasp onto your branches. I beg now your teachers that they may remain like clusters of grapes from which flow strength to your weakest ones, and the fragrance of your countenance like apples,

---

[begun in 6:10]. Now it is the *Shechinah* who is addressing the Jewish exiles who are dispersed among the nations (*Rashi*):

אָמַרְתִּי אֶעֱלֶה בְתָמָר — [lit., *I said, I will rise* (or: *climb up in*) *the palm tree.*]

[Israel is being compared to the palm tree; אֶעֱלֶה is understood in the sense of *I will rise up*, i.e., be glorified, uplifted, elevated *through*, i.e., by virtue of, this nation Israel. As *Rashi* comments:] "I boast about you among the Celestial Hosts, that I am elevated through your actions on earth when My Name is hallowed by you among the nations of the world."

Following *Alshich*, Israel replies: "If so, I will return and repent. I will *ascend* and scale spiritual heights — *tall and erect as a palm tree.* And even if I cannot attain this level of perfection, at the very least *I will take hold of its branches* — i.e., I will grasp onto whatever I possibly can." [The verse continues with God's reply; see comm. below.]

אֹחֲזָה בְּסַנְסִנָּיו — [lit., *I will take hold of its branches.*] *Rashi* continues: "And consequently I will grasp and

cleave to the branches [i.e., children, of this palm tree, Israel]" (*Rashi*).

[And He thus admonishes them:]

וְיִהְיוּ־נָא שָׁדַיִךְ כְּאֶשְׁכְּלוֹת הַגֶּפֶן וְרֵיחַ אַפֵּךְ כַּתַּפּוּחִים   [lit., *and let your bosom be like clusters of grapes, and your breath* (lit., *the scent of your nostrils*) *like* (the scent of)[1] *apples.*]

[*Rashi* perceives this as an exhortation to the *bosom*, i.e., the righteous and wise who, by their good example, nurture and inspire the young — in age or intellect — by withstanding and responding vigorously to the taunts of their heathen neighbors who wish to lead Israel astray.]

Metzudas David interprets this verse as a Divine promise that if God's admonition is heeded, in a short time He will respond by alighting unto His *palm tree*, Israel, clinging firmly to its *branches*; its *bosom* [king and high priest] will then be abundantly flowing like *clusters of grapes* [see comm. to previous verse] and *the scent of your breath* — i.e., the savor of its sacrifices — will be as pleasing to Him as [the scent of] *apples* ... [see next verse].

---

1. The simile comparing finest scents to that of an apple orchard occurs in the *Talmud*. Commenting upon the verse in *Genesis* 27:27: *like the fragrance of a field which* HASHEM *had blessed him*, the *Talmud* [*Taanis* 29b] identifies the beautiful fragrance as "the scent of a field of apples" (*Harav David Feinstein*).

י וְחִכֵּךְ כְּיֵין הַטּוֹב הוֹלֵךְ לְדוֹדִי לְמֵישָׁרִים
י-יב יא דּוֹבֵב שִׂפְתֵי יְשֵׁנִים: אֲנִי לְדוֹדִי וְעָלַי
יב תְּשׁוּקָתוֹ: לְכָה דוֹדִי נֵצֵא הַשָּׂדֶה נָלִינָה

10. וְחִכֵּךְ כְּיֵין הַטּוֹב — [lit., (And let) your palate (i.e., mouth) be like choicest wine.] I.e., exercise caution, and let your response to the taunts of the heathens be [as clear and potent] as fine wine (Rashi).

According to Divrei Yedidiah: That which emanates from the mouths of the Sages who decide the halachah should be as clear and refined as choicest wine.

Israel interjects with a declaration of assurance (Rashi).

הוֹלֵךְ לְדוֹדִי לְמֵישָׁרִים — [lit., it flows (or: goes) for my Beloved in righteousness.]

[This is Israel's reply of assurance:] I am cautious to stress in my response to them that I will stand firm in my faith, that my palate should flow forth before my Beloved in righteous sincere love [אַהֲבַת מִישׁוֹר, see on 1:4: מֵישָׁרִים אֲהֵבוּךָ], a sincere love of the heart — and not feigned (Rashi).

According to Metzudas Tzion, God is still the speaker. He interprets לְדוֹדִי, to my Beloved, as an apocopated version of the plural לְדוֹדִים, for lovers, and in Metzudas David he renders the verse: And your words — i.e., prayers — will be as acceptable to Me as the choicest wine, [הוֹלֵךְ לְדוֹדִי]ם, לְמֵישָׁרִים, which passes between lovers in expression of their love.

— Divrei Yedidiah: And let your mouth constantly utter, "I go for my Beloved in righteousness" — i.e., let all

your deeds be for the sake of Heaven.

דּוֹבֵב שִׂפְתֵי יְשֵׁנִים — [lit., causing the lips of sleepers to speak.] I.e., a love so intense that even my departed ancestors will rejoice in me and be thankful for their lot (Rashi).

The Talmud comments that if a pupil repeats the teachings of his departed teacher, he causes the lips of the latter to murmur in his grave. This is compared to a cluster of ripe grapes which, at the mere touch of a finger, causes an abundant flow of juice. Similarly, at the mere mention of the words of departed sages, their overflowing wisdom is manifested as though they were again discoursing as they did in their lifetime (Yevamos 97a; Maharsha; Torah Temimah).

— I.e., wine strong enough to "move even the lips of a sleeping person" — an exaggerated statement which describes the power of choice wine to make even usually reticent people talkative. Allegorically, God is saying: "Just as these wines stimulate the spirit, so do your words jubilate Me" (Metzudas David).

11. And the following is Israel's firm reply to the heathens (Rashi):

אֲנִי לְדוֹדִי וְעָלַי תְּשׁוּקָתוֹ — [lit., I am my Beloved's and His longing is upon me.] I.e., I am my Beloved's and He longs for me (Rashi).[1]

The relationship is mutually complementary, says the Zohar:

1. [The interpretation of וְעָלַי תְּשׁוּקָתוֹ, His longing is upon me, is possibly open to a dual interpretation. In one sense the verse is interpreted as a quid pro quo statement: "I love My Beloved,

VII

10-12

...Israel
to God:

...to the
nations

...to
God:

¹⁰ *and may your utterance be like finest wine.*

*I shall heed Your plea to uphold my faith be-
fore my Beloved in love so upright and honest
that my slumbering fathers will move their lips
in approval.*

¹¹ *I am my Beloved's and He longs for my
perfection.*

¹² *Come, my Beloved, let us go to the fields where
Your children serve You in want, there let us lodge
with Esau's children who are blessed with plenty yet*

"What is the cause of my being my Beloved? — *because* His desire is toward me" ... I must be my Beloved's *first*, preparing the way, so to speak, for His dwelling among us, and, *in response*, His desire is toward me ... for he who comes to be cleansed is assisted from Heaven [*Shabbos* 104a]; similarly, he who is deserving that God's desire be toward him, that person is sent the inspiration from above to serve God properly.

Rav S.R. Hirsch [to *Genesis* 3:16] explains תְּשׁוּקָה, *longing*: שׁוּק, *market*; שׁוֹק, *thigh*; שׁוֹקֵק, *a strong mass movement of locusts or horses*, the basic conception accordingly, *to move oneself powerfully toward one direction*; hence, תְּשׁוּקָה, *the direction of feelings and the other efforts toward one's goal; striving*

toward; longing.

According to *Metzudas David's* thematic interpretation, this verse is Israel's relieved reply after having heard all of God's admonitions and promises in the previous verses: "I always knew that I am His people and He will not despise me and exchange me for another."

Torah Temimah accentuates the אֲנִי, *I*, in this verse and interprets it as a statement of man subordinating his entire self, his egocentricity, to his Creator by proclaiming: *I am my Beloved's* — my entire self is subordinated entirely to my Beloved, and thus *His longing is upon me.*

12. [And, turning to God:]

לְכָה דוֹדִי נֵצֵא הַשָּׂדֶה — [lit., *Come, my Beloved, let us go forth into the field.*] *Rashi* cites the *Talmud,*

---

and *therefore* He longs for me," as in 6:3, "*I am my Beloved's, and my Beloved is mine.*" This is the interpretation adopted by *Rashi* and most commentators. But possibly, *His longing is upon me* might be interpreted to mean "the longing for Him is upon me" — i.e., I am totally consumed with longing for Him, and upon me is the obligation to love Him with all my heart, soul, and possessions. For one who attains the high degree of being able to say, "*I am my Beloved's,*" upon that person has descended the proper feeling of His longing — i.e., the true longing for God that only the righteous attain — a longing so deep that they become *sick with love*. See *Foreword*, and footnote to 2:5.

It is this interpretation that seems to be reflected in the *Midrash* to this verse, as it comments: "The yearning of Israel is only toward their Father in Heaven." (But cf. parallel *Midrash* in *Bereishis Rabbah* 20:17 to *Genesis* 3:16 where the text reads: "the yearning of God is only toward Israel.")]

פֶּרֶק ז יג בַּכְּפָרִים: נַשְׁכִּימָה לַכְּרָמִים נִרְאֶה אִם־
פָּרְחָה הַגֶּפֶן פִּתַּח הַסְּמָדַר הֵנֵצוּ הָרִמּוֹנִים
יד שָׁם אֶתֵּן אֶת־דֹּדַי לָךְ: הַדּוּדָאִים נָתְנוּ־
רֵיחַ וְעַל־פְּתָחֵינוּ כָּל־מְגָדִים חֲדָשִׁים
גַּם־יְשָׁנִים דּוֹדִי צָפַנְתִּי לָךְ:

Eruvin 21b: "The congregation of Israel spoke before the Holy One, blessed is He: Lord of the Universe. Do not judge me as You would those [affluent ones] who reside in large towns where there exists robbery and immorality; *let us go forth into the field* [i.e., among the rural dwellers and farmers (*Rashi*)] and I will show You scholars who study the Torah in poverty."

נָלִינָה בַּכְּפָרִים — [lit., *let us lodge in the villages.*] [In continuation of the Talmudic interpretation cited by *Rashi:*] Read not בַּכְּפָרִים, *in the villages*, but בַּכֹּפְרִים, *among the disbelievers.* I.e., come, let us lodge [for a short time only (*Midrash*)] among the disbelievers [and in contrast to the Jews], I will show You the children of Esau upon whom You have bestowed much bounty and yet they disbelieve in You.

13. [Israel continues extolling its children by figuratively "inviting" God to come and observe the fine conduct of His nation, Israel:]

נַשְׁכִּימָה לַכְּרָמִים — [lit., *Let us rise early for the vineyards.*] This is an allusion to the synagogues and study-houses [which are already occupied from early morning] (*Rashi; Eruvin* ibid.).

According to the *Midrash, vineyards* refers to Israel, as it says [Isaiah 5:7]: *for the vineyard of*

HASHEM, *Master of Legions, is the House of Israel.* [Compare comm. to 2:15.]

נִרְאֶה אִם־פָּרְחָה הַגֶּפֶן פִּתַּח הַסְּמָדַר הֵנֵצוּ הָרִמּוֹנִים — [lit., *let us see if the vine has budded, if the blossom has opened, if the pomegranates are in bloom.*] *If the vine has budded* is an allusion to the students of Scripture [compare 5:11]; *if the blossom has opened* is an allusion to the students of the *Mishnah* [because, as *Rashi* explains here (and above in 2:13), "blossoming" refers to the period when the blossom falls away and the grapes become visible; the students of *Mishnah* are so described because they are a stage closer to enabling others to benefit from them, the students, by enjoying their teaching (and as *Rashi* explains in the *Talmud* ibid., blossoming is a later stage than budding — so is the *Mishnah* more clarified than Scripture)];

If the pomegranates are in bloom, i.e., in the last stages of ripeness. This alludes to the students of the *Gemara* who have achieved wisdom and are "ripe" and worthy to instruct in Torah matters.

שָׁם אֶתֵּן אֶת־דֹּדַי לָךְ — [lit., *there I will give my love to You.*] I.e., there I will show You my glory and my greatness, the praise of my sons and my daughters (*Eruvin,* ibid.; *Rashi*).

still deny. ¹³*Let us wake at dawn in vineyards of prayer and study. Let us see if students of Writ have budded, if students of Oral Law have blossomed, if ripened scholars have bloomed; there I will display my finest products to You.*

¹⁴*All my baskets, good and bad, emit a fragrance; all at our doors have the precious fruits of comely deeds, both the Scribes' new ordinances and the Torah's timeless wisdom; for You, Beloved, has my heart stored them.*

There will I produce the righteous men and women, the prophets and prophetesses who have arisen from me (*Midrash*).

14. הַדּוּדָאִים נָתְנוּ־רֵיחַ — [lit., *The baskets (or: mandrakes) yield fragrance.*] [The *Talmud* renders דּוּדָאִים, *baskets:*] The baskets of figs, both good and bad figs, as signified in the verse [*Jeremiah* 24:1,2]: *and behold, two* דּוּדָאֵי, *baskets, of figs before the Sanctuary of* HASHEM; *one basket had very good figs ... and the other basket had very bad figs, which were so bad they were inedible. Good figs* are an allusion to those who are righteous in every respect; *bad figs* are an allusion to those who are wicked in every respect. But lest you imagine that their hope is lost and their prospect is frustrated, it was explicitly stated: הַדּוּדָאִים נָתְנוּ־רֵיחַ, *the baskets yield fragrance:* both [the wicked as well as the righteous] will in time to come give forth fragrance — they will all seek out God (*Eruvin* 21a; *Rashi*).

וְעַל־פְּתָחֵינוּ כָּל־מְגָדִים חֲדָשִׁים גַּם־יְשָׁנִים — [lit., *and at our door are all precious fruits — both new and old.*] I.e., we have in our possession the

rewards for many *mitzvos* — *both new and old* — the *mitzvos* instituted by the Scribes as well as those explicitly stated in the Torah (*Rashi*).

דּוֹדִי צָפַנְתִּי לָךְ — [lit., (which) *I have hidden* (i.e., *stored away*) *for You, my Beloved.*] "For Your Name and for Your service have I hidden them [i.e., all the commandments] in my heart" [in order to perform with total dedication]. Or alternatively: "I have hidden [i.e., stored] the good deeds to show you that I have performed the commandments" (*Rashi*).

According to the *Midrash*, God responds: "You store up for Me, and I store up for you. You store up for Me through the performance of *mitzvos* and good deeds, and I store up for you treasures full of more good things than there are in the world." Rav Abba bar Kahana said: His store, however, is greater than ours as it says [*Psalms* 31:20]: *O how abundant is Your goodness that You have stored away for those who fear You, that You have performed for those who seek refuge in You.*

א מִי יִתֶּנְךָ כְּאָח לִי יוֹנֵק שְׁדֵי אִמִּי
ב אֶמְצָאֲךָ בַחוּץ אֶשָּׁקְךָ גַּם לֹא־יָבֻזוּ לִי:
אֶנְהָגְךָ אֲבִיאֲךָ אֶל־בֵּית אִמִּי תְּלַמְּדֵנִי
אַשְׁקְךָ מִיַּיִן הָרֶקַח מֵעֲסִיס רִמֹּנִי:

VIII

1. [In continuity, God had earlier expressed His desire to rest His
Shechinah upon His people once
again. They now continue their
response of 7:10-14 with a longing
plea for His aid and comfort:]

מִי יִתֶּנְךָ כְּאָח לִי יוֹנֵק שְׁדֵי אִמִּי — [lit., *if
only You were as a brother to me,
who had nursed at my mother's bosom!*] I.e., *if only You would comfort
me [in my exile] as Joseph comforted his brothers who wronged him,
as it is said of him [Genesis 50:21]:
and he comforted them (Rashi).*

Divrei Yedidiah applies to the
context of this verse his interpretation of *sister* as alluding to the
filial relationship as manifested by
זְכוּת אָבוֹת, *ancestral merit* [see full
comment to verse 4:9]. According to
this, Israel says to God: Although
You find no personal merit in me,
If only You were a brother to me
— i.e., at least treat me like a *sister* and recall my ancestral merit,
as You have said [*Leviticus* 26:45]:
*But I will remember for them the
covenant of their ancestors.*

אֶמְצָאֲךָ בַחוּץ אֶשָּׁקְךָ גַּם לֹא־יָבֻזוּ לִי — [lit.,
*(When) I would find You in the street
I would kiss You and no one would
scorn me.*] I.e., I would find Your
prophets speaking in Your Name and
I would embrace and kiss them. I am
assured that *no one* [of the prophets]
would scorn me for Your love is

surely so worthy that Your beloved
should go about in search of it (*Rashi*).

This verse is to be understood as
an intensely emotional utterance of
a maiden who craves for freedom of
expression to her Beloved to suit the
purity of her affection: "O that in the
eyes of men You would be only a little brother to me, one who still nursed
at my mother's bosom! Then I could
openly display affection for You,
and no one would look askance."
Allegorically: "O that all the obstacles
toward serving You wholeheartedly
would be removed. I would then be
able to indulge unmolested in Your
Torah and precepts wherever I
went!" (*Metzudas David*).

And no one would scorn me — For
when we perform *mitzvos* publicly
at present, the nations ridicule us, as
in *Lamentations* 1:7: *They gloated at
her Sabbaths* [see comm. to ArtScroll
ed. p. 60] — whereas in the future we
will be able to serve God in sight of
all, *and all the peoples of the earth
shall see that the Name of* HASHEM
*is proclaimed over you, and they
shall be afraid of you* [*Deuteronomy*
28:10] (*Tz'ror HaMor*).

Ibn Aknin explains the symbolism
of the various phrases: *street* connotes
the lengthy duration of the Exile while
Israel finds itself "outside," so to speak,
of its land; *kiss* refers to the prophecy
— transmitted from the "mouth" of
God — which Israel would seek.

VIII
1-2

If only, despite my wrongs, You could comfort me as Joseph did, like a brother nurtured at my mother's breasts, if in the streets I found Your prophets I would kiss You and embrace You through them, nor could anyone despise me for it. ² I would lead You, I would bring You to my mother's Temple for You to teach me as You did in Moses' Tent; to drink I would give You spiced libations, wines like pomegranate nectar.

Harav Gifter points out that this "kiss" may refer to the Torah, also transmitted by the mouth, as in *Proverbs* 2:6, כִּי־ה' יִתֵּן חָכְמָה מִפִּיו דַּעַת וּתְבוּנָה, *For HASHEM gives wisdom; from His mouth come knowledge and understanding.* This is further borne out by תְּלַמְּדֵנִי, *You should "instruct" me*, of the next verse.

2. [And after finding You:]

אֶנְהָגְךָ אֲבִיאֲךָ אֶל־בֵּית אִמִּי תְּלַמְּדֵנִי — [lit., *I would lead You, I would bring You to my mother's house that You should instruct me.*] I.e., I would lead and bring You to the house of my "mother" [allegorically, *House of my nation* (see on 1:6 s.v. אִמִּי)] — i.e., the Temple, *that You should* [again] *instruct me*, as You used to do in the Tent of Assembly (*Rashi*).

[Compare a similar thought in 3:4: *till I brought Him to my mother's house* where chronologically *mother's house* refers, according to *Rashi*, to the Tabernacle. See comm. of *Alshich* cited there.]

Esoterically, Israel's *mother* is the *Shechinah.* Hence, *House of my Mother* refers to the Temple, dwelling-place of the *Shechinah.* For, as the *Talmud* notes: "never has the *Shechinah* departed from the Western Wall" (*Tz'ror HaMor*).

The *Targum* interprets these words as being addressed to the Messiah in reference to the time of Redemption: "I will lead you, O King Messiah, and bring you up to my Temple; and you will teach me to fear the Lord, and to walk in His way. There we will partake of a feast of Leviathan, and drink old wine which has been preserved in the grape since the days of Creation, and eat of pomegranates and fruits which have been prepared for the righteous in the Garden of Eden."

אַשְׁקְךָ מִיַּיִן הָרֶקַח מֵעֲסִיס רִמֹּנִי — [lit., *I would give You spiced wine to drink, of the juice of my pomegranate.*] This refers "to the wine-libations and 'sweet wine' " (*Rashi*).

אַשְׁקְךָ, *I would give You to drink*, is metaphorically understood as "cause You to rejoice in the works of Your creation" (*Sforno*).

Wine is symbolic of the *wine of Torah* [see comm. to 1:2], and the *Talmud* [*Sanhedrin* 37a] homiletically compares precepts to the many seeds of a full pomegranate ... *Juice* refers to the essential joy and "sap" derived from proper performance of the precepts. Allegorically, our verse is thus to be rendered: "I will learn, before You, the Torah with the fragrance of its innermost truths — and perform with utmost pleasure and sincerity the precepts incumbent upon me."

פרק ח ג שְׂמֹאלוֹ תַּחַת רֹאשִׁי וִימִינוֹ תְּחַבְּקֵנִי: ג-ה
ד הִשְׁבַּעְתִּי אֶתְכֶם בְּנוֹת יְרוּשָׁלַ͏ִם מַה־
תָּעִירוּ | וּמַה־תְּעֹרְרוּ אֶת־הָאַהֲבָה עַד
ה שֶׁתֶּחְפָּץ: מִי זֹאת עֹלָה מִן־הַמִּדְבָּר
מִתְרַפֶּקֶת עַל־דּוֹדָהּ תַּחַת הַתַּפּוּחַ עוֹרַרְתִּיךָ

"... And as You instruct me once again in Your proper service, I will respond by offering You *spiced wine*, symbolic of the pleasures of the precepts and good deeds, and *juice of my pomegranate* — the flowing honey of my superior characteristics. All of this is impossible while I am in exile and You are aloof from me; here I cannot properly pursue Your service and I find myself estranged from You" (*Alshich*).

3-4. And now turning and directing her words to the nations (*Rashi*):

שְׂמֹאלוֹ תַּחַת רֹאשִׁי וִימִינוֹ תְּחַבְּקֵנִי — [lit., *His left hand is under my head and His right arm embraces me.*] Know, you nations: Although I complain and lament, my Beloved "holds my hand" and is my support throughout my exile (*Rashi*).

And therefore:

הִשְׁבַּעְתִּי אֶתְכֶם בְּנוֹת יְרוּשָׁלַ͏ִם מַה־תָּעִירוּ וּמַה־תְּעֹרְרוּ אֶת־הָאַהֲבָה עַד שֶׁתֶּחְפָּץ — [lit., *I have adjured you, O daughters of Jerusalem: Why should you wake or rouse the love until it pleases?*] Your efforts will be of no avail! (*Rashi*).

[Cf. comm. to 2:6, and first adjuration in 2:7.]

Your attempts to sway His love from me are in vain for the time will yet come when you yourselves will witness the public manifestation of His love for me — He will cause His Shechinah to dwell among me in love and warm embrace. It is for this reason that *I have already adjured you* against these futile attempts. I have already acquired His love forever! (*Alshich*).

These verses describe the period immediately preceding the Redemption, when delivery is imminent and there need no longer be real fear of what harm the nations may plot. The wording of this adjuration is, therefore, different from the earlier adjuration in 2:7 where they are threatened and adjured *by gazelles or by hinds of the field*. Being so close to Redemption this adjuration carries no threats; its purpose is not to frighten the nations, but to make them know that whatever they plot, their efforts to disturb God's love for the Jews are in vain (*Divrei Yedidiah*).

According to *Targum* it is the Messiah who addresses this verse in exhortation to Israel: "I adjure you, O my people of the House of Israel, why do you war against the nations of the earth to leave the exile? ... Stay here a little longer, until the nations who have come up to wage war against Jerusalem will be destroyed; and after that the Lord of the Universe will recall the love of the righteous, and it will be His will to redeem you."

5. The following is uttered by God and His Heavenly Tribunal [cf. use of *we* in v. 8] in reference to the

³*Despite my laments in exile, His left hand supports my head and His right hand embraces me in support. ⁴I adjure you, O nations who are destined to ascend to Jerusalem, if you dare provoke God to hate me or disturb His love for me while He still desires it.*

HASHEM: ⁵*How worthy she is ascending from the wilderness bearing Torah and His Presence, clinging to her Beloved!*

Israel: *Under Sinai suspended above me, there I roused Your love, there was Your people born; a mother to*

still-exiled Community of Israel (*Rashi*):

מִי זֹאת עֹלָה מִן־הַמִּדְבָּר מִתְרַפֶּקֶת עַל־דּוֹדָהּ — [lit., *who is she that rises up from the desert leaning upon her Beloved?*] I.e., how very worthy she is — she who ascended from the desert bearing wonderful gifts from God; there she was raised up [spiritually] through the giving of the Torah and cleaving to the *Shechinah*. Her friendship was obvious to all — *leaning upon her Beloved*: professing her love for her Beloved while she was still in exile in Egypt (*Rashi*).[1]

[Cf. a similar sequence of verses in 3:5-6. There Israel is quoting the nations whose curiosity was whetted by the sight of the Jews marching in the desert after the Egyptian exile.]

מִתְרַפֶּקֶת is rendered *clinging* by *Rashi* and *Ibn Ezra* who derives it from the Arabic.

Metzudas David, however, perceives *Israel* as speaking these words, trying to elicit her Beloved's favor by indulging in reminiscence of her former loyalty:

"Which other nation believed in You as much as I, following You into the wilderness relying solely on You? ..."

Seeking God's love, Israel interrupts and recalls (*Rashi*):

תַּחַת הַתַּפּוּחַ עוֹרַרְתִּיךָ — [lit., *Under the apple* (tree) *I roused* (i.e., *woke*) *You.*]

Remember, how, beneath Mount Sinai — which was suspended over my head like an apple — *I roused You* — i.e., "I manifested my adoration for You" (*Rashi*).

This is derived from the Midrashic account that God uprooted Mount Sinai and suspended it above their head, as it says: [*Deuteronomy* 4:11]: *and they stood beneath the mountain.*

(*Torah Temimah* suggests that in context with this *Midrash*, Mount Sinai is compared to an apple, since the word תַּפּוּחַ, *apple*, has the same root as

1. In continuity with the *Targum's* thematic interpretation of this chapter, this verse cites the reaction of the inhabitants of the earth upon witnessing תְּחִיַּת הַמֵּתִים, *the revival of the dead*, in the time to come: "When the dead will rise, the Mount of Olives shall be rent asunder, and all Israel's dead will issue from beneath it; and even those righteous ones who have died in exile will come from under the earth by way of caverns and issue forth from beneath the Mount of Olives. The wicked who will have died and been buried in the land of Israel will be cast up as a man throws up a stone with a club.

"Then all the inhabitants of the earth will exclaim: What was the merit of this people,

שָׁמָּה חִבְּלַתְךָ אִמֶּךָ שָׁמָּה חִבְּלָה יְלָדַתְךָ: **פרק ח**

ו וֹ שִׂימֵנִי כַחוֹתָם עַל־לִבֶּךָ כַּחוֹתָם עַל־
זְרוֹעֶךָ כִּי־עַזָּה כַמָּוֶת אַהֲבָה קָשָׁה כִשְׁאוֹל
קִנְאָה רְשָׁפֶיהָ רִשְׁפֵּי אֵשׁ שַׁלְהֶבֶתְיָה:

נפח, *to inflate.* Homiletically, Mount Sinai resembled an "inflated balloon" as it floated above their heads.)

The *Midrash* homiletically notes: Why is Sinai compared to an apple tree? Because just as an apple tree produces its fruit in Sivan, so the Torah was given in Sivan [i.e., so did Sinai bear its fruit — the Torah — in Sivan (*Torah Temimah*)].

"It was *I* and no other who sought out Your shade under the apple tree to which You are compared [see 2:3], and I jumped at the opportunity to cry out נַעֲשֶׂה וְנִשְׁמָע, *we will do and we will obey!"* (*Alshich*).

שָׁמָּה חִבְּלַתְךָ אִמֶּךָ שָׁמָּה חִבְּלָה יְלָדַתְךָ— [lit., *There Your "mother" was in travail for You; she who "bore" You was in travail.*] I.e., there did Your אֻמָּה, *nation* [allegorized as *mother* — see comm. to 3:11 s.v. אמו, *His "mother"*], become a "mother" [i.e., a "mother unto nations" (see ibid.)] and subject herself to travail [allegorized as pains of "childbirth"] by virtue of this association (*Rashi*).

[The bracketed comments inserted above remove many of the surface difficulties in this otherwise difficult *Rashi*, which can be understood fully only by referring to the comm. to 3:11 as indicated.]

[The *travails* indicate the enmity Israel experienced on the part of the heathen world as a direct result of receiving the Torah and, thereby, being elevated to its new status and responsibility. (As in the Talmudic comment [*Shabbos* 89a; see *Iyun Yaakov*]: "Why is it called Mt. Sinai? Because it was there that שִׂנְאָה, *hatred,* of the nations for the Jews descended upon the world.") *Torah Temimah* explains the "prenatal travail" Israel experienced as alluding to the anxiety at having the mountain suspended above them.]

The *Midrash* comments in this context: It is as when a man escapes safely from a dangerous place, and others meeting him say to him: What danger you were in! Your mother has really borne you there! It is as though you were created afresh! [At Sinai, too, you were created afresh by receiving the Torah!]

שִׂימֵנִי כַחוֹתָם עַל־לִבֶּךָ כַּחוֹתָם עַל־זְרוֹעֶךָ **.6**— [lit., *set me as a seal upon Your heart, as a seal upon Your arm.*] And because of that love, seal me upon Your heart so that You do not forget me (*Rashi*).

[The symbolism refers to seals which were suspended from the neck with a cord and worn either over the heart or on the hand.]

myriads of whom have come up out of the earth, as on the day when they came up out of the wilderness to the land of Israel, and who delight themselves with the love of their Lord. as on the day when they were seen at the foot of Mount Sinai to receive the Law?

"At that moment, Zion — the mother of Israel — shall bear her children, and Jerusalem shall receive her captive sons."

*other nations, there she endured the travail of her
birth.* ⁶*For the sake of my love, place me like a seal
on Your heart, like a seal to dedicate Your strength
for me, for strong till the death is my love; though
their zeal for vengeance is hard as the grave,
its flashes are flashes of fire, the flame of God.*

Set me near Your heart so Your
love for me will never depart, *and as
a seal upon Your arm* by manifesting
Your love in deed as well (*Alshich*).

The metaphor of *arm* is illustrated
in the anthropomorphic use of God's
arm in the phrase זְרוֹעַ וְזוּזָיָה, *an outstretched arm,* indicating the dis-
play of His might (*Divrei Yedidiah*).

And You will perceive ...

כִּי־עַזָּה כַמָּוֶת אַהֲבָה — [lit., *that love is
strong as death.*] I.e., to me the extent
of my love for You is as strong as the
deaths which I suffered for Your sake
[i.e., my love for You is so strong that
I endure death for its sake] (*Rashi*).

... Because it is due to our great
love for You *that for Your sake
we are killed all the days* [*Psalms
44:23*] (*Alshich*).

— "My love for You is so strong
that I would even choose death
rather than give up this love. It is
therefore only proper that You do
not remove Your love from me"
(*Metzudas David*).

The intent of this statement is
to portray the magnitude of the
love Israel feels for God — a love
so great that even death is dwarfed
in comparison to it. It is similar to
such earlier statements as *for I am
sick with love* (2:5), and *my soul
departed as He spoke* (5:6).

קָשָׁה כִשְׁאוֹל קִנְאָה — [lit., *jealousy is
hard as the grave*] referring to the
unjust complaints, rivalries, and jeal-
ousies which the nations provoked
against me because of You.[1] (קִנְאָה,
jealousy, is used in Scripture to convey feelings of revenge, zeal — *Rashi*.)

Alshich explains this as the burning, deathlike feelings of envy that
the Jews feel at seeing the wicked
nations prosperous and at peace
while they themselves are alone and
downtrodden ... but in spite of it all
[next verse] even many waters could
not extinguish Israel's love for God.

"On that day shall the Children of
Israel say unto their Lord: We beseech
You, set us as the seal of a ring upon
Your heart, as the seal of a ring upon
Your arm, so that we shall never again
be exiled; for strong as death is our love
for You, and powerful as Gehinnom
is the jealousy which the nations bear
against us. The enmity which they
harbor against us is as the coals of the
fire of Gehinnom, which the Eternal
created on the last day of Creation,
with which to burn the worshipers of
strange idols" (*Targum*).

רְשָׁפֶיהָ רִשְׁפֵּי אֵשׁ שַׁלְהֶבֶתְיָה — [lit., *its
flashes are flashes of fire which is
a flame of God.*] I.e., its flashes are
of a fierce fire emanating from the
flames of Gehinnom (*Rashi*).

1. [Cf. *Lamentations* 1:21: כִּי אַתָּה עָשִׂיתָ, *For it was You Who did it* (i.e., my misfortune emanated from Your will). See comm. to *Eichah*, ArtScroll ed. page 71.]

פֶּרֶק ח ז מַיִם רַבִּים לֹא יוּכְלוּ לְכַבּוֹת אֶת־
ז-ח הָאַהֲבָה וּנְהָרוֹת לֹא יִשְׁטְפוּהָ אִם־יִתֵּן
אִישׁ אֶת־כָּל־הוֹן בֵּיתוֹ בָּאַהֲבָה בּוֹז יָבוּזוּ
לוֹ: ח אָחוֹת לָנוּ קְטַנָּה וְשָׁדַיִם אֵין לָהּ

[Although the subject of this phrase is ambiguous, it seems, according to *Rashi*, to refer to the *hatred* (jealousy) of the nations; or, according to others, to Israel's *love* for God.]

Metzudas David interprets רִשְׁפֶּיהָ, *its glowing coals*, and compares Israel's love for God to coals which keep glowing, and more so to a roaring blaze which [next verse] not even the strongest waters can extinguish.

According to *Tz'ror HaMor*, the subject is the קִנְאָה, *zeal*, of the preceding stich: "These flashes of zeal are like flashes in my heart — a flame of God."

7. God replies, continuing with the simile of love and fire:

מַיִם רַבִּים לֹא יוּכְלוּ לְכַבּוֹת אֶת־הָאַהֲבָה — [lit., *Many waters cannot extinguish the love.*] Even abundant water cannot extinguish it (*Rashi*).

Many waters is a reference to the heathen nations [as in *Isaiah* 17:12,13] (*Rashi*) — [i.e., even the most vile attempts of the heathen nations cannot wrest the love of God from the heart of Israel]. And since love was described in the preceding verse as a flame, this simile follows naturally.

And Israel has endured the test over the centuries by having withstood the tortures of fire and water without weakening her love for God (*Alshich*).

וּנְהָרוֹת לֹא יִשְׁטְפוּהָ — [lit., *and rivers cannot drown it.*] I.e., nor can their

leaders and kings drown it, neither by force or terror, nor by seductive enticement (*Rashi*).

"Even though all the nations, compared as they are to the waters of the Great Sea, were to gather themselves together, they could not quench the love which I bear You; and even though all the kings of the earth, likened to the river flowing with a strong current, were to join together, they could not blot You out of the world" (*Targum*).

[And God, hearing Israel's words, declares (*Rashi*):]

אִם־יִתֵּן אִישׁ אֶת־כָּל־הוֹן בֵּיתוֹ בָּאַהֲבָה בּוֹז יָבוּזוּ לוֹ — [lit., *if a man would give all the substance of his house in exchange for love* — i.e., to barter away your love for Me — *he would be laughed to scorn* — i.e., he would be utterly ridiculed for the attempt] so strong is the opinion of God and His Tribunal as to how Israel "leans" on her Beloved (*Rashi*).

[The flow of the verses is that nothing can extinguish true love, nor can love be bought with even great treasure.]

Most commentators, however, do not see a change of speakers in this verse, and interpret this as being spoken by Israel. Their intent is: And therefore, dear God, do not remove Your love for us (*Alshich*).

Ramban approaches this verse from an entirely different perspective. Interpreting יָבוּזוּ as related to

VIII

7-8

7 *Many waters of heathen tribulation cannot extin- guish the fire of this love, nor rivers of royal seduc- tion or torturewash it away.*

HASHEM: *Were any man to offer all the treasure of his home to entice you away from your love, they would scorn him to extreme.*

8 *Israel desires to cleave to us, the small and humble one, but her time of spiritual maturity has not come.*

בִּזָּה, *spoils*, he renders the verse: "If one would give all his heart, soul, and substance of his house to reach the full level of cleaving to God and loving Him [in the man- ner of the verse (*Deuteronomy 6:5*): *And you shall love* HASHEM, *your God, with all your heart, and with all your soul, and with all your possessions*] — then בּוֹז יָבוּזוּ לוֹ, *to him will be the spoils* — i.e., for publicly sanctifying God's Name, honor and glory will come to him. He will scale the loftiest peaks and will deserve to one day welcome the *Shechinah*."[1]

Ramban is thus following the in- terpretation of the *Targum* who para- phrases: "And if a man were to give all the substance of his house in order to acquire wisdom during the captiv- ity, I would restore it to him in double portion in the Hereafter, while all the spoils which men would take from the camp of Gog would be his also."

8. And the Heavenly Tribunal re- flects ...

אָחוֹת לָנוּ קְטַנָּה — [lit., *We have a little sister.*] אָחוֹת, *sister*, is allegori- cally interpreted by *Rashi* from the

verb אחה, *to join together, mend* (as in the *Talmud:* אֵלּוּ קְרָעִים שֶׁאֵין מִתְאַחִין, *these are the rents that may not be mended* — *Moed Ka- tan 26a*). קְטַנָּה, *little*, is understood as *humble, belittled*. He renders: "There is, among the humans, one [nation] who longs to join with us — one who is little and belittles herself among all the nations (as it is written [*Deuteronomy 7:7*]: *Not be- cause you are more numerous than all the peoples did* HASHEM *desire you and choose you, for you are the fewest of all the peoples*).

[On the symbolism of *sister* see 4:9, and above, verse 1.]

According to *Ramban*, the meta- phor of *little sister* alludes to Israel who is spurned while in exile.

"At that time, the angels of Heaven will say one to the other: We have one people on earth whose merit is clear, but it has no leaders to go forth and wage war with the camp of Gog. What are we to do for this sister when the nations will speak about going up against her in battle?" (*Targum*).

וְשָׁדַיִם אֵין לָהּ — [lit., *but she has no bosom.*] I.e., she is not yet ripe for

---

1. It is perhaps in this sense that the *Midrash* records the following incident:

Rav Yochanan was once going on foot from Tiberias to Sephoris, accompanied by Rav Chiya bar Abba. As they passed a certain field, Rav Yochanan said: "This field used to belong to me, and I sold it so that I could devote myself to the study of the Torah." They came to a

מַה־נַּעֲשֶׂה לַאֲחֹתֵנוּ בַּיּוֹם שֶׁיְּדֻבַּר־בָּהּ:
ט אִם־חוֹמָה הִיא נִבְנֶה עָלֶיהָ טִירַת כָּסֶף
וְאִם־דֶּלֶת הִיא נָצוּר עָלֶיהָ לוּחַ אָרֶז:

Redemption — the opposite of *her bosom is firm* [*Ezekiel* 16:7] which connotes readiness for Redemption (*Rashi*).

Ramban interprets the phrase as: *she is bereft of her source of nourishment* for she has been exiled from Eretz Yisrael, the Land of Life, and separated from the place of Torah, as it says [*Isaiah* 2:3]: *For Torah shall go forth from Zion*, whereas in exile, Scripture says [*II Chronicles* 15:3]: *For a long time Israel had been without the true God, and without a teaching priest, and without Torah.*

— She presently has no great leaders, like Moshe or Aaron [cf. comm. to 4:5 s.v. שְׁנֵי שָׁדַיִךְ] to fend for her (*Tz'ror HaMor*).

Ibn Aknin conjectures that the reference to *bosom* might allude, as it did in 4:5, to the twin Tablets of the Covenant. *But she has no bosom*

might refer to the fact that the Ark [repository of the Tablets] was one of the things Israel did not have in the Second Temple. [See comm. of *Ramban* cited in footnote to 5:7; and comm. to 6:5.]

מַה־נַּעֲשֶׂה לַאֲחֹתֵנוּ בַּיּוֹם שֶׁיְּדֻבַּר־בָּהּ — [lit., *what shall we do for our sister on the day she is spoken for?*] [I.e., how will we comport ourselves toward her when the nations plot against her and she seeks our protection?]

As *Rashi* explains: When the heathens murmur against her to cut her off as it is written (*Psalms* 83:5): *they say, Come, let us cut them off from nationhood.*

— By what means can we sustain her and give her hope while in exile? (*Ramban*).

According to *Metzudas David*, this verse echoes the words of the Jews who, upon reflecting upon the promise of imminent Redemption,

vineyard and Rav Yochanan said: "This vineyard used to belong to me, and I sold it in order to devote myself to the study of the Torah." They passed an olive press and he said the same thing. Rav Chiya began to weep.

"Why are you weeping?" he asked. Rav Yochanan replied: "I am weeping because you have not left yourself anything for your old age." He said to him: "Chiya, my son, you think so little of what I have done in selling a thing which was presented after six days, as it says [*Exodus* 20:11]: *For in six days HASHEM made heaven and earth?* But the Torah was given after forty days, as it says [ibid. 34:28]: *And he was there with HASHEM forty days.*

When Rav Yochanan was laid to rest, his generation applied to him the verse, "*If a man would give all the substance of his house for love* — like the love which Rav Yochanan bore for the Torah — בּוֹז יָבוּזוּ לוֹ, *he would be the recipient of the spoils* — his reward would be abundant."

[The above interpretation of the *Midrash* agrees with the *Targum* and the commentary of *Yefei Kol*. On the parallel *Midrash* in *Vayikra Rabbah* 30:1, however, *Yefei To'ar* [by the same commentator] explains the *Midrash* as meaning: "If anyone would want to follow Rav Yochanan and give up all his life's luxury, emulating the love which Rav Yochanan bore to the Torah — בּוֹז יָבוּזוּ לוֹ, *he would be laughed to scorn*. Rav Yochanan, however, paid no heed to scorn. He did not care for material things and clung to the Torah."]

VIII
9

What shall we do for our cleaving one on the day the nations plot against her?

⁹ *If her faith and belief are strong as a wall withstanding incursions from without, we shall become her fortress and beauty, building her city and Holy Temple; but if she wavers like a door, succumbing to every alien knock, with fragile cedar panels shall we then enclose her.*

---

are concerned about the fate of their brethren, the ten tribes still scattered about the countries of their captivity. The ten tribes, quite unprepared for Redemption, had not had leaders and prophets to nourish them with the "milk" of the wisdom of Torah. "By what merit," Israel asks, "will they become deserving of Your deliverance at the predestined time?"

"All depends upon how they comport themselves," God answers in the following verse.

9. [Our response depends upon how she conducts herself in the interim while in exile:]

אִם־חוֹמָה הִיא — [lit., *If she be a wall.*] If Israel will gird herself with faith and act toward the nations as if fortified with *copper* [*Jeremiah* 1:18] which they cannot infiltrate, i.e., if she will neither intermarry nor intermingle with them (*Rashi*)...

[Then] ...

נִבְנֶה עָלֶיהָ טִירַת כָּסֶף — [lit., *we will build upon her a turret of silver.*] I.e., we will become unto her a fortified city [= טִירָה, *turret*]; a crown and adornment [= כֶּסֶף, *silver*], and we will rebuild the Holy City and Temple (*Rashi*).

וְאִם דֶּלֶת הִיא — [lit., *but if she be a door*] which revolves on its

hinges and opens whenever someone knocks. Similarly, if her conduct is such that she is open to all blandishments, then ... (*Rashi*).

נָצוּר עָלֶיהָ לוּחַ אָרֶז — [lit., *we will enclose her with panels of cedar.*] I.e., [rather than fortifying her with non-corroding silver,] we will line her doors with wood panels which rot and are eaten away [thus leaving her exposed to danger and pillaging] (*Rashi*).

"If she will be as a wall among the nations, then shall we be with her, encompassing her as scaffoldings of silver, and the nations shall have no power to rule over her. And even though she be destitute of precepts, we shall implore on her behalf mercy from Heaven, and the merit of the Torah which the young study shall He recall in her behalf — written as it is upon the tablet of the heart, ready as a cedar to oppose the nations" (*Targum*).

Metzudas David interprets this verse differently: "If she conducted herself properly, then we will provide her with a luxurious dwelling place and rebuild the Temple for her; but if she conducted herself licentiously, then we will barricade her with cedar panels, i.e., we will let her remain exiled from her land."

אֲנִי חוֹמָה וְשָׁדַי כַּמִּגְדָּלוֹת אָז הָיִיתִי בְעֵינָיו י

יא כְּמוֹצְאֵת שָׁלוֹם: כֶּרֶם הָיָה לִשְׁלֹמֹה בְּבַעַל

הָמוֹן נָתַן אֶת־הַכֶּרֶם לַנֹּטְרִים אִישׁ יָבִא בְּפִרְיוֹ

יב אֶלֶף כָּסֶף: כַּרְמִי שֶׁלִּי לְפָנָי הָאֶלֶף לְךָ שְׁלֹמֹה

---

10. [Israel replies proudly and reassuringly. "Your fear is unjustified!":]

אֲנִי חוֹמָה וְשָׁדַי כַּמִּגְדָּלוֹת — [lit., *I am a wall, and my bosom is like towers.*] I.e., [I comport myself not like the *door,* but like the *wall* You mentioned] — strong, in the love of my Beloved ... [And though You thought me not ripe for Redemption, know that I am quite ripe:] *my bosom,* i.e., my synagogues and study-houses, which nurture Israel with words of Torah, *are like towers* [i.e., fortifying and serving as towers of strength for all] (*Rashi*).

"I am strong as a wall in the performance of the Torah's precepts, and my sons are stout as a tower. Then will the Assembly find favor in the eyes of God, and all the inhabitants of the earth shall seek her welfare" (*Targum*).

Homiletically, the Talmud comments: Rav Yochanan said: *I am a wall* refers to the Torah [which protects Israel like a wall (*Torah Temimah*)]; *my bosom is like towers* refers to scholars [who nurture the people of Israel with their Torah wisdom]

(*Pesachim* 87a; *Bava Basra* 7b).[1]

Ibn Aknin explains that although bereft of the primary sources of nourishment — the twin Tablets of the Covenant; Moses and Aaron; and the Prophets — nevertheless, Israel proudly proclaims that she has scholars who, by expounding Torah to the people and nourishing them, become the new beacons of spiritual sustenance. אָז הָיִיתִי בְעֵינָיו כְּמוֹצְאֵת שָׁלוֹם — [lit., then (i.e., *therefore*), I am in His eyes like one who found peace.] Like a bride who was found שְׁלֵמָה, *perfect,* and who finds peace in her husband's home (*Rashi;* cf. *Pesachim* 87a).

Israel thus turns to her companions and says: "אָז, *then,* upon my so reassuring God of my virtue, I became endeared to Him, as one who seeks peace" (*Metzudas David*).

And it is therefore fitting that we thereby merit the Messiah (*Sforno*).

11. [Israel reminisces on the circumstances of her current plight in exile:] כֶּרֶם הָיָה לִשְׁלֹמֹה בְּבַעַל הָמוֹן — [lit., *Shlomo had a vineyard in Baal Hamon.*] [Shlomo, as noted in 1:1,

---

1. The interpretation of *Rabbeinu Gershom* on *Bava Basra* (ibid.) is most interesting: אֵלּוּ ת״ח שֶׁלּוֹמְדִים זֶה מִזֶּה כְּתִינוֹק הַיּוֹנֵק מִשָּׁדֵי אִמּוֹ. The exchange of views among Torah scholars is an integral part of the process of Torah truth; so great is the submergence of self in this devotion to truth as to be comparable to the sustenance of a suckling babe at the mother's bosom,

Yad Ramah (ibid.) explains further: The contemporaries of the Sages derive spiritual sustenance from them just as an infant derives nourishment from his mother. The Torah of the Sages protects the generation like fortified towers.

Harav Gifter amplifies that not only are people nourished by the Sages, but they are as *totally dependent on this nourishment* as a suckling is on his mother, his sole source of sustenance. The maximum benefit from the Sages can be derived only if it is appreciated that *like watchmen* they stand above the generation and see from afar — interpreting the long-forgotten past, and preparing for the future; they are not shortsightedly mired in the fleeting present.

Israel: ¹⁰*My faith is firm as a wall, and my nourishing synagogues and study halls are strong as towers! Then, having said so, I become in His eyes like a bride found perfect.*

¹¹*Israel was the vineyard of Him to Whom peace belongs in populous Jerusalem. He gave His vineyard to harsh, cruel guardians; each one came to extort his fruit, even a thousand silver pieces.*

HASHEM: ¹²*The vineyard is Mine! Your iniquities are before Me!*

Nations: *The thousand silver pieces are Yours, You to Whom*

---

refers to God, מֶלֶךְ שֶׁהַשָׁלוֹם שֶׁלוֹ, *the King to Whom peace belongs.*]

Rashi explains that *vineyard* is an allusion to Israel as in the verse [*Isaiah* 5:7]: *for the vineyard of* HASHEM, *Master of Legions, is the House of Israel.* [Cf. comm. to 2:15; 7:13.] *Baal Hamon* [lit., *the owner of the multitude*] refers to Jerusalem, the greatly populated city, inhabited by הֲמוֹן רָב, *a great multitude of people;* בַּעַל, meaning *plateau, plains*, as in *Joshua* 12:7: בַּעַל גָּד, *the plains of Gad.*

[Allegorically, then, the phrase means: "God had a nation, Israel, who inhabited Jerusalem."]

The *Midrash* explains that הֲמוֹן, *multitude*, is an apt appellative for Jerusalem: "because *multitudes* of foreign powers longed for it."

נָתַן אֶת הַכֶּרֶם לַנֹּטְרִים — [lit., *He gave over the vineyard to guardians.*] I.e., He gave over His people into the hands of harsh rulers: Babylon, Media, Greece, and Edom [i.e., Rome. See comm. to *Eichah* 4:21, ArtScroll ed. p. 127].

אִישׁ יָבָא בְּפִרְיוֹ אֶלֶף כָּסֶף — [lit.,

everyone would bring for its fruit a thousand silver pieces.] I.e., the "keepers" would extort whatever they could: they would impose exorbitant levies and taxes and keep it for themselves (*Rashi*).

[The *thousand* implies exorbitance. See response in next verse, and comment of *Rashi* there, s.v. וּמָאתַיִם.]

12. Following *Rashi*: God will not forever countenance this injustice. On the Day of Judgment, He will proclaim to the nations:

כַּרְמִי שֶׁלִי לְפָנָי — [lit., *My vineyard, which is Mine, is before Me.*] Although I transferred it to you, it is nevertheless Mine. I am the sole owner. All the injustices you perpetrated by plucking their "fruit" for yourselves are before Me; nothing that you filched from them eludes Me (*Rashi*).[1]

To which the nations will reply (*Rashi*):

הָאֶלֶף לְךָ שְׁלֹמֹה — [lit., *You, Shlomo, can have Your thousand.*] I.e., whatever we filched from them [previous verse] will all be returned to You (*Rashi*).

---

1. The *Midrash* offers the following parable:
   Rav Chiya taught: God is here likened to a king who was angry with his son and handed him

פרק ח

יג וּמָאתַיִם לְנֹטְרִים אֶת־פִּרְיוֹ: הַיּוֹשֶׁבֶת בַּגַּנִּים יג־יד
יד חֲבֵרִים מַקְשִׁיבִים לְקוֹלֵךְ הַשְׁמִיעִנִי: בְּרַח |
דּוֹדִי וּדְמֵה־לְךָ לִצְבִי אוֹ לְעֹפֶר הָאַיָּלִים עַל
הָרֵי בְשָׂמִים:

וּמָאתַיִם לְנֹטְרִים אֶת־פִּרְיוֹ — [lit., *and two hundred to the tenders of its fruit.*] And additionally, we will add on even more of our own and recompense Israel's leaders and Sages, in the manner that it is written [*Isaiah 60:17*]: *In place of the copper I will bring gold; and in place of the iron I will bring silver* (*Rashi*).

Rashi goes on to explain that *tenders of its fruit* refers to the Sages [perhaps because it is they who nurture the fruit, i.e., the young, of Israel], and it is they who will benefit from the return of the spoils as in the verse [*Isaiah 23:18*]: *for to them that dwell before* HASHEM *shall be her merchandise* ...

Rashi adds that the *thousand* and *two hundred* in this verse are not arbitrary figures. They allude to the *halachah* that הַנֶּהֱנֶה מִן הַהֶקְדֵּשׁ, *one who benefits [unjustly] from consecrated property*, must repay the principal plus a penalty of an additional fifth. Israel is *consecrated unto* HASHEM ... [*all who devour it*

shall be held guilty] (*Jeremiah 2:3*), and hence the nations are making the gesture of returning the principal [the *thousand* they are accused of filching in verse 11] plus an additional "fifth" of two hundred. [*Rashi's* interpretation follows the opinion of Rav Yonasan in *Bava Metzia 54a.*]

13. And now, God turns to the Community of Israel and says (*Rashi*):

הַיּוֹשֶׁבֶת בַּגַּנִּים — [lit., *O you who dwell* (or: *sit*) *in the gardens.*] You who are dispersed in the Diaspora, tending the gardens of others, and who dwell in the synagogues and study-houses ... (*Rashi*).

חֲבֵרִים מַקְשִׁיבִים לְקוֹלֵךְ — [lit., *companions are attentive to your voice.*] I.e., the Ministering Angels, your *companions*, hearken, and congregate to listen *to your voice* [prayers; sound of Torah-study] in your synagogues (*Rashi*).

The appellation חֲבֵרִים, *companions*, as an allusion to the Ministering Angels is somewhat

over to his servant. The latter thereupon began beating him with a stick, saying, "Don't listen to your father." The son said to him: "Stupid fool! The only reason why my father handed me over to you was because I did not obey him, and you say to me, 'Don't listen to your father!' "

So, too, when in consequence of Israel's iniquities the Temple was destroyed and the children of Israel were exiled to Babylon, Nebuchadnezzar said to them, "Do not listen to the law of your Father in Heaven, but *you shall fall and prostrate yourselves to the statue that I have made*" (*Daniel 3:15*).

The Jews said to him: "Stupid fool! The only reason why God has delivered us into your hand is because we bowed down to *a statue*, and you say to us, 'Fall down and prostrate yourselves to the statue that I have made!' Woe to that man!"

Thereupon God said: *My vineyard, which is Mine, is before Me.* [I.e., My nation is again before Me — and speaks up in defense of our love!]

peace belongs, and two hundred more to the Sages who guarded the fruit of Torah from our designs.

HASHEM: ¹³*O My beloved, dwelling in far-flung gardens, your fellows, the angels, hearken to your voice of Torah and prayer. Let Me hear it, that they may then sanctify Me.*

Israel: ¹⁴*Flee, my Beloved, from our common exile and be like a gazelle or a young hart in Your swiftness to redeem and rest Your Presence among us on the fragrant Mount Moriah, site of Your Temple.*

ambiguous. According to *Rashi*, they are *Israel's* companions, both Israel and the angels being referred to as בְּנֵי אֱלֹהִים, *children of God*.

According to others — e.g., *Ibn Aknin* — the phrase has the connotation of *Divine* companions in the *pluralis majestatis*.

It would seem from the *Midrash* that the inference is that the angels are companions to *one another*: Bar Kappara said: Why are the Ministering Angels called companions? Because there is among them neither enmity nor jealousy nor hatred nor quarreling nor altercation.

Additionally, as *Ibn Aknin, Divrei Yedidiah*, and *Markevos Ami* point out, there is a reference here to the leaders of the heathen nations [cf. comm. to 1:7 עַל עֶדְרֵי חֲבֵרֶיךָ] who are attentive to see if Israel serves its God actively and sincerely; waiting, as it were, for it to weaken so they can pounce upon it and pillage it. This

is implied in the Midrashic maxim [*Bereishis Rabbah* 65:16]: "When Jacob's voice is heard [i.e., when the Jews are religiously active], then Esau's [i.e., the heathens'] hands cannot overpower them" ...[1]

Therefore, according to this interpretation, render, "O you who dwell in the *gardens* of your exiles: The nations are hearkening to hear your voice, ready to pounce upon you. Therefore הַשְׁמִיעֵנִי, *raise up your voices loud*, so they will be powerless against you."

הַשְׁמִיעִינִי — [lit., *let Me hear it.*] [*Let Me hear your voice*, interjects God,] for after you are finished, they will commence to sanctify Me ...

As the *Midrash* comments: It is written [*Job* 38:7]: *when the morning stars sang in unison* — this refers to Israel; and only after that [ibid.]: *and all the "sons of God" shouted for joy* — this refers to the Ministering Angels (*Bereishis Rabbah* 65:17; *Rashi*).

1. ... As it is reported in the *Midrash* (*Genesis* 65:16):
All the heathens assembled before one of their wise men and asked him: "Do you think that we can subjugate this people?"

"Go around to their synagogues and schools," he replied, "and if you find there children with voices uplifted, you cannot subjugate them; if not, you can, for thus did their ancestor assure them: *The voice is the voice of Jacob* — when the voice of Jacob rings out in the synagogues, Esau's might is powerless against them."

This is in consonance with the *Talmud:* "Israel is dearer to God than the Ministering Angels ... For the Ministering Angels do not begin to sing praises in heaven until Israel has sung below on earth" (*Chullin* 91b).

14. [And in her ecstatic desire to return finally and forever to her Beloved, Israel turns to God and beseeches Him:]

בְּרַח דּוֹדִי — [lit., *Flee, my Beloved*] from this exile and redeem us from their midst (*Rashi*).

[I.e., *Flee away with us, O God* Who has accompanied us throughout every exile! And let us leave this exile together.]

וּדְמֵה־לְךָ לִצְבִי אוֹ לְעֹפֶר הָאַיָּלִים — [lit., *and be like a gazelle or a young hart.*] And hasten the Redemption and cause Your *Shechinah* to abide among us (*Rashi*). [Compare comm. to similar plea in 2:17 where the *Midrash* comments: "hasten Your deliverance like a gazelle or a young hart."]

עַל הָרֵי בְשָׂמִים — [lit., *upon the mountains of spices.*] I.e., Mount Moriah and the Holy Temple, may it be rebuilt speedily in our days. Amen (*Rashi*).

— And where You will savor us favorably for the sake of our ancestors whose savor ascended to You like the fragrance of spices (*Midrash*): *fragrance* throughout this Book alludes to the widespread effect of the mitzvos (*Divrei Yedidiah*).

And the *Midrash* concludes: Rav Acha said in the name of Rav Yehoshua ben Levi [*Isaiah* 60:22]: *I am Hashem, in its time I will hasten it:* If you prove unworthy, it [the Redemption] will be in its due time, but if you prove worthy, I will hasten it. So may it be God's will speedily in our days. Amen.

The *Targum* beautifully paraphrases this verse:

"O my Beloved, Lord of the Universe, flee from this polluted earth, and let Your Presence dwell in the high heavens. In times of trouble, when we pray to You, be like a gazelle which, while it sleeps, has one eye closed and one eye open [an allusion to its readiness to awake at the least sound of danger]; or like a young hart, which, in running away, looks back. So look upon us and regard our pain and affliction from the high heavens, until such time when You shall be pleased with us and redeem us, and bring us up to the mountain of Jerusalem, where the priests shall burn before You the frankincense of spices."[1]

תם ונשלם שבח לאל בורא עולם

Fifth day of Chanukah 5736
Brooklyn, New York

1. *Harav David Feinstein* points out that the Second Temple was destroyed because of שִׂנְאַת חִנָּם, *causeless hatred* (*Yoma* 9a), of which לְשׁוֹן הָרַע, *evil speech*, gossip and slander, is a form. The Temple will not be rebuilt nor Redemption achieved while this sin is still rampant among us. The *Talmud* notes that the קְטֹרֶת, *spices* [incense], atones for evil speech (*Yoma* 44a).

Thus, *mountains of spices* in our verse is symbolic of Israel's plea that God remove the obstacles of Redemption and build the Third Temple where we wish to attain eternal atonement for our sins and indulge in them no longer. Render thus: "*My Beloved, flee from exile and speed my redemption so that I may find atonement for my sins on Your mountain where incense is offered,*" בִּמְהֵרָה בְּיָמֵינוּ, אָמֵן.

Bibliography
of Authorities Cited in the Commentary

Italics are used to denote the name of a work. **Bold italics** *within the biography indicate the specific book of that particular author cited in the commentary.*

An asterisk (*) precedes the names of contemporary figures.

Akeidas Yitzchak

see *Arama, Rav Yitzchak b. Moshe.*

Albo, Rav Yosef

Spanish philosopher of the 15th century. Author of **Sefer Halkkarim**.

Little is known about his life, and the dates of his birth (1380) and death (1444) can only be conjectured. He was a student of Rav Chasdai Crescas, and according to some historians, he was a student also of Rav Nissim Gerondi (The "Ran").

His most famous work, **Sefer Ha-Ikkarim** ("Book of Principles"), is an important treatise on Jewish philosophy and faith. The book is divided into four parts, the first of which was originally intended to be an independent work. The other three parts, which elaborate upon the first part, were added later. The entire work was completed in Castile in 1425.

The work was first printed in 1485, and, having achieved great popularity, it has been reprinted many times since.

Alkabetz, Rav Shlomo HaLevi

(b. 1505-Salonica; d. 1576 Safed)

One of the greatest Kabbalists and mystical poets of his day. Author of the *Piyyut* "*L'chah Dodi*" recited every Friday evening. He was a contemporary and friend of Rav Yosef Karo, author of *Shulchan Aruch.*

He is often cited by early commentators, by whom he is referred to in various ways: *Rashba HaLevi; Rav Shlomo HaLevi; Harav ibn Alkabetz HaLevi.*

He wrote commentaries on most of the Bible, the Passover *Haggadah,* on Kabbalah, and was a noted *Paytan.* His kabbalistic commentary to *Shir HaShirim* is entitled **Ayeles Ahavim**. It was first published in Safed, 1553.

In his *Piyyut,* "*L'chah Dodi,*" he speaks of the sufferings of the Jewish people and their aspirations for Redemption. Probably no other *Piyyut* has reached the popularity of "*L'chah Dodi*"; it is recited every Friday evening by all Jewish congregations throughout the world.

Almosnino, Rav Moshe

Distinguished Rav and commentator. Born in Salonica, 1516, died in Constantinople about 1580.

His family originally dwelt in Aragon. Rav Moshe's grandparents were burned at the stake during the Inquisition, and his parents escaped and settled in Salonica, where he was born.

He was Rav of the Neve Shalom Spanish community in that city, and later of the Livyas Chen community.

Rav Almosnino was famous for his erudition and knowledge in both Torah and secular matters. In 1565 he represented the Jewish community before their sultan Selim II petitioning for the confirmation of their civil rights. After six attempts, the sultan acceded to his request and issued a proclamation guaranteeing equal rights to Jews.

He published many works, both in Hebrew and Spanish. Some were published during his lifetime, some posthumously. Many of his works are extant in manuscript form, others have been lost.

Among his works are: *Tefillah l'Moshe* on *Chumash; Pirkei Moshe* on *Avos; M'ametz Koach,* a collection of sermons; *Regimento de la Vida* (Way of Life) in Spanish. His commentary to the *Five Megillos* entitled **Yedei Moshe** was published in 1572.

Alshich, Rav Moshe

[Also spelled Alshekh]

Rav, *Posek*, and Bible Commentator. Born in Andrionople in 1508, he studied Torah there in the yeshivah of Rav Yosef Karo. Settled in Safed where he spent most of his life and was ordained there by Rav Karo with the full *Semichah* reintroduced by Rav Yaakov Berav. Among his pupils was Rav Chaim Vital, whom he ordained in 1590.

He died while traveling in Damascus before 1600.

He wrote commentaries on most of the Bible and published a collection of 140 of his halachic Responsa.

His commentary to *Shir HaShirim*, **Shoshanas HaAmakim,** was originally published in 1608. The abridged form of his commentary appearing in many editions of the Bible as **Kitzur Alshich** was edited by Rav Elazar Tarnigrad, Amsterdam, 1697. Tarnigrad added much original material to this abridgment which he attributed to the Alshich but which cannot be found in the Alshich's commentary.

Alter, Rav Yitzchak Meir

(1789-1866)

Gerrer Rebbe; founder of the Gerrer Chassidic dynasty. Rav Yitzchak Meir was a disciple of the Maggid of Koznitz, and later of Rav Simcha Bunem of *Peshish'cha*, and of Rav Menachem Mendel of Kotzk.

After the Kotzker's death in 1859, Rav Yitzchak Meir was acknowledged Rebbe by the majority of Kotzk Chassidim.

His influence was far reaching. Although his leadership lasted only seven years, he had a formative influence on the development of Chassidus in Poland. Gerrer Chassidus became a powerful element in Orthodox Polish Jewry.

He is most famous for **Chiddushei HaRim**, novellae on the Talmud and *Shulchan Aruch*, and was frequently referred to by the name of his work, "The Chiddushei HaRim."

Alter, Rav Yehudah Aryeh Leib

(1847-1903)

Gerrer Rebbe; known by his work, "Sefas Emes."

His father, Rav Avraham Mordechai, a great but chronically ill man, died when Yehudah Leib was only 12 years old. His upbringing fell to his grandfather, the illustrious Chiddushei HaRim. Yehudah Aryeh would study eighteen hours a day as a youth. It became widely known that a fitting successor was being groomed for the Chiddushei HaRim.

He was 19 years old when his grandfather died. Despite the pleas of the Chassidim, he insisted he was unworthy to become Gerrer Rebbe. Several years later, after the death of Rav Henach of Alexandrow, he acceded to their wishes and molded Ger into the largest Chassidus in Poland.

A prodigious and diligent scholar, he nevertheless found time to counsel tens of thousands of disciples every year and to become an effective leader in Torah causes. His discourses were distinguished for profundity and originality.

Although he never wrote for publication, his writings were posthumously published as **Sefas Emes**, separate volumes of novellae on Talmud, and chassidic discourses on Torah and festivals.

Altschuller, Rav Yechiel Hillel ben David

Bible commentator of the 18th century.

In order to promote the study of the Bible, Reb Yechiel Hillel's father, Reb David, planned an easy-to-read commentary of *Neviim* and *Kesuvim* (Prophets and Hagiographa) based on earlier commentators.

His commentary to *Psalms, Proverbs,* and *Job* was published before he died in 1753.

Rav Yechiel edited his father's remaining manuscripts and completed the missing books himself. By 1780, the entire completed commentary was published. It consisted of two parts: **Metzudas Tzion** which explains individual words; and **Metzudas David** which provides a running commentary to the text. Due to their simple and concise language, the dual commentaries have become almost indispensable aids in Bible-study. They have attained great popularity and have been reprinted in nearly every edition of the Bible.

Anaf Yosef

See *Rav Chanoch Zundel ben Yosef.*

Arama, Rav Yitzchak ben Moshe

(1420-1494)

Spanish Rav, philosopher and preacher. He was Rav of Calatayud where he wrote most of his works. After the expulsion of the Jews from Spain in 1492, he settled in Naples where he died two years later.

He is best known for his book *Akeidas Yitzchak,* a collection of allegorical commentaries on the Torah. First published in 1522, it has been reprinted many times and has exercised great influence on Jewish thought.

Because of this work he is often referred to as the *"Baal Akeidah"* ["author of the *Akeidah"*].

He also wrote a *Commentary on the Five Megillos* which was printed together with his *Commentary to the Torah* in Salonica, 1573.

He wrote *Yad Avshalom,* a commentary on *Proverbs,* in memory of his son-in-law, Avshalom, who died shortly after his marriage.

ARIzal

See *Luria, Rav Yitzchak.*

Ashkenazi, Rav Shmuel Jaffe

16th-century Rav in Constantinople.

Not being satisfied with any commentary to the *Midrash,* Rav Shmuel devoted himself to writing a comprehensive commentary to *Midrash Rabbah* and to the *Aggados* in the *Talmud.*

His first published work was *Yefei Mar'eh* on the *Aggados* in the Jerusalem *Talmud* (1597); *Yefei To'ar* to *Midrash Rabbah: Genesis, Exodus, and Leviticus* (1606); *Yefei Anaf* to *Ruth, Esther,* and *Eichah* (1691); and *Yefei Kol* to *Song of Songs* (1739).

His commentary to *Ecclesiastes* and his halachic writings are still in manuscript form.

Avodah Zarah

Talmudic tractate in *Seder Nezikin.*

Azulai, Rav Chaim Yosef David

Known by his Hebrew acronym CHIDA.

Born in Jerusalem in 1724; died in Leghorn in 1806. Halachist, Kabbalist, and bibliographer-historian, he possessed great intellectual powers and many-faceted talents. He went abroad as an emissary and he would send large sums of money back to Israel. He ended his mission in 1778 in Leghorn where he spent the rest of his life.

His fame as a halachist rests on his glosses to *Shulchan Aruch,* contained in his *Birkei Yosef,* a work constantly cited by later authorities.

He was the author of the famous bibliographic work *Shem HaGedolim.* Among his many works was the homiletical **Nachal Eshkol** on the *Five Megillos.*

Baal HaTurim

See *Rav Yaakov ben Asher.*

Bass, Rav Shabsai ben Yosef

Born in Kalisz, 1641; died in Krotoschin, 1718.

His parents were killed *al Kiddush Hashem* in the Kalisz massacres of 1655. He went to Prague where he excelled in the yeshivah there. Possessing a fine voice, he served as a member of the choir in the famous Altneuschul in Prague, hence his surname Bass.

Between 1674 and 1679, when he traveled through Europe and visited libraries, he became profoundly interested in bibliographic studies. He established a publishing house in Breslau where his books were famous for their beautiful appearance. The first book he published was the then new commentary *Beis Shmuel* on *Even HaEzer*.

In 1680 he published his own work, *Sifsei Yesharim*, a well-arranged bibliographical listing of all books published till his time.

His most famous work is **Sifsei Chachamim** – a commentary on *Rashi's* interpretation of *Chumash* and *Five Megillos* – where he clarifies with admirable brevity the surface difficulties in *Rashi's* commentary. It is an almost indispensable aid toward understanding and appreciating *Rashi* and is printed alongside *Rashi's* commentary in most large editions of the Bible. It has also been condensed and appears in many editions as *Ikkar Sifsei Chachamim*.

Bava Basra

Talmudic tractate in *Seder Nezikin*.

Berachos

Talmudic tractate in *Seder Zeraim*.

Berlin, Rav Naftali Zvi Yehudah

(1817-1893)

Known by the acronym of his name: Netziv.

One of the leading rabbis of his generation and Rosh Yeshivah of Volozhin for some 40 years.

He was born in Mir, and was already known as a great Talmudic scholar in his early youth. In 1831 he married the daughter of Reb Yitzchak of Volozhin – son of Reb Chaim of Volozhin who was the head of the important yeshivah in that town.

The Netziv spent the next twenty years of his life in intensive study and his fame spread. He was also known as a *tzaddik* and gentle in his every mannerism.

When Rav Chaim died in 1851 he was succeeded by his elder son-in-law, Rav Eliezer Yitzchak. When the latter died in 1854, the Netziv succeeded

him, transforming that institution into a spiritual center for the whole of Russian Jewry.

The spirit of his students was profound. For twenty-four hours a day, the sound of Torah-learning could be heard resounding in the walls of the *Beis Midrash*, and the Netziv's relationship with his students was one of parent and child. Under him, the yeshivah grew to over 400 students.

In his last years, he came into conflict with the Russian authorities as a result of their instructions to reduce the number of students at the yeshivah, and to introduce secular subjects into the curriculum. This resulted in a government decree to close the yeshivah in 1892, and the Netziv and his family were exiled. His health was so seriously affected by the closing that he was unable to carry out his desire to settle in Eretz Yisrael. He died in Warsaw about 18 months after his departure from Volozhin. His sons were Rav Chaim Berlin and Rav Meir Berlin.

Among the Netziv's works were the comprehensive commentary to the *She'iltos* of Rav Acha Gaon entitled *Ha'amek She'elah* (Vilna 1861); *Ha'amek Davar*, commentary on the Torah (Vilna 1879); **Rinah Shel Torah**, commentary to *Shir HaShirim* (Vilna 1879); and his responsa *Meishiv Davar* (2 vols. Warsaw).

Chagigah

Talmudic tractate in *Seder Moed*.

Rav Chanoch Zundel ben Yosef

(d. 1867)

Rav Chanoch lived in Bialystock, Poland, where he devoted his life to writing commentaries on the *Midrash* and the *Ein Yaakov*.

He published two commentaries which appear side by side in the large editions of the *Midrash Rabbah* and *Ein Yaakov*: **Eitz Yosef**, in which he strives to give the plain meaning of the text; and **Anaf Yosef** which is largely homiletical.

Rav Chanoch also published a commentary to *Pirkei Avos*, but his commentaries to *Yalkut Shimoni* and the *Mechilta* are still in manuscript.

Chasman, Rav Yehudah Leib

(1869-1935)

Born in Lithuania, he studied in Slobodka, Volozhin, and Kelm. He was strongly influenced by three of the Mussar giants of the era: Rav Simcha Zisel Ziev of Kelm; Rav Yitzchak Lazar of St. Petersburg – both of whom were among the foremost disciples of Rav Yisrael Salanter – and Rav Nosson Zvi Finkel of Slobodka.

Rav Chasman held several positions as Rav and lecturer of *Talmud*. He found his place in Shtuzin, Lithuania, where, after assuming the rabbinate in 1909, he established a yeshivah that grew to 300 students. However, the destruction and dislocation brought about by World War I destroyed the Torah life of the city.

After the war, Rav Chasman was a vital activist in rebuilding Torah life in the city.

The call to become *"mashgiach"* (spiritual guide) of the Hebron Yeshivah in Eretz Yisrael gave him the opportunity to become a seminal figure in the development of the Torah *Yishuv*.

Or Yohel, published posthumously by his students, is a collection of his lectures and writings.

Chavatzeles HaSharon

Homiletical commentary to *Shir HaShirim* by *Rav Zev Wolf Samuelson*, Rabbi in Baltimore, Maryland at the turn of the century. Published in Philadelphia, 1905.

Chazis

Another name for the *Midrash Rabbah* to *Shir HaShirim*. See *Midrash*.

Chida

See *Azulai, Rav Chaim Yosef David*.

Chiddushei HaRim

See *Alter, Rav Yitzchak Meir*.

Cordovero, Rav Moshe

(1522-1570)

Known by his acronym RAMAK.

Leading Kabbalist in the period before the ARI. He lived in Safed and studied Torah from Rav Yosef Karo, author of the *Shulchan Aruch*. He was ordained with the full *Semichah* re-introduced by Rav Yaakov Berav.

Ramak was the brother-in-law of the Kabbalist Rav Shlomo Alkabetz who initiated him into the mysteries of Kabbalah – then being propagated in Safed. His stature was such that even the ARIzal referred to him as "my master and mentor."

One of Ramak's most important works was his *Pardes Rimonim*, elucidating the tenets of Kabbalah.

He is also the author of **Tomer Devorah**, the famous Mussar work which is widely studied even today.

Derech Hashem

See *Luzzatto, Rav Moshe Chaim*.

Dessler, Rav Eliyahu Eliezer

(1891-1954)

One of the outstanding personalities of the Mussar movement. He was born in Homel, Russia.

In 1929 he settled in London. He exercised a profound influence on the teaching of Mussar, not only because of the profundity of his ideas, but also on account of his personal, ethical conduct.

In 1941 he became director of the Kollel of Gateshead Yeshivah in England.

In 1947, at the invitation of Rav Yosef Kahaneman, he became *Mashgiach* of Ponovez Yeshivah in Bnei Brak, Israel, and remained there until his death.

His teachings reflect a harmonious mixture of Mussar, Kabbalah, and Chassidus.

Some of his ideas were published by his pupils in **Michtav Me'Eliyahu** (3 vols. 1955-64).

Divrei Yedidiah

Encyclopedic commentary to *Shir HaShirim* by Rav Aryeh Leib ben Yedidiah Lipmann Lipkin. Rav Aryeh

Leib was a nephew of the great Mussar leader Rav Yisrael [Lipkin] Salanter. Little is known of him personally, but, as evidenced by his commentary, he was a man of profound acumen and great Torah scholarship. In his commentary, wherein he divides *Shir HaShirim* into two Songs, he thematically traces the history of the Jewish people from the Egyptian Bondage – culminating in the descent of the *Shechinah* upon the Temple yet to be built in the days of the Messiah.

In this commentary – published in Vilna, 1895 [and soon to be republished as a public service by ArtScroll Studios/ Mesorah Publications] – he draws heavily on Biblical parallels and Talmudic passages to lend an added dimension of continuity to the verses.

[A great debt of gratitude, as pointed out in the Preface, is due to Hagaon Rav Yaakov Kaminetzky *shlita*, for lending us his copy of *Divrei Yedidiah*. It aided immeasurably in the compilation of the commentary of the ArtScroll edition.]

Eidels, Rav Shmuel Eliezer ben Yehudah HaLevi

(1555-1631)

(Known as Maharsha – "Moreinu Ha-Rav Shmuel Eliezer.")

One of the foremost Talmud commentators, whose **commentary** is included in almost every edition of the Talmud.

Born in Cracow, he moved to Posen in his youth. In 1614 he became Rav of Lublin, and in 1625 of Ostrog, where he founded a large yeshivah.

Eiger Chumash

A medieval manuscript found in Prague containing a commentary to the *Siddur* and a short running commentary to **The Five Megillos**. Published in 1846.

Einhorn, Rav Zev Wolf

Rav in Vilna, end of 19th century.

Author of **Peirush Maharzu,** comprehensive and well-detailed commen-

tary to *Midrash Rabbah* appearing in the Romm edition.

Emunos V'Dei'os

See *Rav Saadiah Gaon.*

Epstein, Rav Baruch HaLevi

(1860-1940)

Born in Bobruisk, Russia. He received his early education from his father, Rav Yechiel Michel Epstein, author of *Aruch HaShulchan.*

Rav Baruch later studied under his uncle, Rav Naftali Zvi Yehudah Berlin [the Netziv].

He was the author of several works, but he is best known for a brilliant commentary to Chumash **Torah Temimah,** in which he quotes and explains the halachic and aggadic passages on the various verses. He also wrote **Gishmei Berachah** on the *Five Megillos.*

Eruvin

Talmudic tractate in *Seder Moed.*

Eshkol HaKofer

See *Saba, Rav Avraham ben Yaakov.*

Eitz Yosef

See *Rav Chanoch Zundel ben Yosef.*

Even HaEzer

One of the four divisions of the *Tur* and *Shulchan Aruch.* It deals primarily with halachos related to matrimony and divorce.

Eyebeschuetz, Rav Yonasan

Rav, and one of the greatest Torah-scholars of his generation.

Born in 1690 in Cracow; served as Rosh Yeshivah in Prague. Served as Rav of the "Three Communities" – Altona, Hamburg, and Wandsbek – until his death in 1796.

Rav Yonasan published extensively on Halachah and Bible. His most famous halachic works were *Urim V'Tumim* on *Choshen Mishpat* (1775), and *Kreisi U'pleisi* on *Yoreh Deah.* His homiletic work, **Yaaros D'vash,** published posthumously, was reprinted many times.

Because of his friendly relations with the government officials, he secured the right to reprint the entire *Talmud* – something which had been prohibited for centuries until that time.

Rav Yonasan's use of amulets sparked off a bitter controversy between him and Rav Yaakov Emden, repercussions of which lasted even after Rav Yonasan's death. All who knew Rav Yonasan vouched for his righteousness, scholarship, and sincerity.

Galico, Rav Elisha ben Gavriel

Prominent Talmudist and Kabbalist of the early-16th century.

Rav Elisha was a student of Rav Yosef Karo, author of the *Shulchan Aruch,* and was a member of his Rabbinical Court in Safed.

Rav Elisha was the teacher of Rav Shmuel de Uzeda, author of *Iggeres Shmuel* and *Lechem Dimah* (see bibliog. in ArtScroll ed. of *Ruth* and *Eichah).*

Rav Elisha's halachic responsa are quoted in *Knesses HaGedolah.* He published a commentary to all *Five Megillos.* His *Commentary to Shir HaShirim* was published in Venice, 1587.

Gishmei Berachah

See *Epstein, Rav Baruch HaLevi.*

Gittin

Talmudic tractate in *Seder Nashim.*

Heller, Rav Yechiel

(1814-1863)

Russian Rav and author. Rav Heller was a descendant of Rav Yom Tov Lipmann Heller [author of *Tosafos Yom Tov*].

He served as Rabbi of Plungian until his death.

A disciple of Rav Yisrael Salanter, Rav Heller was known as a popular preacher in the Mussar movement.

Among his published works were: *Amudei Or,* responsa on the four parts of *Shulchan Aruch; Or Layesharim,* on the Passover *Haggadah;* and **Oteh Or** on *Shir HaShirim.*

Hirsch, Rav Shamshon Raphael

(1808-1888)

The father of modern German Orthodoxy. He was a fiery leader, brilliant writer, and profound educator. His greatness as a Talmudic scholar was obscured by his other monumental accomplishments. After becoming Chief Rabbi and member of Parliament in Bohemia and Moravia, he left to revitalize Torah Judaism in Frankfurt am Main which he transformed into a Torah bastion.

His best-known works are the classic six-volume **Commentary on Chumash,** noted for its profound and brilliant philosophical approach to Biblical commentary, and his **Commentary to Psalms,** and **Horeb,** a philosophical analysis of the mitzvos.

Horowitz, Rav Yeshayah

Kabbalist and *Tzaddik.*

[Called *Shelah HaKadosh* – The Holy Shelah – from the initials of the title of his major work: **Shenei Luchos HaBris.**]

The Shelah was born in Prague, 1565. As a youth, he moved to Poland with his father who was his first teacher. He also studied under Rav Yehoshua Falk, author of *Sema* [*Sefer Meiros Einayim*]; Maharam of Lublin, and Rav Moshe Isserles (Rama). He gained a reputation among Polish scholars while still young.

He served as Rav in various cities, among them Dubno, Frankfurt, and Prague, where he served as Rabbi and *Dayan* until 1621. In that year after the death of his wife, he moved to Eretz Yisrael and settled in Jerusalem, where he remarried and became the Rav of the Ashkenazi community, greatly strengthening and expanding it.

The *Shelah* was greatly impressed by the manuscript notes of the ARIzal, Rav Moshe Cordovero, and Rav Yosef Karo, "those three outstanding *tzaddikim,* truly angels of HASHEM." They increased even more the kabbalistic elements of the *Shelah's* teachings, which he believed was "the teaching of the sages of truth who penetrated the secret of HASHEM, received in unbroken tradition by word of mouth from Moses at Sinai."

The *Shelah* is famous mainly for his *magnum opus: **Shenei Luchos HaBris*** [Twin Tablets of the Covenant] known by its initials **Shelah**. It was first published in Amsterdam, 1649.

In this extensive work, Halachah, homiletics, and Kabbalah are combined to form a work which includes the spectrum of ethical Jewish living.

The work is divided into two parts: *Derech Chayim*, containing laws according to the order of the festivals in the calendar, and *Luchos HaBris*, summarizing the 613 commandments in the order in which they appear in the Bible.

Additionally, the *Shelah* wrote many other works, among them a commentary to the *Siddur* entitled *Sha'ar Ha-Shamayim*, which was published by his great-grandson in 1717.

Ibn Aknin, Rav Yosef ben Yehudah

(1150-1220)

Philosopher and *paytan*. He was born in Barcelona, Spain, and, as a result of persecutions, he moved with his family to Fez, Morocco where he spent the rest of his life. He and the Ramban met each other during the latter's sojourn in Fez, and Ibn Aknin wrote a sad couplet on the sage's departure for Egypt.

Little else is known of the Ibn Aknin's life, and nothing is known about his family or descendants.

He wrote a compendium of Halachah, *Sefer Chulaim U'Mishpatim*, no longer extant, which he refers to as his "major work"; a treatise on the weights and measurements in the *Talmud*; *Introduction to Talmud*; *Sefer HaMussar* – commentary to *Pirkei Avos*.

His *magnum opus* was his commentary to **Shir HaShirim**. The commentary, written in Arabic under the title, "*The Divulgence of Mysteries and the Appearance of Lights*," was translated into Hebrew by A.S. Halkin, and published in 1964.

The commentary starts from the premise that it would be preposterous to believe that the wise King Solomon would compose a love story or engage in erotic banter. According to his interpretation, **Shir HaShirim** is a description of the mutual craving of the rational soul and the active intellect and the obstacles in the path of their union. Ibn Aknin was the first to explain the allegory in this way. This approach was followed later by Ramban, the kabbalists, and has found expression – with modification – in the almost-contemporary commentary of Malbim.

Nevertheless, Ibn Aknin did not reflect the Talmudic explanation of the allegory. His commentary offers a tripartite explanation of each verse: the first is an explanation of the grammatical forms; the second, what he calls the rabbinic interpretation, is an allegory of the love between God and Israel (which is the most widely accepted allegorical interpretation); and the third, which he consistently opens with the phrase "and according to my conception," is his original explanation, referred to above.

Ibn Ezra, Rav Avraham

(Born 1089 in Toledo; died 1164)

Famous poet, philosopher, grammarian, astronomer, and, above all, Biblical commentator. He also wrote a *Commentary on the Five Megillos*.

In all his Bible commentaries he strived for the plain, literal meaning of the verse. His aim was to explain the etymology of difficult words within their grammatical context. Next to Rashi, his commentary on the Torah is most widely studied, and appears in almost all large editions of the Bible.

His commentary to *Shir HaShirim* is divided into three parallel parts. In the first part, he deals with etymology; in the second part, he provides a running commentary to the literal meaning of the parable; and in the third part, he explains the allegory in the historical sequence of the Jews from the time of Abraham through their exiles.

In France, he met Rav Yaakov Tam [Rabbeinu Tam], grandson of Rashi, and a deep friendship between the two followed.

According to some, he married the daughter of Rav Yehudah HaLevi, and had five sons.

Legend has it that he once met the Rambam and dedicated a poem to him on the day of his death.

Ibn Janach, Rav Yonah

Born in Cordova, c. 985; died in Saragossa, first half of 11th century.

One of the foremost *Baalei Dikduk* (grammarians and philologists) of the early middle ages. Little is known of his life.

He published one of the first Biblical grammar books and dictionaries, the earliest to have come down to us in its entirety. It was originally written in Arabic and later translated into Hebrew by Rav Yehudah Ibn Tibbon. It is divided into two parts: *Sefer HaRikmah*; and **Sefer HaShorashim**.

He is often quoted by later Bible commentators and Hebraists such as: Ibn Ezra; Ibn Daud; Kimchi; Mizrachi; Rambam.

The notable exception is *Rashi*, who seems to have been unacquainted with his work (or who may have chosen not to quote him).

Ibn Janach was also a physician. He published several treatises on medicine which have been lost.

Ibn Yachya, Rav Yosef

Bible commentator; member of the famous Ibn Yachya family of which many scholars were descendants.

He was born in Florence, Italy in 1494.

His parents fled to that country from Portugal.

He relates in his preface to his *Torah Or* that in her first month of pregnancy with him, his mother, under threat of being ravaged, had thrown herself off a roof in Pisa in order to preserve her modesty, and she was miraculously saved.

She then fled to Florence where he was born.

His **Commentary to the Five Megillos** was published in Bologna, 1538. Two of his other works, *Derech Chaim* and *Ner Mitzvah*, were consigned to flames at the burning of the *Talmud* in Padua in 1554.

Rav Yosef had three sons, one of whom was Gedaliah, the author of *Shalsheles HaKabbalah*.

Rav Yosef died in 1534. Ten years after his death, his remains were brought to Eretz Yisrael. *Rav Yosef Karo* arranged for his burial in Safed.

Kara, Rav Yosef

French Bible commentator, c. 1060-1130. [Not to be confused with Rav Yosef Karo, 15th-century author of *Shulchan Aruch*.]

Rav Yosef was the student of his illustrious uncle, Rav Menachem Chelbo, whom he often cites in his commentary.

Rav Yosef resided in Troyes, the same city in which Rashi lived, and he frequented Rashi's house, where he made the acquaintance of Rashi's grandson, *Rashbam*.

Rav Yosef wrote a commentary on Torah – based upon Rashi's commentary – which he enlarged and expanded. He also added glosses to Rashi's commentary which Rashi himself agreed with and later incorporated into his own manuscript.

Rav Yosef also wrote an independent commentary to most of *Tanach*, including **The Five Megillos**.

In his commentaries, he followed the general style of Rashi but was not as brief. Sometimes whole sentences are translated into French. He cared more for the sense of the whole sentence than for the grammatical dissection of a single word. Although he preferred the simple, allegorical implication of the text, he did not altogether hold aloof from aggadic interpretation – which he held was an adornment of the text and was necessary to "render Torah great and glorious."

Kedushas Levi

See *Rav Levi Yitzchak* of *Berditchev.*

Kereisos

Talmudic tractate in *Seder Kodashim.*

Kesubos

Talmudic tractate in *Seder Nashim.*

Kimchi, Rav David

French grammarian and commentator; known by his acronym RADAK.

Born in Narbonne, 1160; died there in 1235.

His father, Rav Yosef, also a grammarian, died when Rav David was a child, and he studied under his brother, Rav Moshe, who had also published several volumes on grammar.

Radak's commentary on *Prophets* is profound, and is included in most large editions of the Bible.

Many have applied to him the saying from *Pirkei Avos:* "Without *kemach* ['flour,' i.e., 'Kimchi'], there is no Torah"; such was his great influence.

His main work was the **Michlol,** the second edition of which came to be known independently as the *Sefer HaShorashim* (not to be confused with a work by the same name by Ibn Janach).

In his commentary, he stressed the *derech ha'p'shat,* the plain sense, wherever possible, striving for clarity and readability rather than the compression and obscurity of some of his contemporary commentators.

Kranz, Rav Yaakov

(1741-1804)

Known as the "Dubno Maggid."

Born near Vilna; Rav Yaakov demonstrated his skill as a preacher at an early age, and was barely 20 years old when he became *darshan* in his city. He later became *darshan* in several cities, but he achieved his fame as a preacher in Dubno where he served for 18 years.

He came into frequent contact with the Vilna Gaon, who, it is said, enjoyed

his homiletical interpretations, stories, and parables.

The Dubno Maggid's works were printed posthumously by his son, Yitzchak, and his pupil Baer Flahm. Among these works were: *Ohel Yaakov* on *Chumash;* **Kol Yaakov** on the *Five Megillos;* Commentary on the Passover *Haggadah;* and *Mishlei Yaakov,* a collection of his parables.

Rav Levi ben Gershom

(Known by his acronym RALBAG; also known as Gersonides.)

Born in Bangols, France in 1288; died 1344.

One of the most important Bible commentators of his time, he was also a mathematician, astronomer, philosopher, and physician.

He wrote commentaries to the *Torah; Job,* the *Five Megillos, Early Prophets, Proverbs, Daniel,* and *Nehemiah.*

His philosophic and esoteric commentary to *Shir HaShirim* was written in 1340.

His Bible comments showed the work of a profound philosopher. He also had a great skill in analyzing a text and extracting the ethical and religious teachings inherent in them.

His commentary to *Job* was one of the first books printed in Hebrew (Ferrara, 1477).

Rav Levi Yitzchak of Berditchev

(1740-1810)

Chassidic *tzaddik* and Rebbe. One of the most famous personalities of the third generation of the Chassidic movement.

He was born into a distinguished rabbinic family to his father, Rav Meir, who was Rav in Hoshakov, Galicia. It is said that at the moment of Rav Levi Yitzchak's birth, the Baal Shem Tov remarked that a great soul had just descended from heaven who was destined to be the greatest intercessor of the Jewish people.

He was drawn to Chassidus by Rav Shmelke of Nikolsburg, and he became one of the foremost disciples of Rav Dov Ber, the Maggid of Mezeritch.

He succeeded Rav Shmelke in Richwal, and later became Rav in Zelechov; thus, he was known as the "Rebbe of Zelechov" by many of his Chassidim.

He ultimately moved to Berditchev in 1785, and served as Rebbe there until his death. His fame grew throughout the world as a Torah scholar and *tzaddik*.

Under him, Berditchev became a great Chassidic center and many – including great Torah Sages – flocked to consult with him.

His great love for every Jewish soul – always seeking the good side of every Jew, never the bad – permeated his very essence and he became the subject of many legends.

In his writings, he noted that "only he who admonishes Jewish people gently, elevates their souls, and always extols them righteously is worthy of being their leader."

Although he did not found a dynasty, he had many pupils and left an indelible mark on Chassidim.

His most famous work is **Kedushas Levi,** a commentary on the Torah and some holidays. It was published during his lifetime in 1798. An expanded edition – supplemented by his sons from his manuscript – was published posthumously in 1811.

Lorberbaum, Rav Yaakov ben Yaakov Moshe of Lissa

(Polish Rav and *Posek*. Known as the "Lissa Rav"; or "Baal Nesivos.")

(1760-1832)

He was the great-grandson of "Chacham Zvi." His father, Rav Yaakov Moshe, died before Yaakov was born, and his relative, Rav Yosef Teomim, brought him up.

After he published – at first anonymously – his *Chavas Da'as* on *Yoreh De'ah,* and *Nesivos HaMishpat* on *Chosen Mishpat,* he became acknowledged as an outstanding *posek*.

His contemporaries said of him that his learning was so pure and *"lish'mah,"* that his halachic decisions were as acceptable and unquestionable as if "from Moshe at Sinai."

Together with Rav Akiva Eiger and the Chasam Sofer he vehemently attacked and opposed the *Maskilim* and Reformers.

In 1809 he responded to an invitation to become Rav in Lissa where he enlarged the yeshivah to an enrollment of hundreds of students.

In 1822 he left Lissa due to community strife, and returned to Kalish where he spent his time publishing many more of his books.

Among his writings were *Imrei Yosher,* a comprehensive commentary on the Five Megillos, each published separately under different names. His profound commentary to *Koheles,* entitled **Tz'ror HaMor,** appears in most large editions of the Bible.

Luria, Rav David

(1798-1855; known as RADAL.)

Lithuanian Rav and *posek*. Student of Rav Shaul Katzenellenbogen of Vilna. After the death of his mentor, the Vilna Gaon, Radal was considered one of the Torah leaders of his generation. His scholarly writings embrace almost all of Torah literature. Among his works is his commentary to the Midrash, **Chidushei Radal,** printed in the Romm edition of the *Midrash Rabbah*.

Luria, Rav Yitzchak

(Known as *ARIzal [from the initials of HaEloki Rabbi Yitzchak, zichrono livrachah]*.)

The fountainhead of modern kabbalistic thought.

Born in Jerusalem, 1534, to his father, Rav Shlomo Luria, a relative of Maharshal.

While still a child, he lost his father. His mother moved the family to Egypt, and he was brought up by his wealthy uncle Rav Mordechai Francis in Cairo.

He studied at the Yeshivah of Rav

David ben Zimra (Radvaz), his teacher *par excellence*, in Torah and *kabbalah*. He was a student/comrade of Rav Betzalel Ashkenazi (author of *Shittah Mekubetzes*) who himself was a student of Radvaz.

ARIzal was beloved by his uncle, and, at the age of 15, was given his cousin in marriage. He was thus enabled to continue his studies undisturbed.

His holiness manifested itself at an early age and students flocked to him, extolling his virtues and saintly qualities.

In 1570, at the age of 36, he moved to Eretz Yisrael and settled in Safed where he formed a circle of kabbalists among whom were Rav Moshe Cordovero (Ramak); Rav Shlomo Alkabetz; Rav Yosef Karo; Rav Moshe Alshich; Rav Yosef Chagiz.

He entrusted his kabbalistic teachings to his disciple Rav Chaim Vital, who, according to ARIzal, possessed a soul which had not been soiled by Adam's sin.

After the ARIzal's death in 1572, Rav Chaim Vital collected notes that the ARIzal's students had made of their master's teachings, and published them.

Among the works so published were: *Eitz Chaim; Hadras Melech, Marpei Nefesh, Tikkunei Shabbos; Commentary to Zohar Chadash;* and *Shulchan Aruch* of the ARIzal, which incorporated his halachic customs. These customs are quoted extensively by later halachic authorities, and his influence has been immense.

ARIzal revealed many of the sepulchers of Sages whose locations had been forgotten until his time. He is also credited with composing the Sabbath *Zemiros: Azamer Bish'vachin, Asader liSeudasa,* and *Bnei Haichalah.*

He died in Safed, 1572, at the young age of 38.

Luzatto, Rav Moshe Chaim

(1707-1746)

Kabbalist; author of Mussar ethical works; poet.

Born in Padua, Italy, Rav Moshe Chaim was regarded as a genius from childhood having mastered *Tanach, Midrash,* and *Talmud* at an early age. He later went on to delve into kabbalistic and ethical studies.

He is most famous for his profound ethical treatise, **Mesillas Yesharim** (*The Path of the Upright*), which, alongside the *Chovos HaLevavos* of Rav Bachya ibn Paquda and *Shaarei Teshuvah* of Rabbeinu Yonah, became the standard ethical-Mussar work.

Among his kabbalistic works were: *Razin Genizin,* **Megillas Sesarim**; *Maamar HaGeulah;* **Derech Hashem**.

In 1743, he emigrated to Eretz Yisrael. He lived a short time in Acre, and died there, with his family, in a plague.

Maharal

See *Rav Yehudah Loewe ben Bezalel.*

Maharsha

See *Eidels, Rav Shmuel Eliezer ben Yehudah HaLevi.*

Maharzu

See *Einhorn, Rav Zev Wolf.*

Malbim

(1809-1879)

Rav, *Darshan,* and Biblical commentator.

The name Malbim is an acronym of Meir Leibush ben Yechiel Michel.

He was born in Volhynia, and was a child when his father died. He studied in his native town until the age of 13. He then went to Warsaw where he was known as the "*iluy* [prodigy] from Volhynia." He was Rav in several cities but he suffered much persecution because of his uncompromising stand against Reform, leading to his short-term imprisonment on a false accusation. He wandered much of his life, serving as Rav in several cities for several years at a time – even serving for a short while as Chief Rabbi of Rumania.

His fame and immense popularity

rests upon his commentary to the Bible which was widely esteemed. His first published commentary was on *Megillas Esther* (1845). His commentary to the remaining books of the Bible were published between then and 1876. His commentary to *Shir HaShirim* – which interprets the Song as a series of dialogues between the soul "imprisoned" in the body, and its Beloved God [see *Ibn Aknin*] – is entitled **Shirei Nefesh**.

His commentary on the Bible [as the author sets forth in his introduction to *Isaiah*] is based upon three fixed principles: in the text of the Torah and the figurative language of the Prophets there are no repetitions of mere synonyms; consequently, every word in a sentence is essential to the meaning in accord with the rules of language, despite the fact that they seem to be mere synonymous repetitions. Every statement conveys a sublime thought; all metaphors are of importance and replete with wisdom for they are the words of the living God.

Markevos Ami

Homiletical commentary on *Shir HaShirim* gleaned from early commentators by Rav Chaim Flenzburg. Published in Vilna, 1900.

Mashal Umelitzah

Collection of homiletic interpretations on the Torah by Rav Avraham Naftali Galanti. Published in New York City during the last generation. (Not to be confused with the Bible commentary of the same name by Rav Yitzchak Eliyahu Landau.)

Matnos Kehunah

See *Rav Yissachar Berman HaKohen.*

Megillah

[As differentiated from *Megillas Esther* – the Biblical Book of *Esther.*] Talmudic tractate in *Seder Moed.*

Megillas Sesarim

See *Luzatto, Rav Moshe Chaim.*

Mesillas Yesharim

See *Luzatto, Rav Moshe Chaim.*

Michtav Me'Eliyahu

See *Dessler, Rav Eliyahu Eliezer.*

Michlol

See *Kimchi, Rav David.*

Midrash; Midrash Chazis

See *Midrash Rabbah.*

Midrash Lekach Tov

Midrash on various books of the Bible attributed to **Rav Toviah ben Eliezer** in the 11th century. The work achieved great popularity and was quoted by many *Rishonim* such as Rabbeinu Tam, Rambam, Baal Halttur, Or Zarua, Shibbolei HaLeket. Ibn Ezra also refers to it in his commentary.

This *Midrash* has been published at separate times on the various books of the Bible as the manuscripts have been re-discovered. **Koheles** was published together with *Eichah* in 1908.

Midrash Rabbah

[Lit., *The Great Midrash.*]

The oldest Amoraic classical *Midrash* on the *Five Books of the Bible* and the *Megillos.* [Note: *Throughout the commentary of this Book, whenever "Midrash" alone is shown as the source, the reference is to Midrash Shir HaShirim, also called Midrash Chazis.*]

Midrash Zuta

Also called *Shir HaShirim Zuta* (Minor *Shir HaShirim*). This *Midrash* was probably compiled before the 10th century. It is quoted by the author of *Midrash Lekach Tov* which was written in the 11th century.

It was published by Buber from a Parma manuscript in 1894.

Migdal David

Homiletical commentary to *Shir HaShirim*, by Rav Shmuel Dov Sobel, Rabbi of Adath Israel Anshei Mir, New York. Published in New York, 1907. [I am grateful to Reb Eliezer Katzman for lending me this volume.]

Minchas Shai

See *Rav Yedidiah Shlomo of Norzi*.

Rav Moshe ben Maimon

(1135-1204)

Known by his acronym RAMBAM; Maimonides.

One of the most illustrious figures in Judaism in the post-Talmudic era, and among the greatest of all time. He was a rabbinic authority, codifier, philosopher, and royal physician. According to some, he was a descendant of Rav Yehudah HaNasi.

Born in Cordoba; moved to Eretz Yisrael and then to Fostat, the old city of Cairo, Egypt.

At the age of 23, he began his *Commentary on the Mishnah,* which he wrote during his wanderings. His main work was **Mishneh-Torah Yad-HaChazakah,** his codification of the spectrum of Halachah until his day. This was the only book he wrote in Hebrew, all his other works having been written in Arabic, a fact he is said to have regretted later in life.

He is also known for his profound and philosophic **Moreh Nevuchim** *(Guide for the Perplexed),* and for his many works in the field of medicine, hygiene, astronomy, etc.

Truly it may be said, "from Moshe to Moshe there arose none like Moshe."

Rav Moshe ben Nachman

Known by his acronym RAMBAN; Nachmanides.

(1194-1270)

One of the leading Torah scholars and authors of Talmudic literature during the generation following Rambam; also a renowned philosopher, Biblical commentator, poet, and physician.

Born in Gerona to a famous rabbinic family, he is sometimes referred to as Rabbeinu Moshe Gerondi, after his native town. He spent most of his life in Gerona, supporting himself as a physician. He exercised extensive influence over Jewish life. Even King James I consulted him on occasion.

Already at the age of 16 he had published works on Talmud and Halachah.

Among his works were: *Milchemes Hashem,* in defense of the Rif against the *hasagos* (disputations) of Rav Zerachiah HaLevi in his *Sefer HaMaor; Sefer HaZechus,* in response to the *hasagos* of the Ravad on the Rif; *Sefer HaMitzvos; Iggeres HaRamban; Iggeres HaKodesh;* and his profound and encyclopedic **Commentary on the Torah,** which is printed in all large editions of the Bible. His **Commentary to Shir HaShirim** is included in *Kisvei Ramban* ed. by Rabbi Ch. Chavel.

In 1263 he was coerced by King James I into holding a public disputation with the apostate Pablo Christiani that resulted in a victory for the Ramban, but aroused the anger of the Church and resulted in his forced exile from Spain just in time to escape the death penalty. He then emigrated to Eretz Yisrael. In 1268 he became Rav in Acco, successor to Rav Yechiel of Paris.

He died in 1276; his burial site has not been definitely ascertained.

Nachal Eshkol

See *Azulai, Rav Chaim Yosef David*.

Nachmanides

See *Rav Moshe ben Nachman [Ramban]*.

Netziv

See *Berlin, Rav Naftali Zvi Yehudah*.

Niddah

Talmudic tractate in *Seder Tohoros*.

* Ohel David

Novellae on the books of the Bible by *Harav David Cohen,* noted Talmudic scholar, lecturer, and contributor to various Torah publications. Published in Brooklyn in 1976.

Or Yohel

See *Chasman, Rav Yehudah Leib*.

Oteh Or

See *Heller, Rav Yechiel.*

Pesikta Rabbasi

Ancient *Midrash*; a collection of discourses dating from the first half of the first century, C.E. Divided in *Piskas* [sections] and containing discourses on the holidays, festivals, and special Sabbaths. Several *piskas* are devoted to Tishah b'Av, the Destruction, and ultimate Comfort and Restoration.

Pirkei d'Rabbi Eliezer

Ancient aggadic work attributed to the first-century *Tanna*, Rabbi Eliezer ben Hyrcanos.

*Pirkei Emunah

A brilliant collection of lectures on Mussar and *Hashkafah* by the Telshe Rosh HaYeshivah, Hagaon Harav Mordechai Gifter.

Pri Tzaddik

See next entry.

Rabinowitz, Rav Tzadok HaKohen

(1823-1900)

Born in Kreisburg, Latvia, young Tzadok attracted attention as a phenomenal genius. Orphaned at the age of 6, he was raised by his uncle near Bialystock. Such was the child's reputation, that Rav Yitzchak Elchanan Spektor of Kovno made a point of testing him when he happened to be nearby. He prophesied that "the boy will light a great torch of knowledge in Israel."

In later years, Rav Tzadok lived in Lublin where he became acquainted with Rav Leibele Eiger, a disciple of Rav Mordechai Yosef of Izbica. Rav Tzadok became their disciple, and, with their passing, became Rebbe of the Chassidim of Izbica. He became known far and wide as the "Kohen of Lublin." The breadth and depth of his thoughts were astonishing. Many considered him the greatest Torah scholar in all of Poland.

Pri Tzaddik is a collection of his discourses on the weekly portion and festivals. He was a very prolific writer.

Although many of his works have been published, he left many unpublished manuscripts that were destroyed during World War II.

Among his other works are Responsa *Tiferes Zvi; Meishiv Tzaddik;* and *Resisei Layla.*

Radak

See *Kimchi, Rav David.*

Radal

See *Luria, Rav David.*

Ralbag

See *Rav Levi ben Gershom.*

Ramak

See *Cordovero, Rav Moshe*

Rambam

See *Rav Moshe ben Maimon.*

Ramban

See *Rav Moshe ben Nachman.*

Rashba HaLevi

See *Alkabetz, Rav Shlomo HaLevi.*

Rashbam

See *Rav Shmuel ben Meir.*

Rashi

See *Rav Shlomo ben Yitzchak.*

Resisei Layla

See *Rabinowitz, Rav Tzadok HaKohen.*

Rosh Hashanah

Talmudic tractate in *Seder Moed.*

Rav Saadiah (ben Yosef) Gaon

(892-942)

Rosh Yeshivah of Sura, and one of the most important figures of the illustrious Geonic period.

Rav Saadiah was made Gaon by the *Reish Gelusa* (Exilarch) David ben Zakkai in 928, and the ancient academy in Sura, founded by Rav, then entered upon a new period of brilliancy.

He was a sage in every sphere of

Torah knowledge, had a full grasp of the secular knowledge of his time, and was a dynamic leader, fighting a valiant battle against the growing influence of Karaism.

He published in many areas: halachah, responsa, philosophy, grammar, but most of his works are lost or scattered among the *genizos* (repositories of worn-out manuscript books), waiting to be published.

Among the most important of Rav Saadiah's works to have come down to us are his translation of and partial **Commentary to the Bible**, which was the first translation of the Bible from Hebrew into Arabic, and has remained the standard Bible for Arabic-speaking Jews; his *Siddur*, the first systematic compilation of prayers for the whole year; *Sefer HaAgron*, on grammar; and his profound **Sefer Emunos V'Dei'os** (*Book of Belief and Doctrines*), originally written in Arabic and translated in Hebrew by Rav Yehudah Ibn Tibbon. This major philosophic work is the earliest such work to have survived intact.

There is hardly a figure after him who does not pay generous and laudatory tribute to his pioneering work: the philologist Rav Menachem ben Yaakov (often quoted by Rashi); Ibn Janach; Ibn Ezra, all praise him in the greatest of superlatives.

Even Rambam, who disagreed with Rav Saadiah on many fundamental points, states in his *Iggeres Teiman*: "were it not for Rav Saadiah, the Torah would have well-nigh disappeared in the midst of Israel."

Saba, Rav Avraham ben Yaakov

15-16th-century Kabbalist, Bible commentator, and *Darshan*.

Rav Avraham was among those expelled from Spain in 1492. He moved to Portugal where he wrote his commentary **Eshkol HaKofer** to the *Chumash*, the *Five Megillos*, and *Pirkei Avos*.

In his youth, many of his works were lost, and he was forced to rewrite them later in life from memory.

His commentary to the *Chumash* was entitled *Tz'ror HaMor* [not to be confused with the commentary to *Shir HaShirim* by the same name].

According to the *Shem HaGedolim*, he died on board a ship on Erev Yom Kippur 1508.

Sanhedrin

Talmudic tractate in *Seder Nezikin*.

Sefas Emes

See *Alter, Rav Yehudah Aryeh Leib*.

Sefer Chassidim

See *Rav Yehudah HaChassid*.

Sefer HaIkkarim

See *Albo, Rav Yosef*.

Sefer HaYashar

An early Hebrew Midrashic work which retells and elaborates upon Biblical narratives, especially commentary on the Pentateuch. Its origins are obscure. Some have believed it to be one of the books mentioned in *Joshua* 10:13 and *II Samuel* 1:18, although there are many indications that it is a later work. Traditional scholarship ascribes its authorship to the Second Temple period, although the introduction and several embellishments were probably added at a later date.

Sforno, Rav Ovadiah

(1470-1550)

One of the greatest Italian commentators and literary figures of the Renaissance period.

Little is known of Ovadiah's youth, except that he excelled in Torah studies, and at an early age his halachic opinions were sought by many. His decisions are quoted by Rav Meir Katzenellenbogen (Maharam Padua), who refers to him with great esteem.

Sforno studied medicine, the profession he followed.

He finally settled in Bologna where he was a major force in organizing the religious life of the town and established a *beis medrash* which he headed until his death.

Sforno's great fame, however, rests with his commentary to most of the Bible, in which he tried to explain the text literally, usually regarding the verse as a complete entity rather than philologically dissecting it. He usually avoided esoteric or kabbalistic interpretations. His commentary to the *Chumash* was edited by his brother, Chananel, after his death. The **Commentary to Shir HaShirim** was first published in Venice in 1555.

Shaar Bas Rabim

Scholarly and erudite anthology on the Torah and *Megillos* by Rav Chaim Aryeh Leib Yedvavnah; late-19th century. See *Horowitz, Rav Yeshayah.*

Shabbos

Talmudic tractate in *Seder Moed.*

Shelah

See *Horowitz, Rav Yeshayah.*

Shem HaGedolim

See *Azulai, Rav Chaim* Yosef David.

Shevach Viy'kar

Commentary to *Shir HaShirim* by Rav Yeshaya Hammer, Cracow, 1897.

Shir Chadash

Commentary on *Shir HaShirim* by Rav Dov Ber Treves. Little is known of Rav Dov Ber. He served as Rav in Hungary, and from 1760-1790 (contemporary with the period of the Vilna Gaon), he was head of the *Beis Din* in Vilna.

He was the author of the famous commentary to *Chumash*, *R'vid HaZahav* [published in Grodno, 1797].

When he was well advanced in years, and retired as *Dayan*, Rav Dov Ber undertook his brief but ingenious commentary to *Shir HaShirim*, **Shir Chadash**, to "nourish him in his old age," as the author writes in his preface. His commentary is noted for its erudition and brevity, successfully seeking the "simple" interpretation of the allegory. The volume was first published in Vilna in 1800. The author died in 1803.

[I am indebted to Harav Mordechai Gifter for lending me his personal copy of this *sefer* containing Harav Gifter's own marginal glosses.]

Rav Shlomo ben Yitzchak

(Known by his acronym RASHI)

Leading commentator on the Bible and *Talmud.*

He was born in Troyes, France in 1040 – the year in which Rabbeinu Gershom Me'or HaGolah died. According to tradition, Rashi's ancestry goes back to Rav Yochanan HaSandlar and to King David.

The summit of Rashi's commentaries was his commentary on the *Talmud* – an encyclopedic and brilliant undertaking. Nothing can be compared to the impact this commentary has had upon all who study the *Talmud.* Rashi's commentary has opened to all what otherwise would have been a sealed book. Without his commentary, no one would dare navigate the "Sea of *Talmud*": Every word is precise and laden with inner meaning. Rashi's corrections of the *Talmud* text were, for the most part, introduced into the standard editions and became the accepted text.

Rashi's **Commentary to the Bible**, too, made a similar impact, and virtually every printed Bible contains his commentary which is distinguished by its conciseness and clarity.

[It is Rashi's commentary that forms the basis for the anthologized commentary and allegorical translation in this volume.]

Many halachic works from the "School of Rashi" have come down to us: *Sefer HaOrah; Sefer HaPardes; Machzor Vitry; Siddur Rashi;* and responsa.

Rashi died on Tammuz 29, 1105. His burial place is not known.

Rav Shmuel ben Meir

(Known by his acronym RASHBAM)

Bible and *Talmud* commentator and

Tosafist. Born in Northern France in 1080 to Rav Meir, one of the first Tosafists and disciples of Rashi, whose daughter, Yocheved, Rav Meir married.

Thus, a grandson of Rashi, he was also the brother of the prominent Rabbeinu Tam, and a colleague of Rav Yosef Kara.

Rashbam studied under his father, but later was most influenced by his grandfather. They spent much time together in legal and exegetical discussions. In many instances, it is noted that Rashi accepted his grandson's opinion in exegesis.

Rashbam lived a simple life. He would always pray that he might be privileged to perceive the Truth and to love peace.

He is most famous for his commentary to the Bible which is characterized by his extreme devotion to *p'shat*. He constantly refers to "the profound literal meaning" of the text. In many ways, he considered his commentary as complementing that of Rashi. In many cases, his commentary is exactly identical with his grandfather's.

He was also known as a Talmudic commentator. His commentary to portions of *Pesachim* and *Bava Basra*, where Rashi did not manage to complete his own commentary, were annexed to Rashi's.

Sifri

Name of the Tannaitic *Midrashim* on *Numbers* and *Deuteronomy*.

Sotah

Talmudic tractate in Seder *Nashim*.

Targum

The ancient, authoritative translation of the Bible into Aramaic. The *Targum* on *Chumash* is attributed to Onkelos while the *Targum* on *Nach* is attributed to Yonassan ben Uziel.

Teitelbaum, Rav Moshe

(1759-1841)

Founder of the Sigheter dynasty. A pupil of the Chozeh of Lublin. A re-

nowned *tzaddik*, he was among the first to spread Chassidus in the Northern and Central districts of Hungary in his capacity as Rav of Vjhely. Author of **Yismach Moshe**, considered one of the classic works of Chassidus.

Tomer Devorah

See *Cordovero, Rav Moshe*.

Torah Temimah

See *Epstein, Rav Baruch HaLevi*.

Tz'ror HaMor

See *Lorberbaum, Rav Yaakov of Lissa*.

Wolf, Rav W.

Born in Cologne, Germany, in 1877. He studied in Cologne under his uncle. In 1939 he emigrated to Britain where he assumed a rabbinical post as a member of the London Beis Din.

While in Germany, he authored a German-language contemporary commentary on *Shir HaShirim* which was first published in 1908. It stressed the role of the Jews in their march along the road of Divine destiny from *Galus* to Redemption. The work was translated into English in 1958 and published – along with others of his essays – as part of the Publication Program of the Union of Orthodox Hebrew Congregations of Great Britain.

In 1959, he settled in Monsey, New York, where he spent the rest of his days. He died in 1964.

Rav Yaakov ben Asher

(1270-1340)

Posek and codifier; *Baal HaTurim*.

Son of Rav Asher ben Yechiel (the ROSH) under whom he studied. He was born in Germany. In 1303 he accompanied his father to Toledo, where he lived in great poverty and devoted his life to Torah.

Rav Yaakov's enduring fame rests on his encyclopedic halachic codification *Arbaah Turim*, which is the forerunner of our *Shulchan Aruch* today. As a result, he is referred to as the *Baal HaTurim*.

The arrangement and wealth of content made it a basic work in halachah and it was disseminated widely through the Jewish world. It became so widely accepted that when Rav Yosef Karo wrote his major work, *Beis Yosef*, he decided to base it upon the *Turim* "because it contains most of its views of the *Poskim*."

Rav Yaakov also wrote a comprehensive commentary on the *Chumash* anthologizing the literal explanations *(p'shat)* by earlier Bible commentators. To the beginning of each section he added "as a little appetizer, *gematrios* and explanations of the *Masorah*, in order to attract the mind." Ironically, the whole work was printed only twice. It was just these "appetizers" that were popularly published alongside most editions of the Bible under the title *Baal HaTurim*.

Among Rav Yaakov's students was Rav David Abudraham.

According to *Shem HaGedolim*, Rav Yaakov died en route to Eretz Yisrael.

Yalkut Shimoni

The best-known and most comprehensive Midrashic anthology covering the entire Bible.

It is attributed to Rav Shimon HaDarshan of Frankfurt who lived in the 13th century.

The author collected *Midrashim* from more than 50 works, arranging them into more than 10,000 statements of *aggadah halachah* according to the verses of the Bible.

Rav Yedidiah Shlomo of Norzi

Rav and Commentator.

Born in Mantua in 1560; died in 1626. Became Rav in Mantua in 1585.

Rav Yedidiah consecrated the greater part of his life to studying the *Masorah* of the Bible: by studying every previously printed *Masorah* text, comparing the various readings scattered through Talmudic and Midrashic literature, as well as in published and unpublished manuscripts.

The resulting work was entitled *Poretz*

Geder, but was published under the name *Minchas Shai*.

This work, which was as perfect as thorough learning and conscientious industry could make it, has become the most accepted work in establishing the *Masorah*. The *Minchas Shai* is printed in the back of all large Bibles.

Yefei Kol

See *Ashkenazi*, Rav *Shmuel Jaffe*.

Rav Yehudah (ben Shmuel) HaChassid

(c. 1150-1217)

One of the main teachers of the "Chassidei Ashkenaz" and one of the most profound ethical teachers to have lived.

Author-editor of *Sefer Chassidim*, a profound ethical halachic treatise which has come down to us in two separate editions. The book has achieved great popularity and was reprinted many times.

Rav Yehudah's father, Shmuel, was a renowned Rosh Yeshivah in Speyer, and Rav Yehudah studied under him. His saintly life was revered by all.

His contemporaries said of him: "Had he lived in the time of the Prophets, he would have been a prophet; in the time of the *Tannaim*, he would have been a *Tanna*; in the time of the *Amoraim*, an *Amora* . . ."

Rav Yehudah Loewe ben Bezalel

Known as the MAHARAL of Prague.

One of the seminal figures in the last 500 years of Jewish thought, Rav Yehudah was born c. 1512 and died in Prague in 1609. His genealogy can be traced to King David.

Although he was universally acknowledged as one of the rabbinic greats of the era, his life was not an easy one. He delayed his marriage for 20 years due to financial difficulties. He was Chief Rabbi of Moravia, residing in Nikolsburg for 20 years. Then, in 1573, he transferred his yeshivah to Prague, the Torah metropolis of Europe. Upon two different occasions, he accepted the rabbinate of Posen in order to settle communal strife.

He was elected Chief Rabbi of Prague in 1597 as a very old man. It appears that the position had been denied him up to then because of his outspokenness in attacking social evils and religious laxity.

Though commonly known as a folk hero and miracle worker, his greatest contribution was his formulation of a self-contained system of Jewish thought. His many books and lengthy sermons formed the basis for much of the significant writing of succeeding centuries.

Among his many erudite works were: *Novellae* on *Shulchan Aruch Yoreh De'ah*; **Gur Aryeh** on the Torah; *Be'er HaGolah* on the *Passover Haggadah*; **Derech Chaim**; *Netzach Yisrael*; *Nesivos Olam*, etc. Many of his works are extant and were recently republished in an 18-volume set: *Sifrei Maharal*.

Yerushalmi, Peah

Tractate *Peah* in the Jerusalem *Talmud*.

Yevamos

Talmudic tractate in *Seder Nashim*.

Yismach Moshe

See *Teitelbaum, Rav Moshe*.

Rav Yissachar Berman HaKohen

Known as Berman Ashkenazi.

16-17th-century commentator on the *Midrash*. Very little is known about him except that he was born in Sczebrzesyn, Poland, and that he was a student of the Rama (Rav Moshe Isserles).

He is the author of the famous commentary to the *Midrash Rabbah*, **Matnos Kehunah**, first published in 1584, and appearing subsequently in nearly every edition of the *Midrash*.

Rav Yissachar makes it very clear in his introduction that he was very concerned with establishing the correct text for the *Midrashim*, basing his text upon all the various printed editions up to his time and on various manuscripts.

Yoma

Talmudic tractate in *Seder Moed*.

Rabbeinu Yonah of Gerona

Spanish Rav and Moralist of the 13th century.

Rabbeinu Yonah was a cousin of Ramban (Nachmanides). He was one of the most prominent students of Rav Shmuel ben Avraham of Montpellier ("Min HaHar").

Rabbeinu Yonah was one of the people who banned the Rambam's (Maimonides') *Moreh Nevuchim* out of fear that philosophical influences – rampant at the time – would cause untold harm to the religiosity of the people. But when he saw that this anti-Rambam controversy was getting out of hand – and even resulted in the public burning of the *Talmud* in the same place where the philosophical writings of Rambam had been destroyed – Rabbeinu Yonah publicly admitted that he was wrong in all his acts against the works of Rambam. In his repentance, he vowed to travel to Eretz Yisrael and prostrate himself over the grave of the great teacher and implore his pardon in the presence of ten men for seven consecutive days.

He left France with that intention, but was detained. He died in 1263 before he was able to fulfill his plan.

Rabbeinu Yonah wrote many works, among them commentaries on portions of *Tanach*; commentary of *Avos*; *Chiddushim* on several tractates of the *Talmud*; and his famous Mussar works, later reprinted: *Iggeres HaTeshuvah*; **Shaarei Teshuvah;** and *Sefer HaYirah*.

Rabbeinu Yonah established yeshivos. Among his most prominent pupils was Rav Shlomo Aderet (Rashba).

He stayed in close contact with his cousin, Ramban, and Ramban's daughter married Rabbeinu Yonah's son. When Rabbeinu Yonah died, Ramban's daughter was pregnant. When she gave birth to a son, Ramban told her to name the child Yonah so that he would assuredly excel in Torah and piety.